JESUITS AND THE POLITICS OF
RELIGIOUS PLURALISM IN
EIGHTEENTH-CENTURY TRANSYLVANIA

For John Padberg, SJ

Jesuits and the Politics of Religious Pluralism in Eighteenth-Century Transylvania

Culture, Politics and Religion, 1693–1773

PAUL SHORE
Saint Louis University, USA

Routledge
Taylor & Francis Group
LONDON AND NEW YORK

First published 2007 by Ashgate Publishing

Published 2016 by Routledge
2 Park Square, Milton Park, Abingdon, Oxon OX14 4RN
711 Third Avenue, New York, NY 10017, USA

Routledge is an imprint of the Taylor & Francis Group, an informa business

Copyright © Paul Shore 2007

All rights reserved. No part of this book may be reprinted or reproduced or utilised in any form or by any electronic, mechanical, or other means, now known or hereafter invented, including photocopying and recording, or in any information storage or retrieval system, without permission in writing from the publishers.

Notice:
Product or corporate names may be trademarks or registered trademarks, and are used only for identification and explanation without intent to infringe.

Paul Shore has asserted his moral right under the Copyright, Designs and Patents Act, 1988, to be identified as the author of this work.

British Library Cataloguing in Publication Data
Shore, Paul J., 1956–
　　Jesuits and the politics of religious pluralism in eighteenth-century Transylvania : culture, politics and religion, 1693–1773 1. Jesuits – Romania – Transylvania – History – 18th century 2. Transylvania (Romania) – Church history – 18th century 3. Transylvania (Romania) – History – 18th century
　　I. Title II. Jesuit Historical Institute
　　271.5'3'04984

Library of Congress Cataloging-in-Publication Data
Shore, Paul J., 1956–
　　Jesuits and the politics of religious pluralism in eighteenth century Transylvania : culture, politics, and religion, 1693–1773 / by Paul Shore.
　　　　p. cm.
　　Includes bibliographical references and index.
　　ISBN 978-0-7546-5764-4 (alk. paper)
　1. Jesuits–Romania–Transylvania–History–18th century. 2. Religious pluralism–Romania–Transylvania. 3. Religion and politics–Romania–Transylvania–History–18th century. 4. Christianity and politics–Romania–Transylvania–History–18th century. 5. Transylvania (Romania)–Church history–18th century. I. Title.

BX3745.R6S56 2007
266'.24984–dc22

2006020641

ISBN 9780754657644 (hbk)

Contents

Publishers' Note		*vii*
Preface		*ix*
1	Uneasy Neighbors	1
2	The Uniate Church	27
3	The Institution of Union	55
4	Schooling	89
5	*Jesuitae Fabri*: The Society Constructs a Presence	111
6	Theatre in the Jesuit Schools	133
7	Social Order	147
8	Community: Looking Westward?	163
9	The 1743 Mission to Moldavia	175
10	Conclusion	181
Bibliography		*197*
Index		*229*

Publishers' Note

This volume is a co-publication between Ashgate Publishing and the Jesuit Historical Institute.

It is the 61 volume in the Jesuit Historical Institute's series *Bibliotheca Instituti Historici Societatis Iesu*.

ASHGATE

Ashgate Publishing

Institutum Historicum Societatis Iesu

Preface

The idea of writing about the Jesuits of Transylvania was born some years before the actual research began. Transylvania seemed to me an important component of the Jesuit enterprise in eastern and central Europe, one whose story might even shed light on larger patterns of Jesuit activity elsewhere. The Grand Principality was a relatively early destination of the Society, but the Jesuit presence in the region often appeared to lie outside the view of many who wrote in western European languages about the world-wide activities of the Jesuits. In addition I found that the Jesuit enterprise, as a unified undertaking, sometimes occupied a position of secondary or unclear significance in narratives focusing on the political and military history of Transylvania. While the role of the Jesuits in the cultural and confessional history of the region has always been acknowledged, discerning the nature of this role is complicated by the deep-seated ethnic and nationalistic sentiments of historians, literary scholars and others who addressed the Jesuit presence. The ethnic or national analysis of the decades of Jesuit activity in the region is by no means invalid, but in the case of a world-wide organization such as the Society, it is not the only valid approach.

This small book does not claim either to redress this situation nor is it a definitive history of all Jesuit undertakings in Transylvania in the period leading up to the suppression of the Society. Instead, by focusing on the activities of Jesuits in one of their most important communities, that of Cluj, I hope to raise questions about how the Jesuit missions in Transylvania are evaluated and understood. In particular, while calling attention to the achievements of individual Jesuits, this work endeavors to identify the Jesuits as a body of men with common goals, visions and faith. The pragmatic, political and competitive elements of the Jesuits' labors in Transylvania are undeniable, but so are the less easily isolated factors of belief and collective identity. If this book increases our understanding of these factors, it will have succeeded in its purpose.

I have been fortunate to have had the opportunity to conduct research for this book in many excellent libraries and archives. The Archivum Romanum Societatis Iesu in Rome and the Hungarian National Archives provided hospitality on many occasions, as did the National Széchényi Library in Budapest, whose General Director, Dr. István Monok, was an unfailing source of encouragement and assistance. Dr. Mariann Rozsondai at the library of the Hungarian Academy of Sciences has always been helpful, supportive and resourceful. Professor Adam Chmielewski smoothed the path for access to the University of Wrocław Library. The staff of the Romanian Academy of Sciences Library in Cluj and the Regional State Archives in that city provided valuable assistance on each of my visits. Likewise the library staff at the Pannonhalma Benedictine Abbey, and in particular Father Miksa Béla Banhegyi, OSB, graciously guided me to important document collections. Access to collections at Harvard University and Eötvös Loránd University gave me greater understanding of the significance of archival materials located elsewhere. The hospitality of the Jesuit community at Campion Hall, Oxford enabled me to make use of the libraries of that great university.

Thanks also the Institute of Jesuit Sources, the National Council for Eurasian and East European Research, and the International Research and Exchanges Board (IREX) for their support of this project. The Beaumont and Mellon Funds, and the Marchetti Jesuit Endowment, all administered by Saint Louis University, made travel to research sites possible. Hal Parker, Michael Yonan, Paul Michelson and Mordechai Feingold made valuable suggestions, as did my wife, Ilene Odegard Shore, who as ever has supported me every step of the way. I am also grateful for insights provided by the anonymous reviewers of this book, and for the editorial support of Father Thomas McCoog, SJ, as well as the technical support provided by Adam Hoose.

Finally, I owe a special debt of gratitude to Louis Takacs, whose linguistic and historical knowledge, coupled with his fine research instincts, greatly aided in the completion of this project.

P.J.S.
St. Louis, April 2006

Author's note

Hungarian names are normally written with the family name first, followed by the given name. This practice has been followed in all references to contemporary Hungarians, and also to those Hungarians living in the seventeenth and eighteenth centuries, except thoss (mostly Jesuits) whose names appear in a Latinized form. These last names appear with the Christian name first, as they would have appeared in contemporaneous documents.

CHAPTER ONE

Uneasy Neighbors[1]

I

At the close of the seventeenth century the Habsburg court of Vienna looked eastward across an expanse of newly conquered territory that only a few years before could not have been counted as part of Christendom.[2] As recently as 1683, the Turks, the last of the great non-Christian, expansionist empires to rise out of the east, had pressed up against the very walls of the "Residenzstadt" of the emperors, only to be driven forever from the region by an international alliance of Poles, Germans and other hired troops whose cosmopolitan composition reflected the complexity of the relations between the Habsburg domains and its allies. The hasty retreat of these infidels down the Danube to Belgrade and beyond left the Hungarian plains open to renewed contact with the Catholic and Imperial culture that emanated from Vienna and which had struggled to maintain contact with Hungary throughout the previous century.[3] The river-bound cities of Győr and Esztergom had long been strongholds of orthodox Hungarian Catholicism and had already been incorporated without much fuss into the patchwork of territories the Habsburgs laid claim to.[4] Further downstream, Buda, the historic royal capital of Hungary, was liberated in 1686, by a Habsburg army with Jesuit fathers in its train.[5] But far to the east, across the Danube and its tributary the Tisza, beyond the wasteland of the Hortobágy, in the hills and mountains that rise in the farthest reaches of the Carpathian Basin, lay a land historically connected with Hungary, but with a recent past that had separated it from Hungary and from much of the rest of Europe. This land was Transylvania. Transylvania was a Principality ruled by an elected Prince, a region that had in the previous century made its own peace with the Turks, and whose nobility, burghers and peasants did not consider themselves merely another Catholic territory waiting to be liberated by the Church's champions, the Habsburgs. The Principality had for five

---

[1] Portions of this chapter appear in a slightly different form in the author's "Cluj: A Jesuit Educational Outpost in Transylvania," *Catholic Education* 5, 1 (2001), pp. 55–71.

[2] Gerhard Herm, *Aufstieg, Glanz und Niedergang des Hauses Habsburg*. (Düsseldorf/Wien/New York, 1994); Robert Kann, *A History of the Habsburg Empire 1526–1918* (Berkeley, CA, 1974).

[3] *Documenta Missionaria I. Ex Tabulario Romano Sacrae Congregationis de Propaganda Fide*, eds Sávai János and Pintér Gábor (Szeged, 1993).

[4] The Society of Jesus erected a church in Győr as early as 1641; although besieged by the Turks, Győr remained under Habsburg control throughout the seventeenth century.

[5] Gyenis András, *A jezsuita rend hazánkban: rendtörténeti vázlat* (Budapest: Stephaneum Nyomda, 1940), pp. 14ff. Seven years later, Jesuit priests from Cluj would assist the incoming Imperial army. ARSI, *Aust. 155, An. Prov. Aust. 1697*, folio 70r.

centuries been part of the historic Kingdom of Hungary, whose power structure was annihilated in the battle of Mohács in 1526 and which had then been divided among the Turks, Habsburgs, and Transylvanian princes. For 150 years, the Principality, now largely cut off from the intellectual and political currents of Western Europe, had gone her own way, led by elected rulers who sought to retain the autonomy of the region through a *realpolitik* that sometimes required alliances with the Ottoman Turks and usually pitted its resources against those of Austria.

Transylvania was, and remains today, neither entirely within the influence of the traditions of Western Europe, nor completely excluded from the cultural history of the West.[6] Its medley of nationalities have long looked various directions for cultural orientation, while the key position of Transylvania near the Habsburg, Russian and Ottoman empires made it a point of intersection among competing political and religious powers from the sixteenth through the eighteenth centuries.[7] Transylvania was regarded by Vienna much as the Western European colonial powers viewed their colonial possessions. But unlike the overseas colonies of Spain, Portugal, France, England and Holland, Transylvania was not separated by vast distances and bodies of water from the imperial power that sought to govern her, nor was she heavily populated with strange-looking "natives" whose customs might be considered beyond the pale of European (and Christian) expectations for behavior.[8] Transylvania was always regarded as part of Europe, and in claiming Transylvania for Christendom,

---

[6] Ştefan Pascu, *A History of Transylvania*, trans. D. Robert Ladd with a foreword by Paul E. Michaelson (Detroit, MI, 1982); Cornelia Bodea and Virgil Cândea, *Transylvania in the History of the Romanians* (Boulder, CO, 1982); Béla Kópeczi (ed.), *Erdély rövid története* (Budapest, 1989); Dominic Kosáry "Gabriel Bethlen: Translyvania in the xvii Century," *The Slavonic and East European Review* 17 (1938–39), pp. 162–72; David Prodan, *The Struggle of the Romanians in Transylvania during the Eighteenth Century* (Bucharest, 1971); H. Klima, "Die Union der Siebenbürger Rumänen und der Wiener Staatsrat im theresianischen Zeitalter," *Südost Forschungen* 6 (1941), pp. 249–56; Nicolae Iorga, *Istoria poporului românesc*, ed. Georgeta Penela (Bucureşti, 1985); Toader Nicoară, *Transilvania: La Începtutrile Timpurile Moderne (1680–1800)* (Cluj-Napoca, 1997). The historic location of Transylvania as a bridge between the "advanced" Holy Roman and Austro-Hungarian Empires and the "backward" East is explored in László Kürti, *The Remote Borderland: Transylvania in the Hungarian Imagination* (Albany, NY, 2001), pp. 13ff.

[7] The conflict over the region where these Imperial powers intersected is addressed in many works, one of the best of which is Victor L. Tapié, *The Rise and Fall of the Habsburg Monarchy*, trans. Stephen Hardman (New York/Washington, DC/London, 1971).

[8] An exception to this generalization would be the Roma or Gypsies, who from the first were recognized as belonging to a different cultural and ethnic group, one singled out for particularly harsh treatment. Elliot H. Glassman, "Denial and recovery: Legal Politics perpetrated against the Romans in the Hapsburg Monarchy." http://lgi.osi.hu/ethnic/relations/1/roma.htm. Jews would also have been considered "alien," but were a barely visible minority in seventeenth-century Transylvania. However, at least one Jesuit found positive things to say about the Roma, whose skill as blacksmiths he acknowledged, and whose musical talents he rated as second to none in Transylvania. Andrea Illia, *Ortus et Progressus Variorum in Dacia Gentium et Religionum* (Claudiopoli, 1730, reprinted 1767), pp. 3–4.

the political and religious forces that converged on it as Turkish influence receded sought at each step of the way to reinforce the features that it shared with Europe.[9]

Many of these shared characteristics could be easily identified. Transylvania, in its religious and ethnic diversity, mirrored some of the conditions that had existed a century or more earlier in many parts of Europe, when in the wake of the first waves of the Reformation religious minorities had struggled for legal recognition within the political frameworks of France, the Netherlands and the Empire, a circumstance that had faded with the assertion of policies that disenfranchised nonconformists. Powerful nobles resisted central authority, and residents of "free Imperial cities" clung to their ancient privileges. Feudal relations compelled peasants to work four days each week for their lords, plus give one-fourth of the produce of their own land to their lord.[10] Yet despite this significant resemblance to Western Europe, Transylvania was unique in other ways. Its polity was made up of three *Nationes*: Szeklers (Székely), Hungarian speakers who had been identified with Transylvania since the ninth century, Hungarians, whose ties were to Royal Hungary, and "Saxons," the descendants of the German-speaking settlers who had arrived several centuries later, many of whom were Lutheran.[11] A defining feature of each of these *Nationes* was language, but the possession of a mother tongue by a distinct group did not assure that group's inclusion in the polity of Transylvania. The ethnic Romanians, who made up a sizable minority if not a majority of inhabitants at this time, were not recognized as having the rights of the other *Nationes*, and were denied any role in governance and were considered to occupy the at best outermost fringes of the European culture of the region. Romanians were also discriminated against in many other ways, some subtle, others less so.[12] The politically silenced presence of this large segment of the population of Transylvania added greatly to the inherent instability of the Principality, and will play an important role in our story.

---

[9] Joachim Bahlcke, "Catholic identity and ecclesiastical politics in eanrly modern Transylvania," in Maria Crăciun, Ovidiu Ghitta and Graeme Murdock (eds), *Confessional Identity in East-Central Europe* (Aldershot, 2002), pp. 143–52.

[10] John R. Lampe and Marvin R. Jackson, *Balkan Economic History 1550–1950: From Imperial Borderlands to Developing Nations* (Bloomington, IN, 1982), p. 25. In 1714, the *robota* was defined as three days' service to the lord each week. Georges Castellan, *A History of the Romanians*, trans. Nicholas Bradley (Boulder, CO/New York, 1989), p. 106.

[11] Ernest Wagner, "The Saxons of Transylvania," in *The Transylvanian Saxons: Historical Highlights* (Cleveland, OH, 1982), pp. 7–92. Even after decades of Habsburg efforts to promote religious conformity, Lutherans often dominated the councils of Saxon towns: "in plurimis sedibus Saxonicalibus habetur, totus magistratus est Lutheranus." Letter of F. Maximillianus à S. Catharina to Garampi, Cluj, 3 May 1777, in *Românii în Arhivele Romei* (secolul xviii). I. Dumitru-Snagov (ed.), (Cluj-Napoca, 1999), p. 272. Contemporaries often viewed the Transylvanian Saxons as a group distinct from other ethnic Germans. In neighboring Moldavia in the late seventeenth century, "germanice" and "saxonice" were regarded by at least one Franciscan missionary as two distinct languages. *Moldvai Csángó-Magyar okmánytár*, ed. K. Benda (2 vols, Budapest, 1989), vol. 2, p. 677.

[12] In Brașov, in 1679, if a Romanian died without issue his estate was automatically awarded to the closest residing member of the "Saxon" nation. Étienne Meteș, "La vie menée par les Roumains du XVIe au XVIIIe siècle," in *La Transylvanie* (Cluj, 1938), p. 268.

This diversity of languages, creeds and ethnicities bred, if not tolerance in the modern sense of the word, at least a workable truce among the most powerful elements that was reflected in the religious arrangements of the land, so that in the seventeenth and eighteenth centuries Transylvania possessed a reputation for heresy that profoundly troubled orthodox Catholics.[13] Moreover, the manner in which the three united nations of Transylvania had been split into four more or less self-contained religious categories – Roman Catholic, Calvinist-Reformed, Evangelical-Lutheran and Socinian-Unitarian – was offensive to devout Catholics and perhaps to the Habsburg court as well. This luxuriant flowering of competing heresies was itself a standing challenge to the mission and goals of the Jesuits.[14] In 1568, the Proclamation of Turda had established religious freedom within the Principality, a measure taken in large part because of the demands of its nonconforming Protestant subjects, many of whom belonged to noble landowning families who held the right to elect the Prince.[15] The most remarkable expression of this religious freedom was the relative toleration granted Unitarians (who were generally known as Arians in the seventeenth century), even during the period when the Jesuits were attempting to reduce the influence of this native group.[16] Tolerance appeared to work in several directions, although pressures invisible to the modern researcher may also have played a role in compelling civil authorities to accept the presence of various confessions. In the sixteenth century, while *cuius regio ejus religio* was the rule in Germany, civic bodies in Turda and Cluj that counted Lutheran and Unitarians in their numbers had even allowed Jesuits to come into their communities, where presumably the fathers taught and sought converts.[17] This at least grudging acceptance of the Society, whose missionary activities were far from secret, would be a characteristic of the second period of Jesuit efforts in Transylvania as well.

Other groups, while not recognized as part of the polity of Transylvania, added to the mix of languages, beliefs and customs.[18] An Armenian community, numbering

---

[13] Graeme Murdock, *Calvinism on the Frontier 1600–1660: International Calvinism and the Reformed Church in Hungary and Transylvania* (Oxford, 2000).

[14] Ioanna Costa, "Supplex Libellus Valachorum 'E quatuor [sic] receptis non est,'" Unpublished paper presented at the East-West Seminar, Berlin, July, 1997.

[15] Béla Király, *Hungary in the Eighteenth Century: The Decline of Enlightened Despotism* (New York, 1969), pp. 114–20. The religiously mixed nature of Transylvania was reflected in its great landed Protestant families, all of which by the middle of the eighteenth century had Catholic branches. Charles D'Eszlary, *Histoire des institutions publique* [sic] *hongroises* (3 vols, Paris, 1959–65), vol. 3, p. 371. See also Ladislau Gyémánt, "Religious domination and national Renaissance. The Transylvanian Romanians in the xviiith–xixth centuries," in Maria Craciun and Ovidui Ghitta (eds), *Ethnicity and Religion in Central and Eastern Europe* (Cluj-Napoca, 1995), pp. 276–83.

[16] Even after eighty years of Jesuit efforts to confine Unitarian influence, enough residual Unitarian sentiment remained for a work entitled *Summa Universae Theologiae Christianae secundum Unitarios* to be published in Cluj in 1787. Reported in Georgius Bucsánsky, *Epitome Historiae Religionis et Ecclesiae Christianae* (Posonii, 1801), p. 85.

[17] Orban Balázs, *Torda város és környéke* (Budapest, 1889), p. 189.

[18] Elke Josupeit-Neitzel, *Die Reformen Josephs II. in Siebenbürgen* (München, 1986), p. 12; Otto Mittelstrauss, *Historisch-Landeskundlicher Atlas von Siebenbürgen* (Heidelburg, 1992).

in the thousands, flourished a short distance from Cluj (Kolosvár).[19] Jesuit records also suggest the presence of a handful of Muslims, although some of these may have been prisoners of war captured in campaigns against the Turks.[20] In the remote mountains were peasants and shepherds whose religious practices, despite centuries of exposure to Christianity, were still strongly flavored by animism.[21] While Austrian mercantilism attempted to penetrate the region in the eighteenth century and military conscription brought some uniformity of experience to the adult male population, elements of the Transylvanian mix were exotic or even shocking by Western European standards.[22] Rom were scattered throughout the region, and were still being bought and sold as slaves in neighboring Bukovina until 1775.[23] Vienna did not help this situation by passing laws in 1750, 1753 and 1754 that called for the deportation of "ruffians" from its western regions to Transylvania.[24] Thus the region, while far closer to the regained Catholic heartland of Central Europe than either Peru or the Philippines, remained from a Habsburg or Roman point of view particularly alien and troublesome, a territory whose social conditions were without exact parallel in Western Europe, whose peasants still suffered the deprival of rights enshrined by the fifteenth century *Ius Tripartitum* of Werböczy István, and whose local nobility were identified according to unique and ancient categories.[25] Memories of earlier Jesuit setbacks in the region remained vivid; a mission to Transylvania was a journey to both an exotic location where heroic martyrdom might crown one's

---

[19] The Armenians arrived in Transylvania in the seventeenth century, and Szamosújvár (now known as Gherla), north of Cluj, was officially styled "Armenopolis." R.J.W. Evans, *The Making of the Habsburg Monarchy 1550–1750: An Interpretation* (Oxford, 1979), p. 424. The total number of Armenian families in Transylvania in 1672 was about 3,000, a number that declined during the disruptions of the Rákóczi rebellion. Judit Pál, "Armenier in Donau-Karpaten-Raum, im besonderen in Siebenbürgen," in *Siebenbürgisches Archiv, 35. Minderheiten, Regionalbewusstsein und Zentralismus in Ostmitteleuropa*, Heinz-Dietrich Lowe, Gunther Tontschand and Stefan Troebst (eds) (Köln/Weimar/Wien, 2000), p. 127.

[20] A Turkish woman was converted by Cluj Jesuits in 1695. ARSI *Aust. 155, An. Prov. Aust 1697*, folio 79r. Other Muslim converts may have been orphans, another consequence of war: "Bini item parvuli Turcae in fide Catholicâ ... instructi." ARSI *Aust. 158, An. Prov. Aust. 1701*, folio 23r.

[21] Many of these practices survived into the late twentieth century, when even the efforts of a repressive Communist regime could not eliminate them. Gail Kligman, *The Wedding of the Dead: Ritual, Poetics and Popular Culture in Transylvania* (Berkeley, CA, 1988).

[22] Victor Papacostea, *Civilizaţia Românească şi Civilizaţia Balcanică*, ed. Cornelia Papacostea-Danielopolu (Bucureşti, 1983), p. 225.

[23] Jerome Blume, *The End of the Old Order in Rural Europe* (Princeton, NJ, 1978), p. 244.

[24] Paul P. Bernard, "Poverty and poor relief in the eighteenth century" in Ingrao (ed.), *State and Society in Early Modern Austria* (West Lafayette, IN, 1994). p. 243.

[25] Konrad Müller, *Siebenbürgische Wirtschaftspolitik unter Maria Theresia* (München, 1961), 32; Joseph Benkő, *Imago Inclytae in Transylvania Nationis Siculicae Historico-Politica* (Cibii and Claudiopoli, 1791), vols 2–3, pp. 43–53. Johann Baptist Szegedi, who taught at the Jesuit lower school in Cluj, wrote on the *Ius Tripartium*. Alexius Horány, *Memoria Hungarorum et Provincialuim Scriptis Editis Notorum* (3 vols, Viennae, 1775), pp. 3, 333–6.

efforts, and also where the earlier failures of the Society might be redeemed.[26] Late in the eighteenth century Transylvania would also serve as a place of internal exile for fractious non-Catholics from Bohemia, thereby confirming the region's reputation as a cultural and spiritual frontier.[27] Habsburg arms, coupled with good luck and, on occasion, favorable timing, brought Transylvania within the Catholic-dominated control of the House of Austria after 1686. Yet it would take additional measures to win the population of this distant and little understood Principality to the True Faith, and even more was required to make these peasant burghers and petty nobles into Habsburg subjects who even roughly exemplified the ideal of *Kaisertreue*.[28] And while until the sole rule of Joseph II (1780–90), having a schooled population was never a goal of the Habsburgs (who often feared heresy was the stepchild of exposure to unorthodox religious literature), the extremely low levels of literacy and general poverty of Transylvanian peasants made systematic religious instruction a different sort of undertaking than it would have been in another more prosperous and bookish land.[29] There were other warning signs. The tendency of Romanian peasants to follow Messianic leaders such as Gheorghe Crăcium, the "black man," was an indicator of the desperation of the common people.[30] By any measure, the reclamation of Transylvania called for resolve, flexibility and a willingness to remain with the mission for the long haul. The Society of Jesus, as renowned for its educational and missionary projects as it was for its devotion to the culture of post-Tridentine Catholicism, seemed ideally suited to undertake the assignment converting, and connecting Transylvania to the Habsburg polity.[31]

---

[26] F. Weiser, *A katholikus iskolaügy magyarországon* (Colozae, 1885), vol. 2, p. 400.

[27] Charles O'Brien, "Ideas of religious toleration at the time of Joseph II," *Transactions of the American Philosophical Society* New Series 59/7 (1969), p. 28.

[28] Habsburg forces, led by Charles, Duc de Lorraine, were in Transylvania as early as 1686, occupying Cluj. The Treaty of Karlowitz, signed on 26 January 1699, confirmed control of the region for Austria. Ivan Parvev, *Habsburgs and Ottomans between Vienna and Belgrade* (Boulder, CO, 1995), p. 56; Kann, *Habsburg Empire*, p. 67.

[29] Joseph I asserted in a 1768 memorandum to his mother that only one in a thousand Transylvanians could either read or write in his own language. Cited in C.M. Knatchbull-Hugessen, *The Political Evolution of the Hungarian Nation* (2 vols, London, 1908), vol. 1, p. 96.

[30] Crăcium made his appearance in 1659, about the same time that the false Messiah Shabbathai Zebi was luring equally desperate Jews to his cause. Pascu, *History of Transylvania*, p. 129.

[31] The Jesuit missions in eighteenth-century Transylvania are described in Petru Tocanal, "Attestamento delle missioni in Bulgaria, Valachia, Transilvania e Moldavia," in *Sacrae Congregationis de Propaganda fide Memoria Rerum.* (Rom/Freiburg/Wien, 1973), *Vol. II 1700–1815*, pp. 727–42. See also Louis Châtellier, *The Religion of the Poor: Rural Missions in Europe and the Foundation of Modern Catholicism*, trans. Brian Pearse (Cambridge, 1997). Gernot Heiss has pointed out that the Jesuits had, during the sixteenth century, been major supporters of the policy known as "confessionalisation," which rejected "the view that religious unity could be restored through discussion and minor concessions." Germot Heiss, "Princes, Jesuits and the Origins of the Counter-Reformation," in R.J.W. Evans and T.V. Thomas (eds), *Crown, Church and Estates: Central European Politics in the Sixteenth and Seventeenth Centuries* (Basingstoke, 1991), p. 103. This policy remained officially in force well into the

This book is the story of how the Society's attempts to bring Transylvania into the world of the eighteenth-century Catholic Habsburgs were conducted by the Jesuits in one place, Cluj, or Kolozsvár, a small walled city located in the heart of Transylvania.[32] This undertaking, in its organized and openly supported stages, lasted eighty years, from the organized return of the Society of Jesus to Cluj in 1693, to the suppression of the Society by the pope in 1773.[33] Yet narrow though this study must be in a strictly geographic sense, it cannot ignore issues that spill across a far wider geographical area, nor can it entirely confine itself entirely to the activities of the Jesuits in the immediate vicinity. To make sense of the Jesuit mission in Cluj we must also confront the religious policy of the House of Habsburg in the eastern reaches of its domain and the forces that helped shape this policy.[34] This is in part because of one distinctive feature of the Jesuit "way of proceeding," which took members of the Society out of the monastic seclusion common to many other Catholic religious orders and placed them in direct daily contact with lay people.[35] It is also because the Habsburg vision of Catholicization or recatholicization was broad and never confined to the goal of "regaining" of a single isolated town or district, but instead combined the conversion of communities with the securing of the region for the dynasty and the pacification of elites and peasantry alike. Like the endeavors of the Society to take the message of the Gospel into all corners of the

---

eighteenth century, although, as we shall see, the Society made its own adaptations, depending local circumstances. For works relating directly to the Society's activities in the region see Ladislaus Polgár, *Bibliographia de Historia Societatis Jesu in Regnis olim Corona Hungarica Unitis 1560–1773* (Romae, 1957).

[32] The origin of the name Cluj/Kolozsvár is probably related to the Hungarian "kolostor" or monastery.

[33] The diplomatic maneuvering that resulted in the Suppression of 1773 is most completely covered in J. Crétineau-Joly, *Clement XIV et les Jésuites ou histoire de la destruction de la Compagnie de Jésus* (6 vols, Paris, 1848). Additional correspondence of the Habsburg court is found appended in Alfred, Ritter von Arneth, *Geschichte Maria Theresia's* (10 vols, Wien, 1863–79). In neither of these studies, however, are eastern Hungary and Transylvania given special attention, probably because the relevant documents were not available.

[34] The question of Habsburg religious policy and its intersection with economic and diplomatic policy has not received sufficient attention, although recent Romanian scholarship has recognized the importance of this theme, especially as regards the Uniate Church. Nicolae Gudea, *Biserica Română Unita (Greco-Catholica – 300 de anni – februarie 1697– februarie 1997* (Cluj-Napoca, 1994), p. 11. The diplomatic history of the eastern regions of the Habsburg dominions is detailed in Karl E. Roider, Jr., *Austria's Eastern Question 1700–1790* (Princeton, NJ, 1982).

[35] While the *Constitutions* of the Society enjoined Jesuits to "abstain as much as possible from secular employments" such as a business, the mission of the Society from its inception placed Jesuits in direct contact with the cultures around them, and the success of the Society's schools often depended on how knowledgeable Jesuit teachers were about these cultures. *The Constitutions of the Society of Jesus*, trans. with an introduction by George E. Ganss, SJ (St. Louis, MO, 1970), p. 263. See also Isbella Csikszentmihályi, "Flow in a historical context: The case of the Jesuits," in *Optimal Experience: Psychological Studies of Flow in Consciousness*, in Mihály Csikszentmihályi and Isabella Selega Csikszentmihályi (eds) (Cambridge, 1988), pp. 232–48.

world, Habsburg ambitions to create a religiously homogeneous community were born of a vision of unity and uniformity of belief. For the dynasty, the vision had emerged from the chaos and frequent setbacks of the seventeenth century, and was driven simultaneously by the need for security and by an ambition for new territorial acquisitions. The motivations of the Society as a missionary and educational institution were often compatible with those of the Habsburgs, but had different emphases. Jesuit activities in remote and inhospitable localities, both in Europe and abroad, reflected a strong desire among the members of the Society for contact and confrontation on the "front lines" of the spiritual struggle for souls that characterized Baroque Catholicism in the late seventeenth and eighteenth centuries.[36] Transylvania filled the bill in each of these categories: remote, risky, exotic and important to the spiritual health of Europe, it was a natural place for the Society to concentrate its attention, and a logical setting for the continuation of its world-wide mission.

For the first two centuries of its existence, the Society focused much of its efforts on building a network of schools and missions that spanned the globe, and which sought to bring the people whom it served into closer contact with Church teachings. Jesuits were spurred to interact with cultures world-wide only in the sense that they were "athletae" or warriors for God, a notion promoted in training centers such as the Collegium Germanicum in Rome.[37] The story of the Society thus becomes to some degree intertwined with the story of the lands in which it worked, and the cultures it encountered.[38] While the Jesuits' attempts to develop a profound knowledge of the culture in which they conducted its missions were not always successful, the stated intent of the Jesuits to draw upon those elements already present in a culture that was compatible with Church teachings and incorporate them into their own mission efforts sets the Society's missions apart from many other Christian missionary endeavors, both Catholic and Protestant, of the period. Even their opponents acknowledged the impressive accomplishments that Jesuit educators and missionaries achieved, and critics who scorned the so-called "Jesuit style" in the visual arts had to concede its effectiveness in communicating its intended message. In the late nineteenth century, when the prestige of the Baroque aesthetic was at a low ebb, a noted Hungarian historian still had to grant that the "empty, flashy" Jesuit architectural style conveyed splendor and wealth that impressed enemies as well as friends.[39] There is therefore little disagreement that the Society made a major impact on the cultural history of historic Hungary and Transylvania during its second sojourn in these regions after 1693.

---

[36] B. Duhr, *Geschichte der Jesuiten in den Ländern deutscher Zunge* (4 vols, Freiburg in Breisgau, 1907–28).

[37] Friedrich Paulsen, *Die Geschichte des gelehrten Unterrichts* (2 vols, Leipzig 1919–1921) vol. 1, p. 288.

[38] William V. Bangert, SJ, *A History of the Society of Jesus*, 2nd edn (St. Louis, MO, 1986). In recent years, the need to locate the activities of the Jesuits in the places where they worked has increased. For an example of this newer trend in scholarship relating to Brazil see "Fanatics of Christ" http://www.brasil-brasil.com/p26dec97htm.

[39] Hendrik Marczali, *Magyarország története a szatmári béketöl a bécsi congressusig* (Budapest, n.d.), p. 346.

Yet beyond the simple acknowledgement of the great impact of the Society in Transylvania and elsewhere, the deeper motives of the Jesuits have often been questioned, and were being questioned increasingly throughout the eighteenth century by those within the Catholic Church. Each facet of the Jesuits' work found itself scrutinized and then criticized by groups who found that the Society no longer addressed their needs.[40] The diverse approaches used by the Society, its influence in high places, and the very nature of its successes prompted questions. Was the Society merely trying to co-opt long-established local forms of religious expression in an endless quest to bring all people under the authority of Rome, or did Jesuits acquire a real understanding and appreciation of the cultures they encountered?[41] Did the interest the Jesuits demonstrated for expressions of what would today be called "folk culture" or popular culture reflect nothing more than a cynical exploitation of the less educated by an order that elsewhere prided itself on its intellectual achievements? Was the Jesuit penchant for theatrical (in both the figurative and literal senses) expositions of religious principles an innovation developed from a perceptive and sympathetic reading of humankind's taste for drama, and the need to act out expressions of penitence, or was it something darker, a cynical manipulation of emotion and superstition?[42] Did the highly evolved Jesuit school theatre that flourished for several centuries in Hungary reveal a broad and insightful understanding of how religious and moral principals might be conveyed outside the classroom, or was the Jesuit incorporation of drama, along with dancing and fencing, merely evidence of how worldly and materialist the Society had become?[43] Was the Society's project to reunite Orthodox believers with Rome derived from actual concern for the souls of

---

[40] Central among these deficiencies was the insufficiently vocational and social aspects of the Jesuit education of elites. Ernest Wangermann, "Reform Catholicism and political radicalism in the Austrian Enlightenment," in Roy Porter and Mikuláš Teich (eds), *The Enlightenment in National Context* (Cambridge, 1982), pp. 128ff.

[41] Twentieth-century historians viewing the adaptability of the Jesuits, especially in non-European settings, have seen "anthropologists preaching a religious relativity." H.R. Trevor-Roper, *The Crisis of the Seventeenth Century: Religion, Reformation and Social Change* (New York/Evanston, IL, 1968), p. 130. Related to the criticism of excessive flexibility in religious matters was the charge that Jesuits sought to bring the peoples among whom they worked under their own control. The most memorable example of this set of charges centered on the Jesuit Reductions in Paraguay. The extensive (and frequently inaccurate) publicity the Reductions received is relevant to the experience of the Society in eighteenth-century Europe, as the Paraguayan controversy undoubtedly shaped attitudes towards all Jesuit enterprises. Typical of the popular literature, of dubious origin, circulating in Europe at the time was *Nicolas Premier Jésuite et roi de Paraguai* (Buenos Aires, 1761).

[42] The relation of drama to the sacrament of penance is explored in Michel Foucault, *Religion and Culture,* ed. Jeremy R. Carrette (Manchester, UK, 1999), pp. 171ff. Jesuit school drama in Hungarian-speaking regions is analyzed in a broad context in Jablonkay Gábor, SJ, *Az iskoladrámák a jezsuiták iskoláiban* (Kalosca, 1927).

[43] See William H. McCabe, SJ, *An Introduction to the Jesuit Theatre*, ed. Louis A Oldani, SJ (St. Louis, MO, 1983). Hungarian scholars have been generally positive in their assessment of Jesuit school dramas, which have been seen as an important element in the development of Hungarian Baroque culture. Bálint Hóman and Szekfű Gyula, *Magyar Történet* (Budapest, 1935), vol. 4, pp. 385–7. A rare and important collection of images taken from Jesuit Baroque

these Christians, or had the Jesuits only become fellow travelers in the expansionist plans of the Habsburgs? Why were the Jesuits so unpopular with some of the more aristocratic strata of Habsburg society in which they placed their greatest hopes?[44] And finally, when Jesuit scientists continued to test the boundaries of existing knowledge, did they do so as Jesuits, as scientists in the Enlightenment sense, or as both?[45] The Jesuits of the Cluj community found themselves engaged in each of the activities that engendered these controversies, and any study of the Society's activities in this region must confront these issues as well.

An investigation into the activities of the Society in Eastern Europe during the early modern period also must address the tension between revealed and scientific knowledge to which individual Jesuits in the seventeenth and eighteenth centuries perhaps unknowingly contributed. Mircea Elidae has argued that with the advance of Enlightenment ideas of causality, materialism and linear time, non-religious people gave up the notion of transcendence, and accepted the relativity of the "reality" they encountered daily.[46] Jesuit scientists added to the body of knowledge that fostered this shift in world-view towards what would later be called "modern," a transformation that gained acceptance in the elite salons of Western European capitals and later in university lecture halls.[47] Yet in their world-wide mission activities, including within the reaches of the Habsburg domains, the Jesuits, as an institution, and in their individual activities pressed home the older message of transcendence as a keystone to its theological teaching. The message of a transcendent reality that all should seek also informed the Jesuit educational enterprise. The art, music and rhetorical performances promoted by pre-Suppression Jesuit teachers were based upon exacting standards of execution and frequently attained an outstanding artistic level, but the aesthetic they utilized was that of the pre-scientific, pre-rational Baroque, reveling in dramatic display and calling upon the viewer to make intuitive, pre-rational connections to a metaphysical reality. Thus while some Jesuit scholars and scientists throughout Europe were helping create the standards and the vocabulary

---

stage designs in Hungary is found in M. Fagiolo, É. Knapp, I. Kilián and T. Bardi, *The Sopron Collection of Jesuit Stage Designs,* trans. D. Stanton et al. (Budapest, 1999).

[44] For example the Diets of Széchény and Ónod in 1705 and 1707 condemned the political and educational activity of the Society. Marczali, *Hungary,* p. 272.

[45] After the election of Benedict XIV in 1740, the receptivity of the Holy See towards scientific inquiry increased, thereby encouraging many Habsburg Jesuits to test the limits of acceptable research. Vincenzo Ferrone, *The Intellectual Roots: Newtonian Science, Religion and Politics in the Early Eighteenth Century,* trans. Sue Brotherton (Atlantic Highlands, NJ, 1995), p. 263. Jesuits in the Bohemian Province and probably elsewhere were thus teaching Newtonian physics in the middle of the eighteenth century. Domokos Kosáry, "L'education en Europe Centrale et Orientale a l'âge des Lumières," in *Les Lumières en Hongrie, en Europe Centrale et en Europe Orientale* (Budapest, 1984), p. 218.

[46] Mircea Eliade, *The Sacred and the Profane: The Nature of Religion,* trans. Willard R. Trask (New York, 1959), pp. 202–203.

[47] Antonio Trampus, *I gesuiti e l'illuminismo: Politica e religione in Austria e nell'Europa centrale (1773–1798)* (Firenze, 2000); Robin Briggs, "Embattled faiths: Religion and philosophy in the seventeenth century," in Euan Cameron (ed.), *Early Modern Europe: An Oxford History* (Oxford, 1999), pp. 177–205.

of a rationalist, Enlightenment, empirically defined understanding of reality, their brethren were perpetuating a world-view that the Enlightenment would seek to destroy. Habsburg Jesuits, including those working in Cluj, were caught between these two worlds at the same time that they found themselves struggling to bridge the differences between western and eastern Habsburg culture. The actual impact of the Society on the evolution of attitudes regarding this new understanding of "reality" is therefore harder to trace, and yet without an assessment of its contribution in this area, any examination of the work of the Society is incomplete.

II

Each of these points of controversy, considered in its broadest world context, merits a study far beyond the scope of this volume.[48] Nevertheless, the relationship of the Jesuits who worked and lived in Cluj to the unusually diverse ethnic and religious communities raises questions as to both the motives of these men and the larger political and social environment in which they moved; we must also consider the speculations concerning these motives that have played such a large role in the historiography of the Society.[49] This acknowledgement of the larger world and the temptation to generalize about the relations of the Jesuits of Cluj to their neighbors is tempered by the fact that this study focuses on a town of scarcely eight thousand inhabitants in the eighteenth century, located in a distant region and regarded as remote and even barbarous by many in Western Europe. This circumstance, even allowing for the reality that some of the players belonged to an influential and controversial international organization, might seem at first glance to relegate any account of the town's history to the level of local antiquarianism.[50] But in Transylvania, as elsewhere in Eastern Europe, local history always has ramifications for large questions of national and ethnic history, and the political events of the past hundred years have shaped the way that historians have approached the history of

---

[48] Confessional bias in the study of the "Counter-Reformation" has decreased perceptibly in recent decades, but this trend only overlaps, and is not identical with the problem of the historiography of the Jesuits. Martin D.W. Jones, *The Counter Reformation* (Cambridge, 1995), p. 1ff.

[49] An almost endless series of quotations reflecting this speculation (generally very negative) regarding the motives of the Jesuits might be cited: the following may be considered representative: "... it cannot be denied that Jesuits have often overstepped the bounds of spiritual commitment. This was especially true during the Renaissance and the Reformation periods, when religious quarrels were inseparable from political conflict and wars." Alain Woodrow, *The Jesuits: A Story of Power* (New York, 1995), p. 105. The writer thanks Rich Sanker for making him aware of this work.

On the positive side, Arnold Toynbee praised the Jesuits' willingness to challenge existing understanding of intellectual and spiritual life, noting that they "were as right as they were brave in resolutely wielding the winnowing fan." Arnold Toynbee, *An Historian's Approach to Religion*, 2nd edn (Oxford, 1979), p. 265.

[50] The town's population never rose above 8,000 during the eighteenth century, and in 1714, probably owing to the plague, sunk to as low as 5,000. Ştefan Pascu, Josif Pataki and Vasile Popa, *Cujul* (Cluj, 1957), p. 60.

this important regional center. Small though Cluj was, it has always possessed a special significance in the cultural history of Eastern Europe.[51] The Western reader, unfamiliar with the vicissitudes of political and ethnic history, may not realize that Transylvania, and Cluj in particular, constitute modern-day bones of contention between Hungarian and Romanian nationalists. Both these groups see the region and the city as their own patrimony, and regard the history of both as the special property of their own ethnic groups. This is for several reasons. First, the key role that Cluj (as the Hungarian Kolozsvár) plays in the narrative of Hungarian cultural identity of the sixteenth through eighteenth centuries, when many other cultural centers were under Turkish domination, gives the town an importance out of proportion to its size at the time.[52] In particular, during the first years after the Society returned to the area, Cluj continued to be a center of Protestant Hungarian-language publishing activity, with the work of the Calvinist pastor turned printer Misztótfalusi Kis Miklós being the most distinguished.[53] At the same time, Romanian historians of the past century have been at pains to show not only that Romanians were living in Cluj in the seventeenth and eighteenth century, but that Romanians attended Jesuit schools there and even that Jesuit writers of non-Romanian descent took a special interest in the history and manners of the "Dacians," and consciously linked Romanian Transylvanians with the ancient Roman settlers of the region.[54] More recent events continue to

---

[51] Kürti, *Borderland*, pp. 26–31.

[52] As an example of the cultural importance of Cluj in the decades before the return of the Society, the "Várad Bible" ranks high. After Turks captured Várad, a city lying to the west on the edge of the Hungarian Plain, in 1661, the bible, one of the most ornate Hungarian-language books of the century, was completed in Cluj. *Szent Biblia az az Istennek o es uj Testamentomban Foglaltataott* (Varadon: MDCXI). Exhibit 169, Ráda Collection, Bible Museum, Budapest. The Jesuits were part of this earlier narrative as well, having operated a *collegium seminarium* in Cluj from 1585 until their expulsion in 1613. Ştefan Pascu, *Die Babeş-Bolyai Universität aus Cluj* (Cluj, 1972), p. 9ff. The university library assembled there by the Jesuits in sixteenth century is reconstructed in Klára Jakó, *Erdélyi könyvesház. I. Az első kolozsvári egyetemi könyvtár története és állományának rekonstrukciója 1579–1604* (Szeged, 1991). The eighteenth-century Society took an interest in the activities of its predecessors, publishing Georgius Darorczi's *Ortus et Progressus Collegii Academici Societatis Jesus Claudiopolitani ab Anno M. D. LXXVI* (Claudiopoli, 1737). Nor was the significance of Kolozsvár limited to Catholic history of the period, as several notable Protestant religious figures also lived in the community in the seventeenth and eighteenth centuries.

[53] Misztótfalusi Kis, also known as Tótfalusi Kis, a Calvinist printer trained in the Low Countries, published *Új Testmentom* (Amestelodámban, Kis Miklós által, 1687) (a New Testament) and *Szent David Királynak és Profetanak Szazötven Soltari ...* (Amstelodaman, 1686) (a collection of fifty psalms) that enjoyed wide distribution.

[54] The implication being that by taking note of the Romanian inhabitants of the region, Jesuit writers were bestowing legitimacy on the Romanian claims of being the descendents of Roman colonists of the second century CE. The most important of works penned by Cluj Jesuits, *Dacia Nova*, was written by the Cluj Jesuit Franciscus Fasching and published by the Jesuit academic press there in 1743. Another book that deals with the various religious and ethnic groups of the region is Andrea Illia, SJ, *Ortus et Progressus variarum in Dacia Gentium et Religionum cum Principalum ejusdem usque ad a. 1722* (Claudiopoli, 1730) (reprinted in 1767).

drive these historiographic themes. The loss of Transylvania to Romania following World War I and the separation of two million Hungarian speakers from Hungary are events few Hungarians, even today, regard with anything approaching indifference. The brief return of the Cluj region to Hungary following the 2nd Vienna Award of 1940 is still remembered with bitterness by many Romanians, while the treatment of ethnic Hungarians in the region by the Ceaucescu regime – and its successors – is a subject of ongoing debate and recrimination.[55] Both the post-World War I era and the interlude of Hungarian repossession of Transylvania after the Vienna Awards had an immediate impact upon the historical writing of the time as scholars sought to justify current policy by retelling the history of the region from differing perspectives. These more recent developments lie at some distance from the eighty-year period under consideration here, but they must be kept in mind as the historian picks a path through both the Romanian and Hungarian secondary literature of the past 150 years, and the Western secondary literature, which is derived to a significant degree from these sources. Ownership of the cultural legacy of the Cluj region is as much of an issue today as it was three centuries ago. Modern conceptions of nation and history, which everywhere in this region compete with the desire to preserve a perceived ancestral heritage, are particularly significant in the telling of the history of Cluj, whether from a Hungarian or Romanian standpoint.[56]

III

Thus while the encounters of the Cluj Jesuits with their neighbors have some of the features of a special case study, their eighty-year undertaking also consists of elements representative of the crucial interaction among cultural and religious communities that have continued to shape the destiny of a much larger region. This interaction cannot be characterized, as some have tried to do, simply as an encounter between East and West, between dominant and oppressed groups, or even as one between Catholicism and Orthodox Christianity. While East-West and Catholic-Orthodox relations form an important part of the Jesuit era in Cluj, the story is complicated both by the other groups present in the region, and by larger questions concerning the Uniate Church and the relation of modern-day Romanian intellectual and spiritual life to that of the rest of the Christian world.[57] For some Catholics, the Uniate Church has represented a sensitive compromise between the traditions of two branches of Christianity, while for many Orthodox Romanians, the Uniate Church that was established in 1692 by an Imperial diploma was a Trojan horse forced upon an unwilling populace that fled in

---

[55] The territorial changes that occurred during World War II are summarized in Charles Sudetic, "Historical Setting," in *Romania: A Country Study* (Washington, DC, 1989), pp. 40–42.

[56] On the competing notions of "preserving ancestral roots" and "catching up with modernity," see David Lowenthal, *The Heritage Crusade and the Spoils of History* (London, 1997), pp. 72–3.

[57] Ion Aurel Pop, "Medievalism and Enlightenment in Romanian Historiography" in Teodor Pompiliu (ed.), *Enlightenment and Romanian Society* (Cluj-Napoca, 1980), pp. 180–92.

large numbers to avoid it.[58] While undoubtedly the Society viewed the Transylvanian Uniate clergy as a bridgehead into the fundamentally hostile Orthodox environment, the dynamic between the Jesuits and Uniates was colored by factors as diverse as the educational level of the Uniate clergy, the tensions between married and celibate clergy, and the differing social roles of each group in a traditional society. Prejudice towards all aspects of traditional Romanian culture of the part of ethnic Hungarian Jesuits, including teachers, missionaries and chroniclers, likewise must not be discounted. That the Jesuit record, within its strengths and drawbacks, so completely dominates the primary sources as of yet identified only increases the challenge to the researcher seeking a balanced presentation.

This study will endeavor to shed light on this web of relationships from a standpoint that extends beyond the nationalistic and confessional ones that have predominated in the historiography of Hungary and Romania as they relate to the Cluj region. Instead, the starting point will be the set of schools established by the Society in Cluj, the missionary endeavors of the Society, and the Uniate Church, which was the special project of the Jesuits throughout their sojourn in Transylvania.[59] In each of these instances the Society achieved many practical goals and made a lasting impact on the region, although the Jesuit fathers failed to create an educational institution that survived intact after their own suppression in 1773. This apparent failure has colored assessment of all of the Society's undertakings in the region. At the same time an evaluation of the Jesuit heritage in Transylvania has been drawn into the debate concerning the cultural achievements of the Romanians and Hungarians respectively, and the rights of each group to ownership of the region.[60] This debate has somewhat obscured both the actual accomplishments and activities of the Society by placing them in an anachronistic, overly nationalistic paradigm that presupposes the existence of nation states that emerged over a century later and that would have made little sense to Jesuits of the time, while simultaneously neglecting relevant recent work done on popular culture in the West.[61]

---

[58] Constantine C. Giuescu, *Transylvania in the History of the Romanian People.* (Bucharest, 1968), pp. 59–60.

[59] Keith Hitchins, "Religion and Rumanian National Consciousness in Eighteenth Century Transylvania," *The Slavonic and East European Review* 57 (1979), pp. 214–39; Marcel Stirban, "L'église des Roumains Uniates sous l'évêque Petru Pavel Aron," *Transylvanian Review* 6/1 (1997), pp. 36–50. The seat of the Uniate Bishop of Transylvania, Blaj, was the center of Romanian intellectual activities during the first phase of the Enlightenment in that region. Teodor Pompiliu, "The Romanians from Transylvania between the Tradition of the Eastern Church, the Counter Reformation and the Catholic Reformation," in Maria Craciun and Ovidiu Ghitta (eds), *Ethnicity and Religion in Central and Eastern Europe* (Cluj, 1995), p. 181.

[60] Szász Zsomoborde, *The Minorities in Romanian Transylvania* (London, 1927), pp. 16ff; Endes Miklós, *Erdély három nemzet és négy vallása autonmiájának története* (Budapest, 1935).

[61] Michael Mullett, *Popular Culture and Popular Protest in Late Medieval and Early Modern Europe* (London, 1987) is just one example of a study whose challenges to notions of a monolithic popular culture can shed light on the complex situation in the eastern Habsburg realms. See also Jones, *The Counter-Reformation*.

While the Jesuits as individuals possessed a nationality, the Society of the late seventeenth and early eighteenth centuries was truly international in its educational program and overall outlook, and no administrative unit of the Society illustrated this better than its Austrian Province. The Austrian Province of the Society, established as early as 1563, included all of historic Hungary and Transylvania, and counted many different nationalities among its members.[62] Its operations extended to the edge of Ottoman Serbia, while Belgrade, which was part of the Austrian domains from 1719 to 1739 was visited by Jesuits of the Croatian and Austrian Provinces.[63] Jesuits of the Austrian Province even penetrated the southern Balkan regions of the Ottoman Empire, although without notable success in conversions, while their brethren labored in Moldavia, seeking out isolated communities of Catholics.[64] The eastern reaches of the Austrian Province were likewise a staging area for systematic reporting on regions to the east and south. A member of the Austrian Province, assigned to Transylvania, may have been the author of a seventeenth-century treatise on the status of the Catholic religion in Moldavia, while a few Jesuits of the same

---

[62] The Austrian Province counted 751 priests and over a thousand *coadjutores temporales* in 1750. *Catalogus Provinciarum, Collegiarum, Residentiarum, et Missionum universae Societatis Jesu* ... (Tyrnavae, 1750). See also Ladislaus Szilas, SI, "Die Österreichische Jesuitenprovinz im Jahre 1773. Eine historische-statistische Untersuchung," *AHSI* 47 (1978), pp. 97–158, 297–349. A map of the Austrian Province appears in *Ungarisches Magazin.* (Pressburg, 1781), vol. 1, pp. 398–9; Anton Peter Petri, *Die Jesuiten in der Perwardeiner Mission (1716–1773) (Neue Benater Bücherei XIX*, Mühldorf/Inn, 1985). The creation of the Austrian Province in 1563 is located on a charter illustrating the evolution of all pre-Suppression administrative developed from the original German Province in Fridricus Weiser, SJ, *Tabulae exhibentes Sedes Antiquae Societatis Jesu: Missionum Stationes et Collegia, 1556–1773 Provinciae Bohemiae et Silesiae* (Viennae, 1899), p. 26.

[63] Anton Peter Petri, *Die Jesuiten in der Belgrader Mission, Neue Benater Bücherei XVIII* (Mühldorf/Inn, 1985). The records of the Society's Belgrade mission appear with the Catalogus I of the Austrian Province for 1720, although it is not clear if all administrative responsibility resided in Vienna. The Society made serious efforts to bring both the Belgrade and Timişoara missions within the ambit of the Western European Jesuit tradition when it installed bells "juxta musurgia Kicheri ad sex tonos musicos." ARSI, *Austria 176, An. Prov. Aust. 1719*, p. 113. Rudolf Bzenszky, born in Bohemia but a member of the Austrian Province, was present at the capture of Belgrade. OSzK, 2039 FMI/1608 *Historia anno 1716*, pp. 183–4. The only region penetrated by Austrian troops in the 1710s that was not proselytized by the Society was Oltenia, in western Wallachia, perhaps because of the solidly Orthodox makeup of the population. N. Dobrescu, *Istoria Bisericii Române din Oltenia în timpul ocupaţiunii austriace (1716–1739)* (Bucureşti, 1906).

[64] The failure of the Society to win many converts in the Ottoman lands resulted in the Habsburgs not being able to play the role of protector of Ottoman Roman Catholics that the Romanovs were able to play regarding Orthodox Christians under the Sultan. Roider, *Austria's Eastern Question*, p. 16. Two Jesuits, Paulus Beke and Marinus Desi, each identified as "Ungarus," were working in Iaşi, Moldavia in 1648, ministering to the "Csángó," a Hungarian-speaking minority there. Benda (ed.), *Moldvai*, vol. 2, p. 451. Charles VI, after victories against the Ottomans, even raised the possibility that Moldavia might become a tributary state of Austria, a development, that if it had come to pass, would moved this principality closer to the Society's Austrian Province. Roider, *Austria's Eastern Question*, p. 52.

Province traveled as far as Poland and Muscovy. Meanwhile Jesuit-run universities in Graz and elsewhere trained students from Croatia and the Dalmatian littoral regions who would go on to help shape the development of literary Croatian.[65] In modern-day Slovakia, a region of mixed Slovak and Hungarian speakers and then a stronghold of Lutheranism, Jesuits made use of small town trade guilds to promote conversions.[66] In Trnava, further to the west and not far from Vienna, in what is also now Slovakia, a Jesuit college founded within the lifetime of St. Ignatius trained teachers and missionaries who spread Catholic doctrine and Habsburg culture throughout the Carpathian Basin as well as scholars who help develop the first form of literary Slovak.[67]

The Austrian Province was in many ways a project of the Habsburg dynasty, which had long had a special relationship with the Society. Jesuits, both from within and outside of the Austrian Province, had served the Habsburgs on political and diplomatic missions as far back as the sixteenth century, and at other times had served as mediators between the dynasty and rulers in the region.[68] The administrative heart of the Province was Vienna, and Viennese Jesuits often had connections to the aristocratic families who supplied the political and military leadership of the Empire. Jesuits served as chaplains in Hungarian regiments, which after 1715 were directly subordinate to the Emperor.[69] Like the Habsburg domains themselves, the Austrian Province had a mission that was not confined to the linguistic or cultural origins of many of its members, and which spread the visual and literary aesthetic of the Viennese court wherever it went.[70] Hungarian Jesuits played a key role in the

---

[65] Zoran Ladić, "Students from Croatia at Universities in Graz, Austria and Trnava, Slovakia during the 16th and 17th centuries," in *Jesuits among the Croats: Proceedings of the International Symposium: Jesuits in the Religious, Scientific, and Cultural Life among the Croats, October 8–11, 1990*, ed. Valentin Pozaić (Zagrabiensis, 2000), pp. 298–308.

[66] R.W. Seton-Watson, *Racial Problems in Hungary* (New York, 1972), p. 33.

[67] Stanislav J. Kirschbaum, *A History of Slovakia: the Struggle for Survival* (New York, 1995), pp. 296, footnote 26; pp. 6, 9, 78. Starting in 1714, Trnava was also the point of dispersal of Stobäu's letter of 1598 instructing theologically trained Jesuits how to root out Protestantism in Styria, another example of the transfer of Central European tactics to the Habsburg eastern frontier. Evans, *Making*, p. 273. The establishment of the Trnava seminary in 1679 was in anticipation of the reconquest of the Danube Basin and perhaps territories to its east as well. PFK 118.E. 41, *Jesuitica documenta* ... folios 829r–836v. Dedicated to the Virgin, the Trnava complex was situated in a geometrical town plan whose rationality would be echoed in the construction of the Cluj Jesuit complex several decades later. A small plan of the town appears in the insert facing the frontispiece in *Metamorphoses seu Natales Poëtici submontianarum Superioris Hungaria Urbium et Vinearum honoribus ... A Reverendo Patre Bartholomeo Zarubal è S. J ... .* (Cassoviae, 1728).

[68] A Jesuit, Antonio Possevino, had served as moderator between the Habsburg court and the Prince of Transylvania at a point when Transylvanian influence had been at its peak. John Patrick Donnelly, "Antonio Possevino, SJ as Papal Mediator between Emperor Rudolph II and King Stephen Báthory," *ARSI* 59 (2000), pp.3–56.

[69] Király, *Hungary*, p. 7. Jesuit priests of the Cluj residence assisted the Habsburg army as early as 1692. ARSI, *Aust. 155, An Prov. Aus. 1697*, folio 70r.

[70] The study of late Baroque Jesuit art in Europe is still underdeveloped. The best analysis of the Baroque Jesuit art in general is *Baroque Art: The Jesuit Contribution*, Rudolph

management of this Province, even while they encountered direct opposition from the nobility in many of the counties of Royal Hungary.[71] And although Hungarians were sometimes associated in the memories of the Imperial Court with rebellion, and despite the fact that the relative number of Hungarians in the Danube Basin was probably declining throughout the eighteenth century, Hungarian Jesuits seemed individually to receive more than fair treatment from Vienna, where the Imperial court counted many Jesuits in its retinue.[72] Indeed, many Hungarian Jesuits had the explicit support of the Habsburg court in the completion of projects that focused on Hungarian themes.[73] On an institutional level, the Habsburgs took a keen interest in the internal politics of the Austrian Province, playing what appears to have been a decisive role in the decision not to split it into two parts.[74] Like the Habsburg domains, the Austrian Province in the eighteenth century had its origins and center of strength in Central Europe but faced eastward; and although it included within its borders Alpine lands closer to France than to eastern Hungary, its orientation was never strongly towards Western Europe. Instead, the educational and missionary programs of the Society consistently addressed the agenda of the Habsburgs. Yet merely asserting that the agenda of the dynasty (as it was perceived from its base

---

Witkower and Irine B. Jaffe (eds) (New York, 1972).

[71] OSzK, 2039 FMI/1608 *Historia anno 1722*.

[72] The territory occupied by Hungarian speakers decreased relatively during the eighteenth century, in part because of the increases in other groups, notably the Serbs. Both groups may have been fairly mobile throughout the period. Károly Kocsis and Eszter Kocsis-Hodosi, *Hungarian Minorities in the Carpathian Basin: A Study in Ethnic Geography* (Toronto/ Buffalo, NY, 1995), pp. 15–16; Jeroen Duindam, "The court of the Austrian Habsburgs," in John Adamson (ed.), *The Princely Courts of Europe 1500–1750: Ritual, Politics and Culture under the* Ancien Régime (London, 1999), pp. 181–2.

[73] One of the most famous of these was the Jesuit historian Hevenesi Gábor (1656–1715), who compiled historical records now housed in the Bibliotheca Batthyaneum in Alba Iulia. György Hölvényi, *A magyar jezsuita történetírók és a jezsuita rend* (Budapest, 1974). The key Jesuit position linking political and religious concerns in the region is exemplified by Hevnesi's great project of more than 140 volumes, never published, of a history of the Church in Hungary. Carlos Sommervogel, Augustin de Backer, Auguste Carayon and Pierre Bliard, *Bibliothèque de la Compagnie de Jésus: nouvelle edition* (Bruxelles: 1890–1932), vol. 4, p. 360; Erik Molnár, "Historical Science," in *Science in Hungary* (Budapest, 1965), p. 163. See also D. Dümmerth, "Les Combats et la Tragédie du Père Melchior Inchofer," *Annales Universitatis Scientarum Budapestiensis de Rolando Eötvös nominate: Sectio Historica 27*, p. 106. A later generation of Jesuit polymaths and historians is represented by Georgius Pray (1723–1801), who wrote the first history of Hungarian music and performed groundbreaking work on the earliest period of Hungarian literature. Bence Szabolcsi, "Musicology," in *Science in Hungary* (Budapest, 1965), pp. 246–58; Sommervogel et al., *Bibliothèque*, vol. 6, pp. 1182–1192. While neither of these Jesuits worked in Cluj, their scholarship would have been well known to the Cluj community and would have further strengthened the sense of connection to Hungary.

[74] In 1712, Charles VI (King Charles III of Hungary) declared, "Hinc propositam provinciam seperatam ... necdum concedi." Cited in Lukács László, *A független magyar Jezsuita rendtartomány kérdése és az osztrák abszolutizmus (1649–1773)* (Szeged, 1989).

in Vienna) was a major concern of the Jesuits of the Austrian Province does not tell us very much about the cultural impact of that dynasty on the day-to-day activities of the Society since the very nature of the culture fostered by the dynasty during the first half of the eighteenth century remains a subject of debate. The Habsburg court and capital, during the first decades covered by this study, have in fact been variously assessed as vibrant cultural centers, or as a stagnant region of intellectual obscurantism.[75] Nor does claiming a tie between the Habsburgs and the Jesuits say very much about the quality of the schools and universities run by the Society with the dynasty's blessing, or about what the dynasty's hopes and expectations were regarding these schools.[76] We must also look at the implementation of Habsburg policies in the more remote regions of the Habsburg lands, including Transylvania, not neglecting the actions of the dynasty during the final years of the Society's presence in the region.[77] The manner in which the Habsburgs were described by the Jesuits can also provide a clue as to how the Society regarded its patron dynasty. By examining what evidence is available the relationship between the dynasty and the Society will become clearer, since the Jesuits, venturing ever further into remote and distant districts, depended increasingly on material and moral support from Vienna.

The Habsburg territories and with it the dynasty's ambitions, survived the century, just as the Austrian Province survived intact until the final catastrophe that brought down the Society. While tensions surfaced periodically among some ethnically Hungarian Jesuits who wanted their own province, the institutional integrity of the Province was never compromised, and its existence down to 1773 formed a close institutional parallel to the Habsburg control of the region.[78] Both the dynastic realm (the Habsburg lands were not designated an "empire" until 1804) and the Jesuit Province worked to strengthen their corporate identities in various ways. During the eighteenth century, both set about the task of strengthening their institutional structures, so that while throughout the eighteenth century the Society wrote, compiled and forwarded to Rome its own records concerning its activities in the Principality, the Austrian Chancellery simultaneously issued a "Decretum

---

[75] The Oriental Academy of Vienna, which included in its curriculum chemistry and other "practical" subjects of interest to the dynasty, was staffed by Jesuits. Günther Hamann, "Zur Wissenschaftspflege des aufgeklärten Absolutismus," in Erich Zöllner (ed.), *Österreich im Zeitalter des aufgeklärten Absolutismus* (Wien, 1983), pp. 158–60. For the debate on the cultural attainments of Charles VI's court, see C.A. MacCartney, "The Habsburg Dominions," in *The New Cambridge Modern History* (Cambridge, 1963), vol. 7: *The Old Regime 1713–1765*, p. 398. A more positive assessment of Habsburg leadership in the arts is offered by Ernest Wangermann, *The Austrian Achievement* (London, 1973), pp. 45ff.

[76] It has been a commonplace to claim that while the schools of the Jesuits contributed greatly to the cultural milieu of the Habsburg lands, the universities of the region, all of which except Salzburg were run by the Society, were mediocre. Jean Bérenger, "The Austrian church," in William J. Callahan and David Higgs (eds), *Church and Society in Catholic Europe of the Eighteenth Century* (Cambridge, 1979), p. 97.

[77] For an overview of policy throughout Hungary see Éva H. Balázs, *Hungary and the Habsburgs 1765–1800: An Experiment in Enlightened Absolutism* (Budapest, 1997).

[78] For the question of the establishment of a "Hungarian Province," see Lukács, *Rendtartomány*, p. 110.

instructivum" requiring the collecting of important state and dynastic documents, as first step towards a self-conscious compilation of dynastic history.[79] Thus the rationalization and bureaucratization of the eastern domains of the Habsburgs and of the Principality were simultaneously accomplished step by step by both the dynasty and by the Jesuits, each of whom took surprising measures in their search for security. And as the Habsburgs negotiated to pay for their large military presence in Transylvania and Hungary, even going so far as to consider having their sometime enemies the Turks pay some of their bills, so the Society strengthened ties with Uniate Christians, who a few years earlier, as Orthodox believers, had been opponents of the Roman Church.[80] Both institutions, the dynasty and the Society, had a complex and not always positive relationship with the local nobility, whose own loyalties typically lay with local institutions and traditions, and who were supported by ancient privileges that did not require the endorsement of a Universal Church or an Imperial bureaucracy.[81] And both institutions, as we shall see, never completely grasped the nuances of the intergroup relations of early modern Transylvania.

Given the durability of both the dynasty and the Society, and the drive both demonstrated towards rationalization and organization of its activities in ways that disregarded ethnic distinctions, one might be tempted to discard completely the nationalist emphasis in the historiography of the region. Instead, one might approach the interaction between Jesuits and the Cluj community as the meeting of a monolithic religious institution, backed by an ambitious and centralizing Imperial bureaucracy, with a cluster of local cultures whose distinct characteristics were to be co-opted and absorbed. But such an approach, while it contains more than a grain of truth, would overlook salient features of the Society itself as it functioned in the pre-Suppression era. The uniform and distinctly rigorous training of Jesuit priests, encouraged by the decrees of the Council of Trent and specified in the *Constitutions* of the Society, allowed these men the chance to transcend a local or national orientation by joining an organization that had transnational goals and methods, and a universalist understanding of its basic spiritual message.[82] The basic curriculum that all future Jesuit priests studied was spelled out in the *Ratio Studiorum*, which had reached its final form as early as 1599 and which also provided the structure for the schools founded by the Society.[83] These factors, along with the generally formulaic manner in which the Jesuits often kept their own records, make it easy to see only the repetitive,

---

[79] 13 September 1749. Ioan Dordea, "Les archives transylvaines," *Transylvanian Review* 4/3 (1995), p. 11.

[80] By 1771, the Porte was entertaining proposals from Vienna concerning the Ottoman subsidizing of Imperial troops. Roider, *Austria's Eastern Question*, pp. 111–21.

[81] Systematic work in a Western language on Transylvanian nobility is lacking. Henrik Marczali, *Hungary in the XVIII Century* (Cambridge, 1910) remains the best overview of the upper social strata of the Hungarian-speaking regions.

[82] *Constitutions*, pp. 174ff.; P. Joseph de Guibert, *La Spiritualité de la Compagnie de Jésus: Esquisse Historique* (Rome, 1953). See also Paul Shore, "Universalism and Rationalism among the Jesuits of Bohemia (1770–1800)," in D. Dawson and V. Cossy (eds), *Progrès et violence au xviiie siècle* (Paris, 2001), pp. 71–84.

[83] *The* Ratio Studiorum *of 1599*, trans. Allan P. Farrell (Washington, DC, 1982). A brief and accurate summary of how the *Ratio* was actually implemented up until the time of the

uniform, and increasingly outdated features of the Jesuit missionary and educational activities.[84] Yet the truth about the Society's Cluj projects lies elsewhere, between two polar extremes of interpretation. One pole is the straitjacket of the nationalist historiographic paradigm that sees most if not all of the moves made by the Society in Transylvania driven by political and ethnic considerations, and individual Jesuits capable of protean twists of character and tactics in order to serve the changing worldly goals of the Society and its allies. On the other hand, an uncritical reading of records left behind by the Society where the uniform and universalist elements are most prominent suggests a united and unchanging front, free of ethnically derived or pragmatic motives. Determining the exact location of the point of balance between these two interpretations is not easy.

IV

A major "primary" source for this study is the *Litterae Annue* or annual letters submitted by the Austrian Province to Rome.[85] These "letters," sometimes also identified as *Annales*, are in reality systematic reports on each phase of Jesuit activities in the Province, compiled from no longer extant reports submitted by individual missions and communities, and perhaps supplemented by other correspondence from Jesuits.[86] The "letters," common to most provinces of the Society during the eighteenth century, are therefore primary-source documents in terms of their date of composition and as reflections of the institutional culture of the Society.[87] Yet there are also records of events that were in the past when they were recorded, concealing

---

Suppression is found in John W. Donohoe, SJ, *Jesuit Education: An Essay on the Foundations of its Idea* (New York, 1963), pp. 63–70.

[84] Mikes Kelemen (1690–1761), the page of the exiled Ferenc II Rákóczi, complained in a letter dated 1727 that the students of Jesuit schools learned "Latin and nothing else … this learning for eight or nine years, is useful neither for him, nor for the country." Quoted in Domokos Kosáry, *Culture and Society in Eighteenth-Century Hungary*, trans. Zsuzsa Béres (Budapest, 1987), p. 108.

[85] The Latinity of the *Literae* and other Latin documents produced by the Jesuits of Transylvania follows a model of style set by the *Ratio* and other foundational documents of the Society, but some terminology peculiar to the region occurs. See Antonius Bartal, *Glossarium Mediae et Infimae Latinitatis Regni Hungariae* (Lipsiae, 1901).

[86] The *Literae*, as established in the "Formula scribendi" of the *Institutes* of the Society, "ad Nostrorum consolationem ac proximorum aedificationem pertinent: ex quibus selegant optima quaeque, atque, in ordinem redacta … ." The reader should take into account what might have been considered "optima" by the redactors. Writers were also instructed to keep a record of all things that merited recording but that anything "tamen propter aliquam causam non expediat omnibus vulgari, id scribent seperatim integre et perfecte." *Institutum Societatis Iesu Volumen Tertium* (Florentiae, 1893), pp. 43–4. A contemporaneous compendium of the *Institutes*, the type that would have guided the writers of reports in the field, states simply "Discretae sint literae", free of any hint of suspicion or improbity. *Epitome Instituti Societatis Jesu* (Pragae, M.DC. XC), p.426.

[87] Analyses of the terms and literary techniques found in Jesuit histories are rare. A glossary of terms used by historians of the Society is found in *Historia Residentiae Walcensis Societatis Jesu ab anno 1618 avo*, Max Rohwerder (ed.), (Köln/Graz, 1967), pp. 291–7.

the implicit values and mores of the institution that brought them into existence even as they record the activities of the institution.[88] To a lesser degree, the "letters" are also expressions of the individual Jesuits who composed, transcribed, or edited them. Moreover, these "letters" are secondhand in their formulation, a circumstance further complicated by the desire of the leadership of the Province to present a picture of unity and success to Rome and to itself, and the desire for the Roman leadership of the Society to record its undertakings as successful and unified.[89] The issue is not merely that nationality and ethnic diversity, as we understand them today, as well as explicit diplomatic activities, fail to appear as an explicit focus of concern in these documents, but also that the very formulaic nature of the *Litterae* dominates the narratives, being a reflection of the emphasis on repetition found in Jesuit schooling.[90] Differing circumstances and events were shaped by successive Jesuit correspondents, editors and revisers into frequently monotonous narratives that stressed the universal nature of the goal sought, and the inevitable success of the Society in its pursuit of this goal.[91] Careers of individual Jesuits were often compressed and retold in obituary notices that obscure significant accomplishments, smooth over conflicts, and fail to address the ethnic and linguistic identity of the players, or their experiences before entering the Society.[92] Infrequently the general records of the Cluj community would take note of natural phenomena, although such reports lacked detail or adequate context. On the Calends of March, 1718, for example, a strange light appeared to the east of Cluj, and moved northward.[93] It is unclear whether this light was a comet or some other meteorological event, and no mention is made of this occurrence in subsequent entries in the *Historia*. And while the Cluj community also produced additional sets of records known as the "first" and "second" catalogues, which help flesh out the references provided in the *Litterae*,

---

[88] In this regard, Michel de Certeau writes, "a mise en scène of a (past) reality, that is, the historiographical discourse itself, occults the social and technical apparatus of the professional institution that produces it." Michel de Certeau, "History: ethics, science, and fiction," in *Social Science as a Moral Inquiry*, eds Norma Haan, Robert Bellah, Paul Rainbow and William M. Sullivan (New York, 1983), p. 130.

[89] For a discussion of a similar, but not entirely identical set of issues related to the *Litterae Annue* of the Bohemian Province, see my *The Eagle and the Cross: Jesuits in Late Baroque Prague* (St. Louis, MO, 2002). The greater size and cultural diversity of the Austrian Province placed even greater strains on any effort to produce a uniform narrative.

[90] Even a Jesuit historian with apologetic tendencies confesses that "Truly, the Jesuits made a pedagogical cult of repetition." William J. McGucken, SJ, *The Jesuits and Education* (New York, 1932), p. 37.

[91] These features are hallmarks of Baroque Jesuit writings. See Trevor Johnson, "Blood, tears and Xavier-Water: Jesuit missionaries and popular religion in the eighteenth century Upper Palatinate," in *Popular Religion in Germany and Central Europe, 1400–1800*, eds Bob Scribner and Trevor Johnson (Basingstoke, 1996), pp. 183–203.

[92] Jesuit obituaries might be considered a literary genre in their own right, often saying as much about the Society's institutional culture and the values promoted in that culture as about the deceased. See Martin Svatoš, "Antonín Koniáš SJ von seinen Ordensbrüdern dargestellt," *Humanistica Lovaniensia* 43 (1994), pp. 411–24.

[93] OSzK, 2039/ FMI/1608, *Historia anno 1718*, p. 211.

these catalogues, too, record information in a formulaic fashion that sometimes requires reading between the lines.

The Jesuit chroniclers frequently conceived of the interactions of the Jesuit fathers and brothers with the surrounding Cluj community in strict categories that conform with the objectives of the Society's mission and educational work. And within these categories, descriptions of the interactions are likewise frequently formulaic. Conversion experiences take on an almost ritualistic quality as reported, while educational setbacks and proselytizing failures can often only be inferred from the narrative. Noble or royal patrons are described in the predictable language of the Baroque, and competing religious groups – Jews, Muslims, Calvinists, and so on – receive undifferentiated criticism.

Yet beneath the uniformity of the Jesuit *Literae* and the official histories of schools that were composed by the Society can be detected some of the complexity and tension which characterized much of the Jesuit experience in Cluj and elsewhere in the eastern Habsburg realms. While Jesuits received a systematic, uniform academic formation, the isolated journey that each Jesuit who undertook the *Spiritual Exercises* of St. Ignatius experienced was an equally important feature of Jesuit training.[94] More than most other Catholic religious orders and notwithstanding its famous "fourth vow" of obedience to the Pope, the Society has always attracted individualists who test limits and seek avenues for self-expression, albeit within the Society's stated mission. The isolation and de facto autonomy which distant missions such as those in Transylvania placed on the shoulders of individual Jesuits could only increase the possibility that some Jesuits would respond in an individual fashion to the challenges they encountered.[95] Tensions in the Jesuit mission manifested themselves in other ways: in anomalies in the quantitative data reported and in passages where the curtain of formulaic language parts enough to provide a glimpse of interactions between Jesuits and others. Other categories of records kept by the Society suggest the flexibility the Jesuits were actually capable of. A list of children housed (and presumably schooled) in a "Domus Neoconversorum" in Cluj in 1769 for example included the name of a Gypsy (Rom) girl, something for which the original *Ratio* had made no allowance.[96] The very exceptional nature of such references cautions us against automatically viewing them as evidence of more usual occurrences passed over in silence, but the large cast of characters reported in the Jesuit *Literae* is a reminder of the diversity of human contacts that occurred. Ultimately, Jesuit history in Cluj, like Jesuit history in other settings, is supported by voluminous documentation, yet often seen through a glass darkly. The repetitive

---

[94] Joseph Tetlow, *Ignatius Loyola: Spiritual Exercises* (New York, 1992). All Jesuits complete the exercises, and throughout the seventeenth and eighteenth centuries, Jesuit spiritual advisers guided many laypersons through them.

[95] Because the fourth vow includes the promise to go anywhere, including "among the Turks and infidels," the very sweeping nature of the commitment opens the door to situations where it would not be possible to consult authorities when faced with a dilemma. Ganss (ed.), *Constitutions*, p. 68.

[96] Paul Shore, "Jesuit missions and schools in eighteenth century Transylvania and Eastern Hungary," in I.I. Monok and P. Ötvös (eds), *Lesestoffe und kulturelles Niveau des niedrigen Klerus: Jesuiten und die nationalen Kulturverhältnisse* (Szeged, 2001), p.106.

features of Jesuit record-keeping are easily spotted, but the potential adaptability of Jesuit intellectual activity, as exemplified by the pre-Suppression Society's support of the theologically controversial position of probabilism, is also present, if often less obviously so.[97]

The following chapters will show that the Jesuit contribution that flowed from their work in Cluj had both direct and indirect consequences for the community and the region. The direct results can be traced in the record of buildings erected, students enrolled, conversions reported, processions and pilgrimages undertaken, and acts of charity performed: the data so often reported in the *Literae*. These works, as conceived and completed, are the product of the Society of Jesus as an institution, a religious order within the Catholic Church, but characterized by its own "way of proceeding" which produced indirect results as well.[98] As time passed and the Jesuit community began to encounter the surrounding population in a variety of contexts, the contacts between Jesuit and non-Jesuit took on a special quality, transcending the level of interactions or negotiations, for, as John J. O'Malley puts it, "The reality of the reciprocity between Jesuits and those for whom they ministered was even more profound."[99]

Likewise Jesuit schools did more than simply present a morally neutral body of knowledge to a passive student body. The program outlined in the *Ratio* raised the status of the teacher, placing upon him a moral agenda that encompassed both curriculum and instruction.[100] At the same time, since many Jesuit teachers in the lower faculties of the *collegium* were simultaneously students in the higher faculties, casting the role of both student and teacher in a new light.[101] Jesuit teachers also served as missionaries, librarians, private tutors and administrators at various points in their careers. In short, the institutional and individual faces that the Society presented to the Cluj community were complex, changing, and ones whose legacy must be traced in many directions. Their ultimate significance may have taken forms that the Jesuit chroniclers of the time could neither have envisioned nor articulated.

Before we can begin to assess the concrete, immediate contribution of the Jesuits we must see the place in which they did their work. The next two chapters will trace the development of the program to unite Orthodox Romanians with the Church of Rome, an endeavor that, while it did not produce the results desired by the Jesuits, nevertheless had a lasting impact on the Orthodox Church and on subsequent Romanian cultural history. Chapter Four will take up the story of the schools founded

---

[97] William B. Ashworth, Jr., "Catholicism and early modern science," in David C. Lindberg and Ronald L. Numbers (eds), *God and Nature: Historical Essays on the Encounter between Christianity and Science* (Berkeley, CA, 1986), p. 157.

[98] This phrase can be traced back to the earliest years of the Society, and has been attributed to Ignatius. O'Malley, *Jesuits*, p. 8.

[99] John J. O'Malley, "The Historiography of the Society of Jesus," in John W. O'Malley, SJ, Gauvin Alexander Bailey and Stephen J. Harris, and T. Frank Kennedy, SJ (eds), *The Jesuits: Cultures, Sciences and the Arts, 1540–1773* (Toronto, 1999), p. 26.

[100] Karl Hengst, *Jesuiten an Universiäten und Jesuitenuniversitäten* (Paderborn/München/Wien/Zürich, 1981).

[101] Philippe Ariès, *Centuries of Childhood*, trans. Robert Baldick (New York, 1962), p. 152.

by the Jesuits in Cluj, and retrace the careers of some of the more notable Jesuits who taught in them as well as the students who attended them. One of the points of their departure is the *Metamorphosis Transylvaniae*, the memoir of Apor Péter, a graduate of the Jesuit academy in Cluj. This essay is a record of the ideas and memories of a Transylvanian aristocrat whose relations with other ethnic and religious groups is startlingly different from what many nationalistic historians of the region have emphasized in their writings.[102]

In Chapter Five an attempt will be made to locate the Jesuits of Cluj within the context of the physical environment that they created. Debate continues as to whether one can speak of a "Jesuit style" in the arts and music.[103] Despite the remote location and their limited resources, the Jesuits of Cluj produced or supervised the construction of an impressive array of buildings, commissioned artists and left a lasting stamp on the landscape of Cluj.[104] Here we will attempt to place these contributions in context, drawing upon the scholarship dealing with the controversies that impacted Eastern European art in the early modern period.[105]

The major impact of Jesuit drama on the cultural history of Central Europe has already been alluded to. Cluj was one of the most important centers of production of Jesuit plays. Chapter Six will review the characteristics and significance of these dramas, and how they projected the values of the Society, and in particular the values of the predominantly Hungarian Jesuits who wrote them. Jesuit plays were part of a larger drive to promote an aesthetic that had been little known in Transylvania before the arrival of the Society, one that linked classical, baroque and at times exotic elements to win over an audience. Jesuit dramas therefore included universalist elements that characterized other forms of public performance promoted by the Society, and as we shall see, the factors that made these plays a success are a key to other, less obvious components of the Jesuit enterprise in Cluj and elsewhere. The relationship of the Society to various communities that were encountered in and around Cluj will be the theme of Chapter Seven, which will also examine the type of social order the Society sought to introduce or even to impose on the region. Chapter Eight will look at the community that the Society created for its own members ("Nostri") during the eighty years it flourished in Cluj, and will attempt to identify some of the patterns that helped shape the lives of the men who lived in this community.

Finally, in Chapter Nine the Transylvanian Jesuit missions to Moldavia in the eighteenth century will be considered. These expeditions were sponsored by the Austrian Province, and in several instances had their geographical origins in or near Cluj. But their connection to the Cluj mission runs deeper than this. Like Transylvania, Moldavia was a multi-ethnic, polyglot principality with a Catholic minority. But unlike Transylvania, Moldavia never passed under the domination

---

[102] The *Metamorphosis* appears in published form in *Monumenta Hungariae historica*. Második osztály, ed. Irók. Klazinczy Gábor (Pest, 1863), vol. 2.

[103] "'Le style Jésuite n'existe pas': Jesuit corporate culture and the visual arts," in O'Malley et al. (eds), *Jesuits*, pp. 38–89.

[104] Sas Péter, *A. kolozsvári piarista templom* (Kolozsvár, 1999).

[105] Sergiusz Michalski, *The Reformation and the Visual Arts* (London/New York, 1993).

of the House of Habsburg, nor did it ever become formally a part of the Austrian Province of the Society. Instead it was ruled by a puppet of the Ottomans, and where relations with his Hungarian and Catholic subjects were sometimes stormy and whose interest in the fostering of Western culture varied from ruler to ruler. The Moldavian missions provide a useful comparison with the longer lived and more successful Cluj enterprise because Moldavia and its capital Iaşi lay beyond the limited of what eighteenth-century Europeans saw as their own civilization. Yet some of the same Jesuits who worked in Cluj traveled to this eastern outpost, thereby creating a link between the "European" goals of missions lying within Austrian territory and the possibilities and challenges of "foreign" missions in lands beyond the pale of Western Christendom. That Moldavia and Transylvania would later be united into a Romanian state whose historians strongly desired the development of a unified "national" historical narrative adds to the importance of this comparison.

Chapter Ten will attempt to draw conclusions concerning the long-term impact of the eight decades during which the Society's Cluj project was undertaken. This impact took the form of educational institutions, social organizations, the establishment of an educated elite who shared the experience of Jesuit schooling, and the introduction of state-supported Catholicism and a state-endorsed Uniate Church. In each case, the impact of the Jesuit presence was not precisely what the original Jesuits who arrived in 1693 had envisioned.

Let us turn now to the single most ambitious and controversial component of the Jesuit mission in Transylvania, the Uniate Church.

CHAPTER TWO

The Uniate Church

I

The thirty years leading up to the Society's official return to Transylvania was a period of constant growth throughout the Austrian Province. As the Habsburg dynasty strengthened its control over its hereditary possessions to the west and gradually expanded its influence in the east, Jesuits followed, reestablishing schools and restoring missionary programs that had been interrupted a century earlier. Between 1661 and 1694, six new *collegia* were established, the majority of them in the newly liberated Hungarian regions.[1] The replanting of Catholic culture in these territories was undertaken in the face of the privations brought on by the Turkish occupation, a period of destruction and confusion for much of the region that left some districts uncultivated wastelands. The withdrawal of the Turks was immediately followed by the immigration of mostly Slavic and Romanian Orthodox believers from the south and east. In a few instances these immigrants included Catholic refugees from areas still under the control of the Porte, but even in such instances the immigrants were from ethnic groups whose cultures were distant from the High Baroque idiom promoted by the Habsburgs.[2] This immigration of non-Catholics was less pronounced in the central Danube Basin, which, while it contained some Orthodox believers who had settled there during the Turkish occupation, had never become a center of Orthodoxy in Eastern Europe. The Catholic roots of the Danube Basin region ran deep, and were exemplified by the title of "Apostolic King of Hungary," bestowed by the pope in the eleventh century and held by the Habsburgs since their acquisition of Hungary in 1526. Moreover, the relative proximity of the basin to the Habsburg hereditary territories of Upper and Lower Austria, which by now had been aggressively recatholicized, made the reintroduction of Catholicism to the heartland of Hungary still a challenging but by no means impossible task. This

---

[1] Joseph Brucker, *La Compagnie de Jésus: Esquisse de son Institute et son Histoire (1521–1773)* (Paris, 1919), p. 621. By the time of the Suppression, the Society had eighteen *collegia*, twenty smaller houses, and eleven missions in Hungary. Puskely Mária, *Kétezer év szeretesége: Szeretség és müvelődéstörténenti enciklopédia* (2 vols, Budapest, 1998), vol. 1, p. 553. As early as 1649, there were already twenty "domicilia" in Hungary, and numerous smaller missions. Lukács, *A független magyar jezsuita rendtartomány*, p. 41, *Catalogus Provinciarum, Collegiarum Residentiarum Seminariorum et Missionum universae Societatis Jesu* (Tyrnaviae, 1750).

[2] After the Peace of Karolwitz returned Bulgaria to Turkey and Western armies withdrew, Catholic Bulgarians who had staged an abortive uprising were compelled to flee to Wallachia or Transylvania. Charles A. Frazee, *Catholics and Sultans: The Church and the Ottoman Empire 1453–1923* (Cambridge, 1983), p. 110.

task of reclaiming Hungarian lands "for Europe" was aided by the belief that resettlement or even perhaps colonization might accompany recatholicization,[3] thereby allowing a new culture, unsullied by earlier disputes, to develop. Rooting out Protestant institutions in the Carpathian Mountains north of the Basin was at times tougher, but with Habsburg support Jesuits regained control of churches and schools by the late 1680s, aided in the replanting of the latter by the reputation for flexibility their educational institutions still enjoyed.[4] In contrast to the situation it encountered when it returned in force in the Danube Basin, when the Society began to resume its full-scale activities in Transylvania it found that the overwhelming majority of the ethnic Romanian inhabitants of the region were members of the Orthodox Church, whose presence had been established there almost a millennium earlier, and which claimed ties to Christians who had settled there when the territory had been part of the Roman Empire.[5] A significant number of the ethnic Romanians who made up the overwhelming majority of the Orthodox population were the descendants of settlers who had arrived centuries before, from a time before the region had been part of the Kingdom of Hungary. Others had probably come during the seven centuries when Transylvania was ruled by Hungarian kings, and this immigration from Walachia and Moldavia continued in the seventeenth century. The number of Orthodox believers already settled in the mountains and valleys of Transylvania was also constantly augmented by refugees fleeing from regions within the Ottoman Empire, and who generally found the porous borders between the two realms capable of passage.[6] In addition to refugees entering Transylvania, Transylvanian villagers might also travel in the opposite direction, lured into Moldavia or Wallachia by recruiters sent by boyars who needed laborers in depopulated regions.[7] Among these were Transylvanian Catholics who emigrated to Moldavia, where they settled permanently, thereby creating a cultural tie between

---

[3] Wolff, *Inventing*, p. 164.

[4] Oswald Redlich, *Weltmacht des Barock: Österreich in der Zeit Leopolds I*, 4th edn (Wien, 1961), p. 417. It was well known, for example, that one could begin schooling at any age between ten and seventeen. John Stoye, *Marsigli's Europe: The Life and Times of Luigi Ferdinando Marsigli, Soldier and Virtuoso* (New Haven, CT, 1994), p. 15.

[5] The question of when the Orthodox Church was established in Transylvania is closely connected to the debate as to the date of the arrival of the ancestors of the modern-day Romanians in the region, a controversy that casts a shadow over the entire historiography of the region. Orthodoxy was present from at least the eleventh century (Pascu, *History*, p. 60), but whether the recently Christianized and Roman-oriented Magyars, who subdued the region in the same century, brought with them their own religious institutions, both pagan and Christian, is less certain.

[6] For example, Bulgarians migrating northward out of the Ottoman Empire settled in an abandoned village near Alba Iulia around the year 1700. Nilles, *Symbolae*, vol. 2, pp. 1061–2. It is not possible, however, to determine the actual number of emigrants from the Ottoman Empire who became permanent residents of Transylvania.

[7] Vlad Georgescu, *The Romanians: A History*, ed. Matei Calinescu and trans. Alexandra Bley-Vroman (Columbus, OH, 1991), p. 89.

Catholic Transylvania and the east.[8] Yet the presence of an Eastern Christian tradition, one well established and closely identified with the indigenous culture of the inhabitants, marked out the Principality as something different from other solidly Catholic or previously Protestant territories to the west acquired by the Habsburgs over the previous centuries. The challenge of the Orthodox population of Transylvania, while particularly difficult, could be viewed as simply a more extreme example of conditions existing everywhere in the newly acquired Habsburg possessions. In the east, the political, religious and dynastic loyalty of all segments of the population remained a basic question facing the dynasty, and likewise drove its efforts to repopulate north-eastern Hungary with foreign landowners it could depend on.[9] Orthodoxy was and is, for its Romanian followers, more than a religious tradition; it was also a connection across national boundaries to a wider cultural heritage spread throughout Eastern Europe, whose origins stretch back to the Late Roman period when the division of the Empire fostered and institutionalized the inherent differences between the societies from which Western and Eastern Christianity had sprung.[10] While linguistically the ethnic Romanians were distanced from their Slavic and Hellenic neighbors, the common bonds of Orthodox dogma, tradition and liturgy linked them to the Bulgarians, Greeks and Ukrainians (also known in this period as Ruthenians), each of whom had also struggled to free themselves from the Turk, and who each saw themselves as heirs to the Byzantine religious and cultural traditions.[11] Each of these national churches was also deeply alienated from the Roman Church, which was seen not merely as a rival, but as a source of aggression against its eastern neighbor and a fountain of heretical belief.[12] In the centuries after the Great Schism of 1054, relations between the national Orthodox Churches and Rome had ranged from cool indifference to calculated negotiations to violent hostility, and although

---

[8] In 1714, Stanislau Jezierski, Bishop of Bacau reported that 8,000 Catholics had arrived in Moldavia from Transylvania, and by 1767 24,000 families from Transylvania were reported to have settled in the region. Dumitriu Mărtinaş, *The Origins of the Changos*, eds Vasile M. Ungureanu, Ion Coja and Laura Treptow (Iaşi/Oxford/Portland, OR, 1999), pp. 41, 43. See also Robin Baker, "On the origins of the Moldavian Csangos," *Slavonic and East European Review* 75 (1997), pp. 658–80.

[9] Á. Várkonyi, "Repopulation and the system of cultivation in Hungary after the expulsion of the Turks," *Acta Historica Academiae Scientarum Hungaricae* 16 (1970), pp. 151–70.

[10] The distinctive identity of the Eastern Church can be traced to the Patriarchate of Constantinople. George Every, *The Byzantine Patriarchate 451–1204* (London, 1947), pp. 40ff.

[11] The Romanian Orthodox Church, according to a Catholic observer, was using Old Church Slavonic in the seventeenth century. Juhász (ed.), *Okmánytár*, vol. 1, p. 204. In the eighteenth century, the Romanian Orthodox liturgy was still modeled on that of the Greek Church. H. Daniel-Rops, *The Church in the Eighteenth Century*, trans. John Warrington (New York, 1964), p. 194.

[12] Some of the famous "painted monasteries" of Bukovina, a region directly adjoining Transylvania, portray Catholics, along with Muslims, Tartars and Jews, among the damned. Alan Ogden, *Revelations of Byzantium: The Monastereries and Painted Churches of Northern Moldavia*, introduced by Kurt W. Treptow (Iaşi/Oxford/Palm Beach, CA/Portland, OR, 2002), p. 79.

Jesuit missionaries had traversed the Romanian-speaking lands in the century before the Society's return to Transylvania, these regions had never proven to be fertile ground for conversions.[13] Yet the Jesuit enthusiasm for missionary ventures in the East never slackened, Central and Eastern Europe having been one of the original regions targeted for special attention in the earliest years of the Society.[14] Ethnic Hungarian Jesuits, riding the crest of the liberation of their homeland, also felt a connection with the large and well-established Hungarian-speaking population of Transylvania. The "*status catholicus*" or Catholic nobility of the Principality supported the return of the Society, and soon were petitioning the Father General to send Jesuits "of unblemished personal life" to Transylvania.[15] Jesuits arrived in Transylvania from the west on other assignments as well. At the close of the Turkish era, the Habsburgs sent Antonidus Dunod, a member of the Austrian Province, on a diplomatic mission to the Principality as a personal envoy.[16] The strategic location of these lands was also a major consideration in the long-range plans of the Holy See. Transylvania and its neighbors were key territories whose reclamation by the Church was a high priority for Rome as it sought to capitalize on the retreat of the Ottoman Empire and on the supposed openness of the Muscovite and Russian monarchies to contact with the West. The strategies of the late seventeenth-century Society in exploiting these opportunities, however, differed in important ways from those it had utilized in the sixteenth. Earlier, during the first decades of the Counter-Reformation, the Society's position towards the reclamation of the eastern and southern frontiers of Catholic Europe (which is to say, the Habsburg lands) had been decidedly uncompromising in its approach to already established Churches. Jesuits had in general refused to approach the challenge of religious unity through strategies such as discussions with local religious leaders or the granting of minor concessions to existing ecclesiastic institutions.[17] Protestant Churches had come under particularly

---

[13] Seven Jesuits, including Báranyi László Pál, from whom we shall hear again, were based in the "Manastur" mission, near Cluj, as early as 1683, and earlier Jesuit activity can be traced back to 1650. Lucien Periș, *Le missioni Gesuite in Transilvania e Moldavia nel seicento* (Cluj-Napoca, 1998), pp. 144, 128. Correspondence of seventeenth-century Jesuits traveling through the entire region controlled by the Ottomans is collected in *Documenta Missionaria Hungariam et Regionem sub Ditione Turcia Existentem Spectantia* I. Ex Tabulario Romano Sacrae Congregationis de Propaganda Fide I., eds Joannes Sávai and Gabrielis Pintér (Szegedini, 1993).

[14] Except for Salzburg, all the universities in the mid-seventeenth-century Central European territories of the Habsburgs were in Jesuit hands, a process that began as early as 1552 with the opening of a *Collegium* in Vienna in 1552 and which was strengthened considerably by the Society's control over the venerable University of Prague. Bangert, *History*, p. 73. Ivana Čornejová (ed.), *Dějiny Univerzity Karlovy II: 1622–1802* (Praha, 1996), pp. 23ff. See also O'Malley, *First Jesuits*, p. 62, for the spread of the Society into the northern Habsburg lands.

[15] Letter dated 2 March 1702, Alba Iulia, in Benda (ed.) *Okmánytár*, vol. 2, p. 763.

[16] I. Lupaș, *Sfârșitul suzeraniții otomane și începutul regimului habsburgic în Transilvania. Analele Academiei Române Memorile Secțiunii Istorice Serie III Tomul XXV Mem. 19* (1943), pp. 7–8.

[17] Heiss, "Princes," p. 103.

aggressive attack from the Society, but all non-Catholic institutions were viewed as obstacles to be overcome, rather than as building blocks to spiritual and ultimately political unity. This all-or-nothing approach reflected the grave, even desperate situation that the Catholic Church seemed to be facing in the late sixteenth and early seventeenth centuries in almost all regions controlled by the Habsburgs, when even the pulpits of Imperial Vienna were occupied for a time by Lutheran preachers and the emperor himself seemed to be flirting with the Protestants.[18]

The situation had been transformed a century later, in part because of the consequences of the constant pressure applied by the dynasty on its non-Catholic subjects in both the east and west, and because of the establishment of a generally reliable Catholic landed nobility in the critical Bohemian and Austrian regions. By the latter half of the seventeenth century the Society could point to many successes in its own history of conversion and unification efforts, and had established an enviable status as the leading educational organization in the Western world. In the mid-seventeenth century the Society's self-confidence was at a high point, and the prospects for further successes throughout the world seemed excellent. Jesuit publications of the day drew upon a symbolism that suggested continuing victories in the world, and especially continuing triumphs in the educational and missionary realms.[19] Jesuit hopes for regions inhabited by adherents of the Orthodox Church were also spurred on by the acknowledgement from the Congregatio de Propaganda Fide that the issues that required the most attention were not necessarily challenges over centuries-old rites treasured by local populations, but instead focused on continuing disagreements concerning less central points of dogma, some of which (it was hoped) might not ignite the passions in the ways that fundamental changes in liturgy and ritual could.[20] As far as the union of Orthodox believers with Rome was concerned, the approach to dogmatic difficulties was made as simple as possible, and the gauge by which acceptable conformity to Rome would be determined was

---

[18] Heretical preachers in the Imperial capital were suppressed ruthlessly in the seventeenth century and Vienna quickly became one of the great centers of Catholicism. Paul Hofmann, *The Viennese* (New York, 1988), p. 56.

[19] The outstanding example of this emblematically rendered triumphalism was *Imago Primi Saeculi Societatis Iesu*, published in Antwerp in 1640. O'Malley, "Historiography," in O'Malley et al. (eds), *Jesuits*, p. 31.

[20] This point was clarified in an instruction from the Congregatio in 1669 to missionaries working among the Eastern Churches that Eastern Rites were not to be condemned or challenged, and that only the calendar should be replaced so that holidays might be celebrated on the same days. Moreover, missionaries should concentrate on winning converts over to the Catholic Church in terms of dogma alone, making allowances for the "ignorance" of the uneducated, and recognizing that the process would take time. Costa, "*Supplex libellus*," p. 107. This allowance for "ignorance" was readily embraced by the Society, as it roughly paralleled its approach to confession, whereby relatively liberal standards as to what constituted contrition were applied to the penitent. Yet the Jesuits' flexibility on these and other points of doctrine also alerted critics who saw the entire moral system of the Society as fundamentally lax.

derived from the Council of Florence of 1439, which had codified four key articles that separated the Catholic and Eastern Churches.[21] These were:

- The Pope is the head of the Church of the whole world.
- Unleavened bread is used in giving the Eucharist.
- Besides heaven and hell there is also Purgatory, where souls are purified.
- In the Holy Trinity, the Holy Spirit proceeds from both the Father and the Son (the so-called "filioque clause").[22]

Following the initially high hopes raised by the Council of Florence, which had been instituted in part as a response to the impending collapse of the Byzantine Empire and the danger facing the Eastern Church, during the next several centuries Rome was not particularly successful in reuniting Orthodox Churches with the West. Nevertheless the simplicity of the propositions agreed upon as the minimum requirement for such a union kept the Council's program alive for centuries as a tool for promoting unity. At the same time the practical resolution of other issues agreed upon in Florence remained less clear, especially the practical role of any Orthodox Patriarchs who might enter into union.[23] Ultimately, the abbreviated theological disagreements identified in medieval documents concerning the obstacles that had preceded union and which Florence had attempted to resolve played less of a key role in later negotiations between Rome and the Orthodox hierarchy than the Holy See had originally hoped. As the experience of the Jesuits in Transylvania and elsewhere in Eastern Europe repeatedly made clear, the less dogmatically derived issues that had originally stalled union in the fifteenth century would remain prominent in the seventeenth and eighteenth centuries. These were mutual suspicion and mistrust between two proud and long-established ecclesiastical orders with varying symbols and rituals, differing national perspectives that led to potential conflicts between nation states, and language barriers that carried over into issues of liturgy, preaching, and administration. Added to these were questions about the control of wealth held by the Orthodox Churches that would enter into union, and disagreements that antedated the Great Schism itself but were still vivid in the memories of all concerned.[24] This last bone of contention had been aggravated by reports that Jesuits working in Moldavia had used underhanded tactics to gain control of properties controlled by

---

[21] Dozens of other points of disagreement were also identified, but these were regarded as requiring much more time to root out. Nilles, *Symbolae*, vol. 1, pp. 111–19.

[22] Ludwig Pastor, *History of the Popes*, ed. Frederick Ignatius Antrobus (29 vols, London, 1938), vol. 1, pp. 315–16.

[23] Patriarchal authority in all parts of the Orthodox world continues to this day to be one of the most powerful elements of opposition to Rome. David J. Melling, "Council of Florence (1438–49)," in *The Blackwell Dictionary of Eastern Christianity*, eds Ken Parry et al. (Oxford, 1999), pp. 200–202.

[24] Jesuits were no more willing to ignore the historical antecedents of the controversy than were their Orthodox opposite numbers. A supporter of Orthodoxy might be described as a "new Photius," a reference to the ninth-century Patriarch of Constantinople who rejected Rome's authority. ARSI, *Austria 220, An. Prov. Austr. 1765*, folio 5v; "Photius," in *The Oxford Dictionary of the Christian Church*, ed. F.L. Cross (Oxford, 1997), pp. 1283–4.

the Orthodox Church.[25] And, as is always the case, there was a reluctance among many Orthodox prelates to give up their own long-established way of doing things even when what at stake was not mandated by their Church's historic teachings. The bias of some missionaries entrusted with the task of promoting union was also certainly a factor, as was their lack of familiarity with the languages and customs of the people they would encounter, and their not infrequent insensitivity towards local cultures.

These difficulties, coupled with the challenge of accommodating the positions of the Orthodox patriarchs, who were understandably reluctant to surrender any of their direct authority over their flocks, colored all of the Society's initial efforts in Transylvania and set a tone for the events of the eighteenth century.[26] These challenges did not, however, deter the Jesuits, who despite the view held by some in the west that Transylvania was too dangerous for mission work, yearned to return to the scenes of their earlier successes.[27] Armed with a streamlined program to present to prospective converts and cooperative clergy, and heartened by the apparent success of a Uniate Church in Poland made up of clergy who had accepted the conditions of the Council of Florence, the Society first concentrated its efforts in Ruthenia, like Transylvania a mountainous frontier region abutting Poland and already dominated by the Habsburgs.[28] In the course of the seventeenth century, with the help of energetic envoys and a political situation that steadily gave the advantage to the Habsburgs, the Jesuits were able to bring a significant portion of the Orthodox population there into union with Rome.[29] The peace between the

---

[25] A 1671 letter from the residents of Iaşi claimed that even Orthodox believers were scandalized by the Jesuits' reported refusal to take orders from the local ordinary or even the pope, and their summary occupation of the homes of parish priests. Juhász (ed.), *Okmánytár*, vol. 2, p. 663.

[26] Uniate Church history is presented from a Hungarian standpoint in István Pirigyi, *A magyarországi görögkatolikus története* (Nyíregyháza, 1990), vol. 2, pp. 100–108.

[27] As early as 1650, an anonymous Jesuit in the Kolosmănăştur community composed an "Informatio de statu Transylvaniae et ope conversionis." Benda (ed.), *Okmánytár*, vol. 2, pp. 480–81. On the supposed dangers of seventeenth-century Transylvania, which in the seventeenth century was considered "non impar periculis Japonicis," see MAT, Kéz. Történl. 2 133 Sz. *Historia Collegiorum Domorum et Residentiarum Societatis Jesu in Hungaria, et Transsilvani. Ex Collegij Tyrnavensis A. 1652*, pp. 204–205, and Weiser, *Iskolaügy*, pp. 240ff. The reality of these concerns would be brought home in 1719 when the Jesuit mission in Vásárhely was attacked by Turkish janisaries.

[28] Nilles, *Symbolae*, pp. 2, 922ff; Katona, *Historia Critica*, vol. 20, p. 858 *et passim*. The securing of Ruthenia for the Uniate Church protected the rear flank of any attempt to press the frontier of Catholicism into Transylvania, or beyond.

[29] Ruthenia during the early modern period is best understood as a geographical, rather than an administrative or ethnically delimited term. During the seventeenth century, Ruthenia was ruled by the Habsburgs, and was never dominated by the Ottoman Empire. Much smaller than Transylvania, Ruthenia like its larger neighbor lacked a long-standing history of autonomous dealings with its neighbors and the strong sense of loyalty to local leaders that always characterized the Principality. The formal union of the Orthodox Church in regions of Ruthenia or Transcarpathia nevertheless required decades to accomplish. The first steps towards union were taken in 1646 but the "schismatica hierarchia" was not

Turks and the Russians in 1711 provided more security for this project, and thereby strengthened Jesuit efforts in neighboring Transylvania.[30] Simultaneously, a Greek Uniate, Theophanes Mavrocordat, was preaching a union with Rome in the frontier region between Satu Mare and Oradea, where a mixed population of Hungarian and Romanian speakers made their home; as early as 1636 a catechism composed by the Jesuit Peter Canisius had been translated into Romanian for distribution among the ethnic Romanians of Transylvania.[31] Efforts were also underway to create a Greek Uniate Church, an undertaking that bore fruit before the end of the century.[32] Beyond the realms of the Habsburgs, the Society would continue to use other tactics to further its penetration of the lands of the Eastern Rite. In Tirgovişte, a Romanian city under the control of the Porte, Jesuits had promoted the connection between Greek and Roman rites by establishing the first "higher" school of Latin and Greek in Romanian-speaking lands.[33] Polish Jesuits had been active in Moldavia, another Romanian-speaking region, in the late sixteenth century, and in the seventeenth century there were even hopes of establishing a Uniate Church in the Ottoman-

---

eliminated until 1735. In 1743, Michael Olšavsky, a Rusyn (the term currently preferred by many inhabitants of Ruthenia) of noble background, was appointed as local bishop. Michael Lacko, SJ, "Unio Uzhorodensis Ruthenorum Carpatorum cum Ecclesia Catholica," *OCA* 143 (1955), p. 185; Michael Lacko, SJ, "Documenta spectantia regimen episcopi Munkačevensis Michaelis Manuelis Olšavsky," *Orientalia Christiana Periodica* 25 (1959), pp. 53–90; Nilles, *Symbolae*, vol. 2, p. 824ff. The Uniate diocese of Mukachevo (Munkács), once established, was under the authority of the Catholic Bishop of Eger. Kosáry, *Culture*, pp. 77. See also P. Lud. Carrez, SJ, *Atlas Geographicus Societatis Jesu* (Paris, 1900), plate 9. The influence of Ruthenian religious practice elsewhere in the Habsburg lands can be seen in the veneration of the "Diva Ruthenica," a miraculous image of the Virgin, in rural Bohemia. NK 23/19, folio 323r. By the end of the eighteenth century, the Ruthenian Church could count 839 functioning churches. Stephanus Katona, *Historia Critica Regum Hungariae Stirpis Austriacae* (23 vols, Budae, 1794–1817), pp. 20, 858 *et passim*. See also Josef Mach, SJ, "Ecclesiastical unification: A theoretical framework together with case studies from the history of the Latin-Byzantine relations," *OCA* 198 (1974), pp. 1–388.

[30] OSzK, 2039 FMI/1608, *Historia anno 1711*, pp. 107.

[31] Toader Nicoara, *Transilvania. La începtulurile timpurilor moderne (1680–1800). Societate rurală și mentalitati colective* (Cluj, 1997), pp. 98. An abortive effort by Jesuits to enter Transylvania a few years later resulted in their expulsion in 1653. Father Georgius Buitul, SJ, also produced a Romanian translation of Canisius' catechism that was first published in Bratislava in 1636 and then reprinted in "Klus" in 1703, presumably by the Society's press. The author has been unable to locate a copy of this volume. Sommervogel et al., *Bibliothèque*, vol. 2, p. 366. Veress, *Bibliografia*, vol. 1, pp. 152–3; *Régi magyar könyvtár*, II, p. 2155. See also Weiser, *Iskolaügy*, XL–LI and Sas, *Piarista templom*, p. 20. P. Franciscus Szunyogh, SJ (1679–1726) published a catechism in Romanian, using the old Cyrillic alphabet, as early as 1696. Nilles, *Symbolae*, vol. 1, p. 372.

[32] While union with the Greek Church had been proclaimed during the Council of Florence, in practical terms few Greek Orthodox accepted the authority of Rome during the following two centuries. For efforts to bring about union, starting in 1692 see Nilles, *Symbolae*, vol. 2, pp. 937–59.

[33] Victor Papacostea, *Civilizație Romanescă și Civilizație Balcanică* (București, 1983), pp. 259ff.

controlled region of Serbia.[34] And elsewhere in "Țara Romaneasca," the territory reaching south of the Carpathians and north of the Danube, where Romanian was the dominant language, Jesuits in the eighteenth century would play a role they knew well, that of advisers at a non-Catholic monarch's court, this time serving in the retinue of Constantine Mavrokordat, the Orthodox Prince of Walachia.[35]

The Society likewise approached the challenge of conversion and contact with the various Orthodox communities from other angles as well, participating in a papal legation at the Sublime Porte during the turbulent years of the early eighteenth century.[36] By the start of the eighteenth century, the entire region east of the Leitha could now be viewed as potentially reclaimable from campaigns launched from various directions, both to lands under the direct control of the Habsburgs, as well as to those where the weakening Turkish Empire still maintained its rule.[37] There was even the dream, put forward in 1687 by the Jesuit Franciscus Ravasz, of uniting the Serbian, Romanian and Greek Uniate Churches into a Uniate whole whose orientation would inevitably be western.[38] In this campaign, the Romanian lands and Transylvania were key, both because of their strategic location as gateways to the east, and because their mixed populations afforded opportunities for the Jesuit to proselytize in different directions. Jesuit efforts to establish various bridgeheads in Romanian society, whoever controlled it politically, were therefore widespread and ambitious, none of these undertakings more so than the Uniate Church in Transylvania, which the Society recognized as one of the most important of its undertakings in Eastern Europe.[39]

II The Uniate Church and Historians

Yet although the Uniate Church in Transylvania clearly played an important role in the early modern period in Romania, and has been an object of study for Catholic

---

[34] Nilles, *Symbolae*, vol. 2, p. 710. The Jesuits were expelled from Moldavia following an incident at the princely court in Iași in 1731. *Diplomatarium Italicum. Documenti racolti negli Archivi Italiani* (Roma, 1939), vol. 4. Francisc Pall, " Le controversie tra i Minoriti conventuali e i Gesuiti nelle missioni di Moldavia (Romania)," pp. 308–309.

[35] Georgescu, *The Romanians*, p. 82.

[36] P. Franciscus Miroslavich, (1686–1729), a native of Belgrade (!), served in the Constantinople legation for a year and a half, later teaching philosophy at the Cluj *collegium*. ARSI, *Austria 71, Catalogus I Col. Claud. 1723*; Sommervogel et al., *Bibliothèque*, vol. 6, p. 1493.

[37] The only region where Jesuit advances did not parallel Habsburg acquisitions was in Oltenia, a region in western Wallachia occupied by Austria from 1718 until 1739. Archival records show no evidence of Jesuit activities in this heavily Orthodox district during these years. N. Dobrescu, *Istoria bisericii Române din Oltenia în timpul ocupatiune austrice (1716–1739)*. Cu 200 acte și fragmente inedite culese din Arhivelel din Viena. (București, 1906).

[38] Tóth Zoltán, *Az Erdélyi Román Nacionalizmus első százada 1697–1792* (Budapest, 1946), 19; Sommervogel et al., *Bibliothèque*, vol. 11, p. 194.

[39] The contemporary account of a Jesuit, written at the end of the seventeenth century, conveys the significance attached to the Uniate project. Andreas Freyberger, *Historica Relatio Unionis Ecclesiae Walachiae Cum Romana Ecclesia* (Cluj-Napoca, 1996).

scholars, the contributions of the Church have been obscured by the scarcity of surviving records of its own organization and activities.[40] The known activities of the Church have also long been ignored or minimized by nationalist Romanian historians, a trend that may be discerned as early as the first half of the nineteenth century.[41] Ironically, these early nationalist historians had often received their education in Uniate environments, and at least one, Gheorghe Sincai (1754–1816), was probably educated in the Jesuit schools of Cluj.[42] Romanian Uniates posed a persistent dilemma for many Romanian historians, for while the union with Rome could be interpreted as further evidence of the connection between Romanians and Western Europe, the fact that the Uniate Church was introduced with Habsburg backing and was solidified through the efforts of many Hungarian Jesuits inhibited most Romanian nationalist historians from saying anything positive about it. Rumors of the Jesuits' vast wealth within the Habsburg lands and the Society's close collaboration with the House of Austria only increased the tendency of Romanian historians to look askance at what they viewed as the Jesuit project of the Uniate Church.[43] In doing so, these historians were complementing a pattern elaborated elsewhere, for Jesuits in much of the historiography of other Habsburg lands were portrayed as conniving outsiders using money, threats and deception to accomplish their questionable ends. During the twentieth century, this trend was already marked in the interwar years, when relations between Romania and Hungary were continually tense, and when a new Orthodox cathedral was erected in Cluj, reinforcing the message that the city was a center of Orthodox culture and piety, not a cradle of Catholic and Hungarian culture. Following the communist takeover of Romania in 1948 references in standard Romanian history texts to the Uniate Church and its sponsors did not simply become more negative, they were completely eliminated.[44] Nor was this silencing limited to those historians who served as intimidated and almost anonymous functionaries in the Ceausescu regime; even a figure of the stature of Ştefan Pascu did not address the role of the Uniate Church as an institution in the development of early modern Transylvania, choosing instead to dwell upon the accomplishments of individual

---

[40] For example, no visitation records for the Uniate Church in Transylvania have been found for the period before 1750. István Monok, "Libri ecclesiae pastorumque – Zeugnisse der Protocolle der Kirchenvisitatoren," in Monok and Ötvös (eds), *Lesestoffe*, p. 47.

[41] Iossif Fessler, *Relatio historica de Daco-Romanis in Transilvania et Hungaria cum Ecclesia Romana unitis vel uniendis* (Bucureşti, 1942).

[42] David Prodan, *Din istoria Transilvaniei: Studii şi evocări* (Bucureşti, 1991), p. 314.

[43] Although critics of the Society frequently exaggerated its wealth, it is nonetheless true that by 1747 the Society collectively had become a creditor of the Habsburg government, having loaned it a total of 431,000 florins, not counting sizable loans made to individual nobles. P.G.M. Dickson, *Finance and government under Maria Theresia* (2 vols, Oxford, 1987), vol. 2, p. 307.

[44] Michael J. Ruha, *Reinterpretation of History as a Method of Furthering Communism in Romania* (Washington, DC, 1961), p. 49; for the extent of state archival holdings previous to the Communist era, see *Inventarul Archivelor Statului* (Bucureşti, 1939). After 1948, the Uniate or as it is now more commonly known, "Greco-Catholic" Church was forcibly combined with the much larger Romanian Orthodox Church, a situation reversed after the revolution of 1989.

Uniates without considering the distinctive features, good or bad, of the Church as an institution or its collective impact on Romanian culture.[45] Distrust of Western Christian traditions, if not of the West itself, bitter memories of Habsburg domination, and hostility towards all things seeming to come from or through Hungary – all were factors in the suppression or distortion of information about the establishment of the Uniate Church. The abolition of Orthodox archbishoprics such as Maramureş in 1711, a process that paralleled the development of the Uniate Church, was also a sore point.[46] Likewise, discomfort over the probable motivations of some of the Uniate clergy also inhibited Romanian historians, not a few of whom found affiliation with the Habsburg-dominated Romanian Uniate Church *prima facie* evidence of disloyalty to a Romanian identity and a deviance from the proper destiny of the Romanian people.[47] A Romanian national Orthodox Church, with a complete hierarchy and paralleling those that had long existed in other parts of the Balkans, did not appear until 1865.[48] Thus the visibility of the Uniate Church in Romania is disproportionately greater in any historical narrative dealing with this period, as is the possibility that Uniates would serve as lightning rods for writers critical of cultural trends or social conditions. Yet the perceived cultural unity of the inhabitants of what in the following two centuries became Romania, and the notion of Romanian "Latinity" in national historiography prevented writers from denying the connection with the Latin West.[49] The consequences of the founding of the Uniate Church have therefore received some attention from Romanian historians, while the circumstances that brought about its creation have been dealt with in a more perfunctory fashion. The decline in confessional bias that in the last half century has become so noticeable in the study of the Counter-Reformation and the Catholic Reformation in Western Europe is not yet as apparent in the historiography of the Catholic/Orthodox encounter in the eastern Habsburg realms and there is a lingering tendency among some writers to view the Uniate project in a one-dimensional fashion.[50] Yet the web of social and political relationships that the Uniate Church inherited and developed was far more complex than merely a pattern of compromises and massive sellouts by ill-informed and defenseless Orthodox clergy in the face of a powerful outside force. Nor was

---

[45] Pascu's *History of Transylvania*, widely read in the West, contains no reference (even negative) to the influence of the Jesuits in the creation of the Romanian Uniate Church.

[46] Kosáry, *Culture*, p. 77. The replacement of Orthodox bishoprics with Uniate ones probably involved the transfer of considerable amounts of property rather than cash, although specific figures are almost impossible to determine.

[47] This tone suffuses an influential work by Nicolae Iorga, *Istoria Romanilor din Ardeal şi Ungaria. Volumul I-iu. Pânǎ la Mişcarea lui Horea (1784)* (Bucureşti, 1915), p. 357.

[48] Peter Sugar, "The historical role of religious institutions in Eastern Europe and their place in the Communist Party state," in *Religion and Nationalism in Soviet and East European Politics*, ed. P. Ramet (Durham, NC, 1989), p. 49.

[49] Lucia Boia, "Romania," in *International Handbook of Historical Studies: Contemporary Research and Theory*, eds Georg G. Igges and Harold T. Parker (Westport, CT, 1978), p. 343.

[50] Jones, *The Counter Reformation*, p. 2. The work of the late Pompiliu Teodor is an outstanding exception to this tendency. See also R. Po-Chia Hsia, *The World of Catholic Renewal 1540–1770* (Cambridge, 1998).

the Uniate Church without any institutional character save what was bestowed on it externally and artificially by an aggressive Society made up of stooges for the Habsburg dynasty. It is true that the Jesuit sponsors of the Uniate Church ultimately failed to attract sufficient allies among the Orthodox population and to establish the link that they had hoped for between Rome and the broader Orthodox community. Yet the Uniate project left its own distinct mark on Cluj and the surrounding districts, with its legacy taking directions unanticipated by the Society, and in at least one case, opposed to its own interests, retaining throughout the period here under review distinctly Romanian elements that became more apparent with the passage of time. Looking from the West, it is easy to forget the close association between nationality and religion that was understood and accepted without question in eighteenth-century Eastern Europe. While the tendency to view these two concepts as nearly identical was native to many of the groups living in the region, the notion received reinforcement from the Ottoman Empire, which instituted the policy of treating minority groups as religious entities. Thus each ethnic group in Eastern Europe might be understood as having its own "ethnarch," and Uniates in Cluj might view their own bishop the same way.[51] Religious rituals that expressed loyalty to the Emperor in Vienna could therefore take place that emphasized the universality of Habsburg claims to domination without denying the ethnic identity of the celebrants.[52]

III

From a Roman or Imperial perspective the development of the Uniate Church was much more than a missionary project or just a result of the desire to bring together believers separated only by fine points of dogma. The bridging of the gap between the Orthodox and Catholic populations of Transylvania was a practical necessity, born of an unstable political and religious situation in a region only recently acquired by the Habsburgs (and thus "rejoining" Europe) and as of yet demonstrating scant loyalty for the dynasty, its goals and methods. Having failed to reestablish Catholicism as the universal religion within the boundaries of the Holy Roman Empire, the Habsburgs had continued their mission as champions of the Church by working to make their newer, eastern territories Catholic in a distinctly baroque fashion that reflected the dynasty's understanding of piety.[53] The Danube Basin and its adjacent, formerly Hungarian-speaking regions were a matter of particular concern to the Habsburgs and the Jesuits, since the depopulation that had occurred during the Turkish occupation and the subsequent immigration was part of a larger pattern repeated in the southern territories of the dynasty. If Transylvania, arguably the least stable

---

[51] Peter Sugar, "Ethnicity in Eastern Europe," in Peter Sugar (ed.), *Ethnic Diversity and Conflict in Eastern Europe* (Santa Barbara, CA/Oxford, 1980), pp. 432–3.

[52] Michael Mullett, *The Catholic Reformation* (London/New York, 1999), p. 186. Mullett makes specific reference to rituals conducted in Catholic churches during the War of Austrian Succession; records on similar Uniate celebrations have not been located, although under Jesuit direction, Uniate participation in such activities seems very likely.

[53] Anna Coreth, *Pietas Austriaca*, trans. William D. Bowman and Anna Maria Leitgeb (West Lafayette, IN, 2004), *passim.*

and most inaccessible of the newly won Ottoman lands could be secured, there was hope for the less rebellious and more accessible Banat – and perhaps for any other spoils to be gained from the faltering Turk.[54] Jesuits also dreamed of traveling even further east and penetrating the Tartar and Turkish monarchies, thereby continuing a *leitmotiv* of the Society's understanding of itself and its mission, in which great eastern despotism turns to the truth of the Roman Church, to the glory of that Church (and perhaps the Society as well).

At the same time a *laissez faire* approach to the management of Transylvania was not an option for any of the Habsburg rulers, who could ill afford a catastrophe in the east while their fortunes elsewhere still hung in the balance. A newly arrived population beginning to settle on a devastated landscape possessing few reasons to align with the dynasty was a liability, although land left empty on the outer fringes of its realms was equally a risk for the Habsburgs, who were already stretched to the limit of what they could muster in the form of frontier military units. Central Transylvania, while not suffering from the scale of devastation experienced in parts of the Danube Basin, also threatened to become an unstable region, given its diverse population, distance from Vienna, and historic resistance to outside domination. The nobility of Transylvania, chiefly Hungarian in its language and point of view, added to this instability. Even after the defeat of the rebel Ferenc II Rákóczi and the Treaty of Szátmar in 1711, the Hungarian aristocracy, whose loyalty to the Habsburgs was questionable at best, was left in possession of its power and wealth, which given its history of independence, made it a perennially dangerous element in the mix.[55] And while Vienna might try to curb religious nonconformity in Hungary with edicts such as the *Carolina Resolutio* of 1731, a restive and unchecked Transylvania still could spread its dangerous traditions to its neighbor, thus bringing rebellion to the very gates of the capital.[56]

Despite all the drawbacks of a mission to the region, and despite the deep-seated antipathy on the part of many of its inhabitants towards Catholicism, the Society chose to view Transylvania, as opposed to neighboring regions where it also pursued its Uniate projects, as a formerly Catholic territory to be reclaimed, not as a new missionary field with no historical relationship to Rome. By contrast, the Society had always viewed the "Indies" of both hemispheres where it also carried out its other major missionary projects as territory as yet unclaimed for Christianity or

---

[54] Joseph Féleghazy, "Hongrie: Temps moderns," in Marcel Viller and André Rayer (eds), *Dictionnaire de spiritualité ascétique et mystique, doctrine et histoire* (17 vols, Paris, 1951–), p. 695. This pattern was mirrored to an extent by the arrival of Serbian Orthodox settlers in the region south of the Drave, although in this instance many of the settlers were deliberately brought to the Habsburg lands by the dynasty itself. The Jesuit "Missio Banensis" was reported to be doing well in 1688, although the territory was still under Ottoman control and would remain so for three more decades. MTA, 2-R 11352, *Historia Collegiorum ... 1687, 1688*, folios 266r–267r.

[55] Á.R. Várkonyi, "Handelswesen und Politik in Ungarn des 17–18 Jahrhunderts (Theorien, Monopole Schmugglerbewegungen 1600–1711)," *AHSH* 17 (171), pp. 207–24.

[56] Reproduced in Henrik Marczali (ed.), *Enchiridion Fontium Historiae Hungarorum*. (Budapestini, 1901), pp. 706–708.

civilization.[57] This perspective towards distant societies colored the Jesuits' overseas activities, allowing them frequently to take a more tolerant view of Imperial Chinese culture, or to incorporate the folkways of some of the Native American groups they encountered into their liturgies. While this toleration opened the Society up to criticism that it compromised too much in its dealings with non-Europeans, it also gave Jesuits a freedom of action sometimes denied to other Catholic orders. The decision to see Transylvania as a land to be reclaimed had significant consequences for the entire Uniate undertaking, as it placed those who, once offered the Uniate option, remained Orthodox in the category of schismatics rather than pagans or heretics. This designation perhaps denied the Orthodox faithful some of the innocence granted (often in a manner that seems patronizing today) by the Society to Jesuit objects of conversion efforts in non-European settings. On the other hand, not viewing Orthodox as "heretics" spared them the full wrath of Habsburgs such as Maria Theresia, for whom, as M.-E. Ducreaux points out, heresy, with its political implications, was an "obsession" and whose dislike for non-Christians is well documented.[58] Orthodox Transylvania, the former Roman province of Dacia (a point made repeatedly in Jesuit writings), and a territory now under the control of the Holy Roman Emperor, was instead cast in the much more innocuous role of a prodigal or misguided child finally gaining the opportunity to be reunited with the Mother Church.[59]

When Transylvania appeared as the next project of a Society committed to promoting reunion with Rome, this undertaking immediately received material aid from Habsburg policy, both because of the risks the Principality posed to the state and because of the larger policy concerns of the court.[60] Transylvania indeed represented the farthest possible extension of the dynasty in the new direction it had chosen for itself after making a momentous change in its fundamental geographic orientation. In the late seventeenth and early eighteenth centuries the policy of the dynasty, thwarted in its efforts to subdue the Protestant princes in the Thirty Years' War and unable to resurrect the medieval ideal of a powerful Holy Roman Empire, had turned away from its original power center in Germany and in the Empire in search of a new basis for its imperial and transnational ambitions. Consequently, the Habsburgs would steadily reconstitute their possessions as a dynastic empire based

---

[57] MAT, *Notata Summaria*, Kéz történl., pp. 2, 132, 326.

[58] M.-E. Ducreaux, "La mission et la rôle des missionaires dans les pays tchèques au XVIIIe siècle," *Actes du 109e Congrès des Societés savantes, Dijon, 1984. Transmettre la foi: XVIe–XXe siècles*, p. 38. Maria Theresia is said to have spoken to Jews only when a screen shielded their presence from her eyes.

[59] This parallels the view of Prince Eugene, who regarded the European possessions of the Ottomans as stolen from Christendom. Roider, *Question*, p. 42.

[60] As early as 1653, the Archbishop of Esztergom had created a parish of Kolosmănăştur, although Jesuits were at the time still unable to staff it. MAT, *Notata Summaria*, Kéz. Törtenl. 2 132. Sz., p. 135. When the Jesuits finally gained officially sanctioned entry into Transylvania in 1692, they had been working in Cluj and other Transylvanian cities for at least two decades. Osnifor Ghibu, *Catolicismul Unguresc în Transilvania şi Politica Religiosă a Statului Român* (Cluj, 1924), p. 42. For the Baroque vision of a Hungarian kingdom led by its "queen" Mary, see *Magyar művelődéstörténete*, ed. Domanovsky Sándor (Budapest, c. 1940), p. 430.

solely on the territorial holdings of the family, which increasingly they managed in a consolidated manner, and on the allegiance of key elements in each of these holdings. This was a break with the policy of relying on familial and historical claims to an Imperial crown centered on its German-speaking lands, whose significance was by 1700 little more than symbolic.[61] The territories that offered themselves to Habsburg ambitions all now lay, with the exception of the Low Countries (a windfall that proved far more trouble than it was worth), to the east. The solidification of the eastern boundary of the territories of the dynasty had a symbolic resonance as well. Extension of the dynasty's control to the eastern boundaries of pre-Mohács Hungary would confirm the picture of the Habsburgs as the true rulers of a united Hungary, once again enjoying its "natural" borders under its apostolic (if foreign) king. Regarding Transylvania specifically, long before the Principality came under direct Habsburg control, Emperor Ferdinand III had pressed forward a case that Jesuits should be allowed to remain in Transylvania legally, based on the consent of the ruling Prince and his "glorious ancestors."[62] Such a move was a portent, as it both identified the reigning Habsburg prince (whose father Ferdinand II had once mused aloud that he might have become a Jesuit under differing circumstances) as a champion of the Jesuits in the east and also showed to what degree the Habsburgs were willing to try to extend their influence into an eastern region still independent of their direct control. In the meantime a small group of Jesuits lived and worked in Cluj, teaching children.[63]

As this direct control became a reality, the Society, which in its very first years had served as an ally to the beleaguered Emperor Ferdinand I, the first Habsburg to turn his attention eastward, would thus both feel the effects of the reorientation of Habsburgs' new dynastic policy, as well as aid in its completion. In both their roles as missionaries and as emissaries of the dynasty the Jesuits were spurred on not

---

[61] This reorientation has been called a "translatio imperii" involving the symbolism of the dynasty, and reaching its fruition under the latter years of the reign of Maria Theresia (1740–80), and officially acknowledged with the "acceptance" of the new Imperial Crown of Austria by Francis I in 1804, shortly before the dissolution of the Holy Roman Empire. Joachim Whaley, "Austria, 'Germany,' and the dissolution of the Holy Roman Empire," in Richie Robertson and Edwads Timms (eds), *The Habsburg Legacy: National Identity in Historical Perspective* (Edinburgh, 1994), pp, 3–6. The close relationship between the Austrian Province of the Society and the Habsburgs in fact pre-dated this "translatio" by at least a century. A map of the Province published in 1655 bears the inscription "Sub uno terrae principe de august.ma domo Austriaca." Lukás, *Jezsuita rendartomány*, plate facing 24.

[62] When in January 1652 Jesuits in disguise were found to have penetrated Transylvania as far as the prince's court in Alba Iulia, Prince György II Rákóczi expelled them, and a month later the Protestant-dominated diet deprived them of property they possessed in Kolosmănăştur. The emperor's efforts on behalf of the Society caused these decisions to be reversed, apparently without recourse to bribery. Periş, *Missione*, p. 117; Benda (ed.), *Okmánytár*, vol. 2, p. 507. The Society received formal confirmation of its repossession of the revenues from the Kolosmănăştur properties in 1733. Zsolt Trósanyi, *Habsburg-Politika és Habsburg Kormányzat Erdélyben 1690–1740* (Budapest, 1982), pp. 422.

[63] In 1651, three Jesuit priests and two deacons, each in the garb of secular priests, were active in Cluj. *Relationes Missionarum de Hungaria et Transilvania (1627–1707)*, ed. I.G. Tóth (Roma/Budapest, 1994), p. 329.

only by a general commitment to missionary work, but also by a vision of a greater Hungary reclaimed entirely for Catholicism under the queenship of the Virgin, the so-called *Regnum Marianum*.[64] National consciousness, which emerged earlier among Hungarian nobles than among other groups in the Habsburg lands, early on was linked with Catholic piety to produce a powerful motivation for the reclaiming of Transylvania.

But this redirection of effort did not come without difficulties for the Jesuits. The physical and geographical features of the isolated, independent, and eastward looking Province were unlike those found anywhere in Western Europe. Moreover, the nature of the challenges faced by Jesuit missionaries, polemicists and teachers were different from those they had already trained for, encountered, and frequently overcome in Western Europe. In France and in Western Europe in general, seventeenth-century Jesuits, always the center of controversy, had easily identifiable adversaries, whose points of reference were seldom strictly defined in terms of compactly gathered ethnic groups governed by a single monarch.[65] In France Jesuits in particular had to confront Jansenism and its mordant critique of Jesuit theology, both of which found sympathetic hearers scattered among many city-dwellers and university graduates. The weapons in this struggle were ones Jesuits could wield with skill. On the field of confessional conflict, Jansenists and their supporters relied on polemical writings and sophisticated arguments, often promoted by highly placed political allies, to carry on their opposition to the Society. But Jansenism, which the Society had learned to combat in classically polemical fashion, drew largely upon its own mastery of rhetoric and casuistry common to university training in the West and thus remained a Western European phenomenon. It attracted virtually no followers in the Eastern Habsburg lands and was invisible in the universities of the region, most of which had long been under the control of the Jesuits or were otherwise dominated by Catholic religious.[66] But by the beginning of the eighteenth century the opinion of a growing number of educated people was turning against polemical

---

[64] When the Habsburgs sent Antidus Dunod as their emissary to the Transylvanian nobles, offering the Principality the "protection" of Austrian arms, the offer was not well received and subsequently had to be backed up with military pressure. Pascu, *History*, 130. Much later, some of the language and symbols of the Virgin as queen were appropriated by writers of panegyrics to Maria Theresia, who was seen as "guarding" the Virgin, who symbolically ruled Hungary along with the Habsburgs. The Virgin's relationship to the Hungarian crown was traced by imaginative Baroque writers to Stephen I, who, because he was without an heir, was said to have entrusted his kingdom to Mary. Hóman and Szekfű, *Magyar történet*, vol. 4, p. 387; István Bitskey, *Hitviták tüzében* (Budapest, 1978), p. 226. (A late eighteenth-century painting in the Hungarian National Gallery, Budapest, shows two Madonnas, one guiding Hungary and one guiding Transylvania, each territory indicated by its heraldic device.).

[65] The politics of emerging nation states did of course play a role in the polemical controversies in which the Society found itself, as did competition among candidates of various nationalities for the post of Father General. For the struggle between the Spanish Jesuits and supporters of Belgian and Italian candidates, see Christopher Hollis, *The Jesuits: A History* (New York, 1968), pp. 89ff.

[66] Evans points out the presence of Jansenist influences at the abbey of Klosterneuburg near Vienna. Evans, *Making*, p. 328. But while Jansenism made some inroads in the Austrias

approaches to religious differences; like the curriculum of the *Ratio*, Jesuit polemical techniques were starting to appear out of date.[67] Tried and true polemic tactics did not seem as applicable in the east where the opposition was not noticeably urban, educated or oriented towards literary combat. The challenges to the Jesuit program in the most eastern territories of the Habsburgs came from outside Catholicism, but, unlike in the west, not from relatively recently established movements such as the Anabaptists. Instead the challenge to union or conversion was from well-established religions whose hierarchies generally did not desire closer contact with Rome, and which typically did not engage in the elaborate game of literary polemics published in pamphlets and books to get their messages across.[68] The greatest strengths of these locally based churches of the east lay in the close relations between pastoral clergy and the peasantry, and in the effects of preachers moving among the people, speaking the regional vernacular (as opposed to Latin, the traditionally preferred language of Jesuit erudition and of Baroque polemics on all sides of the debate in Western Europe). Although documentation is incomplete, these local preachers appear to have appealed on occasion to the sense of oppression and despair felt by their listeners and did not dwell on fine points of theology. Such preachers, if they hailed from the immediate vicinity and shared ethnic ties with their audiences, probably had a better sense of "doubled meanings," both theological and animistic, that characterized popular religion in the eighteenth century and that frequently took on qualities not easily understood by an outsider.[69] Divisions between ethnic groups and memories of inter-ethnic conflicts were also a feature of the cultural landscape of the east, although one must guard against applying anachronistic notions of a coherent nationalism to these traditional societies.[70] The Society soon came to recognize the difference in cultural climate between the lecture halls of the Sorbonne and the remote fortified villages of the Carpathians; at the *Collegium Hungaricum*, in Rome, united since the late sixteenth century with the *Collegium Germanicum*, it

---

by the latter part of the reign of Maria Theresia, the movement never spread to the eastern domains of the Habsburgs.

[67] Michael Driediger, *Obedient Heretics: Mennonite Identities in Lutheran Hamburg and Altona during the Confessional Age* (Aldershot, 2002), p. 1.

[68] *Storia della Chiesa XIX/I: Le lotte politiche e dottrinale nei secoli XVII e XVII (1648–1789)*, eds E. Précline and E. Jarry, Edizione italiana a cura di Luigi Mezzadri (Milano, 1991), *passim*.

[69] Marc Venard, "Popular religion in the eighteenth century," in William J. Callahan and David Higgs (eds), *Church and Society in Catholic Europe of the Eighteenth Century* (Cambridge, 1979), pp. 153–4. Jesuit records abound with stories that may be instances of encounters with folk religious practices that were not understood as such. A pact between a soldier and a "demon," who gives him a ring, is one such case. OSzK, 2039 FMI/1608, *Historia SJ Claudiopoli 1712*, p. 116.

[70] Keith Hitchins makes a useful distinction between the idea of nation in a national context, which eighteenth-century Transylvanian Romanians did not have, and "ethnic consciousness," which they did. Building upon this consciousness, Uniate clergy occasionally played the "Romanness" card, as when Geronite Cotorea, later Vicar General of the Uniate Church, asserted that the downfall of Romania had come with its abandonment of the Roman Church. Keith Hitchins, *The Romanians, 1744–1866* (Oxford, 1996), pp. 203–204.

set out to train its teachers and missionaries to confront the sort of challenges they were likely to encounter in Central Europe.[71]

The highly developed system of the Jesuits' institutional organization, with individual Jesuits on various assignments submitting reports to rectors, rectors reporting to Provincials and a Father General directing policy at the highest levels was an undoubted aid to the small bands of men who ventured into the hinterlands of northern Hungary, Ruthenia and Transylvania. The region was not unknown to the fathers; it already held a place in the early history of the Society and was gaining visibility again as a geographical region just at the moment when, as Frédéric Barbier puts it, with the help of the Jesuits, "a new geography was being constructed as an autonomous scientific object."[72] Decades before the official return of the Society to the region, individual Jesuits were not only active in the district around Cluj, but had even taken their vows "publicâ" in that city, indicating that a system of support deriving from the local Catholic nobility was already in place.[73] The systematic assessing of prospects by Jesuit administrators, and the access to money from noble and Imperial donors made success seem more probable. Yet even with these significant supports, the Society was still confronted with the difficulties of the remoteness of the eastern reaches of the Habsburg realms, and with the possibility of the local non-Catholic clergy stirring up opposition to their efforts. The peasants who lived in Ruthenia, Transylvania and neighboring regions were themselves not always promising prospects. Even if they became Uniate, bitter controversies over the national identities of their bishops would often cast a shadow over the achievement of union.[74] Frequently driven to desperation by famine and war and suspicious of outsiders, they often maintained strong ties of loyalty towards local aristocrats, who themselves were linked to one another through marriage and common economic interests. That the seventeenth and eighteenth centuries were periods of pietism and popular religious revival throughout Europe was at times an asset to those Jesuits who could exploit some of these tendencies in their own missionary projects, but it was also a liability for union builders who found themselves combating already established popular preachers of rival confessions.[75] The fierce nationalism of the Hungarians who lived among the Orthodox Romanians (and considered themselves culturally superior to them) and the inherent difficulty of the Magyar language only increased the day-to-day isolation and difficulties for missionaries and preachers of union, unless they were themselves Hungarian-speaking. Mastery of Hungarian

---

[71] Dümmeth, "Combats," p. 84.

[72] Frédéric Barbier, "Problématique d'une recherché collective," in Monok and Ötvös (eds), *Lesestoffe*, p. 9.

[73] Joannes Hilber and Michael Henessi both took their fourth vows in Cluj on 15 August 1666. Other Jesuits had performed the same rites two years earlier in Alba Iulia. MOL, F 234 Erdélyi Kincs., Fiscalis Levéltár Szekrény XXV/B., unnumbered folio.

[74] After 1690, when 36,000 Serbian Orthodox families became Uniates, their old bishop remained with them in a new role as a Uniate, but the presence of a Serbian bishop irritated the Hungarian Catholic hierarchy, and in 1720, the bishopric was abolished. W.R. Ward, *Christianity under the ancien régime 1648–1789* (Cambridge, 1999), p. 204.

[75] Ted Campbell, *The Religion of the Heart: A Study of European Life in the Seventeenth and Eighteenth Centuries* (Columbia, SC, 1991), pp. 130ff.

however only addressed half of the problem, since there remained the Romanian-speaking population for whose sake the Union was being promoted. In short, the environment was a difficult one in which to promote union with an outside entity, for the passions that ruled religious controversy in the east were born of basic human needs, not university-bred theological disputes, and sprang from a culture that was fundamentally far more conservative than that of the villages of Germany or even Spain.[76]

Besides the hierarchies and clergy of established churches put on the defensive by the Society's missionary efforts, other groups were natural opponents to the establishment of the Uniate Church. The predominantly Hungarian-speaking landed gentry of the region generally reacted negatively to the idea of a Uniate Church, even if they were Catholic themselves, since their own dominant position over ethnic Romanians was being undermined if Eastern Rite believers were to be given civil rights equal to those of Catholics of long standing.[77] This gentry, despite its sometimes great wealth, tended not to be well traveled, and was the product of a self-reliant aristocratic culture that based its existence on dominance over the peasant class and took little interest in the latter's language or culture.[78] Communion with a Church reaching across the world and with close ties to the ruling political powers was not necessarily a desirable asset to themselves or for their subject peasants. The Jesuit educational program, despite its favorable reputation, held only occasional appeal for these nobles in the case of their own sons; extending it to Romanians was a direct threat to the *status quo*. And since many of the Hungarian-speaking nobility were Calvinist, the legitimatization or at least toleration of Orthodox rituals, such as the veneration of icons, which were regarded by Reformed Church leaders with contempt, only heightened the already considerable degree of alienation these nobles felt toward Vienna and Rome. Not that the Reformed Church was able to maintain a working alliance with the Eastern Church. In fact, Calvinism had made relatively little headway in Transylvania among Orthodox believers in part because of what it had itself become. By the middle of the seventeenth century the ardor that had animated the Reformed Church had subsided and Calvinism in Transylvania had become "hidebound" and "fossilized," its leaders lacking the ingenuity to devise a successful conversion campaign.[79] Isolated and stymied, the Calvinist leadership of the late seventeenth century was in anything but an irenic mood, as it suppressed crosses, music and images in churches throughout Transylvania.[80] Nor was the

---

[76] Péter Szabó, *Az Erdélyi fejedelemség* (Budapest, 1997), pp. 111ff; Ana Dumitran, Gúdor Botond and Nicolae Dănila, *Relaţii interconfessionale româno-maghiare în Transilvania (mijlocul secolului XVI-primele decenii ale secolui XVIII) Román-magyar felekezetközi kapcsolatok Erdélyben a XVI. század közepe – a XVIII század első évtizedei között* (Alba Iulia/Gyulafehérvár, 2000).

[77] Pascu, *History*, p. 133.

[78] Even the Rákóczi family, the most powerful in the region and owners of an impressive library, was underexposed to outside cultures in comparison with its counterparts in Germany or France. István Monok, *A Rákóczi-család könyvtárai 1588–1660* (Szeged, 1996), p. xxv.

[79] See Evans, *Making*, p. 286.

[80] Georg Haner, *Historia Ecclesiarum Transylvanicarum inde a Primis Popularum Originibus* ... (Francofurti et Lipsae, 1694), p. 314.

role of the Society in promoting the Uniate Church well regarded by Hungarian Calvinists of Transylvania, many of whose co-religionists had suffered at the hands of the Jesuits and Habsburgs elsewhere in Hungary. In fact, the Habsburg persecution of Hungarian Calvinists was a European scandal and the subject of a multilingual literature, while the cruelty of the Imperial forces reclaiming Ottoman territory towards Protestants that fell into their path was well known.[81] As the Society sought to win converts from the Reformed Church and to establish a union with Eastern Orthodox clergy, it would have to overcome the negative aspects of association with a regime that had few natural allies while confronting linguistic and ethnic fissures in Transylvanian society that limited the number of its own allies.

Once the Uniate Church was legitimized after the Second Leopoldine Diploma, Romanians eventually felt secure enough to begin erecting schools in some districts, a development that modified the master-serf relationship that had always denied education to all but a few.[82] On the other hand the installation of a Jesuit *theologus* at the side of the Uniate bishop antagonized the Romanians, who were understandably suspicious of a position that seemed as much that of an Imperial functionary as a religious adviser.[83] The elevation of the status of Uniate priests to a level theoretically equal to that of the Catholic clergy created other tensions, notably resentment on the part of Orthodox clergy who felt that they were being outflanked by the Jesuits and their allies. The growth of a Uniate Church in Transylvania threatened to redefine relationships and challenge notions of what was appropriate conduct for the "Wallachs."[84]

Vienna was not entirely unaware of these and other problems. The Principality, despite (or perhaps because of) its remoteness, was to be ruled directly from Vienna, as Leopold I had neither recognized the election of five-year-old Mihály II Apafi as the legal Prince, nor was he willing to reunite Transylvania with historic Hungary.[85] At the same time the Emperor did not claim the Prince's title for himself, leaving his brother Charles VI to put forward the dynasty's legal claims many years later

---

[81]   Péter Katalin, "The later Ottoman period and royal Hungary" in Peter F. Sugar (ed.), *A History of Hungary* (Bloomington, IN/Indianapolis, IN, 1990), p. 110.

[82]   Sylvius Dragomir, *The Ethnical Minorities in Transylvania* (Geneva, 1927), p. 14.

[83]   Octavian Bârlea, "Biserica Română Unită şi ecumenismul corifeilor renaşterii culturale," *Perspective* v, 3–4 (19–20) (Ianuarie–Iunie 1983), pp. 1–242.

[84]   When, in 1744, the emboldened Romanians petitioned the Transylvanian Diet for civil recognition, the indignant response of the Hungarian-dominated assembly made clear that a change in the social *status quo* was deeply offensive. Keith Hitchins, *The Romanian national movement in Transylvania* (Cambridge, MA, 1969), pp. 26ff.

[85]   The Transylvanian custom of electing its prince from one of the established aristocratic families was another reason for the Habsburgs to regard the region with suspicion. Ferdinand II had gone to some pains to abolish the elective monarchy in Bohemia, and to secure the crown as a hereditary possession of the dynasty, but Transylvania's great landed families were not as easily removed, converted or subdued as Bohemia's. Kann, *Habsburg Empire*, pp. 126–7. The young Apafi prince never saw his putative domain, however; he died in 1713 in Vienna, under Habsburg "protection." C.A. Macartney, *The Habsburg and Hohenzollern Dynasties in the Nineteenth and Eighteenth Centuries* (New York, 1970), p. 46.

when Apafi had died.[86] Instead, Leopold affirmed the autonomy of the regional administration by issuing on 16 October 1690 the *Diploma Leopoldinum*, which reconfirmed the rights of the four recognized religions.[87] He also refrained from establishing any sort of military administration in the region.[88] This move encouraged the Transylvanian Diet to take an oath of loyalty to Leopold on 7 February 1691, thereby binding the Principality immediately to the Habsburgs, who had vast experience in the business of conversion and recatholicization.[89] The Principality would not be resurrected as a separate administrative unit until 1765, the year that Joseph II, the ultimate Habsburg centralizer, would ascend the throne as co-ruler with his mother, Maria Theresia, and even then it would enjoy only minimal autonomy.[90] In the meantime Transylvania experienced the direct intervention of Vienna in all matters, including economic; this was the region's first experience of direct rule by a Western power.[91] While this intervention was generally heavy-handed and taxes were relatively high, even enthusiastically pro-Romanian historians have conceded that this intervention was far from an unmixed evil.[92] The Uniate clergy benefited from contact with the cultures of Western Europe, and the Principality, if not allowed to develop economically as much as it might have had if it had retained more independence, was at least spared the civil strife that had characterized much of the previous period.[93] The central government had the capability to intervene in times of famine, and did so on occasion.[94] Yet the loss of autonomy could not be denied. A subject Transylvania, its nobles subdued and its population under the observation, if

---

[86] This delay revealed the insecurity of the Habsburg claim to Transylvania during the first two decades of the Jesuits' officially sanctioned presence, and thus reflected on the Society's position in the region as well. MacCartney, *Short History*, p. 103.

[87] Béla K. Király, "The Transylvanian Concept of Liberty and its Impact on the Kingdom of Hungary in the Seventeenth and Eighteenth Centuries," in John F. Cadzow, Andrew Ludanyi and Louis J. Elteto (eds), *Transylvania: The Roots of Ethnic Conflict* (Kent, OH, 1983), p. 79.

[88] In 1764, after the Habsburgs had passed through several severe military crises and faced a near uprising under Sophronius, a "Militärgrenze" was finally created in eastern Transylvania. J.H. Schwicker, *Geschichte der oe. Militärgrenze* (Wien, 1883).

[89] Rona Johnston Gordon, "Patronage and parish: The nobility and the recatholicization of Lower Austria," in Karin Maag (ed.), *The Reformation in Eastern and Central Europe* (Aldershot, 1997), pp. 211–27.

[90] The Transylvanian *Gubernium*, answerable to a Transylvanian Chancellery in Vienna, came into existence as early as 1693, as a result of the first Leopoldine *Diploma*. Victor Ember, "The Eighteenth Century," in *A Companion to Hungarian Studies* (Budapest, 1943), pp. 161–93; Király, *Hungary in the late Eighteenth Century*, p. 115.

[91] Romanian historians have even claimed, though without documentation, that the Cameralist policies of Hörnigk were introduced, a process that should have hastened the connection of the region with Vienna. Susuana Andea and Avram Andea, *Structuri Transylvane în epoca luminor* (Cluj-Napoca, 1996), p. 10.

[92] Statistics on early eighteenth-century Romanian landowners in Transylvania are found in *Vieața Agrară, Economică Românilor din Ardeal și Ungaria: Documente Contemporane. Vol. I 1508–1820*, ed. Ștefan Meteș (București, 41, 1921).

[93] Szász, *Romanian Transylvania*, pp. 16ff.

[94] Georgius Pray, *Historia Regum Hungariae* (3 vols, Budae, 1801), vol. 3, p. 587.

not the direct governance, of the Jesuits, fit into the long-range plans of the dynasty. These plans included the expansion of the authority of the Catholic Church, and ultimately, the mobilization of the resources of the Principality for its military uses against traditional foes such as the Turks.[95] The population also found itself dividing into factions that had never before existed. Uniate Christians were isolated from their Orthodox colleagues, since Orthodox bishops, presumably under pressure from the civil authorities, counseled their flocks to avoid contact with those who had united with Rome, and especially to resist the temptation to call Uniates back to their former affiliations with the Orthodox Church.[96] The shift to the West involved more than changes in liturgy and calendars; it extended to social relationships and even economic dealings. The creation of the Uniate Church therefore arguably divided as many Christians as it united.[97]

The Habsburg reluctance to disrupt the existing degree of religious tolerance and the relatively low level of coercion it applied to non-Catholics in the Principality should not be seen as a lack of commitment to the Catholic program of the dynasty or as a betrayal of its support for the Society.[98] The Habsburg approach was instead a piece of *realpolitk* driven by the relatively weak position of Catholicism in the region and a pragmatic view of how many resources should be expended in the promotion of the True Faith in the east while facing powerful external opponents to their Central European power base and rebuilding institutions elsewhere in their realms.[99] Much as Vienna might wish to concentrate on matters east of the River Tisza, the continent-wide commitments of the House of Austria would not allow this. During the first decades of the eighteenth century alone the Habsburgs were distracted by dynastic preoccupations in Spain, securing their new possessions in

---

[95] Recruitment of Szekler men stirred great resentment: in 1764, a recruitment drive in Csikmádéfalva resulted in violence that claimed tens of thousands of lives and became known as the "Siculicidum" or "killing of the Szeklers." Bernadette Pálfy, "Short history of the Tsangos" in *The Tsangos of Romania: The Hungarian Minorities in Romanian Moldovia*, ed. S.J. Magyarody (Mathias Corvinus Publishing) http://www.hungary.com/corvinus/lib/tsangos/tsangos.pdf.

[96] Dionysius Novakovice, Orthodox Bishop of Buda and Transylvania, to all non-Uniate Christians in his jurisdiction, 15 July 1763, in *Documente Privatóre la Istoria Romanilor*, Vol. 7, 1756–1818 (Bucureşti, 1897), p. 34, no. xxi.

[97] Some hint of this is suggested in the Jesuit records of the Cluj mission for 1715, which report that six apostates were counted among the converts. "Apostates" here may mean converts from Judaism, Protestantism or Orthodoxy; in each case, social pressures to resume one's previous religion were perhaps very great. ARSI, *Aust. 172, An. Prov. Aust. 1715*, p. 91.

[98] For example, when the Society returned to Transylvania, Protestants were not required to pay for the construction of new Catholic churches. Ghibu, *Catolismu*, p. 42.

[99] Aurel Ivi, "Seventeenth century Romanian Orthodox confessions of Faith," in Auril Jiji (ed.), *Orthodox, Catholics, and Protestants: Studies in Romanian Ecclesiastical Relations* (Cluj-Napoca, 1999), pp. 120–43. That the Habsburg policy regarding conversion and reconversion was never fundamentally tolerant in the first half of the eighteenth century may be seen by the aggressive policy pursued simultaneously in Bohemia under Charles VI. Ducreux, "Reconquête," p. 688.

Italy, and by the continual threat posed to their Belgian possessions by Bourbon France.[100]

Despite these factors, the dynasty soon had a program in place that was intended to strengthen the position of the Catholic Church in a land where the majority of the population was neither Catholic nor Uniate, and which had long lacked an active Catholic ecclesiastical hierarchy.[101] In 1692, Leopold I issued an Imperial patent declaring that all Uniates of the Eastern Rite who had formally united with the Church of Rome were to be granted all the rights and privileges that members of the Catholic Church already possessed. While the offer was open to all communicants of the Eastern Church, Leopold's patent had particular appeal to the Orthodox clergy, many of whom lived in poverty-stricken circumstances scarcely different from those of the most humble serf. Such priests could also see which way the wind was blowing. In the coming decades, the Habsburgs would issue a series of directives promoting the Catholic faith and those allied with it, including a decree returning formerly Catholic churches in Transylvania to Catholics, the imposition of fines on any Catholic in Hungary proper who converted to Protestantism, and in the 1744 Transylvanian diet, under pressure from Vienna, would move to remove all restrictions on the practice of Catholicism.[102] To be allied with the Catholic dynasty was to be spared the disabilities (or worse) meted out to others who opposed the Habsburgs, their religion, or their allies. Such punishments were severe and widely publicized. The response of Imperial troops to the resistance Sibiu (Nagyszeben, Hermannstadt), one of the "Saxon" towns of Transylvania, had offered in 1688 to the prospect of being incorporated into the Habsburg realms must have made a considerable impression on all who heard of it: leaders of the city's resistance had been beheaded, their severed heads impaled on sticks, after the city had been shelled and captured. Jesuit chroniclers (in each instance, of Hungarian extraction) reported these events without disapproval.[103] By contrast, some of the rewards offered allies of the dynasty were primarily material or stood separate from ecclesiastical dignities: in title-obsessed Transylvania, Catholic bishops of Transylvania would receive the noble title of "baron," as would one Uniate bishop, Inochentie Micu, who would play

---

[100] The relationship between Charles' failed aspirations to the Spanish throne and his commitments in the eastern Habsburg realms is dealt with in Roider, *Austria's Eastern Question*, pp. 36–40.

[101] In 1760–62, 66.46 per cent of the population of Transylvania was identified as ethnic Romanian. Jean Nouzille, *La Transylvanie: Terre de contacts et de conflicts*. (Strasbourg, 1993), pp. 182–3. Assuming a roughly similar ratio and a minimal number of ethnic Romanians who were not Eastern Rite, we may hypothesize that roughly two-thirds of the country was Orthodox in 1690. The Catholic hierarchy had been effectively eliminated at the beginning of the seventeenth century.

[102] Charles d'Eszlary, *Historie des institutions publique* [sic] *hongroises*, 3 vols (Paris, 1959–65), vol. 3, p. 371. At the same time, Charles announced a "wanted dead or alive" offer to whomever could locate Jozsef Rákóczi, son of the rebellious prince.

[103] MAT, Kéz. történl. 2 133 *Historia Collegorum* ... , p. 467. A similar fate awaited those who resisted Imperial troops in Blaj. Pascu, *History*, p. 130.

a major role in Jesuit/Uniate relations.[104] Yet whether such honors would translate into real political power to be retained and built upon, remained to be seen.

Inochentie Micu (Klein), the most important figure in the history of Transylvanian Uniate Church during the eighteenth century, was both a product of Jesuit education and formation and the most important example of Uniate resistance to what was perceived as the agenda of the Society in Transylvania. Born in 1692 in the village of Szád near the border with Walachia, Klein came from a poverty-stricken community whose inhabitants, while free, faced the danger of being forced into serfdom. Klein was educated for a time by the Jesuits in Cluj (school records document his attendance for the years 1719 through 1724, thus suggesting that his primary education may have occurred later than was usual) and was the protégé of the leading Jesuit member of the Cluj community. It appears that Klein originally intended to become a Jesuit himself, but abandoned his training in Trnava for unknown reasons.[105] Once appointed as the Uniate bishop of Transylvania in 1729, Klein launched a campaign to raise the economic, social and educational level of the Romanian peasantry, and to eliminate all inequality between the Romanian and the three "nations."[106] Significantly, Klein wove into his arguments the point that ethnic Romanians had a continuous presence in the region stretching back to the time of Roman Dacia, a position supported by the scholarship of some of the Cluj Jesuit community. Klein's strategy was to bombard the Habsburg court with a flood of memoranda and petitions that culminated in the *Supplex libellus* of 1744, a summary of reforms that were couched in terms that would preserve the *robota* and the existing "nations" themselves. While Klein was unable to find support for these reforms, he was able to solidify the position of the Uniate clergy *vis-à-vis* the Transylvanian Diet, which probably contained no Uniates and had long opposed any move that would have granted political recognition to ethnic Romanians.[107]

Because Klein's *Supplex libellus* included no challenges to traditional legal arrangements, Pascu and other Romanian historians have labeled him a supporter of "notions whose time had passed."[108] Nevertheless, Klein, who was made Baron of Szád in 1732, was viewed in some quarters as a rebel and a troublemaker. In any case his articulation of the desires of the Romanian put Klein at odds with elements

---

[104] Maria Someşan, *Începtulurile Bisericii Române Unite cu Roma* (Bucuresti, 1999), p. 61. It should be noted that some ethnic Hungarians were probably included among the disenfranchised. In 1769, Transylvania claimed a noble population of 6.7 per cent, the highest in Europe.

[105] Adolf Vorbuchner, *Az erdélyi püspökség* (Brassó, 1925), p. 69. *Brève histoire de la Transylvanie*. Constantin Daicoviciu and Miron Constaninescu (eds), (Bucarest: Editions de Académie de la République Socialiste de Roumanie, 1965), p. 143. For a less favorable assessment of Klein by a Hungarian scholar, see Miklós Asztalos, "Erdély története" in Miklós Asztalos (ed.), *A Történeti Erdély* (Budapest, 1936), pp. 293ff.

[106] Augustin Bunea, *Episcopu – Ioan Inocentiu Klein (1728–1751)* (Blas, 1900).

[107] Ion Ratiu, "Contribuţia Biserica Romane Unite cu Roma la dezvoltarea vieţii romaniesti de la 1697 incoace," in *Un Destin Istoric: Biserica Romana Unita* (Targu-Mureş, 1999), pp. 33–6; Asztalos Miklós, " Erdély története," p. 293.

[108] Pascu, *History*, p. 136. Pascu refers to Klein as a "Greek Catholic," a technically correct designation, but one that masks Klein's relationship to the Jesuits.

of the Society that wanted to maintain close control over the Uniate Church. In September 1746, the Jesuit *theologus* Ladislaus Balogh was excommunicated, largely as a result of Klein's efforts.[109] But this victory came at a high price, for Klein was compelled to remain in Vienna, and eventually to resign his episcopal office, under threat of dismissal.[110] Klein's many years abroad spent laboring for better conditions for his people, his promotion within the Uniate hierarchy and his ultimate fall from influence provide an additional perspective from which to view the dynamic between the Uniates and Jesuits of Cluj. While Klein's career was exceptional, and his increasingly anti-Jesuit rhetoric strident even by the standards of the eighteenth century, his training, aspirations and experiences with the Catholic hierarchy are suggestive of the way in which many Uniate clergy must have experienced union. Their junior-partner status was imposed from the start, and while it was occasionally possible to bypass the Society as Klein had done in order to accomplish their goals, in general the Habsburg bureaucracy was unsympathetic to appeals for change and most importantly, did not view the Uniate Church as a future source of leaders of Transylvania. The second-class position of ethnic Romanians in Transylvania could not be divorced from the relationship of the Uniate Church to the Catholic Church and to the Habsburgs, nor could Uniates find champions for their cause beyond the Catholic hierarchy or the Jesuits assigned to them. The tone of a letter written by Klein to the powerful Cardinal Kollonitz explaining Klein's reasons for traveling to Vienna and the calumnies he faced at home place the vulnerability of even the most influential member of the Uniate clergy in high relief.[111]

While the immediate response of the Transylvanian Orthodox clergy to the Patent was hardly a stampede to embrace Catholicism or even to enter into a union with Rome, the apparent shift in allegiances did reach down to the village level, where it created stresses between the celibate Jesuits and their new Uniate brethren. While the Society might point with pride at its tradition of celibacy, the Orthodox Church put no special premium on the celibacy of its own priests.[112] The shift to the West also meant that Easter and other holy days, points of reference in the lives of the peasants, were to be moved. The newcomers were immediately seen to have the upper hand in the conflicts that developed, even if the backing the dynasty provided was not always advertised. The two groups of clergy had received very different sorts of training, used different languages in their liturgies, and had notably distinct views

---

[109] Barlea, *Biserica*, p. 85. Klein described Balogh's attempts to control the Uniate diocese as "ad usurpationem fructuum Episcopalium." Letter to Pope Benedict XIV, 8 August 1746, in Dumitriu-Snagov (ed.), *Românii*, p. 154.

[110] Prodan, *Supplex Libellus*, pp. 163ff.

[111] "Conatui meo in cathedram meam inquiriens livor adeo restitit, ut calumniosis ad augustam aulam suggestionibus me ab epi[sco]patu avocari et Viennae contra S. canones, libertatem nobilitatem et fundamentales patriae leges ad incompetens examen constitui evenerit." Letter to Cardinal Kollonitz, 2 July 1746. in Dumitriu-Snagov (ed.), *Românii*, p. 138.

[112] The pride Jesuits took in their celibacy was remarked on not merely by the Society's opponents but also by a former Jesuit, Guilio Cesare Codara, writing after the Suppression. Guilio Cesare Cordara, *On the Suppression of the Society of Jesus: A Contemporary Account*, trans. John P. Murphy, SJ (Chicago, IL, 1999), p. 180.

of the role of the Church in the world.[113] Like other communicants of the Romanian Orthodox Church, Uniate clergy had been brought up in an environment, shaped by centuries of domination by outsiders and cultural isolation, that emphasized how "Latins" were, along with Jews, Mongols and Muslims, all destined for hell.[114] For their part, the Catholic hierarchy had little good to say about the Orthodox clergy: Cardinal Kollonitz, an important Habsburg ally, writing to the Congregatio de Propaganda Fide in 1701, complained that "schismatic" bishops tolerated simony, divorce and bigamy among their own clergy.[115] Political struggles for control of the flock of faithful in Transylvania were thus reflected and intensified by ecclesial differences and incompatible notions of what tolerable behavior was for clergy and laypersons and how transgressors should be dealt with. And while the promotion of the Uniate Church was a high priority for Jesuits throughout Transylvania, this concern did not inhibit the Society's simultaneous efforts to convert adherents of the Orthodox Church to Roman Catholicism. In 1703, thirteen Romanian ("Valachi") families were reported as converted in the Cluj area alone.[116] The impact of such aggressive proselytizing on Uniate clergy, as opposed to Orthodox clergy, is not easy to determine, but conversions directly to the Roman Church cannot have made the Uniate position more comfortable or secure. Presumably one of the principle reasons

---

[113] Most Uniate priests probably did not understand Latin, and the language barrier was widened by the fact that in the eighteenth century written Romanian was still written in an alphabet similar to Cyrillic. This practice continued in some regions well into the nineteenth century. Personal communication with Mihai Gherman, July 2000. An example of Eastern Rite ecclesiastical correspondence from the late eighteenth century in this alphabet is found in *Acte sinodali ale baserecrei romane de Alba Julia* [sic] *si Fagarasiu*, ed. J.M. Moldovanu (2 vols, Blasiu, 1872), vol. 1, p. 118. Moreover, the Orthodox tradition had nothing comparable to the Jesuit activist view of ordered religious life. On the Jesuit side, competence in Romanian was considered unusual enough to receive notice in reports sent to Vienna; missionaries Joannes Baptista Szegedi and Andreas Patai were both able to use Romanian. Nilles, *Symbolae*, vol. 2, pp. 1024–5.

[114] Jews were a rarity in eighteenth-century Transylvania, although there were some sizable communities in Walachia. ASV, Archivo della Nunziatura di Vienna, 196, folio 403r. The Jews had been expelled from the Romanian provinces of the Ottoman Empire in the sixteenth century, but had been allowed to return in the seventeenth century, and among these immigrants were many Polish Jews, who were therefore perceived as "outsiders" for geographic as well as religious reasons. Abram Leon Sacher, *A History of the Jews*, 5th edn (New York, 1964), p. 249. The first general census of Jews conducted in Transylvania in 1799 discovered a mere 221 families with 461 children. Ladislau Gyémánt, "The Jews from Romania – A historical destiny," *Nouvelles études d'histoire* 9 (1995), pp. 81–5. "Hebrea una" is reported baptized in Cluj in 1703. OSzK, 2039 FMI/1608 *Historia anno 1703*, p. 43. There is scant evidence of a native Catholic population in Transylvania larger than at most a few thousand in the first half of the seventeenth century. "Latin" continues to this day to have a negative connotation in Romanian, meaning, "heretic," or "bad person." Ion Popinceanu, *Religion, Glaube, und Aberglaube in der rumänischen Sprache* (Nürenberg, 1964), p. 174.

[115] Kollonitz to the Congregatio, 28 April 1701, in Vasile Bărbat, SI (ed.), *Instituirea Funcției Teologuilui în Biserica Română Unită. Extras din teza de doctorat* (Roma, 1963), p. 8.

[116] OSzK, 2039 FMI/1608 folio 43.

that some high-ranking Orthodox clergy were prepared to become Uniate was to insure the preservation of Orthodox ritual and the other customs associated with the Orthodox Church under a Western-oriented political regime. Thus the defection of laypersons directly to the Church of Rome can only have prompted feelings of betrayal towards their former brethren and doubts about the wisdom of their own decisions.

Even if hastily agreeing to a short list of requirements was all that was needed for Eastern Rite believers to achieve union with Rome, there was still the gap in institutional goals and organization between the Western and Eastern Churches. The Orthodox Church, for example, had no Inquisition with which to pursue sorcerers, magicians and other nonconformists, who abounded in the mountains of Transylvania.[117] The Jesuit response to such goings-on was often to perform exorcisms, while local authorities were more likely to leave things alone.[118] The Orthodox tradition of monastic life was long and deeply rooted, but the period of Turkish domination had seriously injured the vitality of the monasteries, and placed them at a great disadvantage as centers of intellectual activity, while the dominance of Calvinists had further isolated any literary activities undertaken by Orthodox believers. The Orthodox monasteries themselves, even at their most vital, represented an understanding of the organization and day-to-day functioning of a religious community very different from the one put forward by Ignatius and his companions.[119] The largely autonomous and national character of the Orthodox Churches of the East and the autonomous traditions of some Orthodox monasteries also sharply contrasted with the centralizing tendencies of the post-Tridentine Roman tradition and with the structure of the Society, which was as at least in principle a supranational organization with a world-wide mission. Yet at the same time Romanian Orthodoxy in the seventeenth century has been described as characterized by a conservative conformism that looked to the Patriarchate in Constantinople. Thus the Orthodox Church in Transylvania was hampered by the most negative features of national and supranational ecclesial structure, while the Society seemed able to capitalize on the strengths of each.[120] Orthodox educational institutions were focused on the teaching of doctrine to the believer and made few provisions for instruction to non-believers, whereas the *Ratio* placed little emphasis on doctrine and did not forbid instruction

---

[117] The life of the Romanian peasantry was enlivened by the presence of "strigoï" who were said to be able to shift shapes, and the "căluşari" who were men with the voices of women, and could dance in the air. Prime candidates for exorcisms by Jesuits or other Roman clergy, they seem to have endured in Romanian-speaking lands with little persecution. Mircea Eliade, *A History of Religious Ideas*, eds Alf Hiltenbeitel and Diane Apostolos (3 vols, Chicago, IL/London, 1985), pp. 233–4, 225–6.

[118] A characteristic Jesuit report of an encounter with the occult a few years after the Society's return to Cluj has the "malignos spiritus ... in fuga." ARSI, *Aust. 155, An. Prov. Aust. 1697* folio 73v; William Doyle, *The Old European Order* (Oxford, 1978), p. 172.

[119] Jesuits retained the opportunity to travel about while retaining membership in a community. *Constitutions*, 3 [633]. Orthodox monks occasionally were wandering preachers, but such instances were exceptional.

[120] George Schöpflin, "Transylvania: Hungarians under Romanian rule," in Stephen Borsody (ed.), *The Hungarians: A Divided Nation* (New Haven, CT, 1988), p. 121.

to non-Catholics, who sometimes made up a majority of the students enrolled in a Jesuit school.[121] There was moreover no Orthodox parallel to the "fourth vow" of the Society, which bound Jesuits to the Pope in personal obedience.[122] Finally, the entire land tenure system in Transylvania, in which the rural administrative units of the Principality were under the direct supervision of the local great landowner, posed another contrast to the experience of Jesuits from the western Habsburg lands, who were accustomed to considerable autonomy in the management of their own estates.[123] Coupled with the differences in political pressure that could be brought to bear by each side, these contrasts created an apparently insurmountable barrier to serious cooperation, even if both sides had been interested in working together. There is in fact little evidence that such interest ever existed.

---

[121] Daniel L. Schlafly, Jr., "True to the *Ratio Studiorum*? Jesuit colleges in St. Petersburg," *History of Education Quarterly* 37, 4 (1997), p. 422.

[122] This vow is detailed in Chapter One, Part Seven of the *General Examen and Declarations* of the Society. *Constitutions*, pp. 79–80.

[123] Aurel Raduțiu, "Les institutions rurales dans les pays roumains au xviiie siècle," *Revue Roumaine d'histoire* 20, 3 (1981), p. 510.

CHAPTER THREE

The Institution of Union

I

The initial patent of 1692, reinforced by the political and military presence of the Habsburg regime, was followed by substantial enticements: in 1697, Uniates were explicitly identified as eligible for schooling "sine discrimine" and for "omnis generis officia."[1] In February of the same year, a "Great Synod" was held in Alba Iulia, whereby those Orthodox clergy who became Uniates were officially delivered from the domination of the Calvinist "Superintendent" of Transylvania. At the synod Teofil, the Orthodox metropolitan who had been won over by the Jesuits, treated his listeners to an account of the persecutions suffered by the Orthodox Church under the control of the Calvinists, and then related the benefits union with Rome would bring.[2] Paulus Ladislaus Báranyi, a Hungarian Jesuit who had been appointed the head of the Romanian Uniate Church, followed with an explicit assurance that the Greek Rite would be preserved unchanged.[3] History records no objections or questions raised by the attending Orthodox clergy, or by their flocks. The Union of the Churches was announced on 10 June 1697, signed by Teofil and a dozen protopopes or archpriests.[4] In the view of Ştefan Pascu, the synod of Orthodox clergy held in Alba Iulia in 1697 in fact accepted the Union, subject to the granting of "accepted nation" status for the Romanian population.[5] If so, these hopes were to be bitterly disappointed. By the end of year Teofil was dead, poisoned, some said, by Calvinists fearing his defection to Rome and their loss of control over him.[6]

---

[1] Nilles, *Symbolae*, vol. 1, pp. 168–9.

[2] Jean Nouzille, "Les Jésuites en Transylvanie aux XVIIe et XVIIIe siècles," *Dix-Septième Siècle* 199 (1998), p. 321. The tensions between the Calvinists, who despised any images associated with the religious practice, and the Orthodox clergy, were certainly real. The truth of the claim that anxiety over the spread of Calvinism contributed significantly to the willingness of the Orthodox clergy to become Uniates is, however, difficult to establish with certainty. Ronald G. Robertson, "Romanian Catholic Church" in *The HarperCollins Encyclopedia of Catholicism* (New York, 1989), pp. 1131–2.

[3] Báranyi (1657–1719), born in Jázsbérény, devoted most of his career to the reconversion of the region. In 1702, he published a catechism in Romanian, probably the one translated by György Buitul. Sommervogel et al., *Bibliothèque*, vol. 1, p. 877.

[4] The complete text of the Act of Union appears in Wilhelm de Vries, "L'Unione dei rumeni (1697–1701)," *Transylvanian Review* 6/1 (1997), p. 18.

[5] Pascu, *History*, p. 133. The documents edited by Nilles do not support Pascu's interpretation.

[6] R. Jadin, "Fagaras," in *Dictionanaire D'Histoire et de Geographie Ecclésiastique*, ed. R. Aubert (27 vols, Paris, 1912–), vol. 6, pp. 389–90. The theme of poisoning is a persistent one in narratives of ecclesiastical history, especially Jesuit history, during the Baroque era.

His successor, Atanasie Anghel, the son of an Orthodox priest from Bobâlna, a region already largely regained for Catholicsm, was soon calling a "grand synod" of protopopes in Alba Iulia.[7] Atanasie did not impress all of his contemporaries with his maturity and strength, lending credence to the charge that he was merely a pawn of the Jesuits and their allies the Austrians.[8] The new synod, made up of 54 protopopes and 563 priests, rapidly accepted the union with Rome, an agreement that was formally concluded in 4 September 1700, by which time the Jesuits had already entered Sibiu and Cluj with great ceremony.[9] The new Metropolitan, soon to be a Uniate bishop, had signed the Act of Union in 1698, but it is not clear whether the version of the Act to which he subscribed had omitted references to the recognition of Romanian speakers as members of a "nation."[10] Whatever the actual form of the Latin text of the agreement, the laypersons led by Uniate clergy gained no civil rights as members of an identifiable national group, and the Romanian language was denied any special recognition.[11] These apparent omissions were to have far-reaching consequences, creating a divide between the Uniate clergy and their flocks, and confirming the position of the Uniate Church as an institution that seemed to require external support, that is, from the Habsburg court, as there would be little support for it from within.[12] Atanasie himself and all the Orthodox clergy following him were soon excommunicated by the Orthodox hierarchy, not a surprising development, but one that at least confirmed the necessity of looking elsewhere for support and legitimacy.[13] The Imperial court however did offer some gifts to its new supposed allies the Uniates. The new bishop was given 6,000 florins, a considerable sum, with which to buy lands from which he might support himself.[14] Moreover, the

Mathias Tanner, *Societas Jesu usque ad Sanguinis et Vitae Profusionem* ... (Pragae, 1675), a definitive work of Jesuit self-perception, contains many images of Jesuits poisoned by their enemies (often Calvinists), a diminutive serpent rising out of a cup being the emblem of the poison.

[7] Theofil's exact role in the preliminary moves towards union is still somewhat unclear. Contemporary Jesuits claimed to see some of his actions as obstructionist. Nilles, *Symbolae*, vol. 1, pp. 179–81. A table of Uniate bishops of Transylvania, *theologi*, and directors is found in Bărbat, *Institurea*, p. 40.

[8] Atanasie was described at the time of his elevation as "homo jam juvenis, rudis et non usque ad exemplaris." Nilles, *Symbolae*, vol. 1, p. 194.

[9] Thirty-eight proto-popes or archpriests are reported to have become Uniates in the year 1700 alone. Lucian Blaga, *Gîndirea Românească în Transilvania în Secolul al xviii-lea* (Bucharest, 1966). The Jesuits entered Cluj and Sibiu on 21 November 1699, although individual Jesuits had been present in the former community for many years. Endes Miklós, *Erdély három nemzete és négy vállása autonomiájának története* (Budapest, 1953), p. 273. Additional signatures to the Act of Union were obtained at conclaves held on 7 October 1698, 9 May 1700 and 7 April 1701. Nouzille, "Jésuites," p. 319.

[10] Alan Walker, "Romanian Christianity," in Parry et al. (eds), *Dictionary*, pp. 406–12.

[11] The bilingual text of the Act preserved by Nilles contains no mention of the granting of rights to Romanians. *Symbolae*, vol. 1, pp. 201–207.

[12] de Vries, "L'Unione," p. 18.

[13] Nilles, *Symbolae*, vol. 1, p. 343.

[14] Nouzille, "Jésuites," p. 322. Somewhat later, the Society was able to buy houses in Cluj for several hundred florins apiece.

agreement that Atanasie concluded with the civil and religious authorities in Vienna the following year also contained a concrete opportunity for Romanians seeking an education and social advancement: a Romanian-Latin school was to be established in Alba Iulia.[15] This acknowledgment of the potential of Uniate scholars, coupled with the retention of the ancient Orthodox liturgy and the bulk of the "Pravila" orthodox canon law book, was as close as the Catholic hierarchy could come to endorsing the intellectual traditions of the East.[16] But such concessions allowed the seed of schooling to grow. The most important of the new schools was established in 1754 in Blaj, a city that would become an important center of Romanian literary culture in the next century.[17]

Over time, other Orthodox bishops, encouraged by the Jesuit *theologus*, contemplated union, although to what degree the interest in union was a result of coercion is impossible to determine. When in 1711, Serephinus Petrovanu, Orthodox Bishop of Maramureş, expressed his intention to unite with Rome, the process was carried out swiftly.[18] Separate from the actions of the bishops, who were in the political arena whether they wanted to be or not, the motives of at least some lower Orthodox clergy regarding union can be explained variously. Long after the fact, the Romanian nationalist Nicolae Iorga, fired by the desire to tell the entire story of the Romanians in terms of their relationship to Rome and the West (which included the Entente of World War I), and to stress the separation of Romanians from the Slavic and Magyar populations surrounding them, declared, "We remained Romanians because we could not distance ourselves from the memory of Rome."[19] There were, however, much more immediate and practical reasons for becoming Uniate than a proud recollection of Trajan's legions. The Orthodox Church in Transylvania, before the arrival of the Habsburgs, had been under a Calvinist "Superintendent," a circumstance that, considering the Calvinist view of icons, incense, processions and other mainstays of Orthodox ritual, the faithful would have found humiliating.[20] The Calvinists as we have noted forbade devotion to Orthodox saints and in general repressed the more expressive and aesthetic aspects of the Eastern Rite, while the Calvinist dogma of the Elect made it easy for Reformed clergy to look down their noses at Orthodox Romanians. And although Orthodox conversions to Calvinism were negligible, Jesuit writers were genuinely worried about the dangers to Orthodox

---

[15] *Declariatio Ep. Athanasi 7 Aprilis 1701* in Dumitriu-Snagov (ed.), *Românii*, 92; A *katolikus iskolaügy Magyarországban II Literae Authenticae ... Collectae et Editae a sacerdote achidioeceseos Colocensis*, Fasiculus secundus (Coloczae, 1884), pp. 306–307.

[16] Teodor Pompiliu, "The confessional identity of the Transylvanian Greek Catholic Church," in Crăciun, Ghitta and Murdock (eds), *Confessional Identity*, pp. 167–80, 169.

[17] Blaj was called, with some considerable exaggeration, "the Romanian Rome." See Ioan-Aurel Pop, *Romanians and Romania: A Brief History* (Boulder, CO, 1999), p. 81.

[18] Welykyj (ed.), *Litterae episcoporum*, vol. 5, pp. 107–108. Fraciscus Szunyogh, then the *theologus*, had previously taught at the Cluj academy. Sommervogel et al., *Bibliothèque*, vol. 7, p. 1796.

[19] Quoted in Kurt W. Treptow (ed.), *A History of Romania* (Boulder, CO, 1996), p. 188.

[20] Sacra Congregazione per la Chiesa Orientale, *Oriente Cattolico: Cenni storichi e statistiche* (Città del Vaticano, 1962), p. 277.

of exposure to Calvinist heresy.[21] At the same time there were compelling reasons to eschew Union. Mihaela Grancea writes how Transylvania Orthodox believers were "torn between the trust in their religious officials [who were contemplating becoming Uniate] and the hell punishment promised for those who are baptized by 'unclean priests' through the union of the Orthodox Church with the Church of Rome."[22] Even though the explicit documentation of such emotions is hard to come by, the dilemma was undoubtedly real for many Orthodox faithful. And yet the Uniate project went forward, driven by the circumstance faced by Orthodox priests.

The Orthodox clergy had been hemmed in on another side as well. The Orthodox Bishop of Transylvania was appointed by the Metropolitan of Wallachia, subject to the approval of the Prince of Transylvania. The Metropolitan, living in the Ottoman-dominated Principality and many days' journey from Cluj, did not travel to Transylvania and his first-hand knowledge of conditions there would have been very limited. Likewise the material support the Metropolitan of Wallachia could offer the Orthodox clergy in Transylvanian villages or monasteries would have been minimal to nonexistent. The adherents of the Orthodox Church thus had few real material benefits to lose if they acknowledged the authority of Rome, and perhaps a good many to gain as they moved to a status far more desirable than that held by other groups such as the Sabbatarians.[23] From the start Atanasie had already lost the support of the Prince of Wallachia, the nominal protector of the Orthodox Church, and even before his excommunication his contacts with his superior, the Orthodox Metropolitan of Bucharest, seem to have been tenuous. Thus when Atanasie severed these connections he may have felt that he was only acknowledging a *fait accompli* brought on by circumstances.[24] As for the changes in theology required by the Union, neither Atanasie nor his successor ever made an issue of these, and neither, it appears, did the Jesuits. Disagreements over theology, in fact, are barely visible in the records left by all groups concerning Union over the next eighty years. Instead, Jesuit documents place emphasis on the perceived gap between the moral conduct of Uniate clergy and laypersons, and standards of Christian conduct that were taken as universals. While Uniates are not named specifically in many cases, the mention of polygamy among other instances of sexual misconduct in the Jesuit *Literae* may well refer to followers of the Eastern Rite.[25] Add to these difficulties the poverty of the vast majority of the Orthodox faithful and the scattered resources of the Orthodox Church, and it is not hard to see how the Orthodox Church might be perceived by both Jesuits and its own clergy as vulnerable to outside pressures.

---

[21] "Hinc janua ad errores Calvini in ecclesia Valachia aperta ...," Nilles, *Symbolae*, vol. 1, p. 46. Yet apparently few Romanian Orthodox ever converted to Calvinism. The Jesuits claimed, however, that in 1707 a "pseudo-bishop," Czirka, after trying to foment resistance against the Uniate Church, became a Calvinist. Nilles, *Symbolae*, vol. 1, p. 372.

[22] Mihaela Grancea, "Western travelers on Romanians' religiosity: 1683–1787," in Maria Craciun and Ovidui Ghitta (eds), *Church and Society in Central and Eastern Europe* (Cluj-Napoca, 1998), p. 409.

[23] Sabbatarianism, long established in Transylvania, was a special target of the Society. Horányi, *Memoria*, vol. 1, p. 468.

[24] *Declaratio*, p. 92.

[25] OSzK, 2039 FMI/1608 *Historia anno 1718*, p. 211.

At the same time the military Habsburg conquest of Transylvania had not failed to gain the notice of the Orthodox hierarchy: Vienna, and neither Bucharest nor Constantinople, was to be the center of power in the region, as the Ottomans, so recently a dominating force in the region, appeared to be in steep and irreversible decline. Thus it was to Vienna that Atanasie, now designated a Metropolitan, journeyed in 1701 to preach a sermon before Cardinal Kollonitz in the company of Karl Neuratner, a Bohemian Jesuit who had spent several years in Transylvania.[26] Atanasie besought the Imperial Court for assistance in extracting himself from the isolation of remote Transylvania, but to no avail; the young prelate had little leverage to bring to bear in the capital, while at home he came under criticism for, among other things, allowing Gypsies to caper about in his court.[27] A trend had been established that would characterize relations between the Uniate Church and the Habsburgs for the next century, whereby the Uniate hierarchy would look for favors from the Imperial Court, and that Court would bestow them occasionally, while keeping tabs on the activities of the hierarchy through communications with members of the Society.[28] That June the remaining element of the new relationship was established. Neuratner was appointed as the *theologus* to Bishop Atanasie, thereby forging another link between the political apparatus in Vienna and the Uniates in Transylvania.[29] The relationship was to be an unequal one, with virtually all the power residing in the dynasty and its functionaries.[30] The men who held the post of *theologus*, in each case a Jesuit, left little evidence of their understanding of or sympathy with the traditions of the Eastern Rite, nor did their fellow Jesuits who trained them seem well informed regarding Orthodox Christianity. A possible exception would have been Joannes Pataki, born in 1682, who was the rector of the German and Hungarian College in Rome from 1705 until 1710, when he returned to Transylvania, his homeland.[31] Pataki had also studied at the Cluj Jesuit academy

---

[26] Karl Neuratner (1667–1702) had earlier been almoner to the general commanding the Imperial troops in Transylvania. Sommervogel et al., *Bibliothèque*, vol. 5, p. 1284. A member of the Bohemian Province, Neuratner was appointed "causarum auditor generalis" in 19 March 1701 and was officially given the title of *theologus* the following year. Păcurariu, *Istoria*, p. 207; Nilles, *Symbolae*, vol. 1, pp. 179, 181; Silvestru Augustin Prunduş and Clemente Plainanu, *Catolicism şi Ortodoxie Românesă*. (Cluj-Napoca, 1994), p. 69. The connection of Bohemian Jesuits to Transylvania appears in another, intriguing context: Rákóczi I. Ferenc had received his early education (during which it was said that he was forbidden to speak Hungarian) from Jesuits of the Bohemian Province.

[27] Nilles, *Symbolae*, vol. 1, p. 259.

[28] Atanasie was not invested by the pope as a bishop until 1721, leaving him in a particularly vulnerable position. The delay between appointment by the Habsburg monarch and investiture by the Holy See reflected a long-standing custom among Hungarian Catholic bishops, who acquired their title and vestments by right of preferment. Béla K. Király, "The Hungarian Church," in Callahan and Higgs (eds), *Church and Society*, pp. 114–17.

[29] Prunduş and Plaianu, *Catolicisimu şi Ortodoxie Românească*, p . 69.

[30] Lists of all Uniate bishops and their theologi appear in Bărbat, "Instituirea," p. 40.

[31] Carol Capros and Flaviu Popan, "Biserica Unita între anii 1700–1718," in *Biserica Unita: Doua Sute Cinci Zeci de Ani de Istorie* (Madrid, 1952), p. 72. The union of the Hungarian and German Colleges by the early eighteenth century is further evidence of the

and ultimately became Uniate Bishop of Făgăraş.[32] Pataki, despite his Hungarian name (also spelled Patachi and Pataky), which he took from the place of his birth, is described as a "nobilis Rumenus" and may have received some education in a Romanian cultural setting, although his formation was in Jesuit schools, including the academy in Cluj.[33] Pataki's commitment to the reunion of his homeland's Orthodox believers with Rome was sincere and intense, surpassing even the usual level of ardor expressed by Jesuit missionaries of the day. He wrote that he would engage in "quocumque ritu qualicunque modo ... pro salute carae meae nationis Valalchiae ... ."[34] As one of the first of a handful of Jesuits in the region with Orthodox backgrounds, he was certainly intended to serve as a model for future converts and recruits, in the same way that Peter Pázmány, a distinguished sixteenth-century convert from Calvinism, was a model to other Calvinist aristocrats who converted.[35] But few others raised in the Orthodox tradition followed Pataki's model and became missionaries for the Uniate cause.

At the same time the depth of the commitment of many formerly Orthodox clergy who entered into union with Rome remained somewhat suspect. In 1707, Andreas Horvath, SJ, the "superior of the mission for Dacia," summoned a meeting in Alba Iulia in which one of the major topics of discussion was the sincerity of the

---

Society's awareness of the Habsburg shift to the east. *Facultates, Exemptiones, et Priviligia Concessa Collegio Germanico et Hungarico* (Romae, 1720).

[32] Stan Gabriel, *Ioannes Patachi, Episcopus Fogarasiensis (1721–1729)*. MS Thesis, in collection of Pontifical Oriental Institute, Rome. In accepting the position of bishop, Pataki violated a long-standing principal not to assume high ecclesiastical office. Nevertheless, he was nominated "ab Imperatore Carlo VI" as bishop in 1717, a significant use of an Imperial title in a region far removed from the Holy Roman Empire. Welykyj (ed.), *Litterae episcoporum*, pp. 5, 153–4.

[33] Nilles, *Symbolae*, vol. 1, p. 380. Pataki's father was an Orthodox priest, with the family name of Giurgiu. The young future missionary was greatly influenced by his teacher P. Stephanus Csete, SJ, who gained renown for his incognito travels through Transylvania. Ibid., vol. 1, p. 454. Csete, assuming the name Vizkeleti or Wiszkeleti István and the identity of a secular priest, spent nineteen years working in Transylvania; his letters were published in Trnava in 1698. Sommervogel et al., *Bibliothèque*, vol. 2, pp. 1719–21; Horányi, *Memoria*, vol. 1, pp. 620–24; Szinnyei (ed.), *Magyar irók*, vol. 2, p. 1335. There is no evidence that Joannes Pataki was related to Ferenc (Franciscus) Pataki, who taught lower-level classes at the Cluj *Collegium* until his death in 1740. Sommervogel et al., *Bibliothèque*, vol. 6, p. 344; Prundus and Plainu, *Catolicism*, p. 70; Lukács, *Catalogi*, vol. 6, p. 421.

[34] Nilles, *Symbolae*, pp. 1, 87.

[35] Pázmány, the outstanding Jesuit figure of seventeenth-century Hungary, is credited with having converted thirty noble families to Catholicism. Jealous of the prerogatives of the Society, Pázmámy worked to prevent the revival of the once influential Benedictine order in Hungary, with the result that the Uniate project in Transylvania was spared the rivalries that hampered similar efforts in Moldavia. Gaspár Csóka, Kornél Szóvak and Imre Takács, *Pannonhalma: Pictorial Guide to the History and Sights of the Benedictine Abbey*, trans. Catherine Roman and Judith Pokoly (Pannonhalma, 1996), p. 19. See also Szábo Ferenc, *A teologus Pázmány* (Budapest: METEM, 1998).

Uniate converts.[36] Simultaneously, clergy who remained faithful to the Orthodox Church were articulate in their refusal to give up their customs and traditions, not fearing even to invoke the Emperor's protection. In 1698, the Orthodox clergy of the Hácz region submitted a resolution to the Emperor, stating, "we shall hold on to our Romanian, our Greek faith in its entirety, which we do because we expect to find therein the continuing mercy of Your Highness ... ."[37]

Early on, the Uniate project faced opposition from Orthodox clergy, and this hostility did not subside with the passing of years. The Kolosmănăștur Synod of 1728 attempted to deal with challenges from the "schismatic, turbulent popa" Majalt, and implored him, somewhat ineffectually, to cease his efforts against Union.[38] Lest the Jesuits and the Habsburgs forget the strength of the persisting connection between the Transylvanian Orthodox believers and the historic heartland of Christian Orthodoxy, the arrival several decades later of Sophronius, a monk from Trebizond in Asia Minor, reminded them of the difficulties that still lay ahead. "This Greek wolf" preached against the union of Eastern and Roman Churches in many parts of Eastern Europe, including Hungary and Poland.[39] While he was not the first Orthodox monk from abroad to travel the countryside to preach against Union, Sophronius was much more effective than his predecessor Visarion Sarai, who being Serbian, preached in that language, which few in Transylvania understood.[40] Sophronius, although he was also a foreigner, was a skillful orator and rapidly gained a large following among peasants who were uncomfortable with the notion of belonging to a Church other than the one of their ancestors.[41] This challenge was immediately met by Father Georgius Szegedi, a Jesuit missionary in Cluj, who preached against Sophronius. The Catholic hierarchy from Varad eastward was alerted, but large crowds continued to follow the monk.[42] By 1760, the religious movement began to take on the characteristics of a general uprising. Sophronius even sent ultimatums to Imperial military commanders, and although he later entered into negotiations with Austrian authorities and the rebellion petered out, the depth of the unrest and the potential for its exploitation was clear. Maria Theresia, still at war with Prussia and in chronic financial straits, was pressed to issue a decree in 1759 that recognized the legal existence of the Orthodox

---

[36] Zenobie Pâclișanu, *Istoria Bisericii Române Unite*, ed. O. Bârlea (München, 1996), p. 160.

[37] Resolution 250, anno 1698, in Silviu Dragomir, *Istoria dezrobirii religioase a românilor din Ardeal* în *secolul al XVIII* (2 vols, Sibiu, 1920–30), p. 17.

[38] Nilles, *Symbolae*, vol. 1, p. 491.

[39] Nilles, *Symbolae*, vol. 2, p. 868ff.

[40] Visarion was also known as Bessarion. Nilles, *Symbolae*, vol. 2, p. 558. See also the entry for 1730 in *Monumenta Hungaricae Historica*, Vol. 11, Altorjai B. Apor Péter Munkái (Pest, 1863); and M. Lacko, SJ, "Documenta spectantia regimen episcopi Munkačevensis Michaelis Manuelis Olšavsky," *Orientalia Christiana Periodica* 25 (1959), p. 58.

[41] Pascu states that Sophronius, whom he identifies as Stan Popovici, was a native of Transylvania, but this seems unlikely. Pascu, *History*, p. 146.

[42] Szegedi (1711– after 1773) taught philosophy in Cluj and Košice and had served as rector of the *Pazmaneum*. Szegedi published extensively on Hungarian law and also spoke Romanian. Sommervogel et al., *Bibliothèque*, vol. 7, pp. 1749–53; ARSI, *Austria 80 (Catal. I Col. Claud., 1734)*, p. 65; Katona, *Historia*, vol. 20, p. 1005.

religion in her realms, a move that has in modern times been mislabeled a "decree of toleration"; in reality it was merely an acknowledgement of the existing situation that granted no new political rights to Romanian Orthodox believers, although it did open the door to the reestablishment of the Orthodox Bishop of Transylvania two years later.[43] Yet neither of these developments diminished the favored status of the Uniate Church, which continued to have direct ties to Vienna and to the Society.

II

In a region where the number of Roman Catholics had been and would remain low, the Uniate Church would be the principal institution outside of the state bureaucracy to outlast the Society whose orientation was distinctly Western.[44] For this and other reasons, some Romanian writers have indicted the Romanian Uniate Church for not being authentically "Romanian." But such charges generalize about a complex transition and do not take into account the mixture of self-interest, fear, genuine confusion and sincere agreement with the theological positions listed above that undoubtedly influenced those who joined and made use of the opportunities offered to Uniates.[45] While it would not be the single most important medium through which the aesthetic values of the Viennese court would be introduced into the region, the educational path provided by the alliance of the Jesuits with the Uniate Church created a path for young Romanian men seeking a chance to come in contact with Western European culture, as well as providing an advanced education. This connection remained important even when the men acquiring this education did not become or remain Uniates or when they did not complete the entire course of training prescribed by the Jesuits.[46] This tie to the West was a salient feature of the educational program envisioned by the Uniates themselves from the earliest years of the union. At the diocesan synod of 8 June 1702, Atanasie expressed to desire to create a core of educated Uniate priests trained in universities in Cluj, Trnava,

---

[43] Ioan-Aurel Pop, "Medievalism and Enlightenment in Romanian historiography," in Teodor Pompiliu (ed.), *Enlightenment and Romanian Society* (Cluj-Napoca, 1980), p. 189. In the same year, the Transylvanian Parliament, which did not include Romanian Orthodox, ceased to convene, a development that might be read as a gain for Romanian Orthodox and Uniates as well. Barta János, "A felvilágosult abszolutiszmus fogatatása Erdélyben," in Racz (ed.), *Tanulmányok* (Debrecen, 1988), pp. 119–20.

[44] In 1714, there were approximately 30,000 Catholics in all of Transylvania. Joachim Bahlcke, "*Status Catholicus* und Kirchenpolitik in Siebenbürgen, Entwicklungsphasen des Römisch-katholischen Klerus, zwichen Reformation und Josephinismus," in *Siebenbürgishces Archiv 34: Siebenbürgen in der Habsburgermonarchie: Von Leopoldinum bis zum Augleich (1690–1866)*, Zsolt K. Lengyel and Ulrich A. Wien (eds), (Köln/Weimar/Wien, 1999), p. 63.

[45] Radu R. Florescu, *Essays on Romanian History* (Iași/Oxford/Portland, OR, 1999), pp. 159–66.

[46] Among the notable figures in both the Orthodox and Uniate churches who studied at the Cluj *collegium* were Ioan Bob, Vasile Moga and Gheorghe Lazăr. Vasile Lechințan, *Instituții și edifice istorice din Transilvania* (Cluj-Napoca, 2000), p. 82.

Vienna and Rome.[47] Nor was this the only attempt to link the Uniate Church with new educational opportunities. A generation later, Atanasie's successor, Inochentie Micu Klein, had plans to found a seminary in Cluj supported by the contributions of Uniate priests, although after the bishop ran into opposition to his championing of Romanian identity the scheme was never realized.[48] Throughout the eighteenth century, the Uniate Church produced many of the Romanian leaders of Transylvania. It is fair to say that Jesuit centers in Blaj and elsewhere in Transylvania not only fostered the local intellectual culture, but also significantly influenced the direction of Romanian cultural history by providing centers where Romanian speakers could be educated and come in contact with one another.[49] While binding former Orthodox clergy to Rome, the Uniate Church was also binding Romanian clergy to one another, making them aware of their numbers and their potential influence, and providing the context in which Romanian literary works might be envisioned. Whether the Church provided any sort of connection with the West to the illiterate rural population that made up the vast majority of the nominally "Uniate" community is far less certain.

Many of the Jesuits, both priests and *coadjutores temporales*, who arrived in Transylvania were of ethnic Hungarian, or in some instances, Bohemian or German origins; many had traveled long distances from their homelands. Even those who had been born in Transylvania were almost always of Hungarian extraction. Jesuits had long been involved in the both the development of the Hungarian language and in the use of that language to further religious objectives; the first translation of large portions of the Bible into Hungarian had been made, not by a Protestant, but by the Jesuit Gerogius Káldi, in 1626.[50] The advance of Catholicism in the eighteenth and nineteenth centuries has therefore frequently been identified strongly in Romanian historiography with the unwelcome advance of Hungarian culture and language into parts of Transylvania hitherto dominated by Romanian culture.[51] On the other hand, despite efforts at recruitment, Jesuit priests of Romanian or Slavic origins remained relatively rare in all of the eastern regions of the Habsburg realm. In 1773, only one Jesuit priest at the *collegium* in Uzhhorod (Ungvár) appears to have been of Ruthenian origin.[52] Nor was the apparent ethnicity of many of the Jesuit

---

[47] Ioan Marin Malinas Arhimandrit, *Siutuaţia invatamantului bisericesc al Românilor în Contextul Reformelor Scolare din Timpul Domniei împaratesei Maria Tereza (1740–1780) a împaratilor Iosif al II-ea (1780–1790) şi Leopold al II-ea (1780–1792)* (Oradea, 1994), p. 162.

[48] Pascu, *Supplex Libellus*, p. 139.

[49] Teodor Pompiliu, "The Romanians from Transylvania between the tradition of the Eastern Church, the Counter-Reformation and the Catholic Reformation," in *Ethnicity and Religion in Central and Eastern Europe* (Cluj, 1995), p. 181.

[50] Sommervogel et al., *Bibliothèque*, vol. 4, pp. 897–9. The Kaldi translation is almost certainly the version listed in the 1773 inventory of books in the Cluj *Convictus* library. MOL, *Erdély Kincs. Levéltár*, Nos 30, 133.

[51] Osnifor Ghibu, *Catholicimul Unğuresc*. In addition, Catholics who fled Tartar and Turkish pressure in Moldavia, traveling over the mountains into Transylvania in 1686, were probably mostly ethnic Hungarians. Benda (ed.), *Okmánytár*, vol. 2, pp. 94–105.

[52] *Catalogus Personarum et Officiorum Proviniciae Austriae ... MDCC.LXXIII*, columns 38, 39.

missionary priests who appeared in Transylvania the only evidence of what the role of Hungarian language and culture was to be in the new order of things. Official documents dealing with the conduct of Romanian Orthodox priests were sometimes published in Hungarian as well as Latin, but not in Romanian.[53] With the exception of the catechism of Joannes Gyologi the Romanian language was largely ignored or avoided by the Jesuits who came to Cluj, and while an occasional Hungarian word or phrase found its way into the Jesuit *Literae*, no trace of Romanian vocabulary identified as such appeared in these records until 1730, when the Romanian word for church was recorded with an accompanying translation.[54] The absence of the word "Romanian" from Jesuit records is, however less surprising, as this term was very seldom used before the nineteenth century, the term "Valachus" being the preferred designation.[55] At the same time, the level of comprehension of Latin among Uniate clergy must have been very low, especially at first, before the Jesuit academies were able to admit Romanian-speaking students. A list of eighteen signatories to the 1698 Act of Union does not contain one name written in Latin or even in the Roman alphabet.[56] The gulf of mutual non-comprehension would have been very great indeed, with possibly serious consequences, as when the *Acta* of 29 March 1699, dealing with the conduct of "Valach" priests, were published in Latin and Hungarian, but not in Romanian.[57] Despite the presence of Romanian Uniates in the immediate vicinity, the dearth of Jesuit-produced written material in Romanian persisted, while, improbably, Jesuit instructors found reason to teach their students verses in "Illyrico" (Dalmatian), a language understood by several priests who had grown up or had sojourned on the Dalmatian coast.[58] An almost unique exception to this silence was the publication of the Buitul catechism in Romanian in 1703. In 1735, the Cluj Jesuit press produced a small volume containing the "precepts of the faith" in two languages, but it is doubtful whether either was Romanian. The passing years did

---

[53] For example, the "Instructio de usu Caesarei Diplomatis a Statu catholico," published in Cluj on 29 March 1699. Nilles, *Symbolae*, vol. 1, pp. 227–9.

[54] "In templum, quod illi Bessericam appellant ...," ARSI, *Aust. 187, An. Prov. Aust. 1730*, folios 12r–13r. The writer also complains that many peasants do not know how to make the sign of the cross.

[55] "Valachus" does identify the subject with Rome. The term is cognate with the French Walloon, the English Welsh, the German Welsch and the Hungarian olasz, the last two meaning Italian, and all referring to a relationship with Roman Christianity or culture, as perceived by a group outside these categories. While Jesuit records never use the term with a negative connotation, Valach could also have a negative connation, implying "low born" or "crude." Keith Hitchins, *The Romanian National Movement in Transylvania, 1780–1849* (Cambridge: Harvard University Press, 1969), p. 38. The Romanians call themselves roman..

[56] Nilles, *Symbolae*, vol. 1, p. 211. Many names appear in Greek, which was also used as an ecclesiastical language of the Orthodox Church throughout the eighteenth century. Ibid., pp. 2, 565.

[57] This document, published in Cluj, appeared over Atanasie's signature. Ibid., vol. 1, p. 229.

[58] ARSI, *Aust. 177, An. Prov. Aust. 1720*, p. 84. Father Franciscus Csernovics, whose surname suggests a Croatian origin, spoke "Illyrice super mediocriter." *Aust. 74, Catalogus I Col. Claud. 1726*, p. 63.

nothing to change this pattern: when the stocks of the Society's printing press and bookshop in Cluj were seized in 1773, they included many titles in Hungarian, but not one in Romanian.[59] The Jesuits, famed for their compilation of dictionaries and grammars of the languages they encountered in the missionary work, left the writing of a Romanian-Latin dictionary to a Uniate cleric, Grigore Maior.[60] Examination of records of the Society's activities in Transylvania likewise has failed to turn up any evidence of financial or legal negotiations carried on in Romanian; this is in contrast to plentiful documentation of communications between Uzhhorod (Ungvár) Jesuits and local Slovak-speaking peasants during the same period.[61] Aside from language barriers, Jesuit assumptions concerning the cultural characteristics and attainments of Romanians also helped define relations between the two groups. The accepted view of Romanians, be they Uniates or Orthodox, seems to have been that they were not accustomed to prayers recited in a formal setting in church but were better able to grasp the message when they sang together in a choir, an observation that might imply that Romanians were simpler or more sensual souls.[62] Orthodox priests were accused of marrying couples that were only first cousins, something viewed as a failing not so much of Orthodox teaching but of the primitive and crude moral standards in place in Romanian communities.[63]

The behavior of some Jesuits at public events underscored this bias in favor of the Hungarian language, a difficult tongue held in very high esteem by its speakers, and whose use as a language of instruction was a source of controversy long before other languages used in the Habsburg realms became symbols of cultural identity.[64] In 1713, at the funeral for Atanasie, two Jesuit orators delivered eulogies, one in Latin and another in Hungarian, although the majority of the Uniate priests serving under Atanasie probably did not understand either language.[65] The choice of Hungarian as the language of public discourse would have also called to mind the fact that since 1560 Hungarian instead of Latin had served as the language of civil administration in Transylvania, a reminder of the political ascendancy of the Magyars over the

---

[59] MOL, f 477, "Erdély Kincstár Levéltár Exactorius Cameralis Inventarium Universae Substantiae in Civitate Claudiopli post Suppressum ibi Collegium Societatis Jesu apprehensae", No. 30, p. 58.

[60] *Lexicon Compendiarium Latino-Valachicum* ... , ed. Mihai Gherman (3 vols, Roma, 1994–96).

[61] These are found in MOL, "Jesuitica E 152", and include some of the earliest examples of Slovak from this region.

[62] "... ipse etiam populus Valachus potiori ex parte praecationis ignarus multis in festos dies in choreis magis quam in temples exigibat." OSzK, 2039 FMI/1608 *Historia anno 1722*, p. 265. Aside from the implication that Romanians were unequipped to appreciate the subtleties of the Baroque devotional, this passage also raises the question of whether Jesuits composed hymns in Romanian.

[63] OSzK, 2039 FMI/1608 *Historia anno 1723*, p. 264.

[64] The Bohemian Jesuits who had educated the future Prince Ferenc II Rákóczi had allegedly not allowed the youth to speak Hungarian in their presence, a decision, whether or not it had really happened, that irritated later writers. Imre Lukinich, *A History of Hungary in Biographical Sketches*. (Budapest, 1937), p. 176.

[65] Păcurariu, *Istoria*, p. 208.

Romanians and of the Magyar literary traditions associated with Transylvania.[66] Mastery of spoken Romanian, which should have been relatively easy for any Jesuit well versed in Latin, or familiar with French or Italian, was rare enough to be noteworthy among the Society's Transylvanian enterprises, even in regions where the overwhelming majority of inhabitants were Romanian speakers.[67] It appears that Jesuits on occasion relied on Romanians to translate key documents into their own languages, sometimes with bizarre results. In a list of "Canones disciplinares in Synodo condidti" adopted for Uniate priests in 1700, instructions to mention Leopold I in the Divine Office became garbled into a reference to "his highness Emperor Ignatius"(!).[68] That this mistake passed into the permanent records of the Society without correction (and appears without comment in a major nineteenth-century document collection) says a good deal about the level of communication between Jesuits and Romanians, and perhaps about the degree of attention paid by some Jesuits to matters involving Uniates as well. Had the Society not been long noted for its eagerness to take up the study of the languages of peoples wherever it conducted its work, these lapses would not seem so remarkable. Under the circumstances, it is difficult to disagree with the assessment of Romanian historians that these and other similar actions and omissions by Jesuits in Transylvania were felt to be insulting to Romanian speakers, and specifically to Uniate priests.[69]

There was one other way in which the Jesuits did not develop the same literary relationship to Romanian culture and to the Uniate Church that they did in many of their other mission contexts. The pre-Suppression Society's missions in the New World and elsewhere were the subject of *Relations*, detailed and nuanced reports that unlike the *Literae Annue*, reached a wide contemporary audience, including many non-Catholics. The *Relations* served not only as important documentation of the cultures encountered by the Society, they also advertised the Society's undertakings and accomplishments in an engaging style that frequently had literary merit. These remote regions were identified in the public mind with the accomplishments of the Society and were understood through the lens that the Society provided. Since Transylvania, despite its challenging environment and exotic cultural elements, did not count as the "Indies," the traditional designation of all overseas locations where

---

[66] Castellian, *History*, p. 101.

[67] In Iași, Moldavia, Michaelis Salbeck (Szalbeck), SJ, who had been born there in 1709, was identified as having spoken "Valach." "Elogium P. Michaelis Salbeck," Bibliotheca Batthyaneum Szentiványi 691 XI 68. *Annue Residentiae Carolinae* Annus [sic] 1758, folio 63r. Michaelis also taught philosophy and theology in Cluj, where his *Prima quinque Saecula Regni Mariani Apostolici ethicae adumbrata* was published in 1746. Katona, *Historia Critica*, vol. 20, p. 1003.

[68] Nilles, *Symbolae*, vol. 1, p. 254.

[69] Nor should it be thought that Romanian, in its late seventeenth-century form, lacked the precision or clarity to serve in ecclesiastical documents and pronouncements. The acts and decrees of the Synod of 1697 were published in Romanian as well as Latin. Nilles, *Symbolae*, vol. 1, p. 202. Romanian liturgy and ecclesiastical literature was highly developed in the eighteenth century. An example of this is a prayer book, *Eulochion adeca Mltvník.* (Bucurest, 1729).

the Society labored, no *Relations* were ever written or published about Transylvania.[70] The Society's *Literae annue*, intended for a different and much more limited audience, did not aspire to the same kind of reportage, either in richness of detail or in polished literary style.[71] Information about Romanian-speaking lands in general instead was instead provided to the outside world by other sources, most notably the aristocratic scholar Dimitrie Cantimir, whose *Incrementa atque Decrementa aulae Othomanicae* had wide circulation in the eighteenth century, being translated into Russian, French, Italian and English.[72] Thus despite the dominant Jesuit presence in the Principality, the Society never managed to make the story of the reclaiming of Transylvania and its dealing with its inhabitants of the Eastern Rite its "own" in a literary context where the endeavors of the Society and the culture in which it worked were unified into a compelling narrative. This missed opportunity meant that the court in Vienna could not read about the lands it had acquired from the perspective of its allies, and the Jesuits could not remind their distant patrons of the work they were undertaking. This literary isolation, while not decisive by itself, was a contributing factor in the more encompassing experience of isolation that Jesuits experienced everywhere in the Transylvanian missions, including Cluj. Later, when Vienna demanded that the Transylvanian government take steps to defend the Uniate Church, Jesuit lobbying for its allies would no longer be possible.[73]

Despite the suspicions that surrounded it, the Uniate Church came to be identified with a conscious sense of Romanian ethnicity during the eighteenth century, one that grew in part out of the awareness that almost all Romanian speakers shared the same religious traditions.[74] But this ethnic identification should not be understood as synonymous with a developed sense of national identity. A unified Romanian nation state including all regions where Romanian was the majority language had never existed and could not yet be conceived of by peasants or priests, whose cultural horizons, like those of virtually all of the rural laboring classes of Europe, were still narrow. In the late seventeenth and early eighteenth centuries, the memories of Roman (and Christian) Dacia that the Society frankly sought to promote and incorporate into its own mission of expanding the reach of the Universal Church were faint, if not nonexistent, among the general Romanian population and had to be amplified and reinterpreted when necessary. When, in 1743, a statue of "Nicetas,

---

[70] See, for example, *The Jesuit Relations and Allied Documents: Travels and Explorations of the Jesuit Missionaries in North America (1610–1791)*, ed. Edna Kenton with a introduction by Reuben Gold Twaithes (New York, 1954).

[71] In addition to Hevenesi's *magnum opus*, a history of Transylvania was written by the Bohemian Jesuit Joannes Koffler, but like Hevenesi's work, never was published. Johann Nepomuk Stoeger, *Scriptores Proviniciae Austriacae Societatis Jesu.* (Viennae, 1856), pp. 190–91; Sommervogel et al., *Bibliothèque*, vol. 4, pp. 1156–7.

[72] Ștefan Ștefănescu, "Cuvînt înaninte" in *Reflectarea Istoriei Universale în Istoriografia Românească*, Ș. Ștefănescu ed. (București, 1986), p. 5.

[73] Marcel Știban, "L'union des Roumains Uniates sous l'évêque Petru Pavel Aron," *Transylvanian Review* 6, 1 (1997), p. 41.

[74] Ioan-Aurel Pop, "Ethnie et confession. Genèse médiévale de la nation roumaine moderne," in Nicole Bocsan, Ioan Lumperdean and Ioan-Aurel Pop (eds), *Ethnie et Confession en Transylvanie (du XIIIe au XVIIIe Siècles)* (Cluj-Napoca, 1996), p. 59.

the first apostle to the Dacians" was unveiled in the Cluj *Convictus Nobilium* next to a memorial to a Hungarian king, the intended audience was to be aristocratic, not peasant, and predominantly Hungarian.[75] The message was one that stressed the universality of the Faith, not the special identity of the Romanians, who probably made up a minority of those present.[76] In this way, the promotion of the Uniate Church and the conversion of Orthodox to Catholicism proceeded entirely without the special sense of national mission that typified the reclaiming of the Hungarian heartland for the Roman Church, the Apostolic King, and for the Virgin.

The sense of distance experienced on both sides of the Romanian–Hungarian divide had more to do with cultural norms (including, but not limited to liturgy, the church calendar, and the adoration of saints), and in particular with the relations between laypersons and the clergy. Uniate Orthodox clergy, in contrast to the Jesuit newcomers from the West almost always had roots in the immediate vicinity, and since they were not celibate, had ties through marriage with local families, as well as with other Orthodox priestly families.[77] This point is illustrated vividly in a picture of an Orthodox village priest preserved from the late seventeenth or early eighteenth century. The costume of the priest is very similar, if not quite indistinguishable from that of a peasant.[78] This question of personal appearance was not trivial, and symbolized what were perceived as more profound differences between Catholic and Orthodox clergy.[79] While the Society did not have an official habit and its members in fact exercised considerable freedom in their choice of costume, there are no indications that Jesuits in Transylvania, once their presence had been legitimated, made any efforts to dress like the locals, or at least like the local peasants. From the beginning Jesuits were aware of the role of the Orthodox priest in his village and how his lifestyle differed from a Catholic village priest or a Jesuit. Andreas Freyberger, a member of the Bohemian Province, noted in 1702 that Orthodox priests in Romanian-speaking lands performed the liturgy only on Sundays, devoting the rest of the week to agricultural pursuits while going about dressed in goat- or sheepskins

---

[75] Drawing upon more recent events, but using identical terminology, the Jesuits identified Stephanus Apor as one of the "heroes of Dacia" honored by students in *Selecta Heroum Daciae Spectacula. Honori Reverendum, Nobilorum ac Eruditorum Dominorum Dominorum Neo-Baccalorum ... Promotore R. P. Andrea Patai è Soc. Jesu ...* (Claudiopoli, 1731), pp. 26–33.

[76] Nilles, *Symbolae*, vol. 2, p. 570. Nicetas of Remesiana was a fourth- and fifth-century bishop who may not have actually traveled in "Dacia," but was remembered as a staunch supporter of Rome in lands that later were dominated by Orthodox churches. A.E. Burn, *Niceta of Remsiana: His Life and Works* (Cambridge, 1905).

[77] Evans reports, however, that in 1607 the Catholic community in Transylvania "numbered no more than forty priests, (excluding Jesuits), most of them married." Evans, *Making*, p. 270. The phenomenon of married Catholic priests in regions dominated by Eastern Orthodoxy awaits more systematic study.

[78] Mircea Păcurariu, *Istoria Bisericii Românesti din Transilvania, Banat, Crisina şi Maramureş până în 1918* (Cluj-Napoca, 1992), plate 15.

[79] "... in multi suquidem popis nec forma sacerdotis, apparenbat; imo non paucos ebriosos, simoniacos, contentiosos plus ventriae lucris quam gregis mentos ...," OSzK, 20039 FMI/1608, *Historia anno 1712*, p, 250.

like their neighbors.[80] In 1721, a confrontation between Orthodox clergy and Jesuits is recorded from the Jesuit side in terms of personal appearance: the Orthodox priests are negatively portrayed as "obese and wearing long beards," while the Jesuit by contrast is approvingly described as "unbearded," giving him a similar appearance to the young virgin saints who were such an important part of Jesuit iconography.[81] Elsewhere an anonymous Jesuit is quoted as claiming that the Uniate clergy "were led not by supernatural principals, but by temporal necessities."[82] Orthodox clergy thus were still too tied to the world, unable to abandon symbols of their masculinity or hide the evidence of the fleshly appetites and familial relationships, and thus to be compared unfavorably with Jesuit clergy who might be in the world, but were not of it. This assessment of course fits perfectly with the frequent references in Catholic Church records to bigamy and divorce among Orthodox clergy, another evidence of their inability to resist worldly temptation. From the Jesuit perspective, the alleged sensual weaknesses of the Uniate clergy separated them from those who had undergone the journey of the *Spiritual Exercises* and who understood penance as a process whereby sensuality had been taught to obey reason.[83] Paralleling this perceived weakness for the worldly was the problem of the educational attainment of most Uniate clergy, many of whom had not even received extensive training in their own native tongue.[84] The Society sought to remedy these deficiencies by encouraging Romanian boys to enroll in its seminaries, and by 1731 the Cluj seminary could boast of half a dozen "Valach" youths "receiving instruction in both letters and the faith."[85] To the Society's credit, this recruitment of Romanian boys shows that the deficiencies perceived among Orthodox clergy were understood to be the result of failures in their training, not an inherent inferiority as human beings or Christians. In this respect the Jesuit attitude toward the Eastern Rite believer resembled the Society's view of Jews, only in a much milder form: the perceived deficiencies of the individual, as manifested in his religious beliefs, were always remediable – through conversion.

In some instances the Orthodox priesthood was passed on from father to son, fostering a culture centered on village life and that perpetuated family relations, in dramatic contrast to the celibate, frequently solitary life of the traveling Jesuits. The celibacy of the Jesuit newcomers, coupled with a militancy regarding their religious convictions, their frequently distant geographical and linguistic origins and their often ambitious intellectualism, may also have antagonized Uniate and Orthodox laypersons. Laypeople may have seen their own ideas of a balanced and

---

[80] *Historica Relatio Unionis Walachicae cum Romana Ecclesia*, quoted in Nicoara, *Transilvania*, p. 89.

[81] "plures obesi et longobarbi scaredotes." ARSI, *Aust. 178, An. Prov. Aust. 1721*, p. 3.

[82] Quoted in Seton-Watson, *History*, p. 124.

[83] David L. Fleming, SJ, *The Spiritual Exercises of St. Ignatius: A Literal Translation and Contemporary Reading*. (St. Louis, MO, 1978), p. 59.

[84] The ignorance of Orthodox clergy in all parts of Eastern Europe is a persistent theme in Jesuit writings, even cropping up in the narrative of Ruder Bošković, the Dalmatian Jesuit scientist. Larry Wolff, *Inventing Eastern Europe: The Map of Civilization on the Mind of the Enlightenment* (Stanford, CA, 1994), pp. 174–5.

[85] ARSI, *Aust. 188, An. Prov. Aust. 1731*, p. 428.

defensible life, unchanged for centuries, threatened by the arrival of the Society and the difficulties of daily existence multiplied by new requirements and expectations posed by the Jesuits. The striving after an exemplary moral life that was part of the ethos of the Baroque Jesuit did not always inspire admiration, and the recruitment of promising youths for Jesuit-run schools could be viewed as an additional effort to undermine traditional role of the Orthodox priest, by moving him ever farther from the mainstream of village life. Eloquently expressed piety and ostentatious self-denial were not always in harmony with the rhythms of peasant culture, but might instead be read as a rebuke. Writing about anti-clerical sentiment in sixteenth-century Strasbourg, Thomas A. Brady observes:

> If anything, the holiest nuns and the most austere priests threatened their [the laity's] own ideas more deeply than dissolute nuns and whoring priests, for the success of a celibate way of life relativized and therefore devalued, by its own success, their own ideal of the harmonious and hierarchized household.[86]

If such tensions could exist in a culturally homogeneous context such as the Rhineland, the possibility for resentment and resistance in unstable and rebellious Transylvania was at least as great. And to these tensions was inevitably added the cultural gaps between West and East, Hungarian and Romanian, missionary and native, convert and apostate, factors that would have been present even if a religious order other than the Jesuits had led the campaign for union.

The low ratio of Orthodox priests to believers created the potential for a close relationship between the clergy and the laity, a relationship that the presence of Catholic missionaries placed under stress.[87] These factors go a considerable way towards explaining why, despite the clear advantages offered to Orthodox clergy who were willing to join, the Uniate Church was not a resounding success from the standpoint of bringing the faithful of the region more directly under the authority of Rome. In addition, Jesuits charged that the Calvinist Hungarian magnates conspired to turn Uniate Romanians against the "Roman yoke," an accusation that probably had more than a grain of truth in it. Yet Hungarian historians have sometimes viewed the problem from a different angle, asserting that "The Uniate Church was an anti-Hungarian organization, so the Habsburgs were able to create a cultural-political

---

[86] Thomas A. Brady, "'You hate us priests': Anti-clericalism, communism and the control of women in Strasbourg in the age of Reformation," in Peter Dykema and Heiko Oberman (eds), *Anticlericalism in Late Medieval and Early Modern Europe* (Leiden/New York/Köln, 1993), p. 206.

[87] In eighteenth-century Transylvania, there were roughly 555,000 Orthodox believers, 1,000 priests, 1,400 parishes, and 44 proto-popes. Remus Câmpeanu, *Elitele Româneşti din Transilvania veacului al xviii–lea.* (Cluj-Napoca, 2000), pp. 182. There was no complete census of the Principality during the first half of the eighteenth century. Conscription records from 1774 point to a population of about one million. Alfred Garter, *Die Volkszählungen Maria Theresias und Josef II. 1750–1790.* (Innsbruck, 1909), Tabelle 1. The first reliable census in 1790 returned a figure of 1,650,000. Wellmann Imre, "Erdély népsége és agrárfejlödése 1660–1830," in István Rácz (ed.), *Tanulmányok Erdély történetéről*, Szakmai Konferencia, Debrecen 1987, Október 9–10 (Debrecen, 1988), p. 111.

center against the 'dangerous and rebellious Hungarians.'"[88] Documentary evidence falls a good deal short of unequivocally supporting this last claim, but it seems certain that Vienna was eager to build up any institutions whose loyalties would tend directly towards the court and the Catholic hierarchy, rather than towards any more local authority or point of reference. The connection between the Austrian Province and Vienna, and the eagerness with which individual Jesuits pursued the objective of union made the promotion of the Uniate Church as a counterbalance to other local sources of authority a plausible strategy. Yet this goal remained impossible to realize. Resistance to the Uniate Church continued throughout the eight decades of Jesuit presence in Cluj, and in fact can be considered one of the constants of the Jesuit experience in the region.[89]

Beyond the difficulties experienced between the Jesuits and the Uniate clergy remained the reality that the bulk of believers now designated as Uniates (because of the decisions of their priests) in fact experienced little actual change in their religious lives beyond the moving of some feast days. The theological points that made up the minimum requirement for reconciliation with Rome did not affect the basic daily practices of Orthodox faithful who found themselves now to be Uniates. If we can believe the records left by the Society, Jesuits in Cluj and in other parts of Transylvania did not interact as intensively or as continually with the Uniate population as might have been expected. The *Literae,* following true to form, provide more details about the small number of noble Romanian families who converted or otherwise came into contact with the Jesuits. Typical of these was a "nobilis Valachus" who donated money to the weeping image of Mary in the Cluj Jesuit church (probably the former Unitarian church), even though he had not personally seen the painting while it was performing its miracle.[90] In Alba Iulia a "puella Valacha" is reported rescued through conversion to the Latin Rite from the "shadows in which her nation has been miserably encased," but such references are surprisingly rare.[91] What is also lacking is an emphasis on preaching to a specifically Romanian population.

For decades after the creation of the Romanian Uniate Church significant problems remained in the relationship between the Catholics and their new colleagues. The number of actual Catholics in the diocese of Alba Iulia remained small, only reaching 2,000 by the second half of the eighteenth century, which meant that the Church with which Uniates were joining was barely visible as a locally established and rooted institution. Instead its small numbers emphasized its character as a foreign Church, without significant local support.[92] The presence of an Orthodox majority and the

---

[88] Endre Haraszti, *The Ethnic History of Transylvania* (Astor Park, FL, 1971), p. 87.

[89] Octavian Bârlea, *Ostkirchliche Tradition und westlicher Katholicizmus: Die rumänische unierte Kirche zwischen 1713–1727.* Acta Historica Tomus VI (Monachii, 1966), pp. 82ff. See also the account of Uniate resistance to Adam Fitter's "Catholicizing" tendencies in Nilles, *Symbolae,* vol. 1, p. 496.

[90] OSzK, 2039 FMI /1608 *Historia anno 1701,* folio 5.

[91] BB, Szentiványi 691 XI 68, *Annue Residentiae S. J. Carolinae Annus* 1734, folio 26v.

[92] R. Ritzer and P. Serfin, *Hierarchia Catholica Medii et Recentoris Aevi Vol. VI 1730–1799* (Patavii, 1958), *passim.* At the same time, 56,000 "non–Uniates" were reported living in the region in and around Cluj. Beju and Hitchens, *Biserica,* pp. 521–4. A figure of 127,000 "Greco-Catholics" in 1766 is reported in all of Transylvania by Nicoara, *Transilvania,* p. 22.

distance from Vienna and Rome made Uniate clergy bolder; some were less than subtle in expressing the real reasons why they had joined with Rome.[93] Others did not seem to grasp the significance of the step that they had taken, or how the Roman Church's expectations of their conduct might be different from what they had previously experienced. A letter from a Count Seeau, dating from 1706, describes most Romanian Uniates as "rather dense folk, who do not even know themselves what it is they believe."[94] Ultimately, the motivations of many who became Uniate remain obscure.[95]

As the Jesuits went about the task of bringing Orthodox believers into union with Rome, they could draw upon the recruits of such institutions as the German and Hungarian Colleges in Rome, schools enjoying great prestige and whose graduates moved on to prominent positions throughout the Habsburg lands.[96] But while the training and fervor that resulted from exposure to the Roman colleges, or more often the *Pazmaneum*, in Vienna was an asset to missionary endeavors, there were significant drawbacks to the training of Jesuits destined for work with the Uniate Churches. The Society, while acknowledging and paying close attention to the religious practices of the less educated classes, continued to promote formal ecclesiastical structure and the so-called "closed world system" of Aristotle that underlay it. In doing so the Jesuits introduced a rigorously hierarchical system into their teaching, and sometimes their preaching as well, whose foundational notions were different from those familiar to Eastern Rite clergy, to say nothing of the rural peasant communities from which the majority of Eastern Rite clergy originated.[97] Even if matters of doctrine could be reconciled, more visible issues of relationship with the community and institutional loyalty continued to separate Uniate and Jesuit. While both looked to Rome for spiritual and historical reasons, the Uniate had been largely untouched by the upheavals of the Reformation or by the Catholic response,

---

[93] As late as 1744, a bishop addressing a synod in Blaj dared to speak candidly about how he and his colleagues, in order to get the benefits and opportunities available to Uniates, would "unify ourselves even with the Turks." Quoted in Lumperdean, "Nation et confession au XVIIIe siècle. Options et preoccupations pour l'union ecclésiastique de Roumains de Transylvanie," in Bocsan, Lumperdean and Pop (eds), *Ethnie et Confession*, p. 72.

[94] "... die meisten aber seyet plumpe Leuth, wissen selbsten nicht, was sie glauben," in Dragomir, *Istoria*, No. 5, 15.

[95] As is the case with the Orthodox Bishop of Maramureş, who in 1711 expressed the desire to enter into union with Rome. *Litterae Episcoparum Historiam Ucrainae Illustrantes (1600–1900)* Vol. V, 1711–1740, ed. Athanasius G. Welykyj (Romae, 1981), p. 106.

[96] By 1720, the German and Hungarian Colleges were functioning as one unit, a reflection of the Habsburg desire to integrate its newer territories east of the Leitha permanently into the *Totum* of its hereditary lands. *Facultates, Exemptiones, et Privilegia Concessa Collegis Germanico et Ungarico Alexander Papa VIII* (Roma, 1720).

[97] C.A. Patrides, "Hierarchy and order," in *Dictionary of the History of Ideas*. Philip P. Wiener, ed. (New York, 1973), vol. 2, p. 443. While critics of the late Baroque Society have rightly pointed out that the Aristotelian system was regarded obsolete by the end of the seventeenth century, the integration of this system into the culture of the Uniate Churches was a task for the Jesuits who remained committed to an Aristotelian model. The Eastern Orthodox Church, of course, had its own understanding of the hierarchy of knowledge.

while the Habsburg Jesuit saw in the structure of the Roman Church an answer to the anarchy of competing faiths and the dangers of heresy. The tie to Rome for the ethnic Romanian was a distant, dimly perceived ancestral relationship, a link with remembered greatness but lacking in specifics or an awareness of the consequences of reestablishing a real connection.[98] While Rome was increasingly on the mind of Romanian-speaking intellectuals of the later eighteenth century, it was not the Rome of the Bernini colonnade and papal ceremony but that of Trajan's column and Ovid's banishment to the shores of the Black Sea that fired their imaginations. The connection with the Church of Rome was thus as much a means to reach an earlier reference point of identity as it was an end in itself. For the Jesuit missionary the situation was entirely different. Rome and the Holy See were vital forces with which he had established a personal and sacred relationship. Especially for the Hungarian Jesuit, the relationship between the papacy and the Hungarian monarchy was a unique bond. And for any Hungarian cleric, including members of other religious orders who would have received some university training, there was an additional distinction between the West and East, for philosophy and theology were joined together in higher education in a manner unlike anything found in Orthodox priestly formation.[99]

The man chosen by the Society to overcome these differences of experience and perspective was Adam Fitter.[100] Fitter, after many years as a teacher, became rector of the Cluj *collegium*, and then director of the Uniate Church by order of the Aulic Council of Transylvania on 15 August 1728.[101] The Jesuit was chosen in part because of his interpersonal skills ("modum agendi suavem habet") that aided him in dealing with the sometimes uncooperative Uniates.[102] An ethnic Hungarian, Fitter had been born in 1679 to a Lutheran family and had converted as a teenager.[103] After formation and study in Trnava, Fitter had spent half a year at the *Pazmaneum* in Vienna, taking his fourth vow in Cluj in 1714.[104] Fitter spoke Hungarian and some "Slavonice," but in 1714 Jesuit records do not report any knowledge of Romanian. On the positive side, Fitter had received an education superior to that of many other Jesuits

---

[98] Dmitre Cantimir devoted some attention to the relationship between Latin and Romanian, but it remained for scholars coming after the Suppression to illustrate in any systematic way the nature of this connection. See Franz Joseph Sulzer, *Geschichte der transalpinischen Daciens* ... (Wien, 1781–82).

[99] Robert Gragger, "Die Ungarische Universität," *Ungarisches Jahrbücher 5* (1925), pp. 25–40.

[100] A rare portrait of Fitter appears in Aloysius Zelliger, *Pantheon Tyrnaviense* (Tyrnaviae, 1931), p. 61.

[101] Fitter had been "Professor Physicae," in 1715, "Professor metaphysicae et ethicae," in 1716, and "concionator festivus hungaricus" in 1717. Lukács, *Catalogus* VI, pp. 766, 810, 858.

[102] Pâclişanu, *Istoria*, p. 210; Katona, *Historia*, vol. 19, p. 860; Nilles, *Symbolae*, vol. 1, pp. 483–5. A portrait of Fitter appears in Zelliger, *Pantheon Tyrnaviense*, p. 61.

[103] Sommervogel et al., *Bibliothèque*, vol. 3, pp. 761–2.

[104] ARSI, *Aust. 62, Catalogus I Col. Claud. 1714*, p. 35. While not primarily a scholar, Fitter wrote *Disputatio III de Suspensione* now preserved in the Romanian Academy Library in Cluj. BANC-N, Ms C. 761.

in Cluj: he had completed a doctorate in philosophy, had served as the "decaonus linguarum," an attestation to his language skills, and was obviously regarded as one of the most able Jesuits in the region, whose resolve and energy might be equal to the challenges of dealing with the rapidly multiplying problems in the Uniate Church. His experience in cosmopolitan Vienna, brief though it was, would have exposed him to a broader understanding of other Christian traditions, including Calvinism, one that took into account more rationalist and pre-Enlightenment elements and which would have placed Transylvanian Calvinism in a different light.[105] What is not evident in the Society's records on Adam Fitter is any familiarity with Romanian culture or religious practice, or any evidence of correspondence with members of the Orthodox or Uniate hierarchies. Perhaps the Society did not have any candidates better suited to work among the Romanians, or, what is equally probable, the Jesuits did not see previous knowledge of the objects of the Society's efforts as important a quality as steadfastness in the values of the Society and administrative competence.

In the autumn of 1728, Adam Fitter, acting as the "director" during the absence of a bishop in the Romanian Uniate diocese, called a synod of protopopes in Kolosmănăştur, a few miles from the walls of Cluj, where the Society had taken over a church that had originally been Catholic.[106] Among the issues raised by Fitter were questions about the discipline and morality of the Uniate clergy and the founding of a theological school.[107] Both of these issues reveal the discomfort with which some Jesuits viewed the cultural gap between Catholic and Uniate, as well as the intentions of the Society to remedy these deficiencies according to its own standards and practices. Enforcing moral standards would not be easy: any effort in this direction would have the practical effect of distancing the formerly Orthodox priest from his traditional lifestyle, which in everyday practice, not only greatly resembled that of his serf neighbors, but validated their way of life. Fitter did not flinch from the task, however. By being the initiator of reform, Fitter also

---

[105] Hugh Trevor-Roper makes the important distinction between Hungarian and Western European Calvinism, the former having little relation to the Enlightenment ideas that would develop in some Western European Calvinist settings in the eighteenth century. Yet the coexistence of Transylvanian religious pluralism and regional Calvinism should not be ignored. Trevor-Roper, *The European Witch-Craze of the 16th and 17th Centuries* (Harmondsworth, 1969, 1967), p. 139.

[106] This is probably the same settlement referred to elsewhere in Jesuit documents as "oppidum Kolos." Nilles, *Symbolae*, vol. 2, p. 926. Gabriel Patacsi, SJ, "Die unionsfeindlichen Bewegungen der orthodox Rumänen in Siebenbürgen in den Jahren 1726–1729," *Orientalia Christiana Periodica* 26, 2 (1960), p. 356.

[107] The synod found it necessary to inveigh "Contra popas bigamos, ebriosos, convitiatores ... ." Moldovanu (ed.), *Acte*, vol. 1, p. 102; Maria Someşan, *Începtulurile Bisericii Române Unite cu Roma*. (Bucuresti, 1999), p. 60. Jesuit records from 1730 also make reference to bigamy among the "popas" of the region. ARSI, *Austria 187, An. Prov. Aust. 1730*, folios 12rff. See also *Supplicationes Ecclesiae Uniatae Ucrainae et Bielorusjaie Voll II, 1700–1740*, P. Athanasius and G. Welykyj (eds) (Romae, 1962), p. 253, nos 762–3. Bigamy and the general morality of the Orthodox, and by implication, Uniate clergy seem to have been an ongoing concern of the Catholic authorities overseeing the Uniate venture, for thirty-two years earlier, Atanaise had avowed that he would ordain no bigamist. *Declaratio*, p. 92.

reinforced his position of authority over the Uniates, and delivered an indirect critique of the training these clergy had received previously in the Orthodox Church. Likewise the establishment of a seminary under the watchful eye of the *theologus* would shift the cultural context in which Uniate priests received their formation away from traditional Romanian peasant society and towards something more akin to the training of Jesuits, which, while it was in no way divorced from the world, did seek to sustain high moral standards in a context where these standards would serve as a visible model to others.[108] Fitter's efforts appeared to be a strong start in the development of a set of permanent institutions: the creation of a cultural elite was undoubtedly an important part of the Jesuit program in Cluj, and by tying the future of this elite to Habsburg hegemony in the region, as opposed to any other tradition or institution, the Society sought to improve its own position as well. Had the Society survived more than a few more decades in the Cluj region the introduction of such a seminary might have proven to be one of the most significant institutions established by the Jesuits of Transylvania. The coming years, however, saw little progress in the rooting and stabilization of a Uniate Church drawn from the Romanian Orthodox faithful: growth was modest, and the danger of defection remained constant. And the Jesuits of Cluj had other enterprises that were occupying their attention.

III

While the Society struggled to establish a strong Romanian Uniate Church in Transylvania, it simultaneously promoted the union of Armenian Rite Christians with Rome.[109] Armenians were scattered in small numbers throughout Eastern Europe and the Crimea, where after arriving in the Middle Ages they had in many instances assimilated into the existing population.[110] Armenians were also said to have entered Transylvania about 1650 from Moldavia.[111] In the seventeenth century, Jesuits had already come into contact with Armenians in Moldavia, and simultaneously cultivated

---

[108] The connection between priestly formation as understood by the Jesuits and moral development is described in the third Part of the *Ratio Studiorum*. O'Malley points out that the "psychological reality that primarily grounded [the Jesuits'] lives ... was membership in the Society ... ." *First Jesuits*, p. 159. See the passages in the *Constitutions* dealing with the general confession made by candidates seeking admission to the Society. Ganss, *Constitutions*, p. 106. This was a very different starting place from that of most Uniate priests, whose foundation would have often been based on community relationships, often not directly connected with their role as clergy.

[109] Kristof Lukácsi, *Historia Armenorum Transsilvaniae a primoridis gentis usque nostram memoriam e fontibus authenticis et documentis antea indeitis* ... (Viennae, 1859).

[110] Malachia Ormanian, *The Church of Armenia*, 2nd edn, trans. G. Marchar Gregory and ed. Terenig Poladia (London, 1955), p. 47.

[111] P. Marcellus Ciski, "Status Armenorum in Transilvania ... " in I. Dumitriu-Snagov (ed.), *Românii în arhivele Romei (Secolul XVIII) Romeni in archiviis Romanis (Saeculum XVIII)* (București, 1973), p. 326. A "Brevis descriptio Status Armenorum in Transilvania degentium" written in 1780 contains no reference to the Jesuits. ASV Archivio della Nunziatura di Vienna, 196, folios 147r–149r.

contacts with Armenian communities in Poland, claiming at least one Polish Jesuit of Armenian descent, Gregory Zacharyaczewicz.[112] Although the original homeland of the Armenians of Transylvania was even farther from Rome than that of other Eastern Rite Christians, the differences between the Jesuits and the Armenian clergy never appeared as rancorous or insoluble as those the Jesuits found themselves embroiled in with other Eastern Rite and Orthodox communities.[113] Armenians often responded favorably to Jesuit overtures, and the Society responded with a surprising degree of interest and attention, considering the small number of Armenians in the region. In the nineteenth century, these relations might be explained because the Armenian community in the Habsburg realms never posed the challenge to political control that the Romanians or Serbs did. There was no possibility of an Armenian state being founded based on territory controlled by Austria, or of Armenians seeking to join with a larger Armenian polity located beyond the boundaries of the Habsburg empire. In the late seventeenth and early eighteenth centuries, the compatibility of Armenians and Latin Rite Jesuits had more to do with theology than regional politics, and moreover was related to a long-standing tradition of cooperation between this Eastern Rite community and the West. It is also possible that the Society viewed the Armenian Church as a connection to regions far inside Asia where Jesuits had always hoped to evangelize, but where there had so far been only scant opportunities for proselytizing. The Armenians, a small minority without the legal recognition granted to other religious groups, might have seen in a formal relationship with the Society the chance to strengthen their own position in the Transylvanian polity. While the Jesuits could count among the "errors" of the Armenian Church its refusal to recognize the Council of Chalcedon, its symbols and details of its mass, these characteristics are never described in Jesuit documents as presenting the obstacles that Romanian Orthodox Christianity did.[114] Most significantly, Armenians are never denominated as "schismatics," a term that as we have seen carried very negative associations.[115]

Statistics on the Armenian Church in the eighteenth century are almost nonexistent, but in the totality of domains controlled by the Habsburgs in the nineteenth century, there were roughly 15,000 Armenian Rite faithful. These lived in Bukovina (not acquired by the Habsburgs from Turkey until after the Suppression and never a center of the Society's missionary activities), Transylvania, Galicia (part of Poland until 1772) and Eastern Hungary. At least 3,000 of these had emigrated from Moldavia.[116] The Armenian community of Siret in Bukovina, some of whose members were Catholic, had been banished by the local prince; a few of these may

---

[112] Zacharyarczewicz (1740–1814) was a native of Galicia, a territory that passed under Habsburg control in 1772. Sommervogel et al., *Bibiliothèque*, vol. 8, p. 1436.

[113] I am grateful to Francis Brennan, SJ, for pointing out this fact.

[114] Nilles, *Symbolae*, vol. 2, pp. 916–18. Among the most noteworthy of these was the Armenian custom of animal sacrifice, a tradition dating back to late Classical times when the Armenian Church had been founded.

[115] The term "schisma" invariably refers to Orthodox Christians, as in "Ut schisma, de qu' ut ipsi popae suspecti, potiore jure observaremus," ARSI, *Aust. 176, An. Prov. Aust. 1719*, p. 106.

[116] Nilles, *Symbolae*, vol. 1, p. XLIV.

have migrated to Transylvania.[117] In Transylvania proper, the small community of Armenians showed greater enthusiasm than the Romanian Orthodox faithful for union with Rome; by 1697, 2,000 believers had entered into union, along with two bishops.[118] Influenced by their brethren, Armenians from Moldavia likewise joined with Rome.[119] Once they were received by Rome, Armenian communities joined in supporting and adorning Jesuit churches. In 1720, during a time of plague, the Armenians of Gherla (Szamosújvár) offered silver tablets to the Jesuits of Cluj (perhaps for display in the Jesuit church) as a testimonial to their faith.[120] Eighteen years later, Theodorus Buzesco, an Armenian priest from the same town, donated 1,000 florins to the Jesuit *collegium* in Cluj, the interest from which was to go to support an Armenian Rite student, preferably from the Daniel family.[121] Armenian students came and participated in the culture of the Jesuit schools, and Armenian prelates participated in rites celebrated by the Jesuits.[122] Among the performers in a recitation dedicated to St. Nicetas in 1750 at the Cluj *collegium* was Antonius Izikucz, "Armenus Ebesfalvensis."[123] Rome reciprocated in 1751 by paying the expenses of Armenian students returning from schools in the Eternal City to work in Transylvania.[124] An undated list of recipients of bachelor's degrees from the Cluj *collegium* reports something even more remarkable: among the Transylvanian nobility and the occasional "civis" is "Teodatus Abraham Armenus Moldavus" from Iaşi.[125]

Jesuits, too, returned the support and cooperation they received from the Armenians by regarding their rituals and rites with a fair degree of sympathy. A procession of Armenians, including twenty schoolboys, half a dozen women dressed in *chlamydes*, a short mantel fastened at the shoulder, and a Hungarian and Armenian cantor, passed through the town of Ebesfalva, while the Jesuit who recorded the scene remarked positively on the women's modesty.[126] In 1725, Jesuits participated

---

[117] Constantin Cuciuc, *Atlasul Religiilor şi al Monumentilor Istorice Religioase din Romania* (Bucureşti: Editura Gnosis, 1997).

[118] ARSI, *Aust. 155, An. Prov. Aust. 1697*, folio 81v.

[119] Illia, *Ortus et Progressus*, p. 72.

[120] ARSI, *Austr. 177, An. Prov. Aust. 1720*, p. 79.

[121] 13 August 1738, in Jakab, *Oklevéltár*. While Jakab does not state it explicitly, the donor was presumably Uniate.

[122] "Kharginez Civem Armenum Szamos-Ujvarensiem" is among those recorded in an undated list of *Convictus* students from probably the mid-eighteenth century. BARC-N, McC 49, unnumbered folio; "Episcopus Armenus Aladensis Oxendius Virzirescus ad nos pro aliquot dieb. Divererat, at in Penacoste sanctum Confirmationis contulaerat," OSzK, 2039 FMI/1608, *Historia anno 1710*, p. 90. "Adeodato Laszlöffi Armenus" defended a thesis on universal philosophy at the Cluj *collegium* in 1765. ARSI, *Austria 220, An. Prov. Aust. 1765*, folio 66r.

[123] *Gesta S. Nicetae veteris Daciae episcopi et apostoli* ... (Typis Academicis Societatis Jesu Anno MDCCL), p. 76. Elsewhere identified as "nobilis," Izikusz made a defense of logical propositions the following year. ARSI, *Aust. 208, An. Prov. Aust. 1751*, folio 49v.

[124] Welykyj (ed.), *Supplicationes*, vol. 3, pp. 101–102.

[125] BARC-N, MsC 49 1-b, p. 134.

[126] BB, Szentiványi 691, XI, 68, *Diarium Residentiae Marosvásárheliensis*, 30 May 1737.

in the dedication of an Armenian church in Gherla and the Society regarded the event significant enough to record in its annual *Literae*.[127] The Society clearly made efforts to include elements of the Armenian Rite in their own liturgical activities. In 1730, the old church in Kolosmănăștur resounded to the sound of praises sung to the Virgin in three languages: Hungarian, German and Armenian.[128] This points not only to the presence of Armenian Rite believers in the immediate vicinity of Cluj, but also to the willingness of the Cluj Jesuits to bring together Uniate and Catholic worshippers, something not well documented with regard to other Uniate groups (assuming that the Armenian worshippers were not in fact converts to Roman Catholicism, a matter on which the Jesuit record is silent). At the same time, the absence of the "Valach" language from the service, despite the presence of Romanian Uniates in the Cluj community, suggests how differently Armenians and Romanians were regarded by the Society, although this might also be a reflection of the relatively low number of Romanian speakers living in the immediate vicinity.[129] The Cluj Jesuits paid close attention to their Armenian neighbors, who despite their small numbers, had ties to some powerful members of the Transylvanian aristocracy.[130] Armenians, in contrast to Orthodox believers, also made an impression on the Jesuits as a literate community; in 1738, the citizens of "Armenopolis" donated 60 florins to the library of the Jesuit academy.[131] The same year that Armenian hymns were heard in a Jesuit church, Andreas Illia's *Ortus et Progressus* noted that the residents of "Armenopolis," many of whom had embraced Catholicism, had migrated to that city from Moldavia and even from as far away as Armenia itself.[132]

Yet the Armenian Uniates, like others whom the Jesuits sought to reunite with Rome, were not prepared to submerge their identity entirely within the larger institution of Catholicism, and maintained a desire for control over their own affairs. In 1741, a request made by Armenians in the Cluj region to have a bishop of their own, while still maintaining their connection with the Holy See, was turned down by Rome, amid

---

[127] ARSI, *Aust. 182, An. Prov. Aust. 1725*, folio 23v.

[128] ARSI, *Aust. 187, An. Prov. Aust. 1730*, folio 62.

[129] In 1733, an Imperial commission conducted a census of non-Catholics and reported, "Kolosvár: non est papa, 10 incolae." It is not clear whether these data refer to Uniates or Orthodox. Bunea, *Episcopul*, 305. If by "papa" is meant an Orthodox "popa," these data are contradicted by the claim that "Claudiopoli popae triginta." Nilles, *Symbolae*, p. 2, p. 509.

[130] Imre Thököly (1657–1705), the Protestant magnate and father-in-law of Ferenc II Rákóczi who led a rebellion against the Habsburgs and was later reported by Jesuits to be contemplating a conversion to Catholicism, was buried in an Armenian cemetery. *Encyclopaedia Britannica*, 11th edn, (29 vols, Cambridge, 1911), vol. 26, p. 861; Nilles, *Symbolae*, vol. 1, p. 379.

[131] ARSI, *Aust. 194, An. Prov. Aust. 1738*, folio 220r.

[132] Illia, *Ortus et Progressus*, p. 72. The history of Armenians in Transylvania is reviewed briefly in Miklós Gadovits, *Az Erdély örmények történetéből*. (Kolozsvár, 2000) and Peter I. Hadas, "The role of Greeks, Armenians and Jews in the economic life of Transylvania in the eighteenth century,".*Tanulmányok Danyi Dezső 75. születésnapjára*. (Budapest, 1996), pp. 124–30.

fears that this would be the first move towards a return to schism.[133] Other problems plagued the Union: Armenian clergy complained about the conduct of Latin Rite priests, charging them on occasion with immorality. In 1697, an "Admodum Rev. D. Lazari Budachovitz" (not a Jesuit) faced a charge of adultery with the daughter of an Armenian priest.[134] Yet even if the development of the Armenian Uniate Church had been completely free of scandal and difficulty, the Church alone could not have been the centerpiece of a successful Jesuit push to build a network of Uniate Churches in the eastern Habsburg domains. The size of the original Armenian Church, its localization in one community, and its lack of stronger links to other Eastern Rite churches limited its usefulness to the Jesuits and the dynasty. Transylvanian-born Armenian Jesuits remained a rarity, either among the priests or brothers, and no Armenian language publications have been identified among the materials produced by the Jesuit press in Cluj. While the union of the Armenians may be considered the single greatest success of the Jesuits' Transylvanian campaign for union, its ultimate impact on the region as a whole was relatively minor.

IV

This then was the background of the Jesuits' Uniate enterprise in Cluj. The political pressures that played a role in the original decisions of many Orthodox clergy to become Uniates never decreased, and while Hungarian Jesuits sometimes found themselves struggling within the Society for more autonomy, the Cluj Jesuits never enlisted their putative Uniate allies in any significant joint undertakings to strengthen their position *vis-à-vis* the Vienna-based leadership of the Austrian Province. The initial contact between ethnic Romanians and the Society that had showed considerable promise in the late seventeenth century never evolved into a strong and enduring connection.[135] Nor did the Jesuits conduct their mission activities in concert with the Uniates, whose numbers in Cluj proper remained tiny for decades.[136] Language, tradition and mutual suspicions made considering such collaboration highly unlikely, and its execution extremely difficult. The Jesuits, inclined to view even intractable problems in an optimistic light, probably underestimated the hostility felt by those

---

[133] "Transilvania o Weissemburg," in *Dizionario di Erudizione Storico-Ecclesiastica*, 109 vols (Venezia, 1850–79), vol. 79, p. 107. The problem of ordination of Armenian Rite clergy would persist even after the Suppression: in 1782, the Roman Bishop of Transylvania would still be seeking the right to ordain Armenian priests. ASV Nunziatura di Vienna 196, folios 39–40.

[134] ASV, Nunziatura di Vienna 196, folios 159r–163r.

[135] An outstanding representative of this early contact was the Jesuit Gavril Ivul (1619–78), who taught philosophy in Košice and Vienna, and who was credited with building some of the first substantive connections between Romanian culture and the Latin West. N. Cartojan, *Istoria Literaturii Române Vechi*, afterword and bibliography by Dan Simonescu, and preface by Dan Zamfirescu (București, 1980), p. 188.

[136] In 1761, there were 1,221 Uniate families in the Cluj Județ (county), compared with 11,324 Orthodox. Dragomir, *Istoria*, vol. 2, pp. 268–9.

believers who remained Orthodox.[137] The Rákóczi uprising further undermined the stability of the Uniate Church among the few members of the petty nobility who had joined it and paralyzed all of the Society's activities, including the Uniate project, while the degree of comprehension among many lay Uniates concerning the new arrangements remained a question mark.[138] The intermittent threat of the plague, so severe that some Jesuits fled the towns to stay with the nobility in their castles, was an additional impediment to any possible plans for concerted action that would have reached out beyond the cites and towns into the countryside.[139] The attitude of the Orthodox rank and file towards the push for union is hard to assess, since few left written records. Oral history offers a few scraps of evidence suggesting that the Romanian population viewed the relationship between the Jesuits and Uniate Church so close that the credibility of the former was in jeopardy. Petru Major recalled in 1813 that in his youth it had been rumored that Ioan Patachi, the Uniate bishop from 1723 to 1727, had actually been a Jesuit.[140]

Meanwhile some Romanian Orthodox believers emigrated "over the mountains" into Moldavia to avoid the pressure to convert, thereby emphasizing the difference between the lands controlled by the Habsburgs and those under the control of the vassals of the Porte.[141] A logical chief ally of the Jesuits in their efforts to promote the Uniate Church, the Catholic Church hierarchy, was periodically in a state of disarray, and from 1734 to 1743, the Catholic Bishop of Transylvania's seat was even vacant.[142] The seat of the Uniate bishop itself was moved from Alba Iulia, where it had been established in 1699, to the remote town of Făgăraş in 1721 (perhaps deliberately to restrict the influence of the bishop), and then on to Blaj in 1733.[143] While struggling to execute the many other tasks they had set for themselves, the Jesuits simultaneously sought to regulate the flow of information among the relatively small minority of literate Uniates by requiring that all books printed by the "typographia valachia" in Alba Iulia be reviewed and formally approved by the *theologus*.[144] Systematic control of Romanian literature, however, was hampered by poor communications within

---

[137] Robert J.W. Evans, "Die Grenzen der Konfessionisierung. Die Folgen der Gegenreformation für die Habsburgländer (1648–1781)," in *Konfessionaliserung in Ostmitteleuropa: Wirkung des religösen Wandels im 16. und 17. Jahrhundert in Staat, Gesellschaft und Kultur*, eds Joachim Bahlcke and Arno Stromeyer (Stuttgart, 1999), p. 410.

[138] OSzK, 2039, FMI/1608, *Historia SJ Claudiop. 1706*, p. 66; Pascu, *History*, p. 135.

[139] ARSI, *Aust. 175, An. Prov. Aust. 1719*, p. 89.

[140] Mircea Păcurariu, *Pages del'histoire de l'église roumaine. Considerations au sujet de uniatisme en Transylvanie*, trans. M. Alexandrescu (Bucarest, 1991), p. 90.

[141] Such a claim has been made by a Romanian historian, but without documentation. Constintin C. Giurescu, *Transylvania in the History of the Romanian People* (Bucharest, 1968), pp. 59–60.

[142] *Series episcoporum Ecclesiae Catholicae*, ed. P. Pius Gams (Ratisbonae, 1873), p. 382.

[143] Hubert Jedin, Kenneth Scott Latourette and Jochen Martin, *Atlas d'histoire de l'Église* (Bruxelles, 1990), p. 96. The bull establishing the episcopate of Fagăras specifically refers to the see as "Valachorum." PFK, p. 118. E.41, Jesuitica Documenta ... folios 130r–131r.

[144] Weiser, *A katolikus iskolaügy*, vol. 1, p. 10.

the Principality and by the modest but constant presence of Romanian Orthodox publications, both locally produced and imported from neighboring regions.[145] At the same time the impact of the Uniate Church on the intellectual life of literate Romanians was limited to those Romanian-language publications that passed the censor and to the curriculum taught to Uniate students in the Jesuits schools. While the latter was far from negligible, it did not make Romanian culture noticeably more "Roman" or Catholic. Nor did it decrease the ties many Romanians continued to feel towards Orthodox communities with whom they had long shared traditions.

The Society's records moreover suggest that neither close collaboration with Uniate clergy nor the erection of a strong and independent Uniate Church were important or explicit goals of the fathers, who wished to document clearly their own accomplishments and keep a short rein on their newly acquired colleagues.[146] But when we rely as we must on these records, the tendency of Jesuits to be vague about the backgrounds of some of the converts they made becomes obvious. Among the unidentified "covertitae" listed in Jesuit school records may be a number of Romanians.[147] On the other hand, a significant number of Romanian students are identified as such: the status of many of these as "nobiles" perhaps made full reporting easier.[148] Contacts between Jesuits and Uniates, or Jesuits and Orthodox clergy do not seem to have followed any systematic pattern. Apparently an "Olah" (Romanian Orthodox?) church was functioning in Kolosmănăștur, a short distance from Cluj in 1704, although references to it cannot be found in Jesuit records.[149] The few scattered references to sermons preached in "Valach" by Jesuit priests are unaccompanied by commentary on the connections between Jesuits and Uniates.[150] Jesuits in Cluj and throughout Transylvania appear to have put little trust in the Uniate clergy and perhaps even less in its flocks. Instead, Jesuits throughout the region retained a strong sense of their own autonomy and their capability to bring about the spiritual and moral regeneration of the region on their own terms, an attitude perhaps fostered by the seventeenth-century policy of sending Jesuits into

---

[145] Orthodox books published in Transylvania for a few years after it passed under the control of the Habsburgs are found, see Eva Mârza, *Tipografia de la Alba Iulia 1577–1702* (Sibiu, 1998), pp. 85ff. The influence of these religious publications was especially great for those literate in Romanian, as there was very little popular secular literature available. Cornelia Papacostea-Danielopolu and Lidia Demény, *Carti și Tipar în Societata Romanească și sud-est Europeană (secole XVII–XIX)*. (București, 1985), p. 212.

[146] Almost innumerable examples of this focus in Jesuit records on the accomplishments of the Society might be cited; one characteristic instance is the story of a woman freed from the sexual advances of a demon, which had taken the form of her departed husband. ARSI, *Aust. 155, An. Prov. Aust. 1697.* folio 79v.

[147] As, in 1754, a convert in Cluj *collegium* is recorded without a family name. Tóth, *Nacionalizmus*, p. 173.

[148] One such instance is "Gerogius Vilhány nob. Valach" who graduated on an unknown date. BARC-N, MsC 49-1-b, p. 134.

[149] MTA, Kéz. 705, *Néhai Tetinketes Nemzetes Czegei Wass Gyoergy Urnák ... 1704–1705*, p. 94.

[150] For example, ARSI, *Aust. 218, An. Prov. Aust. 1763*, folio 54v.

the region in disguise.[151] Curiously, the Society persisted for decades in a strategy for winning over Orthodox believers that relied on argumentation in baroque Latin, rather than reaching out to clergy who could read only Romanian or whose Latin was probably limited.[152] Even in the years immediately preceding the suppression, the emphasis on Latin in Jesuit publications showed no signs of slacking, nor did the multiple generations of ethnic Romanian Uniate priests educated in Jesuit schools seem to be making much of an impression on the character of the Cluj mission, whose forays into the use of the "Valachica oratio" were rare enough to merit special mention in the *Literae annue*.[153] The Society's commitment to the premier language of the Counter-Reformation may be seen as evidence of a conservatism that gripped Jesuit culture in the decades before the suppression, but the persistence of Latin may also be understood as a prudent decision to concentrate conversion efforts on the Calvinist community, which was conversant in Latin, rather than reach out to a largely illiterate Eastern Rite population.[154]

A scattering of students identified as Uniates do appear in the records of the *Seminarium S. Josephi*, but these young men are not found later among those who joined the Society.[155] While the Jesuits did not leave behind a clearly defined group of Uniate heirs to carry on their work after 1773, the fathers educated some of the secular leaders of Romanian Transylvania. One of the graduates of the Cluj *convictus* who can be identifed as a Romanian Uniate was Boér Jozsef, who was a *fiscalis exactor* in 1714 and *Vicekapitan* for Făgăraş in the Transylvanian civil bureaucracy.[156] Nevertheless, it is noteworthy that in 1773, after a lifetime's work to promote the Uniate Church and to secure conversions to Catholicism, the Jesuits of Cluj could not count one *coadjutor temporalis* with a Romanian surname in their

---

[151] See, for example, the biography of Stephanus Csete in Horányi, *Memoria*, vol. 1, p. 448.

[152] An example of this approach is *Concordia Orthodoxorum Patrum Orientalium et Occidentalium de Spiritus Sancti Processione*, published in Cluj in 1745. Michalis Salbeck is listed as the "promotore" of this publication. Andrei Veress, *Bibliografia Romano-Ungară Românii în literatura ungară şi literatura română. Vl. I 1473–1780*. (Bucureşti, 1931), p. 211.

[153] As was the case in 1765 when a sermon in Romanian was preached at Kolosmănăştur. ARSI, *Austria 220, An Prov. Aust. 1765*, folio 9r.

[154] The occasional topical references found in Latin works published or promoted by the Society in Cluj further point to efforts to reach a relatively broad lay population who could read Latin, many of whom would have been Calivnist. In 1722, the "poëti" of the Cluj *collegium* "originem infelicitatis Transylvaniae indagit" in a public performance. The topic may have been the recent plague. ARSI, *Austr. 179, An. Prov. Aust. 1722*, folio 45r.

[155] For example, "Daniel Marcziani Nob. Valachus Unitus de terra Fogaras," "Petrus Tóháti Valachus Transylvanus Tohatensis." Tóth, *Nacionalsimsus*, p. 59. When Jeusits in disguise penetrated Transylvania as far as the prince's court in Alba Iulia, Prince György II Rákóczi Ferenc expelled them, and a month later the Protestant-dominated Diet deprived them of property they possessed in Kolosmănăştur.

[156] Boér was a student in Cluj from 1712 until 1718. Boér András, who served as the "Registrator" and exactor of the Transylvanian chancellery, also studied in Cluj from 1711 through 1718. Tóth, *Nacionalismus*, pp. 178–179.

community.[157] As the years passed, the Jesuits would continue to work to deepen the commitment of the Uniate clergy, but at the same time, there remained the strong desire among some Jesuits to claim such successes as were obtained for the Society alone. The definition of what was a success lay with the Jesuits themselves who saw themselves as the only ones educated sufficiently to judge the Uniate project. This was partly because the Uniate project included no "ministries among the learned" reaching out to educated elites, such as were found in other Jesuit educational and missionary endeavors. For not only was there no educated elite of note among the Orthodox clergy of Transylvania, but there was seemingly no desire on the part of the Society to foster one.[158] Romanian historians have long complained that Romanian Transylvanians were regarded as cultural inferiors by their Habsburg rulers, and while little in the records of the Jesuits smacks of an explicit attitude of overt cultural superiority, their lack of attention to contemporary Romanian culture is striking.[159] Jesuit writers of the eighteenth century often seemed more interested in the remote early history of "Dacia" than in the customs of Romanians living around them, although Franciscus Fasching, one of the brightest lights of the Cluj Jesuit community, commented on the Romanian alphabet in his *Nova Dacia* (1743).[160]

As was often the case in the pre-Suppression Society, converts and allies of the Society were given few roles of any authority within the institutional structure. Evidence for ethnic Romanian Uniates in even marginally important positions is scarce; in 1747, Moyses Lestyán, one of the "Professores inferiorum scholarum" in Cluj, was a "grammatista, socius catechistae valachii," and in the same year, P. Michalis Salbeck was "missionarius in pagis nostris, catechista et operarius valachus," although in the case of Salbeck, he may have been a non-Romanian fluent in the language.[161] It is not clear whether Alexius Okolitsani, "pervenusto genere," who taught philosophy and polemical theology at the Cluj *collegium* was born Catholic or Uniate, although his Romanian ancestry seems at least possible.[162] Born in 1711 in what is now Slovakia, Okolitsani took his fourth vow in 1744, but never held administrative positions of importance within the Austrian Province. The elusive

---

[157] *Catalogus Personarum et Officiorum Provinciae Austriae ... M.D.CC.LXXIII.*

[158] Stephen J. Harris, "Confession-building, long-distance networks, and the organization of Jesuit science," *Early Science and Medicine* 1, 3 (1996), p. 289.

[159] Jesuits of the Bohemian Province did preach in Romanian when on a mission to Transylvania in 1771. NK 23/19, folio 350r.

[160] Cited in Mălinaş, *Situaţia*, 118. Fasching's scholarship was not without its critics, however. Dobrá Péter said that Fasching's book should have been called *Nova Mendacia*. Tóth, *Nacionalismus*, p. 48.

[161] Lukács, *Catalogi*, vol. 8, pp. 806–807. Lestyán, born in Csík county in 1720, was studying as a scholastic in Cluj in 1746. ARSI, *Austria 93, Catal. I Coll. Claud. 1746*, p. 82. Salbeck published *Prima 5. saecula regni Mariani* (Claudiopoli, 1746), a work that would have supported the theme of the reign of Mary over Hungary. Katona, *Historia Critica*, p. 1003. Father Salbeck was also a mentor of the future Uniate Bishop Petru Paul Aron, when both men were in Vienna. Cipariu, *Acte*, p. 104. Missionary work in "pagis nostris" was distinguished from work further afield.

[162] Stephanus Katona, *Historia Critica* (Budae, 1809), vol. 20, p. 986. Sommervogel et al., *Bibliothèque*, 1878, p. 5 identifies him as Hungarian.

Georgius Buitul, the translator of the Canisius catechism, appears to have come from Romanian stock, but his relationship, if any, to plans for the promotion of the Uniate Church is unclear. Competence in the Romanian tongue of course is not a sure indicator that a Jesuit came from a Romanian Uniate background: Thadeus Manner, SJ (1707–85) served as the "pro officio operarii et missionarii Valachii," in the Cluj region, though his name may point to a German origin.[163] Clearly a few Jesuits acquired knowledge of Romanian through exposure and effort rather than ethnic ties. The *coadjutor temporalis* Georgius Balásovics, described in Jesuit records as an "Ungarus" and born in Pozsony in western Hungary, also achieved a "mediocriter" level of proficiency in Romanian, presumably after his arrival in Transylvania.[164] Joannes Mayer, a glovemaker ("chyrothecarius") and native of Košice, where a Hungarian population mixed with Slavs and perhaps some Romanians, apparently spoke German as his native tongue and Hungarian and Romanian "mediocriter," signs of at least some contact with those populations.[165] Much earlier, Georgius Thomas, another *coadjutor temporalis* who served as a "socius mercatoris" in the Cluj community in 1711, also spoke Romanian, although it is not possible to make even a confident guess at his own ethnic background.[166]

We are on firmer ground with the case of Vasile Dobra, who taught in the Cluj *collegium*. Dobra was undoubtedly of Romanian origin, and was has been identified as coming from a Uniate background.[167] After a career following a typical range of assignments in schools and communities throughout the eastern Habsburg lands, Dobra became professor of dogma in Cluj in 1762, and combined his teaching with missions to the Uniates.[168] It is not clear whether Ladislaus Dobra, who was a scholastic in Cluj in 1746, and who spoke "Valache bene," was related to Vasile, but both his skills and the time of his birth, several decades after the creation of the Uniate Church, would make him a likely candidate for Uniate origins.[169] But these cases are unusual and stand out from the mass of records left by the Society. The general impression left is of an organization that even decades after its arrival in Cluj, had continued to set definite boundaries in its range of serious contacts with the Romanian-speaking population. The emphasis in Jesuit records of conversions of Valach nobility, while it is certainly a reflection of the Society's desire to highlight its dealings with the most powerful, may also be evidence of the restricted contact many Jesuits had with the majority of Romanian speakers who did not speak one of the languages understood by most Jesuits.

A conspicuous feature of the Uniate-Jesuit relationship was the position of the Uniate bishop, who was also restricted in his ability to act as a leader for his flock. Supervised by the Jesuit *theologus*, the bishop was enjoined by the terms

---

[163] Nilles, *Symbolae*, vol. 2, p. 641.
[164] ARSI, *Aust. 99, Catalogus I Coll Claud. 1754*, p. 90.
[165] ARSI, *Aust. 93, Catalogus I Coll. Claud. 1746*, p. 85.
[166] ARSI, *Aust. 59, Catal. I Col. Claud. 1711*, p. 334.
[167] Mălinaș, *Situația*, p. 163.
[168] Veress, *Bibliografia*, p. 163.
[169] Born 14 October 1720, SJ ingress. 1737. ARSI, *Aust. 93 Catal. I Coll. Claud. 1746*, p. 82.

of Article Five of the second *Diploma Leopoldinum* of 19 March 1701 to avoid all communication with non-Catholics, or at the very least to submit all such communications to the *theologus* first. The need to strengthen the Uniate Church as an independent institution and the repudiation of the "errors and abuses of the past" may have been the initial motive for such policies, but the consequence of these restrictions was to concentrate all real decision-making authority in the hands of the Jesuits. The protests of Uniate bishop Inochentie Micu and the silence of Transylvanian Jesuits on the topic of power sharing with the Uniates make it clear that Jesuits understood the nature of the arrangement and by and large agreed with it.[170] Ultimately, the verdict of many Romanian historians on this arrangement was expressed by the twentieth-century writer Osnifor Ghibu: "The [Uniate] Church was an institution of the state," by which is meant the increasingly centralized Habsburg state.[171] While this is an oversimplification of the role of the Church in the lives of the clergy who joined it, the Uniate Church frequently did serve as a tool of the Habsburgs. Was it also a tool of the Society? The answer here must be at most a qualified yes. Jesuits played a major role in the creation of Uniate Church, and as individuals, both in the roles of *theologus* and in less formal capacities they directed the actions of Uniate clergy on innumerable occasions. Jesuit schools educated a significant number of leaders of the Uniate Church, and synods held to determine Uniate policy show the influence of the values and expectations of the Society, at least in the recorded actions of the Uniates. The Uniate bishops received money and support from the Habsburgs, and the dynasty kept a close eye on these bishops. But the Uniate Church did not work overtly (or successfully) to increase the political power of the dynasty, remaining a relatively weak institution preoccupied with dealing with internal and external threats to its own existence. Instead, the leadership of the newly established Church, having been trained to a large degree in Jesuit schools, conveyed such a sense of loyalty to the House of Austria as it could muster automatically, and perhaps unconsciously. This loyalty would have been reinforced in various ways for the students of Jesuit schools in Cluj, where references to the distant dynasty were made at public and formal events, as well as in official Society documents.[172] Petru Pavel Aron, Uniate bishop from 1752 to 1764, attended Jesuit schools in Cluj, as did Atanasie Rednic, who held the bishop's chair from 1765 to 1772.[173] These men were not puppets of the Habsburg-Jesuit alliance, but products of an educational and social formation that turned them towards the West and towards

---

[170] Prodan, *Supplex Libellus*, p. 166.

[171] Ghibu, *Catolicismu*, p. 40.

[172] In 1718, by which time there were already many Romanians enrolled in the Cluj *collegium*, the philosophical theses were presented "under the auspices of the august and invincible Roman Emperor Charles VI." ARSI, *Austria 175, An. Prov. Aust. 1718*, pp. 200–201. Seven years earlier, the election of Charles in far-off Frankfurt had resulted in the performance of the Hymnus Ambrosianus to celebrate the success of the dynasty. OSzK, 2039 FMI/1608, *Historia anno 1711*, p. 108. In 1720, the *Literae Annue* for the Austrian Province begins, not with a description of the current situation facing the Society, but with a eulogy for Elenora Magdalene Theresia, the widow of Leopold I. ARSI, *Austria 177, An. Prov. Aust. 1720*, p. 2.

[173] Capros and Popan, "Biserica Unita," pp. 86, 93.

the bureaucratic and ecclesiastical institutions that provided the ongoing support for their Church.

Our understanding of the Uniate Church as an instrument of Habsburg and even Jesuit policy must take into account the distance between Vienna and Transylvania, and, a factor most important in the case of Cluj, the many other tasks the Society had set for itself in its Austrian Province. Because the Jesuits of Cluj were spread so thinly, they could not have exercised a dominating control over their Uniate colleagues, even if this had been their uppermost concern. The dealings between Jesuits and Uniates were therefore defined frequently by expedience and scarcity of resources in a time of recurring crises. The exclusion of Uniates from major Jesuit undertakings and the domineering role of the *theologus* eventually alienated the influential Uniate Bishop Micu and a major part of the Uniate clergy, and ultimately resulted in the removal and even excommunication of his opponent the Jesuit *theologus* Ladislaus Balogh.[174] Yet these developments did not deter young Romanians from continuing to seek an education at the Jesuit *collegium* in Cluj right down until the time of the Suppression. The attitude of these students seems to have been similar to that of other students throughout history who have attended Church-affiliated schools of varying cultural origins whose mission includes conversion. Romanian students (many if not most of them presumably Uniates), took advantage of the opportunities offered by Jesuit education while by and large steering clear of any change in their religious beliefs.[175] While the Jesuits studied Romanian society and culture, no ethnic Romanian Uniate protégés of the Jesuits emerged from the schools of Cluj to lead his people to union with Rome, and no great Uniate theologian claimed these schools as his spiritual home. From a Romanian perspective, the Uniate undertaking has always been understood as directed towards the incorporation of ethnic Romanians into a polity already established and one that looked westward to Vienna and Rome. While this supposition is largely correct, it is worth recalling that the first Uniate Bishop of Transylvania had as his charge "Graecos, Vallachos, Ruthenos et Rascianos" living in the region.[176] Most importantly, the stated goal of the Society as promoter of this union, whatever the personal feelings of its ethnic Hungarian members, was never the cultural assimilation of any group, but the reuniting of all Eastern Rite believers in acknowledgement of doctrinal points and lines of ecclesiastical authority. When this program was thwarted, Jesuit writers described the attack in terms of the misdeeds

---

[174] Balogh, who had fought with Micu for at least five years, was excommunicated 21 September 1746. Bârlea, "Biserica Română," p. 85. Petru Minor, *Istoria Beserica Românilor* (La Buda, 1813), pp. 88–91.

[175] From the start, Jesuit schools admitted students of various religious backgrounds, so many of the students identified as Romanian in the Cluj *collegium* may have been Orthodox, a circumstance implied by the presence of an audience "a diversis sectis" at the graduation of the first Baccalaureate class of the Cluj *collegium* in 1713. ARSI, *Austria 170, An. Prov. Aust. 1713*, folios 155r–156v.

[176] Ritzler and Sefrin, *Hierarchia Catholica Media et Recentoris Aevi*, vol. 5: 1667–1730, p. 293.

of their rivals the Orthodox "popae" rather than an expression of national or ethnic sentiment.[177]

The level of engagement between the Jesuit aesthetic and cultural ideal and the Orthodox tradition remained minimal in Cluj, which like much of the rest of Transylvania never underwent the full-blown Baroque transformation that took place in the Danube Basin and the western Habsburg realms. This reduced degree of engagement parallels the minimal contacts between Romanian and Hungarian culture that occurred in other important areas of Jesuit endeavor, such as school drama and sodalities, which appear to have been focused to a significant degree on ethnic Hungarians. What the Cluj community did gain were the first representatives of an educated clerical elite that would play a commanding role in the cultural history of Romanian Transylvanians in the nineteenth century. This small but immensely influential elite was armed with both a knowledge of the structure and organization of the Catholic Church, as well as a familiarity with Latin, whose parental relationship to Romanian would be called to mind whenever they used either language.

We turn now to the schools of the Jesuits of Cluj, one arena where young men of various backgrounds did come together, and where the Society's program of introducing cultural models from the West was most successful.

---

[177] When the Uniate Archdeacon of Doboka was deprived of his "dignitate," the cause is a "conjuratione tumulantium poparum." ARSI, *Austria 203, An. Prov. Aust. 1746*, folio 25r.

CHAPTER FOUR

Schooling

Our knowledge of the schools run by the Jesuits in Cluj in the decades immediately before the official return of the Society in 1693 are sketchy; Jesuit records from this period are sparse, although a few suggestive details are known. In the early decades of the seventeenth century, following their expulsion, Jesuits were not to be found sojourning permanently in Cluj. The Transylvanian Diet did however relent from its initially hostile attitude towards the fathers and allowed them to resettle at Kolosmănăştur, a short distance west of the town.[1] At the same time members of the Society, in the garb of secular priests, were teaching in unspecified locations in Transylvania, perhaps including Cluj, as early as 1652.[2] In 1657, a band of Turkish raiders attacked and damaged Kolosmănăştur, which prompted the town authorities to bend and allow the Jesuits to resume their work within the walls of Cluj while continuing to maintain their operations in their former location, although the Society's presence within Cluj proper remained very modest.[3] The silence in formal reports reaching Rome regarding the Cluj enterprise bears witness to the low-profile status of the project, but the Jesuits never abandoned their educational program. In 1665, Giulio Spinola, the papal nuncio in Vienna, reported that the two or three Jesuit fathers and two deacons in Kolosmănăştur "habent scholas usque ad rhetoricam."[4] The location of the Society's school a short distance from the town may have been motivated by a desire to avoid incurring the wrath of the community leaders, who would have numbered among them many Unitarians. This school, located on the previous site of a Jesuit house, remained small. In 1683, among the eight Jesuits listed as working in Kolosmănăştur, only one, Ladislaus Barany[a]i, is denominated a "professor," which simply identifies him as a teacher possibly of lower-level Latin grammar referred to as "parva."[5] Six years later, Andreas Szinder professed

---

[1]   György Lajos, "A kolozsvári római katolikus Lyceum–könyvtár története (1579–1948)." György's study of the entire history of the Jesuit library and its descendents was completed in the late 1940s and remained in manuscript until it was recently put online: http://www.mek.iif.hu/porta/szint/tarsad/konyvtar/tortenet/gyorgy/html/index.htm. Unfortunately this work does not include citations or bibliography, but is nonetheless valuable because of the inclusion of archival data no longer available.

[2]   PFK, 118. E. 41. Jesuitica documenta, Consultata Viennae 2 et 3 Decemb 1652, folio 1034r.

[3]   Bíró Vencel, *A kolozsvári jezsuita egyetem szervezete és építkezése a XVIII. Században.* Erdélyi tudományos füzetek (192) (Kolozsvár: Erdéélyi Muzeum-Egyesület kiadasa, 1945), pp. 12, 10.

[4]   Tóth, *Relationes*, pp. 329, 364.

[5]   Peris, *Missioni*, p. 144. Baranyai's three years of teaching in Kolosmănăştur were sandwiched in between training in Graz; he professed his fourth vow in Cluj in 1692.

the fourth vow of the Society "Claudiopoli," which suggests that the institutional structure needed for the formation of Jesuits was already well in place.[6] About the same time Paulus Szamoroczi arrived in Cluj "in disguise" to begin the teaching of rhetoric, and Paulus Adamovich died in the town.[7]

Each of these facts points to the ongoing existence of a rudimentary organization kept in place by the Society in anticipation of its large-scale return. This evidence is further supported by a fragment of a report apparently written by an anonymous Jesuit for the years 1655 to 1622.[8] In addition, the careers of a few Jesuits native to Cluj provide circumstantial evidence of a continually operating school offering the Jesuit curriculum in the area before 1693. Martinus Zeller, a native of Cluj, entered the Society at the age of 17 in 1646; while Zeller's career as a Jesuit commenced in Vienna, his early education may well have taken place in a Cluj school or he may have received private instruction from a local Jesuit.[9] Another important source on Jesuit schooling in Cluj at the end of the seventeenth century comes from the memoirs of Apor Péter, who was born in 1676 and received his early education from the Society. Decades later Apor recalled that in those early years instruction for the youngest students was carried out in a tiny building within the walled town of Cluj, not far from where the Jesuits later built their complex; in the winter the room was so dark that the teacher could scarcely see the book from which he read, and students had to take up a collection to pay for candles.[10] Documentation of the curriculum offered under such conditions is entirely lacking, but it is not improbable that the *Ratio* was followed closely, since even these limited educational offerings were intended to help train future Jesuits.

When, starting in 1693, the Jesuits began their systematic expansion of the rudimentary school program they had offered through the second half of the seventeenth century, the immediate problem was to obtain facilities adequate to handle a much larger undertaking that would eventually enroll 400 students.[11] Emperor Leopold I, despite his chronic lack of funds, quickly provided 15,000 florins to supplant the meager monies available to the Kolosmănăştur school.[12] In these early years the Society relied on large donations to provide the financial foundations of their academy. In 1698, Count Apor István committed 9000 florins to the teaching of philosophy, a huge sum for the size of the community in which the school was to be located and one that made clear what the relationship between the Society and

---

L. Szilas, "Baranyai Pál László" in *Diccionario*, vol. 1, p. 339; ARSI, *Germania 25*, folios 277–8.

[6] "Professus 4 votorum Claudiopoli 1689 15 Aug. ... 3. Egit missionarium in Dacia." ARSI, *Austria 50, Catalogus I 1696*, folio 136v.

[7] Sommervogel et al., *Bibliothèque*, vol. 7, p. 1742; ARSI, *Austria 47, Catalogus defunctorum*, folio 259r.

[8] ELTE, Kéz. Kaprin xxvi, folios 2r–15v

[9] Zeller died in 1663, apparently without having returned to Cluj. Stöger, *Scriptores*, p. 405.

[10] Apor, *Metamorphosis*, p. 158.

[11] Hets J. Aurelián, *A Jezsuiták iskolái Magyarországon a 18. század közepén*. (Pannonhalma, 1938), p. 17.

[12] Lechinţan, *Instituţii*, pp. 18–19.

the Habsburg-supported elite was going to be.[13] As we have seen, the Habsburgs themselves also contributed significantly to the expansion of the *collegium*, and eventually funds from the Transylvanian state treasury were also used to support Jesuit schools.[14] Thanks to these and other gifts, and to a well-established system of teacher training already in place in the Austrian Province, the instruction offered at the Jesuit schools of Cluj remained free, although a fee was charged for the actual granting of a degree. The cost of being promoted to the bachelor's level was one florin thirty kreutzers, a licenate in theology cost two florins, and a doctorate in theology four florins, a fee scale prescribed for the entire Austrian Province. The Society also prorated the fee charged for public disputations, whereby a "communis quilibet" would pay twelve kreutzers, while a "comes" would be assessed one florin thirty kreutzers for the same exercise.[15] The variation in fees shows that the Society was aware both of the prestige associated with the higher degrees that its schools offered and of the varying financial conditions of its students. In a community as close to starvation and calamity as Cluj frequently was, such responses to the striated financial conditions of many students made up a significant element in the academic culture promoted by the Society, and helped promote the prestige of the Jesuit schools, which successfully sought out aristocratic families as sources of students as well as funds.[16] The Jesuits, at least in the earliest days of their mission, also charged considerable fees for board, which sometimes included wine. Gentlemen's sons paid 100 Hungarian forints annually to dine in the refectory, a healthy sum that would have fed a young nobleman (and his manservant) in a larger Habsburg city.[17] In later years, other sources of income contributed to the support of the overall Jesuit program, probably including the schools. Income from the pharmacy might be applied to everything from church repairs to maintenance of the schools.[18] The exact relation between the income derived from property and the expenses incurred by the schools the Society operated is not clear, but in prosperous years the Jesuits' land holdings would have provided needed cash for a variety of purposes.

Historians have often made the assumption that the curriculum and instructional approach of all of the Jesuit schools was closely modeled on the *Ratio*, and while this is likely, it is also true that the guidelines of the *Ratio* were not infrequently bent to accommodate specific conditions, including the previous training of the students, the availability of books, and special circumstances such as intervening wars and plagues. Modification of Ignatius's original plan for a school of three faculties – Languages, Arts and Theology – had begun in the sixteenth century, and the *Ratio*

---

[13] Weiser, *A katholikus iskolaügy*, p. 74.

[14] Lechințan, *Instituții*, p. 69.

[15] PFK, 119, A. 2. 1–64 (no. 43) "Taxa academica," folio 123r.

[16] The majority of students identified as ethnic Romanian were probably also of noble blood. Pâclișanu, *Istoria Bisericii*, p. 154.

[17] Apor, *Metamorphosis*, p. 158.

[18] Ferenc Szigetváry, "Die Apotekengründungen der Jesuiten," in *Reformation und Gegenreformation in Pannonischen Raum. Schlaininger Gespräche* 1993/1994, eds Gustav Reingrabner and Gerald Schlag (Eisenstadt: Burgenländisches Landesmuseum, 2000), pp. 385–8. The pharmacy was established on 3 March 1731. ARSI, *Austria 188, An. Prov. Aust. 1731*, pp. 501–502.

of 1599 already reflected an awareness of the need for more rudimentary schooling, and for good teaching at all levels.[19] As John W. Padberg notes, the *Ratio* of 1599 was less of a detailed program for higher instruction than it was

> ... a series of quite specific, concrete, and ordered directives, intended for the practical guidance of those to whom particular functions in the schools had been confided ... The general aim of the whole system, from the lowest class of grammar to the highest philosophical or theological discipline, was something which has become a truism, but until the Society enunciated it explicitly, had not at all been so clearly put for the Christian schools: "The harmonious development of intellect and will, mind and spirit ... ."[20]

In the early 1700s, after more than a century of application and adaptation, the *Ratio* was still regarded as the foundational guide for Jesuit curriculum in the eighteenth century. And as the Jesuits' school in Cluj (which was formally designated an academy in 1701) expanded its curriculum, it did so along lines prescribed by the *Ratio*, and in a way that makes clear that the education of parish priests, while one of the tasks the Society took up, was never the focus of its efforts.[21] The study of theology, for example, was formally instituted only in 1712, several decades after the Jesuits' well-financed return.[22] Such changes as were introduced were cast formally as additions following a well-established pattern of expansion, rather than substitutions, although practically, the reduction of emphasis on more traditional elements of the curriculum must have been common. Yet the curricular innovations that arrived at mid-century went well beyond the framework of the *Ratio*. By 1737, historical studies were being introduced systematically into Jesuit schools throughout Transylvania; in Cluj in addition to formal schooling, instruction was conducted in private by "Moderators."[23] In 1747, "Academy" (for example, lower-level *collegium*) students were studying the history of the first seven "duces" of Hungary, which meant that they were receiving a healthy dose of combined patriotic history and hagiography that closely paralleled the publications and art works already initiated by the Society.[24] The promotion of history was closely tied to the Society's commitment to advance the prestige (and acceptability to the general population) of the Habsburgs and their allies, a task that was much more difficult than Jesuit records might suggest. The Jesuits took special pains to make this connection in public contexts. Such an event is recorded in the Latin verses published in Cluj in 1722 on the occasion of the awarding of degrees at the *collegium*. This ambitious poem began by honoring earlier Hungarian heroes such as János Zápolya and Sigmund Rákóczi, and culminated with praise for Charles VI,

---

[19] Karl Hengst, *Jesuiten an Universitäten und Jesuitenuniversitäten*. (Paderborn/München/Wien/Zürich, 1981), pp. 64, 70.

[20] John W. Padberg, SJ, *Colleges in Controversy* (Cambridge, 1969), p. 144.

[21] Kathleen M. Comerford, "Clerical education, catechesis, and Catholic confessionalism: Teaching religion in the seventeenth and eighteenth centuries," in Kathleen M. Comerford and Hilmar M. Pabel (eds), *Early Modern Catholicism: Essays in Honour of John W. O'Malley, S.J.* (Toronto, 2001), p. 254.

[22] Stephan Pascu, *L'Université de Babeş-Bolyai de Cluj* (Cluj, 1971), pp. 16–17.

[23] Private instruction was yet another way by which the Society extended its influence in the community. OSzK, 2039 FMI/1608, *Historia anno 1737*, pp. 412.

[24] ARSI, *Aust. 204, An. Prov. Aust. 1747*, folio 75r.

who, as in other Jesuit sponsored publications, is extolled as Holy Roman Emperor, not as king of Hungary or prince of Transylvania.[25] Local history and the Society's relationship to it might also figure in public performances, as in 1737 when Count Paul Haller von Hallerstein presented an *Epitome chronologica rerum hungaricarum et transsilvanicarum* that noted how the Society had been allowed to return to Cluj in 1603.[26] On other occasions, pagan and Biblical themes were combined with local history to praise the memory of a distinguished family. Ovid, despite his reputation for slightly risqué content, was a favorite of Jesuit masters training their students for public performance.[27] And while the teaching faculty in Cluj could count no notable historian or geographer among its numbers, the Jesuit press did produce an elegiac text on the rulers of Transylvania and, in 1731, Baccalaureate candidates addressed the question of "Quanta orbis terrae pars sit Transylvania."[28] The desire to inculcate students, be they ethnic Hungarian or not, with a sense of Hungarian royal and Catholic history goes far to explain much of the writing undertaken in the Cluj community. But complementing the drive to educate youth in the history of Hungary was a genuine scholarly interest among many Jesuits to record the diplomatic history of Hungarian rulers, and to establish the relationship between contemporary culture and the earliest known history of the region. In addition to Maximilianus Hell's scholarly work in this area, Stephanus Kaprinai devoted himself to the collection of documents relating to the career of Matthias Hunyadi, the fifteenth-century national hero.[29] Kaprinai's work was in fact a continuation of a long-standing tradition within the Society of compiling and annotating historical documents. An enthusiastic amateur quality persisted in the researches of Cluj Jesuit historians: continuing the Kircherian tradition of proposing linkages between modern and faintly understood

---

[25] *Magnus manes Transylvania Principatu, honori Reverendorum Nobilium ac Eruditorum Dominorum DD. AA. LL. Et Philosophiae Neo-Doctorum* (Claudiopoli, 1722).

[26] *Epitome chronologica rerum hungaricarum et transsilvanicarum a divo Stephano ad an M.D.CC.XVII* ... (Anno M.D.CC.XXXVII. mense ... die ... Claudiopoli, Typis Academicics Soc. JESU, per Simonem Thadaeum Weichenberg), pp. 239.

[27] An Ovidian literary model was applied to Biblical themes in a poem that included references to the Kornis family in *Metempsychosis sive Animalium in alia Corpora Transmigratio* ... (Claudiopoli: Typis Acad. Soc. JESU, 1729). For the role of Ovid in the early modern curriculum, see R.M. Ogilvie, *Latin and Greek: A History of the Influence of the Classics on English Life from 1600 to 1918* (Hamden, CT, 1969), pp. 1–33.

[28] *Principes tredecim Transylvaniae, Carmine Elegiaco* (Claudiopoli, 1733), written by Andreas Handler (1726–62), who apparently did not teach in Cluj. Stöger, *Scriptores*, p. 121; BARC-N, MsC 49 a–b, folios 36v–37r. As early as 1696, Gabrielis Hevenesi had published a school text entitled *Parvus Atlas Hungariae* (Vienna, 1696), demonstrating the Society's interest in both the reestablishment of Hungary as a geographical entity known in the West, as well as the Jesuits' claim to being the interpreters of Hungary to its own students. A copy of this atlas is preserved in the Archdiocesan Library in Győr.

[29] "Kaprinai St. Hungaria diplomatica temporibus Matthias de Hunyad. Pars 1–2, Vindobona," appears in the reference catalogue of the Győr diocesan seminary (*A Győri püspöki papnevelőintézet könyvtárának czimjegyzéke* (Győr, 1893)). This works appears to be identical with one published in Vienna in 1767. Sommervogel et al., *Bibliothèque*, vol. 4, p. 917. Kaprinai (1714–85 or 1786), studied in Cluj from 1737 to 1738 and taught in Cluj from 1750 to 1755. Szinnyei (ed.), *Magyar írók*, vol. 5, p. 982.

ancient languages, Rudolphus Bzenszky, arriving in Transylvania in 1696, asserted that the name "Colosvar" was Scythian in origin.[30] The most renowned Jesuit historian to work in Cluj was Samuel Timon (1675–1736), who served as rector of the Cluj *collegium* from 1725 to 1726.[31] Timon, who was born in Vienna, compiled works on ancient and modern Hungary, and like other Hungarian Jesuits, produced practical classroom texts and left behind unpublished manuscripts intended for use by *collegium* instructors. Unlike many of his peers, Timon was spared the rigors of missionary work, since his health was poor. Yet he was as peripatetic as other more robust Jesuits, serving in Uzhhorod, Skalica, Prešov, Buda, Trnava and Košice, where he ultimately died. Like several other literary lights of the Austrian Province, Timon had a limited impact on the Cluj community because of the brief time he spent there.

The flexibility implied in the *Ratio* also allowed the fathers to build a library. In 1737, they purchased works ranging from Euclid and a Hebrew Old Testament to Descartes' *Meditationes de prima philosophia*.[32] Advanced students at the Cluj academy sometimes pursued topics in the fledgling natural sciences. In 1725, the first prize among the master's theses in philosophy was awarded in Cluj to a student debating the question, "An niger an aureus color praestantioris naturae sit indicium."[33] Nine years later, master's students offered a "libellum" dealing with the rudiments of geography, a subject included in the library acquisitions of 1737.[34] Faculty members were also involved in writing about geography. Ladislaus Nedetzki, who taught in Cluj, Győr, Košice and Eger, produced a geography text that was published in 1737.[35] Geography and trigonometry both figured in the examinations of bachelor's candidates in 1751, and circumstantial evidence points to an awareness of Newtonian mathematics and post-Ptolemaic astronomy among some of the faculty of the *collegium*.[36] Some dim awareness, however biased, of conditions outside the Catholic world is apparent in the *Acta Magistri* of 1734, which seem to call attention to the paucity of books published in the Ottoman Empire.[37] At the same time relics of

---

[30] *Transylvania epistolica*, folio 46v.

[31] Katona, *Historia*, vol. 19, pp. 893–4; Sommervogel et al., *Bibliothèque*, vol. 8, pp. 27–9; O'Neill and Domínguez, *Diccionário*, vol. 4, pp. 3802–3803.

[32] OSzK, 2039 FMI/1608, *Historia anno 1737*, pp. 420–21.

[33] ARSI, *Aust. 182, An. Prov. Aust. 1725*, folio 75r.

[34] ARSI, *Aust. 191, An. Prov. Aust. 1734*, folio 79r; OSzK, 2039 FMI/1608 *Historia anno 1737*, pp. 420–21. Ladislaus Nedetski (1703– ?), who taught in Cluj, edited a *Geographicus Symposis*. Katona, *Historia*, vol. 20, p. 984.

[35] Stöger, *Scriptores*, p. 242.

[36] BARC-N, MsC, 49 a–b, folios 36v–37r. The Jesuit press in Trnava, the most prolific in Hungary, had published a *Geographia Nova vetrum locorum regnorumque nominibus et historia synopsi aucta ...* as early as 1725. In the undated *Catalogus Librorum ad Theologiam Heterodoxorum Spectantium* is found *Newton Isaaci Arithemetica Universalis* (Amstelod, 1761) MsC 678, folio 407r. In the same collection is found the undated text *Scriptores Arabici de Judicis Astron.* identified as written by "Albohazen." Folio 387r.

[37] The possibly corrupt text of the *Acta* reads "Turcas Typographiis deinceps etiam carere magis è è [*sic*] re Xstiam orbis quam ab undare [?] ... BARC-N, MsC. 49 a–b, *Acta Magistri, 1734*, folio 267r–v. Between 1726, when the first printing press is reported in Constantinople,

a pre-empirical scientific mindset were sometimes interwoven with topics of current scientific interest. Another "actus" undertaken by a master's candidate in 1749 considered whether the laurel tree was resistant to lightning, a question neither posed in the *Ratio* nor debated by Enlightenment scientists.[38] Each of these innovations are in part a reflection of a development that occurred after 1735, when, under pressure from the Crown, the Society in Hungary had modified its curriculum somewhat and produced the *Typus*, which provided some coverage of more modern subjects such as history.[39] Neither natural science nor post-Classical history can be easily identified with subjects prescribed in the *Ratio*, but instead reflect (albeit in the first instance in a pre-modern and unscientific way) later trends in the evolution of a curriculum that by mid-century had critics even within the Society. The subjects taught in Cluj reflect these innovations, yet with emphases that continued the long-range plans of the Society to keep its proselytizing efforts in the forefront. This arrangement remained essentially the same until the years immediately before 1773, when additional innovations were introduced to the curriculum of the Trnava university.[40] These reforms, however never spread to the pre-Suppression Cluj *collegium*, which did however offer courses in natural law, taught by Father Emericus Boer.[41]

As at other schools operated by the Society, the Jesuit schools of Cluj normally employed scholastics to teach the lower-level courses, often identified in school records as "parva."[42] There is no clear evidence of secular clergy or laypersons teaching in any of the Cluj schools, but we must make allowances for the possibility. But even with the occasional presence of a non-Jesuit teacher, the teaching faculty of the Cluj *collegium* would have had an overwhelming Jesuit tone at all times, one that reflected the Society's use of its own schools as training grounds for future Jesuits. This tone would have profoundly influenced the education of the non-Jesuits who completed the course of instruction. One such graduate was Antonius Szeredai, who

---

and 1815 sixty-three books were printed in the Ottoman capital, in comparison with thousands of titles published each year throughout Europe. Colin McEvedy, *The Penguin Atlas of Modern History (to 1815)* (London, 1972), p. 4. Given the Society's long-standing connections to Constatinople, this information may well have been available to teachers in Cluj.

[38] BARC-N, MsC, 49 a–b, folios 328–32v. A 1761 edition of Newton's *Arithmetica Universalis* is listed in the catalogue of the "Royal Library" of 1797; since many of these works represent theological literature from sects with whom the Society engaged in polemics ("Librorum ad Theologiam Heterdoxorum Spectantium"), the works identified probably came from the old Jesuit *collegium*. BARC-N, MsC, 678, folio 407r *et passim*.

[39] Kosáry, *Culture*, pp. 108–109. What one scholar has dubbed the "highly centralized organization of the order" hampered large-scale reform of the curriculum down through the 1750s. Jerzy Kloczowski, "The Polish Church," in Callahan and Higgs (eds), *Church and Society*, p. 131. The Thomist theological system that was a mainstay of the Society's curriculum went into decline in Trnava after 1753, as a result of reforms instituted by Joannes Baptista Horváth. Csapodi Csaba, "Newtonianizmus a nagyszombati jezsuita egyetem," *Regnum 6* (1944/46), pp. 58–68.

[40] In keeping with the reforms promoted by Vienna, Trnava acquired two chairs in the field of camerilistics: secular rhetoric and history.

[41] ARSI, *Aust. 114, Catal. I Coll. Claud. 1767*, p. 85.

[42] For example, Ignatius Pernkopf, a twenty-year-old scholastic from Komárom, taught "parva" in Cluj in 1761. ARSI, *Aust. 106, Catal. I Coll. Claud. 1761*, p. 95.

earned the "suprema philosophiae laura" in Cluj and went on to study theology in Trnava.[43]

The Jesuits of Cluj agreed with the first curriculum designers of the Society that without books they were like soldiers without weapons, and thus the Cluj community included modest library holdings that went well beyond the readings recommended by the *Ratio*. No complete reconstruction of the Cluj *collegium* library has been possible, nor would a complete list of books in this library necessarily give us a clear picture of the boundaries of Jesuit tolerance, since the presence of a volume would not necessarily imply the Society's endorsement of its contents. György Lajos estimated that when the Jesuits began to expand and formalize instruction at the beginning of the eighteenth century, there were approximately a thousand volumes in their possession, and in 1773, this number had grown to about six thousand.[44] The "Bibliotheca" list compiled by government authorities at the time of the Suppression does not list titles but only provides categories of books, although even this information is highly suggestive: in addition to 156 German and 108 volumes in Hungarian, seven "Ilyirci" works are listed, but not one in Romanian.[45] It is worth noting that in the Jesuit library in Trnava, Lutheran authors were to be found, but in the seventeenth century censors had cut away the names of the offending heretical writers from the title pages.[46] Students were unlikely to have owned many books themselves, and like other Jesuit schools in the Austrian Province, the Cluj schools no doubt relied on lectures delivered in the medieval fashion to students who took notes without the benefit of their own copies of the texts.[47]

Meanwhile the vernacular (or at least one of the spoken languages of the region) had penetrated the curriculum of the *convictus nobilium*, where Jesuit scholastics also taught: in 1751, a new rule allowed the use of German "praeter exercitationes."[48] The curriculum of the *convictus* must nevertheless have closely resembled the instruction found in the lower levels of the *collegium*, as there are numerous instances of alumni of the *convictus* going on to earn degrees from the Cluj *collegium*. We know that in addition to Classical languages the *convictus* students had been undertaking the study of music, arithmetic and unspecified (but probably vernacular) languages "ad ingent. solatium parentium."[49] The role of music in the education offered in the

---

[43] Katona, *Historia*, p. 1007.

[44] György, "Lyceum." The reader is referred to the chapter entitled "A kolozsvári jezsuita Akadémia könyvtára (1693–1773)."

[45] MOL, F-447, *Exactoratus*, p. 58.

[46] *Magyarországi Jezsuita Könyvtárak 1717–ig: Nagyszombat 1632–1690*, ed. Farkas Gábor Farkas (Szeged, 1997), p. 25.

[47] The availability of texts to students in eighteenth-century Jesuit *collegia* is difficult to assess; the Cluj Jesuit press was an active one, however, and while many of the books it produced may have been destined for other Jesuit schools, students might have been able to purchase some of the titles it published. For a list of titles published by the Society in Cluj, see *Magyarország Bibliográfiája 1712–1860*, vol. 8 (Budapest, 1991), pp. 342–7.

[48] ARSI, *Aust. 208, An. Prov. Aust. 1751*, folio 55r. No record survives, however of any similar rule instituted for the speaking of Hungarian, which would have been the native language of perhaps a majority of the *convictus* students.

[49] ARSI, *Aust. 202, An. Prov. Aust. 1745*, folio 155.

convictus had striking prominence not found in other comparable schools. Although specific instructions for the Cluj *convictus* have not survived, a late seventeenth-century document from Trnava spells out objections to the employment of music outside the confines of the institution that may have also applied in Transylvania.[50] The choice of German is significant, as there is no reason to suppose that it was the native language of the majority of either students or teachers, although the relative youth of many of the students may have led teachers to choose a living language for the medium of instruction.[51] German, moreover, was one of the languages used most frequently in the Habsburg army, which was undergoing a steady if slow process of reform and standardization. Reforms in Jesuit schooling were also being imposed from the outside: in 1753, the years of training required in philosophy to be taught in *collegia* in Transylvania were reduced, by imperial *diploma*, from three years to two.[52] The addition in 1769 of dogmatic speculative theology to the curriculum of the Cluj *collegium*, as the request of the local bishop, was less of a break with the past.[53] Collectively, the curricular innovations adopted in Cluj also were a consequence of curricular reforms occurring in Western Europe, although the resistance of the Society to these ideas has often attracted more attention than individual instances of innovation undertaken in Jesuit schools.

The strict instructional regimen outlined in the *Ratio*, with teachers sitting in judgment on student competitions and supervising the moral behavior of their charges, was undoubtedly the goal towards which Jesuit instructors strove, but the role of the teacher had a kinder side as well. The French Jesuit Louis Bourdaoue, addressing a class of orphaned girls in 1671, spoke of the necessity of maintaining a balance between what he characterized as the "two idolatries": making parents godlike in their power over children, and holding children to be like "gods" in the eyes of their doting parents.[54] Jesuit schooling aimed at this balance, seeking to avoid the most severe treatment in the hopes of winning young souls. But sometimes there were difficulties.

The *seminarium pauperum* established in Cluj was a conscious attempt by the Society to take on a parental role that extended beyond the tasks of training future Jesuits and recruiting the sons of the local nobility into the Society's educational system. In histories of Jesuit education, schools created especially for orphans and poor boys have not received as much attention as the schools that grew into universities, or the *convicti* designed specifically for the sons of nobles. In Cluj, as elsewhere, many details about the running of the poor boys' school are lacking, but the

---

[50] "Musicos intertenere in hoc Seminario ex proventibus Seminarii est mnifestè contra mentem, et intentionem Fundatoris." PFK, 118. E. 41., Jesuitica documenta, folio 847c.

[51] The age of admittance to the Cluj *convictus* is not specified, but at the Győr *convictus*, students could be as young as twelve. Ascay Ferencz, *A győri kath. főgymnázium története.* (Győrött, 1910), p. 170.

[52] *Historia Critica Regum Hungariae stirpis Austriacae ... a Stephano Katona* (Budae, 1809), vol. 20, ordine 39, pp. 512–13.

[53] Jakab, *Története*, vol. 3, p. 325.

[54] Lawrence Wolff, "Parents and children in the sermons of Père Bourdaloue: A Jesuit perspective on the early modern family," in Christopher Chapple (ed.), *The Jesuit Tradition in Education and Missions: A 450-year Perspective* (Scranton, 1993), pp. 81–94.

need for such an institution was apparently great: within a few years of its founding roughly a hundred youths were in attendance.[55] In 1717, a year of hardship and hunger, trouble broke out in the Cluj *seminarium pauperum*. A "sedition against the professors" erupted that could be subdued only when the perpetrators, holed up in the *seminarium* itself, were prevented from obtaining loaves of bread and were starved into submission. After the *moderatores academiae* were able to restore order, the ringleaders of the rebellion were flogged in the public square and "sanitas reddit."[56] Jesuit records make no further mention of such breaches of the peace, but the space devoted to the incident in the *Literae annuae* of that year is highly suggestive. Jesuit schools, for all their deserved recognition as innovative and humane institutions, were still creations of their own time. In the early modern period, rebellions by students chafing under the discipline of their teachers or dissatisfied with their food were commonplace, as were severe punishments for such actions. In the seventeenth century, students at a French Jesuit *collegium* had led a mutiny, and armed with muskets, had held the authorities at bay until a confrontation forced the issue.[57] The students in the Cluj *seminarium pauperum*, of all those under the tutelage of the Jesuits, had the least to lose. The training they were receiving did not necessarily lead to higher levels that would have prepared them for study at a university, and their job prospects in the area following the completion of their studies cannot have been brilliant, even in more prosperous times. Were these boys treated more severely than those enrolled in other Jesuit schools? Seven years after the notable rebellion of the *seminarium*, the Jesuit community record speaks of "many [in the *seminarium*], who were unable to bear the rigors of discipline."[58] There is no clear evidence that these students received especially harsh treatment, but it must also be acknowledged that the Cluj Jesuits, like their colleagues in other communities, paid great attention to the social status of their students. Even the poorest youth was certainly capable of redemption, but deeply entrenched social attitudes, combined with interethnic hostilities and the presentation of a curriculum that would have seemed of little use to marginalized youth, may have made life in the *seminarium pauperum* bad enough to risk rebellion.

The school for poor boys receives the least attention in Jesuit records of all the educational undertakings of the Society in Cluj.[59] We are often told more about how many of these unfortunates were fed and clothed than about what they learned or how they demonstrated their skills.[60] By contrast, the *Seminarium S. Josephi* built

---

[55] OSzK, 2039 FMI/1068, *Historia Societatis Jesu Claudiopoli 1701*, folio 21.

[56] ARSI, *Aust. 174, An. Prov. Aust. 1717*, folio 67.

[57] Ariès, *Childhood*, p. 316.

[58] "... plures, qui disciplinae rigorem non ferebant ... ," ARSI, *Aust. 181, An. Prov. Aust. 1724*, folio 63v.

[59] In addition to the orphanage run by the Society, beginning in 1760 another orphanage established by Battyány József, Bishop of Kolocsa, designed specifically to care for (and presumably convert) orphans from Protestant families. It is not improbable that Jesuits played a role in whatever education was provided to these children. Juhász (ed.), *Kronologiája*, vol. 2, p. 578.

[60] In 1718, for instance, 130 "pauperes" were supported by the *collegium* at time when food had to be imported into Transylvania. ARSI, *Aust. 175, An. Prov. Aust. 1718*, folio 227.

a connection between the Society and the elite of the region and is given constant attention in Jesuit records. In 1722, the school could boast an enrollment that included "comitibus octo, baronibus quattuor, perillustribus quinque."[61] Fourteen years later, out of a total enrollment of 73, nine students were identified as "illust." and ten as clergy.[62] The fathers were successful in enlisting the local elite in supporting the *seminarium*; in 1747, Koncz Éva and the wife of Ferenczi Medobéri András donated 2000 florins, and seven years earlier, an anonymous donor gave an equal sum to the school.[63] Down to the time of the Suppression, the Jesuit schools of Cluj, despite fluctuations in enrolment and the interruptions caused by war, were able to avoid curtailing or dismantling any of their programs.[64]

The Jesuits were not the only religious body operating schools in Cluj. The Calvinist academy continued to attract students throughout the eighteenth century, a few of whom went on to attend universities as far away as Frankfurt and Holland.[65] The Franciscans starting in 1729 ran a boarding school connected with their convent that employed three lecturers and offered instruction in canon law and theology.[66] Noble families residing in the countryside also employed tutors who on occasion may have been Jesuits. Thus we cannot resort to the generalization of a Jesuit "monopoly" on higher education used by many historians, since such a statement misrepresents "higher" education as it was understood at the time. In fact, a person tutored privately at home was regarded as just as "highly" educated as the product of a formal school. In addition, schools run by the Unitarians continued to function; Jesuit writers report with obvious pleasure when students left these schools to enroll in the *Seminarium*.[67] There was also a private literary culture alive in the region around Cluj, situated in the homes of those Calvinists who resisted conversion.[68] Yet as the years passed the Society came increasingly to dominate the literate culture of the Cluj region, in part because of the constant stream of money that flowed into its schools and allowed the Jesuits to build up land holdings that would help them sustain all of their operations.[69] The growing network of graduates emerging from Jesuit schools further strengthened the influence of the Society in the region, especially among the families of the local aristocracy. By 1718, the *convictus* had

---

[61] ARSI, *Aust. 179, An. Prov. Aust. 1722*, folio 50v.

[62] ARSI, *Aust. 193, An. Prov. Aust. 1736*, folio 88v.

[63] Jakab, *Története*, vol. 2, pp. 576, 562; Bod Péter, *Magyar Athenas*, p. 114.

[64] Jesuit records note that in 1735, despite warnings from older and wiser heads, the "unhappy youth" enrolled in Jesuit schools exited to participate in distant wars ("Mars exul"). ARSI, *Aust. 192, An. Prov. Aust. 1735*, folio 62v. In 1767, one of the worst scourges of the eighteenth century, smallpox, struck the Cluj complex, and three youths died. ARSI, *Aust. 222, An. Prov. Aust. 1767*, folio 54r.

[65] Jakab, *Története*, vol. 2, p. 551.

[66] Sas Péter, *A kolozsvári ferences templom (*Kolozsvár, 1999), p. 118.

[67] ARSI, *Aust. 229, Fructus Missionum*, folio 122r.

[68] Exemplifying this elite Protestant literary culture is Bod Péter's poem "Tiszta Fényes Drága Bíbor," extolling the accomplishments of the Calvinist noblewoman Bethlen Kata and published in Cluj in 1762. Simon Melinda and Gábor Ágnes, *Bethlen Kata könyvtárának rekonstruckiója* (Szeged, 1997), p. xv.

[69] Jakab, *Története*, p. 514, *et passim*.

built an enrollment that included ten clergy, as well as several dozen other students.[70] As in many of the western reaches of the Habsburg domains, half a century of Jesuit dominance in all aspects of post-primary education produced a situation where a majority of those claiming to have had an education had received it from the Society. This consequence was far from accidental. The plan undertaken during the eighty-year period before the Suppression assumed that fathers would be able to build a base of graduates who would solidify the influence of the Society and create a ready-made clientele to supply their schools in the future, as well as providing a source of future Jesuits. But the Suppression of 1773 prevented this strategy, pursued with considerable success elsewhere, from bearing fruit, as had been hoped. The most successful aspect of this program was the cadre of *seminarium*-trained Uniate clergy whose careers in a few cases stretched far into the next century.[71]

Jesuit schools, wherever they were established, provided a valued service to the community by offering a tried and true curriculum delivered by teachers whose level of training far exceeded that of most other instructors. Families responded to the opportunity to have their children educated by the fathers: enrollment in the Jesuit *collegium* rose from 50 in 1703 to 387 in 1747 to 493 in 1771, figures all the more impressive considering the breaks placed on population growth in the region.[72] From the first, the *collegium* attracted the sons of non-Catholic families as well, some of whom converted.[73] But the role of Jesuit schools in Cluj was more complex than this. The professor's podium, the graduating scholar's platform, the pulpit and the printing press all functioned as dissemination points for crafted rhetoric supporting the House of Habsburg. Thus while Ladislaus Dobra performed as a teacher of dogmatic theology, and preached in Hungarian and Romanian in the towns of Transylvania, he also wrote Latin verse extolling the House of Austria.[74] Stephanus Dobner, completing his doctorate in Cluj in 1725, used the occasion to laud Stephen Bathory,

---

[70] ARSI, *Aust. 175, An. Prov. Aust. 1718*, folios 200, 217. An otherwise successful *convictus* might have another, less savory reputation to live down: six years later an unnamed disease (possibly the plague) devastated the school, resulting in at least one death and the departure of several other students. ARSI, *Aust. 181, An. Prov. Aust. 1724*, folio 62r–v. The obituary for Joannes Raichane, rector of the Cluj *collegium*, notes how his job in Cluj, and his position in Trnava as the rector of the *convictus nobilium* was burdened with famine and disease. ARSI, *Austria 190, An. Prov. Aust. 1733*, folio 278. But by 1768, a period of relative prosperity and high enrolments in the *collegium*, the Cluj *convictus* counted one hundred students. ARSI, *Aust. 223, Lit An. Prov. Aust. 1768*, folio 48v.

[71] Ioannes Bob, who attended the *Seminarium S. Josephi*, served as Uniate Bishop of Făgăraş until his death in 1830. Octavian Bârlea, *Ioannes Bob Episcopus Fagrarasiensis (1783–1830)* (Frankfurt/Main, c.1950), p. 13.

[72] Pascu, *Universität*, p. 9.

[73] For example, three Calvinist boys converted in 1749. ARSI, *Aust. 206, An. Prov. Aust.* 1749, folio 35r. The presence of non-Catholic students may have played a role in the development of remarkably tolerant views expressed by Apor Péter in his *Metamorphoses*, in which he stressed that Calvinists and Unitarians are humans too. But such attitudes were also fostered by the long-standing toleration of limited religous diversity in the Principality.

[74] *Oliva Pacis a Dva Hungariae Patrona haereditariarum domûs Austriae provinciarvm votes retenta* (Claudiopoli, 1746); Szinnyei (ed.), *Magyar irók*, vol. 2, p. 934.

the King of Poland, and Emperor Charles VI as patrons of the Jesuit *collegium*.[75] Jesuit instruction and the literary efforts of Jesuit teachers were of a piece with the plays and other public spectacles the Society delivered to the community. The number and high degree of visibility of these performances suggest the urgency with which the Society pursued the goal of making the region loyal to the Imperial dynasty. This urgency may have been driven by memories of recent rebellions and by the insecurity barely concealed beneath the impressive list of titles held by the Emperor, of the Habsburg dynasty. We must also view these public expressions of support for the dynasty in the context of an educational environment that did not yet include state-supported general schooling. The relationship between monarchies and schools designed for the masses would only begin to take shape after the suppression of the Society, when governments recognized both their responsibility and the potential benefits of schools created for the common people.[76] In the early and mid-eighteenth century, schools, especially those run by the Society, functioned as stages from which dramatic and symbolic representations of the authority and legitimacy of the Habsburgs were enacted. In Transylvania, remote and unstable, this function of schools was especially important.

Finally, the Jesuit *collegium* was the training ground of future Jesuits, some of who would pass their careers in the immediate vicinity, as well as others who would range far from Cluj. In addition to the formal curriculum imparted to scholastics, the Jesuit community was where the mores and culture of the Society were learned. As a representative scholastic, we might consider Paulus Sándor, a native of Komárom on the Danube in western Hungary, who entered the Society in Trenčin at the age of 19 and taught lower-level courses in Cluj in 1743. These assignments would have put him in contact with both the youngest students in the community and the senior Jesuits who would have directed his teaching and further formation.[77] Sándor's daily life within the Jesuit community of Cluj and his participation in the public rituals and private devotions and exercises that were the core of Jesuit experience would have continually shaped his identity as he completed his formation. While there is no record of a specific mentoring relationship between Sándor and older Jesuits, the continuity in the curriculum offered in the lower grades made it likely that the younger teacher drew upon the experiences of older teachers in his community. Jesuits identified and promoted those young men that they felt would continue the mission and values of the Society. Breeding and moral character figured prominently, along with academic expectations, in the acceptance of prospective Jesuits.[78]

---

[75] *Gratii officium Stehpano Bathorio Serenissimo Poloniae Regi ... oblatum a rhetoribus Claudiopolitanis anno 1725...* . Cited in Sommervogel et al., *Bibliothèque*, vol. 3, p. 107.

[76] James Van Horn Melton, *Absolutism and the Eighteenth Century Origins of Public Schooling in Prussia and Austria*. (New York, 1988).

[77] ARSI, *Aust. 90, Catal. I Coll. Claud.1743*, folio 66.

[78] The *examina* of two candidates seeking admission to the Society in 1769 include references to their financial condition, and confirm that the candidates are "legitimo thoronatus," that is, that they were not bastards. PFK, A/2. 1–64 (no. 45), folios 161r, 162v. *Examina* for candidates seeking admission to the Society are also preserved in the records of the Ungvár *collegium*: MOL, *Jesuitica*, E152, Coll. Ungv. 1., folio 113r.

The Cluj complex also served as a place where *coadjutors temporales* gained training and experience that they might carry on to other settings, and pass on to younger men as well. At its best, the community of Jesuits in Cluj constituted a self-perpetuating learning environment, one that combined some of the characteristics of the medieval monastic community with the apostolic goals unique to the Society, as well as responses to the special demands of operating in a remote and unstable environment. The greatest challenge to the success of such an undertaking was the environment in which the Jesuit schools had to operate. Transylvania, subdued by Habsburg arms, did not cease to be a restive region where loyalties and self-identification remained complex and divided. The local aristocracy, the traditional place where Jesuit educators would look to find support for their undertakings, was never entirely supportive of the Society's program, for while Catholicism made many significant inroads into the highest levels of the nobility, a core of Transylvanian aristocrats remained true to Calvinism despite constant pressure to convert. Calvinist colleges, such as the famed school in Miskolc, were forced to close or restrict their enrollment, but the literary legacy of these schools was not forgotten.[79] The Cluj region, and Transylvania generally, remained less than wholly receptive to the Society's efforts to convert and bring about ecclesiastical union with Rome, and the obstacles that slowed the progress of these undertakings drew resources away from Jesuit schools. The tensions that characterized the struggle to advance the Uniate Church may have had echoes in the classrooms of Jesuit schools as well.

A Home for Scholars

Virtually every Jesuit community in pre-Suppression Europe had some members who represented the literary aims of the Society. The mobility of individual Jesuits meant that such individuals might not remain members of the community for long, but this mobility also ensured the introduction of new ideas to even fairly small and remote Jesuit outposts. The Jesuit commitment to the exact sciences had been established in the first decades of the Society's existence. Although neither the *Constitutions* nor the *Ratio* mandated that Jesuits engage in investigations of the physical world, the intellectual reputation fostered by Jesuit schools and the accomplishments of a small group of outstanding Jesuit scholars and scientists early on set the stage for the vigorous activities of Jesuit scientists of the seventeenth century. In the first century of their existence, Jesuits focused on "Aristotelian philosophy and science" in a manner that was completely intertwined.[80] The career of Athanasius Kircher, while it somewhat exaggerates the way in which Jesuit science and pseudo-science mixed in

---

[79] The Calvinist *collegium* in Debrecen survived the entire period of Jesuit domination in Hungary, thereby offering one of the few alternatives to the *Ratio*-driven curriculum. *Methodus quam in Collegio Reformatorum Helveticae Confessionis Debrecensi, Omnes Scholas Inferiores Docentes ...* (Debreceni, 1770).

[80] O'Malley, *Jesuits*, p. 226.

the seventeenth century, is nevertheless provides a useful glimpse of the intellectual climate of the Society at the time of its return to Cluj.[81]

The Cluj *collegium* never claimed to be a major center of scientific research, located as it was miles from major population centers in a region repeatedly harassed by war and plague. Occasionally an academic thesis would reflect interest in natural science, but the studies undertaken appear to have been neither innovative nor influential. In comparison to scientific work undertaken and published in Trnava, the "Magyar Athens," the output of the Cluj community and its press was inevitably modest.[82] Its resources spread thinly in the fields of missionary work, teaching, book publishing, and *cura personalis*, the Jesuit community could devote only a modest amount of money to purely scientific undertakings, and in any case only a handful of the Jesuit teachers had any aptitude or training in the sciences. Despite these handicaps, the Cluj community could claim two outstanding scientific personalities in the eighteenth century. Johannes Fridvaldszky has been remembered as a pioneer in agronomy and geology who dabbled in Roman antiquities.[83] Fridvaldszky, a professor of philosophy and mathematics at the Cluj *collegium* and sometime "historian of the house," who had been educated in Vienna, published a dissertation on the presence of iron ore in Transylvania in 1767, one of the first systematic studies on this topic.[84] He was influential in the establishment of a *Societas Agriculturae* and pioneered the idea of three-field crop rotation, an innovation badly needed in Hungary, which suffered famine in 1771.[85] Fridvaldszky also did pioneering research on topinambur, an important crop somewhat like the potato, which had been infested with a parasite.[86] Following the suppression, the former Jesuit produced a work on the "Skupina," a plant found in the region.[87] Like his brethren in Bohemia and elsewhere, Fridvaldszky was comfortable mixing Baroque piety with his scientific and practical studies. Picking up a favorite theme of Hungarian Jesuits, Fridvaldszky

---

[81] For an overview of methods and goals of Kircher, and in particular his *Oedipus Aegypticus*, see Evans, *Making*, pp. 432–40.

[82] Eighteenth-century Trnava was one of the most important centers for the applied sciences east of Berlin. Its press produced optic tables, diagrams of military architecture, works on hydrostatics, astronomy and mechanics. *Universae Matheseos Brevis Institutio Theoretico-Practica ex Operibus PP. Societatis Jesu*. (Tynaviae: Typ. Acad. S. J., 1752).

[83] *Erdély Rövid Története*. Béla Köpeczi ed. (Budapest, 1989), p. 395; Alexius Horányi, *Memoria Hungarorum et Provinciarum scriptis editis notorum*. (3 vols, Viennae, 1775), vol. 1, pp. 721–4.

[84] *Minerologia magnae Principatus Transylvaniae* (Claudiopoli, 1767); Paul Cernovodeanu, "L'histoire universelle dans l'historiographie Roumaine," *Revue Romaine d'Histoire* 10 (1972), p. 61.

[85] Benkő, *Transsilv. Gener. II, Supplemetum* 605, 1; Kosáry, *Müvelödes*, p. 640; Georgius Pray, *Historia Regum Hungairiae* (3 vols, Budae, 1801), vol. 3, p. 587; Alexa Csetri, *Importanţa primei lucrari agromice de specialitate din Transilvania. Studiul inedit al lui Fridvaldksy Dissertatio de agris fimandis et arandis pro M. Principatu Transylvaniae (1771). Studia Universiatis Babes-Bolyai. Series Historica*. Fasc. I (174), seperatum.

[86] *Diccionário Histórico*, vol. 2, p. 1531.

[87] Cited in *Catalogus Bibliothecae Hungariae*. Tom. I Supplementum I A–Z. (Posoni, 1803), p. 96. Interestingly, this post-Suppression work was published by the Calvinist college in Cluj.

published *Reges Ungariae Mariani* in 1775.[88] After the Suppression, Fridvaldszky appears to have continued to teach at the Cluj *collegium*, in the role of professor emeritus, a position that was probably made easier by the pension awarded to him by Maria Theresia for inventing a new way to make paper.[89]

Even better-known than Fridvaldszky was Maximilianus Hell, one of the most distinguished scientists of his day, and easily the most renowned person ever associated with the Jesuit schools of Cluj.[90] Hell was born in 1720 in Hungary and received his formation in Trečin, where he mastered Latin, German and Slovak, and also acquired the ability to compose verse, another characteristic of the Counter-Reformation Jesuit.[91] His most famous achievement was his journey to northern Finland where he observed a transit of Venus and also identified similarities between Finnish and Hungarian.[92] In Cluj, where he worked after 1755, Hell taught mathematics and physics, conducted research on magnetism and electricity, and published a textbook on mathematics.[93] He also erected an observatory, and an anonymous manuscript table of the altitudes of the sun about the horizon surviving in the Cluj Academy is probably his.[94] Hell did little important scientific work during the years he spent in Cluj, but he did publish a textbook for students on the mathematical principles of natural philosophy.[95]

Hell's later career took him to the University of Vienna, where he was Astronomer Royal to Maria Theresia and survived the suppression of the Society with little

---

[88] Kosáry, *Művelődes*, p. 581. The very late date of this work illustrates the persistence of the mixture of Baroque piety and patriotic sentiment in this region.

[89] Sommervogel et al., *Bibliothèque*, vol. 3, pp. 996–7; *Catalogus pers. Prov. Aust. 1773*, p. 8.

[90] The most complete biographical study of Hell is Emil Kisban, "Hell Miska: A Magyar Csillagász," *Publicationes ad Historiam S. J. In Hungaria Illustrandum* 27 (1942), pp. 5–20. See also L. Koch, *Jesuitenlexikon* (Paderborn, 1934), pp. 786–7; Karl A.F. Fischer, "Jesuiten-Mathematiker in der deutschen Assistenz," *AHSI* 47 (1978), p. 170; Sommervogel et al., *Bibliothèque*, vol. 4, pp. 237–58.

[91] *A Magyar irodalom történet*; Sommervogel et al., *Bibliothèque*, vol. 4, pp. 237–58. Sőtér István (chief ed.), vol. 2. *A Magyar irodalom története 1600-tól 1772-ig*, ed. Tibor Klaniczay (Budapest, 1964), p. 579.

[92] A rare portrait of Hell conducting his research in winter dress is found in *Magyar művelődés történet. barokk és felvilágosodás* ([Budapest?], 1940[?]), p. 371.

[93] ARSI, *Aust. 209, An. Prov. Aust. 1752*, folio 4v; *Elementa Arthmeticae numericae et literalis*, (Claudiopoli, 1725), ed. Szinnyei (ed.), *Magyar írók*, pp. 4, 659–63.

[94] *Cesta Maximiliána Hella do Vardo pri Laponsku a jeho pozorovani prechodu Venuše v Roku 1769*. Prologue by Jan Tibenský, František Hattala trans. (Bratislava, 1977); Hell's putative astronomical calculations are housed in the Cluj-Napoca Academy library. *Tabula Altitudinis Solis supra Horizontem ad Elevationem Poli infrascriptus*, BARC-N, MsC 478.

[95] *Elementa mathematica Naturalis Philosophiae Ancillantia*. (Claudiopoli, 1755). Although he only spent five years in Cluj, Nicholas Jánosi (1700–41) also deserves mention here because of the trigonometry text (*Trigonometria plana et spherica cum selectis ex Geometria et Astronomia problematis*) he published there, and the astronomical observations he conducted from his own room in the Jesuit residence. Sommervogel et al., *Bibliothèque*, vol. 4, pp. 740–41; Heinrich László, *Az első kolozsvári csillagda* (Bukarest, 1978), pp. 20–27.

impairment of his research. Ultimately, a lunar crater was named for the Hungarian Jesuit.[96] While Hell's academic and scientific accomplishments place him firmly within the Enlightenment, he was also a product of the late Counter-Reformation culture of Hungary and one of several Jesuits who became identified with the development of Hungarian national consciousness. Hell gained a sizeable reputation both in his homeland and beyond as a scholar who had furthered understanding of Hungarian linguistics.[97] Yet the Jesuit teacher retained a Counter-Reformation view of confessional differences. In a letter written by Hell after the Suppression, he reveals his contempt for Protestant education, calling Protestant universities "pseudo-universities" that "corrupt students' minds."[98]

The scholarly community in Cluj, such as it was, cannot be considered separately from the wider Jesuit culture. In one sense, men such as Hell and Fridvaldszky were very isolated, and in Hell's case, the time spent in Transylvania may seem to us today like a interruption in otherwise productive careers. Yet the scientific culture of the Society was underpinned by researchers operating in far more remote outposts than Cluj, and the resources needed to conduct experiments in the eighteenth century were modest in comparison to what would be required a century later.

Jesuit Schooling in an Urban Context

Michael Buckley has offered three general categories for grouping the Jesuit undertakings in the years before the Suppression: colleges, missions and the urban churches.[99] The Society left a distinctive mark on each of these, although from the standpoint of what has been left behind materially, perhaps the urban churches were perhaps the most distinctively "Jesuit" of the three. The Jesuits of Cluj participated in each of these undertakings, for the churches they occupied within the town walls of Cluj should be viewed as "urban." This is because whether or not the barely one-sixth of a square kilometer that made up Baroque Cluj answers our modern definition of urban, it certainly represented a significant concentration of political power, cultural attainments and ethnic diversity in overwhelmingly rural Transylvania.[100] This urban identity, while placed under the strains of war and plague, stretched back several centuries and was well documented in the family and civic records of

---

[96] Joseph MacDonnell, SJ, *Jesuit geometers: a study of fifty-six prominent Jesuit geometers during the first two centuries of Jesuit history* (St Louis, MO, 1989), p. 76.

[97] Hell's work was cited, for example, in Christian Engel, *Disquititio Critica, Quo in Loco Nunc Adhuc Cognitio Nostra de Hungarorum Origine et Cum Aliis Gentibus Affinitate Postia Sit?* (Viennae, 1791), p. 114.

[98] The autograph letter is pasted between pp. 176 and 177 in the copy of *Diplomata, Bullae, Priviligia Libertates, Immunitates, Constitutiones ...* (Viennae: Typis Joannis Thomae nobilis de Trattnern, MDCCXCI), OSzK, Sign. 405.558, a volume of documents edited by Hell.

[99] Michael Buckley, SJ, "What have we learned," in O'Malley et al. (eds), *Jesuits*, p. 713.

[100] At the end of the eighteenth century Cluj covered 115 ha. This probably did not include built-up land outside the city walls. Mircea Toca, *Cluj Baroc* (Cluj-Napoca, 1983), p. 136.

the community. The crucial location of Cluj in a relatively sparsely settled region threw even the smaller cultural attainments of the community in higher relief. The bookstore operated by the Society before 1773 was, for example, the only one for many miles in all directions: The nearest one to the north was in Lwow, in Poland, and to the east, one would have to journey to Iaşi, in Moldavia to find a bookseller.[101] The content of Jesuit schooling offered in Cluj was also ambitious and distinctive; born in an urban environment, it retained this flavor even as its teachers periodically served in rural missions. Even in comparison with the thorough education available in Calvinist schools, the instruction in Hebrew, in addition to the more common Latin and Greek, set the Jesuit *collegium* apart.[102] The Jesuits unabashedly set out to present a curriculum whose aesthetic paralleled the Society's accomplishments in the material realm and whose intent was to reshape the societal values, in part through the displays its schools staged, which were of course best suited for production in a town where an audience could be readily assembled. The pursuit of these goals was also easier in an urban setting, even when the "city" involved was as small as Cluj, because of the influences the Society could bring to bear in a self-contained community where Jesuits might bring home their messages to townspeople in a variety of contexts, such as sodalities, processions and architecture. The Jesuits did not always find themselves in an urban environment, but they often transformed the setting in which they worked into one which possessed the essential characteristics of a city. In the case of Cluj, a total transformation was not necessary, for the rudiments of a urban setting were already present. And, as we shall see in Chapter Five, the Society expended considerable effort in refashioning the townscape of Cluj into something closely resembling many Habsburg urban centers. Yet before the physical transformation was undertaken, the Jesuits had worked to promote an intellectual climate in which an urban mission might flourish.

As we have seen, not all the cultural achievements of the community were linked to Jesuit activities and the Calvinist, Lutheran and Unitarian communities continued throughout the eighteenth century to produce books whose titles have found their way into bibliographies of Hungarian literature of the period. A "Demonstratio quadratura circuli" was published in Cluj in 1767, the work of Enyedi Benedek Samuel, a professor at the Evangelical *collegium*.[103] Cluj's Protestant population continued to have an influence on Hungarian Protestant literature well into the eighteenth century and beyond. Cluj did not become an exclusively Catholic community, nor did the surrounding countryside abandon the other confessional influences that had existed there for centuries. The reemergence of non-Catholic educational institutions and attitudes throughout Transylvania in the nineteenth century suggests how deeply rooted these traditions were. The entire time the Society labored in Cluj, the power

---

[101] Paul Robert Magocsi, *Historical Atlas of East Central Europe*. (Seattle, WA/London, 1993), p. 54.

[102] *Forma et Ratio Gubernandi Academiae et Studia Generalia in Provincia Austria*, PFK, 119, A.2/1–64 (no. 43), folio 115v.

[103] Alexius Horányi, *Memoria Hungarorum et Provincialium scriptis editis notorum* (3 vols, Viennae, 1775), vol. 1, pp. 620–24; Szinnyei (ed.), *Magyar irók*, vol. 2, p. 1335.

of these older forces was always to be felt, if less openly expressed than were the Jesuits' performances.

Yet despite the persistence of other traditions, for the majority of the eighteenth century, the outstanding feature of intellectual life in the Cluj community was the range of undertakings of the Society and the energy with which these undertakings were promoted. The Jesuit schools, which drew in students from all of the various confessional groups, had arguably the greatest influence on the burghers of Cluj. While lectures and lessons that formed the core of the educational experience in the *convictus*, the *collegium* and the *seminarium pauperum* have not survived, thanks to the Jesuit commitment to consistency in its curriculum and mode of delivery, it is possible to reconstruct important elements of the academic parts of education provided by the Society in Cluj. This curriculum, expounded in the *Ratio*, reveals an emphasis in Classical languages, and a highly hierarchical plan of studies that culminates in theology, which was also conducted in Latin.[104] The struggles reported at the *seminarium pauperum* give some hint of the discipline employed in the transmission of this content. Yet it would be misleading to describe the educational experience provided by the Society solely in terms of the curriculum or the mechanics of instruction, as the Jesuit teachers were enjoined in the *Ratio* to infuse their teaching with the spiritual, for, while only a half an hour each week was devoted to the explanation of doctrine, the personal example of the instructor and admonitions that presumably were interwoven through lectures, recitations and competitions that were the hallmark of the Jesuit educational program. The nature of the religious experiences of the Jesuits themselves and those of the people to whom they ministered and instructed remain more elusive than the specifics of curriculum and the guidelines prescribed for instruction. The Jesuit mission to bring souls to God was never intentionally compromised by the Society, but the means by which this might be accomplished took a multitude of forms in the pre-Suppression Society. The *Literae annuae* and the official history of the Cluj community, compiled by various hands, of course stress the sheer number of conversions achieved and the dramatic and miraculous, presenting only the Jesuit perspective on these events.[105] By contrast, although the *Spiritual exercises* do not receive much attention in the *Literae*, they were an essential feature of the Society's *cura animarum* and were offered in German in Cluj as early as 1722.[106] The impact of the *Exercises*, in

---

[104] The actual ability of students (and in some cases priests) to use Latin actively is one of the many unresolved questions related to Jesuit education in the Habsburg lands of the eighteenth century. One commentator, writing not long after the fact, has asserted that "the fathers were satisfied if their students could speak Neo-Latin with grammatical accuracy and prosaic clarity." I.A. Fessler, *Die Geschichte der Ungarn und ihren Landsassen* (10 vols, Leipzig, 1814–25), vol. 10, p. 391. Other writers refer to the "Hussar Latin" and "kitchen Latin" used by the graduates of schools throughout the Hungarian-speaking regions.

[105] Trevor Johnson, "Blood, tears, and Xavier-water: Jesuit missionaries and popular religion in the eighteenth century upper Palatinate," in Bob Scribner and Trevor Johnson eds, *Popular Religion in Germany and Central Europe 1400–1800* (Basingstoke, 1996), pp. 183–202.

[106] *Exercitum oder geistlichen Übungen des H. Vatter Ignatius*. Anno 1722. BARC-N, MsC 405.

contrast to the dramatic and public missions conducted by the Society, was that of a private and individual experience, and their role in the lives of the students taught by the Jesuits is extremely difficult to assess. However, given their central role in the mission of the Society from its earliest days, and considering how the *Exercises* often provided the vocabulary with which Jesuits described other experiences, a few general remarks on the intent and organization of this document are not out of order.

The experience of the *Exercises* is the single most distinctive element of Jesuit spirituality, one that helps defines all aspects of Jesuit identity, while at the same time remaining a document inviting the participation of non-Jesuits.[107] Differing from other devotional practices popular during the Baroque period, the *Exercises* make special demands upon the imagination of the participants, who must spend many days progressing through the sequence of encounters. Scenes from the life and Passion of Christ form the centerpiece of the *Exercises*, where concrete images are combined with calls upon the excertant to examine his or her own conscience and undertake a journey in which the Passion of Christ is followed by the building intensity of settings presented to the excertant for reflection. These culminate in the image of a combat between the forces of Christ "The King" and those of His archrival. The tone of the *Exercises* at first glance may seem completely at odds with the patient rationality and accumulated skill building that permeates the *Ratio*, but the relationship between the two documents is more complex than a balance between opposites. Both the *Ratio* and the *Exercises* set the Society apart from its rivals and competitors in the fields of missionary work and education, in large part because of the emphasis on individual experience and initiative that places apostolic work at the center of any outward expression of Jesuit spirituality. While commentators have noted the emphasis in the articulation of this spirituality on a "magnanimous docility on the part of all," the importance of direct experience, imagination and action in the carrying-out of the mission of the Society in all its facets is equally clear.[108] The God of Ignatius is frequently denominated "Creator," and this attention to Creation (with all the potentiality for innovation it implies) informed the practical application of the experience of the *Exercises*. Self-conscious Creation was also part of the process carried forward from the *Ratio* that resulted in the production of plays and poetic performances.

But we cannot credit the *Ratio* by itself with providing the impetus for creativity and innovation, for an equally important component was the circumstances in which individual Jesuits found themselves. In contrast with the reflective and imaginative journey completed by those undertaking the *Exercises* under the guidance of a spiritual director, the educational training prescribed in the *Ratio* did not stress tutorials or private instruction, and instead focused on competitions, examinations and performances conducted openly in the classroom or even before the public. Each of these activities was prescribed in the *Ratio*, which is to say that they were non-negotiable elements of the schools of the Society. By the beginning of the eighteenth

---

[107] Joseph Tetlow, *Ignatius Loyola: Spiritual Exercises* (New York, 1992).
[108] J. Lewis, "Ignatian spirituality," *The New Catholic Encyclopedia*, vol. 7 (New York: McGraw Hill, 1967), vol. 7, pp. 349–51.

century the *Ratio*, once an innovative educational blueprint, had become, at least for the high levels of administration within the Society, "an untouchable document" whose basic premises were not to be revised, even while the practical application of its curriculum underwent revision.[109] At the same time, the topics of public academic defenses show a willingness to address the special circumstances in which a Jesuit school had to function. The answer to this seeming contradiction lies with the long-standing tendency of the Society to allow priests, especially those engaged in missionary projects in remote settings, considerable leeway in determining how to implement the goals of the *Constitutions*, which preceded the *Ratio* in age and importance. While the sheer distance of central Transylvania from the administrative heart of the Austrian Province obviously contributed to the climate that allowed such individual and community initiative, the image of Transylvania as a region requiring first of all missionary work also contributed to this climate. Initiative and innovation, albeit pursued within the boundaries prescribed by the Society, were central to the carrying-out of the Jesuit mission throughout the Habsburg lands. Without men who possessed these capabilities, the Society's mission in Cluj would not have achieved a fraction of the success it did enjoy.

---

[109] John W. Padberg, SJ, "The General Congregations of the Society of Jesus: A brief survey of their history," *Studies in the Spirituality of Jesuits* 6, 1 and 2 (January and March, 1974), p. 32.

CHAPTER FIVE

Jesuitae Fabri:
The Society Constructs a Presence

When the Society arrived in an organized fashion in Cluj in 1693, it found a city that had changed little from the late Middle Ages, one that had been little affected by the transformation of the Principality from sometime Ottoman ally to Habsburg possession.[1] Below the walls of a decaying fortress were hundreds of dwellings stretched along roads leading into the countryside, housing perhaps more than half of the town's population by the middle of the eighteenth century. Many of Cluj's houses, reflecting German influence in their construction, dated from the sixteenth century, before the later influx of Magyars, when the majority of its inhabitants had been Saxons. As with many Transylvanian cities, the Renaissance left little mark on the residential or public architecture of Cluj, and instead, a late medieval aesthetic would persist until the arrival of the Baroque. By the end of the seventeenth century, Cluj was viewed as a Hungarian city.[2] At the beginning of the eighteenth century, a scant few dozen of the residents of Cluj may have been Romanian,[3] a number that did not increase for several decades. About a thousand households were counted both within and beyond the town walls, many living in dwellings centuries old.[4] The town was closely tied to the surrounding countryside. The region around Cluj was not dominated by "magnates," the owners of vast tracts of land, who played a decisive role in the local politics in other Hungarian-speaking territories, although a

---

[1] A mid-eighteenth-century description of Cluj survives in Johann Hubner's *Neu=vermehrtes und verbessertes Reales Staats=Zeitungs und Converations Lexicon* ... (Regenspurg und Wien, 1759), p. 272.

[2] "Plebs adeò facta est Hungara." *Transylvania epistolica sev Historia Transylvaniae Epistolico-historicae narrata, per histrophanum anagnosten R. B. [Rudophum Bzenszky] S.J. in castrenisbus hybernis collecta anno Christi M. D. C.LXXXXVI* ... PFK 118.A.6. 697, folio 45v.

[3] In 1733, ten families were Uniate and presumably Romanian; in 1762, there were seventeen Orthodox and six Uniate families. These numbers increased to 93 and 293 by 1785. Ştefan Meteş, *Domni şi Boieri din Ţările Românii in Oraşul Cluj şi Românii din Cluj* (Cluj, 1935), pp. 22–3.

[4] Ernő Deák, "Ethnisch-nationale Probleme in den königlichen Freistädten," in *Städtisches Alltagsleben in Mitteleuropa vom Mittelalter zum Ende des 19. Jahrhunderts*, Viliam Cicaj and Othmar Pickl (eds) (Bratislava, 1998), p. 120. Perhaps seven thousand people lived in Cluj during the first half of the eighteenth century. Pataki István, Páter Pál and Füzeri György, *Descriptio Civitatis Claudiopolis ab origine repetita* ... OSzK, Fol. Latin 1208, pp. 22ff.

sizable urban nobility lived within the city walls.[5] Guilds, many of them consisting of German speakers, dominated the commercial life of the community and continued to be a visible element of the town into the eighteenth century.[6] This German influence also manifested itself throughout the seventeenth century through the presence of a small but literate Pietist community whose roots lay to the north and west.[7] In the 1660s, the "Polish Brethren," a Unitarian sect with connections to the seventeenth-century Socinian movement, had gained the right to settle in Cluj and resisted Magyarization for several generations.[8] Cluj was in its way a small metropolis: in the late medieval period, it had been the seat of an archbishop and in the middle of the seventeenth century it was both the home of the *Plebeanus* or superintendent of the Unitarian Church in the region and had hosted the Diet of the Principality, a role it would regain in the eighteenth.[9] Briefly, Cluj would also be the seat of the Catholic bishop of Transylvania, Joannes Antalffi.[10] The town's Calvinist academy had been home to several prominent scholars, including Apáczai Csere János (1625–60), who had debated an Anglican divine and was a widely published polemicist.[11] Its importance was enhanced by the fact that the eastern reaches of the Habsburg domains were lacking in sizable urban centers, a pattern that continued beyond the boundaries of Transylvania into the lands controlled by Russia and Turkey.[12] Thus, one might say that partially by default Cluj found itself cast in the role of a key urban center in overwhelmingly rural Transylvania. The most prominent landmark in the central and oldest section of the city or the *ováros* was the Church of St. Michael, which was quickly awarded to the Jesuits after it was taken away from the Unitarians

---

[5] Rebecca Gates-Coon, *The Landed Estates of the Esterházy Princes: Hungary during the Reforms of Maria Theresia and Joseph II* (Baltimore, MD, 1994).

[6] Fritz Valjavec, *Geschichte der deutschen Kulturbeziehungen zu Südosteuropa. III Aufklärung und Absolutismus* (München, 1958), pp. 350–51; Rajka Géza, *Kolozsvári Szabó Céh Története* (Kolozsvár, 1913).

[7] As early as 1670, a Pietist tract was published in Cluj. Szent-Iványi Béla, *A pietizmus* (Budapest, 1936) p. 24. R. Po-Chia Hsia, *Social Discipline in the Reformation: Central Europe 1550–1750* (New York, 1989), p. 176. Jesuits were combating Pietist influences in Cluj in 1722, when a local resident returned from travels in Germany where he had picked up the "contagion" of Halle. ARSI, *Aust. 179, An. Prov. Aust. 1722*, folio 11v. These problems were endemic throughout the eastern regions of the Austrian Province: in 1728, a "biblia Hallentia," originating from the center of Pietist influence, Halle, was seized in Buda. ARSI, *Aust. 185, An. Prov. Aust. 1728*, folio 14v.

[8] Janusz Tazbir, "Les Frères polonais en Transilvanie," *Revue Roumaine d'Histoire* 8, 3 (1969), pp. 699–700.

[9] Cluj would not regain its status as an archiepiscopal city again until 1853, after the abortive Hungarian reution. Jedin et al., *Atlas d'histoire de l'Église*, p. 44. Chistopher Sandius, *Nucleus historiae ecclesiasticae exhibitus in historia Arianorum* (Coloniae, 1676) 431; Stephen Bela Vardy, *Historical dictionary of Hungary (European historical dictionaries, no. 18)* (Lanham, MD/London, 1997), p. 431.

[10] PFK, 118.E.41, Jesuitica documenta, folio 121r.

[11] Frederick Riedl, *A History of Hungarian Literature*, trans. C. Arthur Givener and Ilona de Gjöry Givener (London, 1906), pp. 55–6.

[12] All the large cities of the Habsburg realms were located in the west. Paul Münch, *Lebensformen in der frühen Neuzeit* (Frankfurt am Main/Berlin, 1992), p. 50.

by the civil government.[13] Located in the market square, the towerless, tile-roofed structure was by far the largest building for many miles around. Within its rather dark and austere gothic interior, long stripped of Catholic imagery by the Unitarians, the Jesuits began to hold services within a year of their arrival.[14] But the Society desired a building of its own, wishing, as it did in many other communities in which it pushed forward recatholicization, to set its own stamp on the environment in which its priests would celebrate mass, preach and teach. The Jesuits would continue to use the old church for public displays of their relationship to the Habsburgs, as in 1711 when a temporary funerary monument or "castra dolorum" for the recently deceased Joseph I was erected in St. Michael's replete with emblematic configurations typical of Jesuit visual education in the high Baroque.[15] Such a response to a new setting was typical of the Society in its Baroque phase, where older landmarks were incorporated into revised visual schemata that stressed the sacramental and triumphalist aspects of the Jesuit mission. In Cluj, as in so many other communities where the Society established itself, existing institutions and resources were viewed not merely as a problem to be overcome, but rather as resources to serve the new agenda.

Architecture has been described as "a special preoccupation" of the pre-Suppression Society, perhaps because as an art form it has a permanently public aspect, and because when it is put to work in an ecclesiastical role, it can serve as a bridge between the internal world and the external, sensual world, both of which were of concern to the Jesuits.[16] The Baroque building can also be seen as a larger than life "book" wherein the basic doctrinal messages of Catholicism are written in the imagery and overall composition of the structure; as producers and elucidators of books the Jesuits would have turned to an architectural metaphor for the exposition of the mysteries of the Church.[17] The small scale of Cluj made these changes not only more readily apparent, but also more potent; relatively little modification of such a miniature urban landscape was required to change the relationships between elements and to imprint the message of the Society's arrival and dominance in the area. Spiritual and more worldly lessons were bound up in the elevation of saints

---

[13] Sas, *Szent Mihály templom*, p. 38. Murdock, *Calvinism*, p. 126 says the Unitarians were ousted from St. Michael's in 1716, but this late date would imply that the Jesuits could only make use of temporary quarters elsewhere, a supposition not borne out by the records kept by the Society. The seizure of St. Michael's did not mean the Unitarians had lost a recognized place of worship.

[14] The Jesuit Rudolphus Bzenszky reports that Jesuits were using the church in 1693. Sas, *Szent Mihály templom*, p. 38. It is also likely that the Jesuits brought art from Vienna that was displayed in St. Michael's. *Op. cit.*, p. 40.

[15] OSzK, 2039 FMI/1608 *Historia anno 1711*, p. 108.

[16] Clement J. McNaspy, "Art in Jesuit life," in *Studies in the Spirituality of Jesuits* 5, 3 (April, 1973), p. 95.

[17] One of many examples of this use of the space within a Jesuit building to convey doctrinal messages in symbolic or emblematic forms occurred in 1713 during the funeral for the aristocrat Gabriel Josika: "cum dictis accesseri apparatus symbolico-funebris ex gentilitis defunctis Baronis signis desumptus ..." ARSI, *Aust. 170, An. Prov. Aust. 1713*, folio 17r. The writer acknowledges the East-West Seminar, Berlin, 1997 as the source of this idea.

venerated by the Society, and by the overlaying of Calvinist or Unitarian simplicity with the exuberance of the Baroque.

A short distance from St. Michael's, near the intersection of Torda, Farkas, and Fogoly streets, and close to a Calvinist church that had long been established in the town, the fathers selected a site for their own church, one that was eventually to be surrounded by their schools, to form a complex of structures serving educational, religious and secular purposes, and, not accidentally, establishing the presence of the Society in the community in a distinctive "Jesuit district," a strategy undertaken in other Habsburg cities where the Society worked.[18] While the details of acquiring the property and erecting the buildings were worked out, the Society occupied a site to the north-east that already included a church and living quarters.[19] As early as 1697, they had found space for a printing press as well.[20] Later, after the core complex of buildings was begun, the Society purchased additional properties, both in the vicinity of the Jesuit schools and elsewhere.[21] Thus the Society's presence in Cluj was both focused around its architectural complex and scattered through other neighborhoods. Merely in terms of real estate, it was not possible in eighteenth-century Cluj to ignore the Jesuit presence.

The building of the Jesuit church of Cluj, said to be the first authentically Baroque building completed in Transylvania, would take many years, commencing in 1703 with the arrival of stones from the old Jesuit residence site in Mănăştur, a property that they were also able to repossess.[22] In the meantime, the Jesuits made do with the medieval facilities provided to them when they arrived, and probably made partial use of the unfinished church.[23] The construction of the "Jesuit Church" always

---

[18] Among the many instances of this approach to urban architectural organization Wrocław (Breslau) affords one of the most outstanding examples, with its impressive set of Baroque buildings facing the Odra River. Carsten Rabe, *Alma Mater Leopoldiana: Kolleg und Universität der Jesuiten in Breslau* (Köln, 1999). I am indebted to Michael Yonan for calling attention to the notion of the Jesuit "district."

[19] The core of this site has been a disused Dominican (later Franciscan) monastery. Bíró, "Egyetem," p. 10.

[20] Alexius Horányi, *Memoria Hungarorum et Provincialium scriptis editis notorum*. 3 vols. (Viennae, 1775), vol. 2, p. 91.

[21] Two houses were purchased in 1715 "in usum nostrorum instructiae," and in 1720 two more houses were obtained and a third "à convictu ad cujus fundum sub tenore scholae aedificatur." ARSI, *Aust. 172, An. Prov. Aust. 1715*, p. 91; *Aust. 177, An. Prov. Aust. 1720*, p. 113.

[22] This property was occupied by the Jesuits by 1704, when diarist Czegei Wass György reported that he dined with them there. MTA, Kéz. 705, Néhai tekentetes Czegei György, 1704–1705, p. 94.

[23] Although there is evidence that the Franciscan church was occupied by the Jesuits early on, other documentation indicates that the building was formally handed over on 18 December 1727, to the Jesuits but was later returned to the Franciscans, who redid it in the Baroque style and continue to occupy it today. However, classes in the Jesuit academy continued to be offered in the Franciscan buildings at least as late as 1729. Sas, *Ferences templom*, pp. 118, 180–81. The Society found itself making use of a variety of facilities in the reclaimed eastern territories of the Austrian Province; in Pécs (Quinque-Ecclesiáe), Jesuits converted a former mosque into their church. ARSI, *Aust. 170, An. Prov. Aust. 1713*, folio 93r.

remained a major goal of the Society, and the formal commencement of plans to erect it was a major event for the Cluj Jesuit community, and indeed for the entire town.[24] The decision to erect a major edifice was not undertaken at the most auspicious of times; in both 1711 and 1719, plague swept the town, paralyzing all public affairs, as it would several more times in the century.[25] Political upheavals brought on a critical shortage of food in 1717, the Rákóczi (kuruc) uprising and subsequent siege provided further distractions, as did fire that swept the town several times in the first years of the century.[26] The steady, if occasionally interrupted, progress of the new Jesuit church and other buildings surrounding it stood in contrast to the minimal building activity that took place elsewhere in the town, reinforcing the message that the Society intended to bring about a permanent transformation in the community, despite the current hardships or the limitations on construction faced by others. The Jesuit presence also served to tip the mix between east and west that existed in Cluj, with regard to social organization and political orientation, decisively to the west. "West" in this instance meaning the upper Danube territories of the Habsburgs and specifically the culture that had developed around Vienna.

The architect of the Jesuit church in Cluj is unknown, although the roots of its style are easily traced and the involvement of a German master builder named Konrad Hammer, who erected a basilica in Tîrgu Mureş, is probable.[27] This link to the west was strengthened by four Austrian craftsmen previously employed in Hungary who

---

[24] Sas, *Piarista templom*, p. 30.

[25] *Istoria Clujul*, ed. Ştefan Pascu (Cluj, 1974), p. 186. Jesuit and civil records throughout Transylvania are filled with references to the plague during these years. A Father Stephanus Endesius is described as having survived the plague three times, only to die from it in 1711. Plague remained a scourge of the community down into the late 1720s, with the city government struggling to control its spread by burning clothing and even houses. Nevertheless, on at least one occasion one-ninth of Cluj's population died of the plague. *Székely Oklevéltár. Csíkvármegye Költségén*, ed. Lajos Szádeczky (8 vols, Kolozsvár, 1898), vol. 7: 1696–1750, pp. 269–71; Cluj, Vár. Levélt., Fasc., no. 686, 23 Dec. 1728. In 1719, classes at the Cluj *collegium*, which then enrolled 331 students, were suspended because of the plague. ARSI, *Austr. 176, An. Prov. Aust. 1719*, p. 137. For the fires that plagued Cluj in 1724 see Aurel Rautiu and Ladislau Gyémánt, *Reportoriul Izvoarelor Statistice privind Transilvania 1690–1847* (Bucureşti: Editura Univers Enciclopedic, 1995), p. 89. Fires struck the Jesuit complex as well: in 1722, 200 florins worth of damage was done to the *convictus*. OSzK, 2039/ FMI/1608 *Historia anno 1722*, p. 261. A second wave of plague visited Cluj in September 1738, lasting into the new year. The majority of the population fled the city at this time. The "serpente ... per provinicam lue" that struck the region in 1756 may have been yet another recurrence of the plague. ARSI, *Aust. 213, Lit. An. Prov. Aust. 1756*, folio 99v.

[26] "Claudiopoli panis et vini defectus ... dum barbarus Thrax saeviret in Transilvania." ARSI, *Aust 174, An. Prov. Aust. 1717*, p. 76. When Imperial troops recaptured Cluj, they put to death civilians (including women) who were related to soldiers serving with the kuruc forces. Jesuits, including Gabrielus Kapi, were locked in disputes with the town council over tithes and other financial problems during this time of want. Magyari András, "Kolozsvár az 1703–1711 évi habsburgellenes szabadságharc első szakaszában," *Studia Universitatis Babeş-Bolyai*, Series VI. Fasciculus I (1959), pp. 45–56; OSzK, 2039, FMI/1608, *Historia anno 1705*, p. 62; *anno 1706*, p. 66.

[27] Mircea. Toca, *Clujul baroc* (Cluj-Napoca, 1983), p. 29.

were hired to glaze the church's windows.[28] The church and adjacent school and residential buildings closely followed models found throughout the Habsburg lands from the Tyrol eastward in both Jesuit compounds and governmental structures, and have characteristics shared by many parish churches as well as by churches of other Catholic orders. Yet the Jesuit architecture that flourished in Central Europe in the seventeenth and eighteenth centuries was also a reflection of a specific universalist vision of the Society that reached beyond the Habsburg domains. This unifying vision was mirrored in many other aspects of the Jesuit mission and often took on literary forms, starting with the curriculum of the *Ratio Studiorum*, and including the intellectual ambitions of Jesuits such as the seventeenth-century polymath Athanasius Kircher, whose books sought to tie together virtually all branches of knowledge and were "endlessly reprinted or re-edited," as well as the scholarship of eighteenth-century Bohemian Jesuits who sought to bring together diverse categories of knowledge.[29] The building of the Jesuit church in Cluj provided a visible symbol of these ambitions, and called attention to the world-wide character of the Society at the same time that it proclaimed the saving message of the Gospels. By the time the Society began its construction of the Cluj church, the seventeenth-century architectural pattern was already found with regional (and individual) variations in locations as remote as Mexico, the Philippines or Bavaria. Elements of the Jesuit church in Cluj, such as the high façade and the detail work arranged around a symmetrical model, can also be traced to the mother church of the Society in Rome, the Gesù, which had been erected more than a century earlier.[30] The façades of the Gesù and other Jesuit churches, their flat surfaces rising dramatically above open spaces, can be compared to the stage apparatus of Baroque operas that provide an imposing backdrop to the stage action. While these productions served a very different function from that of a church, and often had themes drawn from pagan mythology rather than Christianity, the comparison has validity, since both the stage designer and the architect sought to use the reworked Classical notions of symmetry to produce a dramatic effect. On a more abstract level, the Jesuit willingness to find moral lessons even in pagan mythology provides a further link between a backdrop of a secular opera and the elements of a Jesuit church visible from the street.[31] For just as Classical mythology presented figures in a logical and hierarchized fashion in which a narrative unfolds (which, in the case of an opera, may contain a discernible moral), likewise the façade of a Jesuit church also leads the viewer's eyes upward

---

[28] OSzK, 2039 FMI/1608, *Historia anno 1722*, p. 261.

[29] Nicolette Mout, "Introduction," in Charles W. Ingrao (ed.), *State and Society in Early Modern Austria* (West Lafayette, IN, 1994), p. 90; Paul Shore, "Universalism, rationalism and nationalism among the Jesuits of Bohemia, 1770–1800" in V. Cossy and D. Dawson (eds), *Progrès et violence au xviiie siècle* (Paris, 2001), pp. 71–83.

[30] Aurelio Dionesi, *Il Gesù di Roma: breve storia e illustrazione della prima chiesa eretta dalla Compagnia di Gesù* (Roma, 1982). The standard English-language work on Baroque Jesuit art is *Baroque art: The Jesuit contribution*, Rudolf Witkower and Irna B. Jaffe (eds) (New York, 1972).

[31] Pierre Gaulruche, SJ (1602–82) developed the notion of extracting moral precepts in mythology in his *L'histoire poetique*. Myroslava T. Znayenko, *The gods of the ancient Slavs: Tatischev and the beginnings of Slavic mythology* (Columbus, OH, 1980), pp. 49–50.

towards the "lesson" that is the culminating component of the composition. In the case of the Jesuit church in Cluj, we are led to this "lesson" by way of the two statues of the Jesuit saints Ignatius and Xavier, executed by the Austrian craftsman Johann König, to the Society's monogram containing the three nails of Christ's passion, and visible to passers-by in the adjacent streets and square.

While the façade of the Cluj church owes much to the Gesù, the most immediate and significant ancestors of the church and its surrounding complex are found in Vienna, whose seventeenth-century Jesuitenkirche had already been an important landmark of the inner city for half a century.[32] The identification of the Cluj church with its Viennese precursor is the single most important influence on the former's style. While the Society was aware of local artistic traditions found in Cluj, there was little in the plans for the new church that could be identified with regional traditions, or with the specific artistic idioms of the Saxons, Romanians, Hungarians and others who made up the population of the town. In this respect, all the Society's building projects in Cluj failed to exhibit the often cited "qualified accommodation" between the universals of the Baroque aesthetic and regional elements that has often been identified as a characteristic of the Baroque in the Habsburg lands.[33] Instead, the Jesuit church, like the dress of the Jesuits themselves, functioned as an outpost of the new transnational and Imperial aesthetic, and as an emblem of the new educational ideal and the new political order, one that drew its inspiration from the west and from Vienna (König, like some of the Jesuits of the Cluj community had lived in the capital), and from the south and Rome. A century later, when the Uniate (now Orthodox) church was completed a short distance away, it too would reflect neither the Byzantine roots of Orthodox architecture nor the cool classicism by then reigning in Vienna. Instead, the Baroque aesthetic imported from the upper Danube region by the Jesuits and ultimately associated with them was the idiom in which this late eighteenth-century church was designed. The net visual effect of the Society's presence in Cluj was therefore to make the community look more Austrian, less individual, less identifiably "ethnic," and more rationally organized.[34] Whether intentional or not, the Jesuit transformation of a portion of Cluj also Europeanized the city, thereby drawing a clearer distinction between those regions reclaimed from the infidels and lands still beyond the direct influence of Europe.

The Jesuits' Cluj church was first opened in 1718 and consecrated in 1725. From these beginnings until the Suppression, the Jesuit church would serve as the focal

---

[32] Grigoire Ionesco, *Historie de l'Architecture en Roumanie: De la Préhistoire à nos jours* (Bucurest, 1972), pp. 368, 371. Plans of the Jesuitenkirche appear in *Třicetiletí Valky*, ed. Jan Skutil (Brno, 1995) plate 5. Petr Fidler, "Několik poznámek k fenoménu jezuitské architektury," also in Skutil (ed.), pp. 182–206, contains a helpful set of sources on Jesuit architecture in the Habsburg lands.

[33] For example, see the discussion in Evans, *Making*, pp. 445ff.

[34] It should be noted that "Austria" at this time referred more specifically to the Habsburg dynasty than to a particular geographic region. Austria was a concept whose physical boundaries might change with the needs of the dynasty. Although the Austrian late Baroque has been contrasted with the spare, rationalist style of Joseph II (1780–90), important rationalist elements were always present in the organization of Jesuit residential and scholastic architecture.

point of the Jesuit project in the region and as the most visible symbol of the Society's presence. Spared damage from fire and the ravages of war, the church and the Jesuit structures that grew up around it permanently altered the character of the óváros, changing its external physical appearance as well as creating new focal points for community expressions of piety and social conformity.

The most precious object housed by the Jesuit church was the miraculous image of the Virgin that had been in existence at least since 1699 and dedicated in the Jesuit church on 8 September 1724.[35] The Jesuits commemorated the dedication of the image with a solemn ceremony and a homily preached by Joannes Gyologi, a Jesuit who had taught at the Cluj *collegium*.[36] The "Weeping Maria," purchased with funds donated by the Father Provincial and Baron Haller György and other nobles, and supported with funds from Count Sigismund Kornis, Governor of Transylvania, has remained a highly visible vestige of the Jesuit era in Cluj down to the present day.[37] The creator of this Madonna is unknown, but the style of execution reflects eastern influences and is in fact the single outstanding example of art owned by the Society in Cluj that betrays influences from the surrounding community.[38] This notable exception to the general tendency of the Jesuits of Cluj to retain an "upper Danubian" style shows that the Society could incorporate an Orthodox approach on occasion. The eastern influence on this painting is reinforced by the Slavic inscription running around its frame.[39] As with some icons venerated by the Orthodox Church, the face and hands of the Virgin appear in a lifelike if visually flat rendition, but are entirely surrounded by an embossed silver plate that contrasts dramatically with the fragments of much darker tempera painting imbedded within it. Unlike other examples of Jesuit painting found in the Habsburg lands, where the viewer is drawn by the emotional intensity conveyed in the gestures of the figures, the elaborate symbolism and emblematics, and the touches of detailed realism, the

---

[35] In 1701, the "Thaumaturgic" Madonna was described as having been brought to Cluj from an unspecified Transylvanian location two years earlier, and was already the object of veneration by several ethnic groups, including Bulgarians. OSzK, 2039 FMI/1608 *Historia anno 1701*, pp. 3–4. Andreas Patai, *Historia Thaumaturgae Virginis Claudiopolitanae ...* (Claudiopoli, 1737), pp. 24–125. Patai (+1756) taught philosophy in Cluj. According to one account, the image had been painted by a Ruthenian named Lukács in 1681. Bálint Sándor and Barna Gábor, *Búcsújáró magyarok: A magyarországi búcsújárás története és néprajza* (Budapest, 1994), p. 333.

[36] Author of *Prima JESV Societatis Claudiopolitana* (Claudiopoli, 1715). Sommervogel et al., *Bibliothèque*, vol. 3, p. 1980; Katona, *Historia critica*, vol. 20, p. 56; Sas, *Piarista Templom*, p. 41.

[37] In 1729, Kornis donated 500 florins to the maintenance of the image. MOL, F 234, Erdélyi kinsctári levéltár. Fiscalis levéltár, Szekrény XXV.B., unnumbered folio. The Madonna is mentioned in a MS prepared by Rudloph Bzenszky in about 1701, MTA, *Notata Summaria* Kéz. Történet. 2 132 Sz., p. 323; ARSI, *Autr. 158, An. Lit. Prov. Aust. 1701*, folio 77v.

[38] A.M. Mansi, "Le icone di Maria: Un camino teologico," in C. Giraudo (ed.), *Liturgia e spiritualità nell'Oriente cristiano* (Milano, 1997), pp. 237–47.

[39] Gy. Rózsa, "Thesenblätter mit ungarischen Beziehungen" *Acta Historica Artium Hungaricarum* 33 (1987–88), pp. 282–3.

Weeping Madonna is not easily approached on this human level.[40] Relatively small and static in composition, the Madonna seems to represent a deliberate attempt to incorporate the aesthetic principles of the traditional style of icon composition in the Orthodox Church. Put another way, the means by which the Weeping Madonna was supposed to induce a sense of reverence in her viewers was fundamentally different from the strategies employed in many other Jesuit churches throughout the Habsburg lands, where dramatic lighting and vivid color combine with contorted or flamboyant gesture to create an arresting overall impression. This painting departed from the more common Jesuit model in which the church functioned somewhat as a theatre, with attention focused on the region around the altar, and where freestanding figures functioned almost like actors in a liturgical drama. Although the Cluj church possesses some of the features of this theatrical model, seclusion and relative visual inaccessibility was intended to promote the feeling of individual devotion and private interaction; theatrical poses of larger than life figures, ancillary *putti* and cheerful blue skies form no part of the picture offered. However, the icon also played an important role in public events staged by the Society, even if it may not have been as accessible to viewers as would have been a larger image; in 1710, the Madonna was paraded through the streets of Cluj in an attempt to ward off the plague.[41] The display of the human features of the Virgin is subdued and lacking the "road signs" that guide the pilgrim to a Baroque set-piece. Here the image must be actively sought out to receive the intimate devotion characteristic of the Eastern Rite.[42] The viewer is reminded that Orthodox churches do not have long naves, but instead often place the worshiper closer to the altar, while holy images, frequently small and dark, are typically displayed in a more vertical presentation to worshippers who are in relatively intimate contact with them as they stand during the service.

If the records kept by the Society may be believed, the strategy of creating a Madonna whose appearance was compatible with local artistic traditions was

---

[40] It should be noted that an oil portrait head of the Madonna surrounded by embossed and jewel-encrusted silver or other metals is not entirely restricted to the orthodox tradition. The "Salus populi Romani," executed in Italy in the early seventeenth century and whose face is framed by a plate of silver, bronze and crystal, reflects this style. Museo della Patriacale Basilica di Santa Maria Maggiore, Catalogue no. II 02. While weeping madonnas resemble human beings, their material splendor and connection to the divine sets them apart from human beings exhibiting the same behaviors. For how the miraculous effluences of weeping statues are "pure" in contrast to those of a human body that "defecates, dribbles and devours," see Mikhail Bahktin, *Rabelais and his world*, trans. H.I. Swolsky (Cambridge, 1968), pp. 315–25.

[41] OSzK, 2039 FMI/1608 *Historia anno 1710*, p. 85.

[42] Stephen Bauer, "Shrines, curiosities and the rhetoric of relics," in Lynne Cooke and Peter Woolen (eds), *Visual Display: Culture beyond Appearances* (Seattle, WA, 1995), p. 24. Icons are frequently kissed by the faithful in Orthodox churches. An engraving of the Cluj Madonna appears on the frontispiece of a small book of poems offered to the Virgin by baccalureate recipients: *Secunda deiparae Virginis laudum minuta post laudes Laurentanas* ... per R. P. Antonium Grueber è S. J. (Claudopoli, 1736).

successful.[43] The history of the Society's work in Cluj is filled with accounts of men and women resorting to the image of the Virgin in times of peril, with miraculous results. For example, in 1704 Matthais Bayr, a "Saxon" surgeon, endangered by a runaway horse, was rescued through the intercession of the Madonna.[44] The Jesuits themselves displayed considerable devotion to the image; at least two members of the Cluj Jesuit community published works on the miraculous picture.[45] Devotion to Mary also manifested itself in Marian sodalities among the students of the *collegium* that assembled its own library while the Cluj Jesuits published a book on how to found other such organizations.[46] Yet this devotion to the Virgin, in her weeping form or in other manifestations, could also lead to disputes. The devotees of the Immaculate Virgin and the Holy Trinity at one point became entangled in a rivalry that made its way into the history of the church.[47] While Marian sodalities and other expressions of devotion built unity among Catholics by providing a focus for religious experience, they also provided forums for the airing of disputes already existing in the community.

Of all the images placed in the Jesuit church the image of the "Weeping Madonna" alone calls to mind the Orthodox aesthetic; and may well have an Orthodox origin. Other references to Mary throughout the Jesuit complex are steadfastly in the Central European Baroque tradition. Over the pulpit appears a monogram of Mary, flanked by *putti*, recalling the monograms found in German or Polish churches, a theme repeated on bells cast for the Cluj church that likewise feature supporting *putti*.[48] These and other details point to the employment of other Austrian artisans, who are known to have been active in Cluj during these years.[49] By contrast, ethnic Romanian artists did not avail themselves of elaborate monograms or chronograms, and had not yet begun to use the symbolic or emblematic elements of Renaissance

---

[43] In 1768, a figure of the Virgin in the Kolosmănăştur convent was also reported to shed tears; testimony on this incident was collected from Calvinists as well as Catholics. ANC, Fondul Liceul Romano-catolic, unnumbered dossier, folios 21r–24v.

[44] OSzK, 2039, FMI/1608 *Historia*, folio 61.

[45] For example, Joannes Simeghi, *Genuina de Lacrimosa Virgine Claudiopolitana* (Claudiopoli, 1714).

[46] *Sodalitatum Marianum in Soc. Jesu gymnasiis erectarum summa utilitas ...* (Claudiopoli, 1744). Three congregations existed before 1773, although all three may not have been active at the same time. These were the Congregatio major B.M. Virginis, the Congregatio minor B. M. Virginis, and the Congregatio Agoniae Christi. MOL F477 Erdélyi kinsctári levéltár. Exactoratus Cameralis Inventarium ... No. 30, pp. 182–3.

[47] Sas, *Piarista templom*, p. 42.

[48] The inscriptions on the church's bells and the Maria monogram are reproduced in *Kolozsvár Története előtti világosító rajzai kőre metszette Haske Ferencz* (Budapest, 1888) p. 7. The Maria monogram as a theme in Hungarian religious art intended primarily for laypersons is illustrated in Knapp Éva and Tüskés Gábor, "Barokk társulati kiadványok grafikai ábrázolásai," *Magyar Könyvszemle* 115(1999), p. 11, plate 12.

[49] Geza Entz, "Cluj-Napoca," in Jane Turner (ed.), *The Dictionary of Art*, 34 vols (New York, 1996), vol. 7, pp. 471–2.

or Baroque visual art; their presence, vividly recorded elsewhere in religious art, cannot be detected in the Jesuit church.[50]

The placing of the image of Mary within a Jesuit church whose plan closely follows the model for other churches throughout the Habsburg lands and which was complemented by a classic Habsburg column provides a useful metaphor for the Society's approach to the problem of bringing together local and more universalist traditions in Transylvania. As an organization committed to evangelical work, the Society was prepared to draw upon local artistic and cultural traditions, so that the faithful might experience personal encounters with holy images in their homes, or in the case of the Weeping Madonna, in the quiet and darkness of a church. Yet much as it was willing to work towards contact with individuals with Orthodox cultural backgrounds, the Society was much less inclined to bend in the matter of larger symbols that occupied public spaces and which might figure in the crafting of its corporate and public image. These larger and more visible symbols, like the processions held by Marian sodalities, retained a quality that linked them to the newly arrived sources of authority and legitimacy and which were in every case redolent of and derived from the Habsburg heartlands and from districts of the Empire that were won back early for Catholicism or were never lost in the first place.[51] There is some danger in claiming to understand all the motives for this rigidity or conformity, although the confrontations that Jesuits and their supporters encountered in the first years of their mission may provide part of the answer. The history of the Cluj college records that in 1713 when a Croatian Catholic soldier stationed nearby brawled with his fellows and had his nose cut off, he then found himself charged with blasphemy by the local authorities and had to be rescued by Cluj Jesuits, who as a result no doubt felt the need to demonstrate their legitimacy and authority to a community where their own students might be in danger.[52] Perhaps there was simply a lack of existing local artistic models that could be employed in designing the public buildings and symbols of the Society, or an unwillingness to invest time and effort in creating a more individualistic plan for the Cluj church. Or perhaps the Hungarian Jesuits who made up a significant portion of the contingent sent to Cluj favored a style already familiar to them from years spent in Trnava and points east.[53] Whatever the reason, the permanent result of the choice made by the Society was to confirm its relationship with those artistic trends originating or mediated through Vienna. The political power now emanating from the Imperial capital provided an additional reason to emulate its architecture. If Vienna was the "new Rome," then Cluj could serve as an important outpost of Imperial civilization,

---

[50] For example, the "Nașterea lui Isus," an eighteenth-century painting by an unknown artist, in Muzeul National de Artă, Cluj.

[51] In 1713, one such procession had as its destination St. Michael's. ARSI, *Aust. 170, An. Prov. Aust. 1713*, folio 106v.

[52] ARSI, *Aust. 170 An. Prov Aust. 1713*, folio 33r. Armed horsemen wounded several students in a fight in 1702. OSzK, 2039 FMI/1608 *Historia*, folio 34.

[53] Johann Kapossy, "Die Stellung des ungarländischen Barock in der europäischer Kunstentwicklung," *Ungarische Jahrbücher* 1 (1931), pp. 49–50; Balázs Dercsény, Hegyi Gábor, Marosi Ernő and Török József, *Katolikus templomok Magyarországon*. (Budapest, 1991), pp. 18, 42, 93, 110, 181, 189, 201, 249 *et passim*.

thereby recalling the relationship of the ancient province of Dacia to the original Rome.[54] These trends would play a dominant role in the architectural development of Cluj for the next two centuries, long after the Society had departed.

The first resting place for the deceased of the Jesuit community was located somewhere in the óváros, perhaps adjacent to St. Michael's.[55] Shortly after the completion of the Jesuit church the crypt that had been constructed under it was opened to hold the tombs of both Jesuits and other prominent members of Cluj's Catholic community. Unlike the more public structures created in the first years of the Society's organized presence in Cluj, part of whose purpose was to establish the image of the Jesuits and the Habsburgs in opposition to some of the existing local sources of power and prestige, the crypt documents relationships within the Society, and in some instances, between notable laypersons and the Jesuits. Among the laypersons entombed in the crypt is an inspector of salt mines named Christopher Prezner, who died on 6 September 1725.[56] The presence of Prezner's tomb among those of many Jesuit fathers (but, significantly, no *coadjutores temporales*) may point to his role as major contributor to the Society's undertakings; his position as a government bureaucrat may also have helped make him significant enough to be buried with the Jesuits. (The salt mines of the region, like the iron mines, were a state monopoly with direct ties to the government in Vienna.[57]) A few other non-Jesuits appear to have been buried in the crypt, which was later used to house the remains of the Piarists who took over the church after 1773. Among these are two noblemen: Sigismundus de Felvinczi de Harasztos, whose body was moved to the Jesuit church almost twenty years after his death, and Georgius Napolyi de Félőr, whose body was also moved to the church long after his death.[58] The inscriptions on a number of Jesuit tombs are still visible, including that of the rector of the community, Antonius Mindszenti, who died 15 April 1732.[59] Above ground, there are fewer indications of the Jesuits' relations with the aristocracy. In the nave of the Jesuit church, in plain view of all visitors, only one prominent layperson was buried. Stephanus Apor (Apor István), Count of Apor, a major benefactor of the Society and of educational projects that furthered Catholic influence, was one of a handful of Transylvanian aristocracy that had benefited immediately from the advance of the Habsburgs.[60] A Catholic in an aristocracy dominated by Calvinists, Apor had been made a baron

---

[54] "Dacia Felix" is still a cultural reference point in modern-day Romanian Transylvania, whether figuring in the name of a locally produced automobile or a bank.

[55] OSzK, 2039 FMI/1608 *Historia anno 1723*, p. 262.

[56] M: D: Christoph: Prezner Inspector Salis Fodin: Defunct: 6. September 1725.

[57] Á.R. Várkonyi, "Historical personalities, crisis and progress in 17th century Hungary," *AHASH* 71 (1970), p. 290.

[58] S: D. Sigismundus Felvinczi de Harasztos defunt: 1706 / Huc trans: 7 Juni 1725; S.D. Georgius Napolyi de Félő ... defunct: 2 Maij 1714/Huc translat: 7 Junij 1725.

[59] R. P. Rector Antonius Mindszenti Hunc Tyrnavinesis obiit 15 Apris anno 1736 Ætatis 49.

[60] Apor's financial support of Jesuit schools is documented in Weiser, *Iskolaügy*, p. 72; Apor also supported orphans and paid for the education of four impoverished noble children in Cluj. Bakk Endre Szentkatolnai, *A Bak és Jancsó család* (Budapest, 1883), p. 223. See also *Altojai gróf Apor István* (Cluj, 1935).

as recently as 1693, and was elevated to the rank of count in 1696.[61] In addition to later becoming a major benefactor of the Jesuit *seminarium*, Apor demonstrated his support of the Society by offering a prize for the best play produced by Jesuit students in 1693, immediately after the return of the fathers.[62] One year after Apor died in Naples in 1724, his body was returned to Cluj where the first important funerary monument of the Jesuit church recalls the count's financial support of Jesuit schools and his devotion to the Catholic faith. His nephew Apor Péter, a graduate of the Jesuit academy, would make a major contribution to Hungarian literature, with his memoirs known as *Metamorphoses Transylvaniae*.

Baroque churches, even ones much more modest in their conception than the Jesuit Church of Cluj, were often set off whenever possible by a square whose centerpiece was a monument whose ornamentation would complement the details of the façade of the church, as well as reinforcing its ideological and theological message. When the urban space available was cramped, as in the case of the Jesuitenkirche in Vienna, the façade would strive to accommodate the limited range of vision by modifying proportions and details, a situation similar to what the Jesuits of Cluj faced when building their own church. Other symbols might also be brought into play to establish further the Jesuit presence within the urban space. In Cluj, the Jesuit Church faced a column completed in 1744 (since destroyed) situated in the small open space in front of the church, and dedicated to the Virgin Mary, echoing the iconic images and inscriptions housed within the church. Like the façade of the Jesuit church, the Mary column in both its form and location followed a stock pattern that could be found throughout the Habsburg lands. The Virgin stood atop a column adorned with wreathes and surrounded by baroque *putti*, urns and other elements of Baroque decoration; while the style of the ornamentation was grandiose, the scale of the monument was relatively modest, in keeping with the scale of the surrounding buildings. The result of the relationships established in the space occupied by the church, school buildings and the column was a miniature urban landscape that stressed, not the unique features of the local community, or even the relation of the community to the larger world, but instead the connection of the redefined urban space to the dominant aesthetic of alliance of Church and dynasty. Coupled with the aesthetic harmony sought by the balance of church and column was the unambiguous message of the triumphant return of the Church to a region regarded as rightfully "its own," and, not coincidentally, the re-incorporation of Transylvania into the culture of Western Europe. Like the inscription within the church offering praise to the Trinity, the public presence of the Mary column affirmed the triumph of Catholic theology over Protestant and Unitarian beliefs that avoided the use of human figures and had reduced or eliminated the sacraments, which play such a large role in the Jesuit program of evangelization. The prominent display of the Virgin and other human figures can also be seen as a repudiation of the Muslim prohibition of images. This repetition of a recognized pattern is to a degree a parallel with the uniformity

---

[61] *Wappenbuch des Adels von Ungarn samt den Nebenländern der Stephans-Krone* (Nürnburg, 1885–87), Heft 1–7, 16. Most Transylvanian noble Calvinist families had a branch that had converted or had remained Catholic.

[62] ARSI, *Aust. 155, An. Prov. Aust. 1697*, folio 71r.

found in Jesuit record-keeping and in the curriculum of the *Ratio*, with one important difference: the images produced by the architectural patterns of the Jesuit compound called to mind the House of Austria as directly as they did Jesuit buildings in other lands. Habsburg and Jesuit building projects often went hand in hand.

While the Society erected its own church and expanded its complex of educational and residential structures, its aesthetic influences spread over Cluj, leaving a distinct stamp on the urban environment.[63] Eight crosses appeared around the town, calling attention to the message of salvation proclaimed by the Society.[64] Baroque details were added to the medieval bulk of St. Michael's and a gate in the Baroque style, topped with a figure of the Archangel Michael slaying a dragon and decorated with statues of St. John Nepomuk, St. John the Baptist, St. Sebastian, St. Francis of Assisi, St. John the Evangelist and St. Roch was erected in 1747 in front of the church. Like the figures on the façade of the Jesuit church, these statues were created by Johann König, whom we have met before and who had also been active in Alba Iulia.[65] This gate, moved in 1899 to another location in Cluj and today in poor condition, was another link to the Habsburgs and the Jesuits of the Austrian Province, since Nepomuk had been utilized by the dynasty to legitimate its control over Bohemia, a process in which the Society had played a major role.[66] Nepomuk was also a special protector of the Society, and had been promoted as a candidate for sainthood by Jesuits who used his legend as a counterpoise to Bohemian Hussite traditions. Here again, as in the façade of the Jesuit church, Baroque theatricality is the mode of expression in a public context, and although there is no documentation that the Society specifically commissioned the execution of these figures, their placement before a formerly Catholic church that had been rendered more austere during its use by the Unitarians before being reclaimed by the Society is highly suggestive. Baroque elements appeared elsewhere in the town: the *collegium* erected near the church in the years 1700 to 1703 harmonized with the themes set forth by the slowly rising new church and suggested what would follow.[67]

In Kolosmănăştur, the old church, located a few miles west of the city walls and rich with associations with an earlier period of Catholic influence in the region, was taken over by the Society and underwent significant renovations. In 1719, thanks

---

[63] An important general work on the architecture of this period in Central Europe is Thomas DaCosta Kaufmann, *Court, Cloister and City: The Art and Culture of Central Europe* (Chicago, IL, 1995). For the Jesuit approach to urban architecture see Pietro Pirri, SJ, *Giovanni Tristano e i primordi della architettura gesuitica*, (Roma, 1955) (Biblioteca Istituti Historici S.J. VI), and J. Valley-Radot, "Le recueil des Plans d'Édifices de la Compagnie de Jésus conservé à la Biblithèque National de Paris" (Roma, 1960) (Biblioteca Istituti Historici S.J. XV). An important recent addition to this literature is Thomas M. Lucas, SJ, *Landmarking: City, Church and Urban Strategy* (Chicago, IL, 1997).

[64] ARSI, *Aust. 171 An. Prov. Aus. 1724*, folio 49r.

[65] Jolán Balogh, *Kolozsvár mûemlékei* (Budapest, 1935), plate 88.

[66] Paul Shore, "The several lives of St. John Nepomuk" in J. Chorpenning (ed.), *"He Spared Himself in Nothing": Essays on the Life and Thought of John N. Neumann, C. Ss. R., Fourth Bishop of Philadelphia, on the Occasion of the 25th Anniversary of his Canonization* (Philadelphia, PA, forthcoming), pp. 3–24.

[67] Jolán Balogh, *Kolozsvár régi lakói* (Kolozsvár, 1942), p. 7.

to the generosity of Kolosvári Pál, the recently deceased "Arianorum Parochus" who had undergone a change of heart, and several "Valachi, qui ritum sequentur Graecum," the church reopened. Three years later, its tower was reroofed and a statue of St. John Nepomuk was installed on the premises, reinforcing the connection to the western Habsburg lands.[68] These developments gave the Society a highly visible base in town, as well as a foothold in the countryside, where Catholicism faced its most entrenched opposition from Orthodox peasants and clergy.[69] The symbolism of both the reoccupation of buildings and the utilization of materials used by the Society during its earlier sojourn in Cluj was also highly significant. After some dramatic successes in conversions, the Jesuits had been driven from the city in 1602 in a violent encounter with the Calvinist community in which at least one father had met a martyr's death and several students had been hurled from the windows of the *collegium*.[70] Almost a century later, the return of the Society to Cluj was accompanied by unambiguous demonstrations of its new strength and of the support it felt it could count on from the west. Jesuits could now, as it were, go public with their identity, a transformation that had consequences in several directions, among which was architecture and dress. In Transylvania, they received in 1700 explicit permission from the emperor to appear in their customary way of dressing ("amicta sua"), which although the Society did not have an officially designated habit, was still significant, as many Jesuits had previously traveled through the region incognito.[71] Throughout the next eighty years, the Society would seek to expand this visibility and attendant influence further into the countryside around Cluj and beyond.[72] Rural churches were repaired or established in Búza, Csisco, Kerestúr and "in oppido Kolos," and a paper mill was established, while in Bács the Society collected tolls from a small bridge.[73] Smaller properties were held in Bogor, Teklie and Gegennye as well.[74] But the focal point of Jesuit demonstrations of physical splendor, political power, future success, and doctrinal fidelity always remained the center of the old walled town, near the architectural anchors of the Jesuit presence, and in the setting of the processions and other public events that the Society staged.

In the town of Cluj itself, the construction of school buildings was a preoccupation of the Society second only to the completion of the church. Because the *Ratio* did not

---

[68] OSzK, 2039, FMI/1608, *Historia anno 1722*, p. 258.

[69] Jesuit properties were constantly augmented by donations, for example, a donation of land made in 1736. MOL F 234. Erdély Kincstári Levéltár, Erdélyi Fiscalis Levéltár Szekrény XXV/B., unnumbered folios.

[70] Antal Molnár, "Sándor Dobokai's Autobiographische Aufzeichnungen 1620," *AHSI* 66 (1997), pp. 75–88; Argenti, *De Societate Jesu*, excerpted in *Jezsuita Okmánytár I/1. Erdélyt és Magyarországot érintő iratok*, ed. Bálazs Mihály (Szeged, 1995), pp. 233–6.

[71] Ferencz Szlilágyi, *Közlemények az erdélyi rómái katholikus egyházi történetből* (Budapest, 1874), p. 5.

[72] In 1702, Father Sigismund Székhely, not having a successor to his post in Marosvásárhely (Tîrgu Mureş), gave the Cluj Jesuit community the right to appoint his successor. ARSI, *Austria 159* (1702), folio 37r.

[73] ARSI, *Aust. 172, An. Prov. Aust. 1715*, p. 78; *Aust. 96 Cat. III 1746*, p. 46; Jakab, *Története*, vol. 3, p. 306.

[74] ARSI, *Aust. 220, An. Prov. Aust. 1765*, folio 77r.

prescribe a curriculum that included medicine or law, the Society's plans for school buildings could be rather more compact and efficient than those of institution-wide broader curricula (although the absence of these disciplines left the Jesuits open to the criticism that they did not operate true universities[75]). Yet the opening of a Jesuit school in 1698 was a ceremonial occasion to which Unitarian and Calvinist clergy were invited. By 1713, the Jesuits' first school, the academy, which had been raised to the rank of a *collegium* in 1701, could boast an auditorium that sat one hundred in the parquet plus space for dignitaries in three stalls. Simultaneously, the fathers were able to begin work on a "*seminarium*" with an endowment from Leopold I, who in 1701 pledged four thousand Rhenish florins to the creation of this school. The "Báthory-*Seminarium*," which was also known as the "*Seminarium* S. Joseph" was a training school for archdiocesan priests, a fulfillment of one of the requirements set down by the Council of Trent that there be a seminary for this purpose in every diocese. As we have seen, Franciscans also attended the *Seminarium*, suggesting the Society's ascendancy over other Catholic orders.[76] Jesuit control of this seminary was yet another instance of how the Society increased its influence in various directions through the community. The Society accomplished this both through the establishment of yet another visible educational institution, and by training priests whose values and outlook would be shaped by their experience under the tutelage of the fathers, who sought financing for the creation of a library for the *seminarium*.[77] Ten years after its initial funding, there were five students enrolled.[78] Still standing today, the Báthory-*Seminarium* (which also received major support from Apor István) presented a face to the street that harmonizes with the two-storey façade of the *Convictus*, helping define the space in which the Mary column once stood.[79] The *Seminarium Pauperum* was originally housed in a former Dominican house, although construction began on a new building for the school in 1726, which was combined with the clerical *seminarium*, providing an added opportunity for the poor boys of the town to be exposed to life in a religious order.[80] The *Convictus Nobilium* or school for noble boys did not itself open until 1735. Built in stages, this structure followed the Jesuit model of a range of residential and teaching facilities surrounding a courtyard. With the completion of the *Convictus* and the addition of a pharmacy in

---

[75] Maria Theresia added a faculty of medicine to the venerable Jesuit university in Trnava in 1769, shortly before the Suppression. Johann Christian von Engel, *Geschichte des Unagarischen Reichs* 5 vols (Wien, 1813–14), IV, p. 334.

[76] Eight Franciscans were enrolled at the *Seminarium* in 1722. OSzK, 2039 FMI/1608 *Historia anno 1722*, p. 260.

[77] In 1721, sixty florins were committed to the establishment of the *Seminarium* library. OSzK, 2039 FMI 1608. *Historia anno 1721*, p. 250.

[78] OSzK, 2039 FMI/1608 *Historia anno 1701*, p. 21; *Historia anno 1711*, p. 104.

[79] An illustration of the *Convictus* appears in *Erdély története*, chief ed. Béla Köpéczi, 2: *1606–tól 1830–ig*, eds Matkai László and Szasz Zoltán (Budapest, 1982), plate 294.

[80] ARSI, *Aust. 181 An. Lit. Prov. Ausr. 1721*, folio 63v; OSZK, 2039 FMI/1608, *Historia anno 1722*, p. 258. Occasionally a student at the *Seminarium pauperum* would choose the chaste life of the ordered clergy. Ibid., *Historia anno 1724*, p. 279; Apor Péter, *Synopsis Mutationum notabiliorum aetete mea in Transylvania et Progressus Vitae Meae*. Kazinczy, G. (ed.), *Monumenta*, pp. 424–5.

1731, the basic framework of the Cluj Jesuit complex was complete.[81] In the coming decades, the ongoing acquisition of lands outside of town would further solidify the Jesuit presence while providing revenue and produce for the Jesuit community.[82] The Jesuits thereby assumed the highly visible identities of landowners and contributors to the local economy simultaneously with their emergence as the dominant educational, religious and aesthetic influence in the district.[83] The commitment of individual Jesuits to the preservation of this presence in the community was underscored by a pledge taken by nine priests and two "magistri" (scholastics, young Jesuits teaching in the lower classes of the *collegium*) to remain in Cluj whatever the "pericula" they might face.[84] While the circumstantial evidence we have seen pertaining to language usage and ethnic affiliation suggests that the Jesuits did not have the same degree of interaction with the Romanian speakers of the region as they did with other groups, no one living in or around Cluj could avoid the presence of the Society.

Given the size of Cluj and its existing buildings, public and private, at the end of the seventeenth century, the overall impact of the Jesuit building program on the character of the community was particularly profound. Not only had a new architectural style been introduced, but the new buildings housed a community and an educational program that provided a link to the west and to the dominant political power of the region. The Jesuit complex, offering both religious succor and rationalized safety, became a haven for refugees fleeing religious strife in Hungary and Transylvania.[85] It was no coincidence that the Cluj Jesuit press published the work of Ernestus Vols, a Styrian Jesuit who expounded on the art of military architecture.[86] The Society saw itself constructing clearly defined spaces for conducting its urban mission, and while such complexes did not take on an overtly defensive character, they nevertheless followed principles of rationality, economy and compactness of design that reflected their role as outposts in a potentially less-than-friendly environment.

The visual presence of the Society in this community was both static and mobile, manifesting itself in human terms as well as in works of art, in references to personalities

---

[81] ARSI, *Aust. 188, An Prov. Aust. 1731*, pp. 501–502. A bookstore was later added to the complex. Jakab, *Története*, vol. 3, p. 325. In 1726, the Society had purchased a printing press for 180 Rhenish florins. ARSI, *Aust. 183, An. Prov. Aust. 1726*, folio 63r.

[82] For example, Fenyes, where the Jesuits owned a vineyard. OSZK, 2039 FMI/1608, *Historia anno 1707*, pp. 73–4. Elsewhere, the Society eventually acquired a fulling mill, a mill and other agricultural buildings. Bíró, "Egyetem," p. 14; ARSI, *Aust. 176, An. Prov. Aust. 1719*, p. 154.

[83] A very rough sense of the degree to which the Society only a few years after its return to Cluj had become involved in the raising of livestock may be gained by noting that during 1704, the Jesuits lost 20,000 florins worth of livestock from various causes, including war. OSzK, 2039 FMI/1608 *Historia anno 1704*, p. 56.

[84] The greatest immediate danger at the time would have been the plague. ARSI, *Aust. 171, An. Prov. Aust. 1714*, sheet before folio 1.

[85] In 1715, four soldiers and a currier charged with a capital crime sought asylum for several months in the collegium. OSzK, 2039 FMI/1608 *Historia anno 1715*, p. 171. A decade earlier Jesuits had fled Hungary, where they were harassed by Protestants, and were lodged in the Cluj Jesuit complex. OSzK, 2039 FMI/20391608 *Historia anno 1711*, p. 111.

[86] Ernestus Vols, *Architecturae militaris tyrocinium* (Claudiopoli, 1738).

and events both close by and remote. The Society strove to be omnipresent on the physical plane while laboring in the spiritual as well: Jesuits descended into the town's prisons to console the condemned while simultaneously raising symbols of their mission and message above the rooftops of Cluj and on the "Mount Calvary" located in Kolosmănăştur.[87] Meanwhile Jesuit *coadjutors temporales*, and possibly paid townspeople as well, cared for the Turkish horses housed in the Society's stables.[88] Leading processions through the streets, publicizing plays produced by students in their schools, grappling for their share of the tithes granted to the Church, preaching in their own and in other churches throughout the area, feeding the crowds who gathered outside the Jesuit residence during times of famine, loaning money to strapped noblemen, and conducting conversion campaigns in the countryside, the Jesuits must have been the most conspicuous and widely discussed group of men in Cluj.[89] Their architectural achievements likewise would have stirred notice, admiration and perhaps controversy as they transformed the liturgical experience of the faithful with a new vision of ecclesiastical architecture and decoration. Some of these monuments were only temporary, as when the Jesuits erected a triumphal arch to welcome Rákóczi II Ferenc upon his entry into Cluj in 1705.[90] But most of these architectural undertakings were intended to have a lasting impact on the greater community. The church erected by the Society afforded residents of this often sorely tried community what one historian has called an "earthly paradise where members of all classes could enjoy luxury otherwise confined to palaces," an experience that might take place even during the funeral services for a local noble.[91] Taking into account the widespread poverty that afflicted town such as Cluj even during the best of times, the splendor and scale of the Jesuit building program must have seemed almost out of scale for the needs and resources of the community. Nevertheless, the Jesuit mandate to bring souls to God was furthered, at least in the eyes of the Jesuits

---

[87] ARSI, *Aust. 170, An. Prov. Aust. 1713*, folio 33r; *Aust. 187, Aust. 1730.*, folios 41v–42r; The "Mount Calvary" was completed by 1714. OSzK, 2039/1608 *Historia anno 1714*, p. 139. Emericus Koermendi (1670–1733) was said to have preached on the "Mount Calvary" five times daily. Stöger, *Scriptores*, p. 189.

[88] ARSI, *Aust. 187, An. Prov. Aust. 1740*, p. 101.

[89] Penitents, perhaps part of a procession organized by the Jesuits, threw themselves into the winter snows. ARSI, *Aust. 189, An. Prov. Aust. 1732*, p. 185. On another occasion, a procession of flagellants with others carrying crosses, made its way through the streets. OSzK, 2039 FMI/1608 *Historia anno 1713*, p. 116. Father Gabrielus Kapi "Superior Missionis Daciarum," is reported to have clashed with the town fathers in 1702 over the proper use of the tithe. Sommervogel et al., *Bibliothèque*, vol. 4, pp. 913–15. In the difficult year 1726, crowds gathered each week to receive assistance from the Jesuits. ARSI, *Aust. 175, An. Prov. Aust. 1718*, p. 227; *Aust. 183 An. Prov. Aus. 1726*, folio 31v. Michael Count Kornis borrowed 11,500 Rhenish florins from the Society's *collegium* on 21 January 1764. MOL F 477, *Erdélyi Kinsctár Levéltár Exactoratus Cameralis ...* No. 30, p. 7. The Cluj Jesuit community operated an ongoing mission in Marosvásárhely (Tîrgu Mureş), as early as 1702. OSzK, 2039 FMI/1608, *Historia anno 1702*, p. 36.

[90] Jakab, *Története*, pp. 3, 6–7. The problem of the relationship of the Cluj Jesuits, ostensibly devoted to the Habsburg dynasty, to Rákóczi, has yet to be resolved.

[91] William M. Johnstone, *The Austrian Mind: An Intellectual and Social History 1848–1938* (Berkeley, CA, 1972), p. 15.

themselves, by their ability to establish a presence in a community, to maintain discipline and cohesion within the Society while remaining in contact with the people they sought to convert. Perhaps many different idioms could have served this function, but the employment of the Austrian Baroque guaranteed an unusual fusion of elements and messages. Friedrich Heer notes that the Austrian Baroque 'not only sought to express the union of diverse peoples, but celebrated the victory of Faith over reason and heresy ... .' 'Spiritual' was equated to worldly, art to science, reason to Faith, Church to empire and Europe to Christianity. All together they made up Austria.[92]

The Jesuit presence in Cluj, and especially, the Jesuit church, can therefore be regarded as ultimately an expression of the Habsburg conception of the world. When this conception changed in the late eighteenth and early nineteenth centuries, the baroque idiom in Cluj, and in dozens of other places under Austrian control, was left with nowhere else to go.

The physical presence of the Society in Cluj may be characterized as threefold, thereby addressing three of the four "dimensions of the world" identified by Martin Heidegger and applied to Baroque art by Václav Richter. These four are "space, time, sacral nature and profane nature."[93] We have already seen how the sacral nature of Jesuit building projects and public manifestations of piety such as processions that existed in time and space, was always intertwined with messages about the Society itself, its relation to other institutions, and its mission to the people. While affirming the universality of their message, the Jesuits were frequently promoters of an aesthetic or a visual language that was initially alien to the communities in which this message was propagated.[94] The introduction of the Baroque aesthetic to Transylvania was moreover not only an innovation, but was also an expression of a shift in political power from a local principality preoccupied with keeping greater powers at bay to a dynasty with pretensions to universal dominion. The message of this new visual aesthetic was repeated in the school-sponsored performances by Jesuit students, which themselves reiterated a Baroque aesthetic.[95] Next, the Jesuit aesthetic and artistic legacy in Cluj glories in beauty. In a non-sacral or arguably profane sense, the Hungarian word "fény," or the German "Pracht," best translated as "splendor" or "magnificence," comes the closest to conveying the effect sought in the interior of the Jesuit church as well as the sound and spectacle of Jesuit public events, the intricacy and emotional charge of Jesuit rhetoric and drama, and even the

---

[92] Friedrich Heer, *The Intellectual History of Europe*, Jonathan Steinberg trans. (Cleveland, OH/New York, 1966), pp. 444–5.

[93] Václav Richter, "Poznámky k barokní uměni," in Milan Kopecký (ed.), *O Barokní kultuře: Sborník statí* (Brno, 1968), pp. 147–60.

[94] Gauvin Alexander Bailey notes that despite their concentrated efforts, the Jesuits' efforts to engage the elites of China and Japan through their displays of visual art were not successful. Gauvin Alexander Bailey, *Art on the Jesuit Missions of Asia and Latin America 1542–1773* (Toronto, 1999), p. 196.

[95] For instance, the "thema" of the highest class of the *collegium*, presented in 1722, was "Vindicata Maiestas in Carlo cognominato Parvo Neapolis et Alteriae Rege." OSzK, 2039 FMI/1608, *Historia anno 1722*, p. 260.

ornate form of Baroque Latinity found in books and tracts produced in Cluj.[96] While relatively modest in comparison with many other Jesuit churches in the Habsburg lands, the Cluj church placed an emphasis on realistic detail in portrayal of the human form combined with the arresting use of symbols designating the sacred not found in the earlier religious and civic buildings of the town.[97]

Finally, the practical and rational elements of Baroque Jesuit architecture, too often overlooked by critics, are conspicuous in the organization of the Society's Cluj complex. The residential and educational facilities constructed during the eight decades of the Society's activities were not intended to be unimpressive outbuildings hidden behind the façades of more imposing structures, but instead were designed to work as a functional whole to complement the more commanding church towers and façade. If the "Jesuit Quarter" was in some ways a stage, backstage would have been the interiors of classroom and residential buildings, not the exteriors of the structures. Seeking to carry the community towards God through a variety of strategies that engaged the populace in specially designated spaces and at prescribed times, the Jesuits appealed to both to the sensuous and the intellectual in designing the physical settings in which they did their work, and the overall effect of the less ornate structures combined with the more deliberately ostentatious buildings was always kept in mind. This orderly physical design, in a physical sense, of Jesuit schools reflected the disciplined curriculum taught within them. As a complement to the rigor and rationality of the *Ratio*, the Jesuit vision of sumptuous beauty as both a delight to those on earth and a metaphor for the glories of heaven was carried out on a more modest scale in Cluj, but remained a dominant force in the selection of materials for liturgical, theatrical and public events. The presentation of images was sustained in an *ancièn regime*, Europe-wide culture that, as Remy Saisselin has noted, did not yet view even a lavish work of art as a symbol of tyranny and oppression.[98] The net impact of the Jesuit complex on the medieval town was to add order and rationality, accented by touches of "fény" on both an educational and a visual level to a community that had up until then grown organically and with competing intellectual and theological points of reference. The claiming of the space in front of the Jesuit church with a monument to Mary, the spiritual queen of the Hungarian lands, established a centerpiece touched with "fény" to the rationalized Jesuit quarter whose political meaning was as easily perceived as was the efficient functionality of the surrounding buildings. This pairing of the rational and the late

---

[96] A procession, honoring the newly beatified French Jesuit Joannes Franciscus Regis (1597–1646) led by the Bishop of Transylvania on 23 August 1716 and including students and townspeople, advanced from the chapel of the *collegium* to the "blare of trumpets and the thundering of kettledrums." ARSI, *Aust. 173, Lit. An. Prov. Aust. 1716*, folio 81r.

[97] The Jesuit Church of the Most Holy Name of Jesus in Breslau, whose interior was also completed in the 1720s and which likewise was located in a province wracked by war, is far more lavish than the Cluj church, but the governing principles of façade, its interior decoration, and organization are very similar. Elżbieta Kotkowska and Monika Raczyńska-Sęzikowska, *Die Kirche zum allerheiligen Namen Jesu*, trans. Bernadetta Szyszka (Wrocław, 1997), p. 5.

[98] Remy Saisselin, *The Enlightenment against the Baroque: Economics and Aesthetics in the Eighteenth Century* (Berkeley, CA, 1992), p. 133.

Baroque would be repeated in another public space at the end of the Jesuit era when work began on the Bánffy palace facing St. Michael's in central square of Cluj.[99]

Ultimately, while the significance of the Society's introduction of the Baroque and accompanying ideology was far from negligible, it was the element of Jesuit rationality that left the most important legacy in Cluj. Long after the Society had been suppressed, its church taken over by the Piarists and its curriculum superseded by Theresian and Josephinian reforms, the school buildings of the Jesuits continued to serve a practical function in a community that was leaving behind its identity as a small, isolated town and was destined in the coming decades to become a burgeoning industrial center bearing little resemblance to the town the Jesuits had known.

---

[99] The Bánffy palace, home to the governor of the region, was completed between 1773 and *1785*. Mariane Sallay, "Koloszvár," in Zádor Anna and Genthon István, *Művészeti lexikon* (4 vols, Budapest, 1965), p. 665.

CHAPTER SIX

Theatre in the Jesuit Schools[1]

The Jesuits of Cluj based their curriculum and extracurricular activities on the guidelines set down in the *Ratio Studiorum* of 1599. In this foundational document the production of school plays is not mandated, but great emphasis is placed on public speaking, on the demonstration of linguistic competence, and on the value of competition in a public or semi-public setting.[2] In the decades following the creation of the Society, Jesuit educators, constructing an educational program in the richly theatrical culture of the late Renaissance, quickly seized upon the idea of using school dramas as means of teaching public-speaking skills and morality. These plays also served as a way of advertising the Jesuit schools themselves, thereby generating not only a long list of original plays but also an extensive literature on the topic.[3] Within the Habsburg lands, Jesuit school drama, developing alongside other forms of public performance such as recitations and academic defenses, played a significant cultural role in the seventeenth and early eighteenth centuries.[4] Within Hungarian-speaking lands, Jesuit drama helped shape both the development of literary Magyar as well as the perpetuation of Baroque Latin as a living language in a nation that continued to use Latin as the language of its government well into the nineteenth century. In particular, Jesuit school dramas, through their sheer numbers, exercised an enormous influence on the development of theatre in Hungary down to the present. During the seventeenth and eighteenth centuries, it is estimated that roughly 7,800 different plays were staged in schools in Hungary (including Transylvania). Of these, an

---

[1] A shorter version of this chapter was published as "Patriotism, Catholicity and the Jesuit plays of Kolozsvár" in the CD-ROM *Proceedings of the international conference "Iskola és Színház" (School and Theatre) Miskolc, Hungary, September 7–9, 2002*.

[2] The 88th Rule for the Provincial of the *Ratio* of 1591 points out that "poetry without drama stagnates" and makes allowances for performances, as long as women do not appear on stage. The regulation banning boys appearing in female roles was later loosened.

[3] Nigel Griffin, *Jesuit School Drama: A Checklist of Critical Literature, Supplement No 1* (London, 1986); Jean-Marie Valentin, *Le théâtre des Jésuites dans les pays de langue allemand. Répertoire chronologique des pièces représentées et des documents conservées* (2 vols, Stuttgart, 1984).

[4] In 1709, a public debate was held in Cluj between Jesuit scholars and the "primarias facultatum Arianarum doctor." OSzK, 2039 FMI/1608 *Historia*, p. 80. A panegyric on Prince Eugene of Savoy, the Habsburg general, was delivered in 1716. OSzK, 2039 FMI/1608 *Historia anno 1716*, p. 203. A eulogy on Joseph I, which cast the emperor in the role of father of his people, was delivered at the Cluj *collegium* in 1710: *Verus Patriae Pater etc. Oratio Funebris ab uno Societate Presbytero Celebrata* (Claudiopol, 1710). *Régi Magyar Könyvtár* II k 2399 sz; also *Josephus Accrescens sat. Publica Parentatio sat. a Quodam Societate Patre ... mens. Jul. die VIII a. 1711* (Claudiopol). *Régi Magyar Könyvtár* II k. 2418 sz.

astonishing 5566 were produced in Jesuit schools.[5] As remarkable as these figures are, they are even more astonishing when we recall that Hungary and Transylvania only numbered a few million inhabitants, that girls were effectively excluded from almost all of the schools that staged plays, and that these regions were convulsed by war and not infrequently threatened with famine. At the same time, Jesuit drama reflected influences from many directions, including France and Germany, making the finished product "cosmopolitan" in ways that school dramas developed in other contexts seldom were.[6] Like many other Jesuit plays of the Baroque era, these dramas were frequently public representations of the struggle between good and evil, between salvation through Christ and the powers of the Devil.[7] Hungarian Jesuit dramas thus contained elements of both the wider world, the post-Tridentine Church, and of the specific historical and cultural context of early modern Hungary.

The visual arts were central to the presentation of many Jesuit school dramas produced in Hungary, and while the sets, costumes and properties used in Cluj themselves have not survived, contemporary drawings reveal the richness and sophistication of the visual display of many Jesuit plays produced in Hungarian-speaking regions.[8] The tradition of using drama to promote Jesuit educational goals reached back to the beginnings of the Counter-Reformation in Transylvania: the original Jesuit *collegium* in Cluj was the site of the earliest known play produced by a Jesuit school in a Hungarian-speaking region, which appeared in 1587. Significantly, this drama focused on the history of the first Christian king of Hungary, St. Stephen.[9] While the expulsion of the Society from Transylvania meant that it did not have the context of functioning schools in which to stage dramas, a program from a Jesuit production staged in 1654 has survived, as well as evidence of another performance in 1684.[10]

Although specifics on the dramas offered by the Jesuit schools of Cluj are often lacking, we can gain glimpses of the Jesuit school theatre in the brief notices it receives in the histories of the Society, while recognizing that these references themselves are less than complete.[11] Summaries of plays have also survived,

---

[5] István Kilián, "Church, school, drama and stage in the 17th–18th centuries," *Publicationes Universitatis Miskoliensis, Sectio Philosophica Tomus IV* (Miskolc, 1998), p. 86.

[6] *A Magyar Irodalom Története*, ed. Beöthy Zsolt (4 vols, Budapest, 1896), vol. 1, p. 494.

[7] Robert Birely, *The Refashioning of Catholicism, 1450–1700* (Basingstoke, 1999), pp. 128–9.

[8] *The Sopron Collection of Jesuit Stage Designs*, preface by Marcello Fagiolo, studies by Éva Knapp and István Kilián, iconography by Terézia Bardi (Budapest, 1999).

[9] *Historia S. Stephani Regis: Acta per Speciem Fabulae in Scena.*

[10] Varga Imre, "A kolozsvári jezsuita színjátszás," in Demeter Júlia and Kilián István (eds), *A magyar színház születése* (Miskolc, 2000), pp. 231–44, 231.

[11] For example, from the 193 Jesuit plays performed between 1701 and 1773, as identified by Staud, only 76 can be identified in the *Historia Collegii Claudiopoli*, which breaks off in 1747 and is water-damaged.

providing some insight into the action and the moral promoted.[12] Jesuit plays were generally performed before an audience that included members of the general public, thereby increasing the influence they would have had on the wider community, a pattern initiated quickly once the Society had returned to Transylvania. During the first year in which the recently reestablished Jesuits operated a school in Cluj, a competition was held for the best play, the prize being offered by Apor Péter, whom we have already met.[13] Different classes and members of the *collegium* community might take part in the production of dramas. Six years later, in June 1699, the Jesuit *collegium* staged a production entitled "Sanctus Carolus Borromeus Tutor et Pater Pauperum."[14] Although St. Charles Borromeo (1538–86) was not a Jesuit, his life embodied many of the goals of the Society, and he was a close ally of the Jesuits and their *Praepostius Generalis*, St. Francis Borgia. The play's title also points to two priorities of the Society: the training and the guidance of the poor, themes that the Jesuits would have wanted to spotlight in any public production associated with their schools.

Public play production rapidly became a feature of Jesuit schools in Cluj. In 1711, the "rhetorices," "poetae," and grammar classes all participated in the production of a series of plays produced "in the public theatre" of the *collegium*.[15] These performances were staged by young students, and were an important element of the culture of the lower Jesuit schools, in which young students and relatively young instructors worked together. Play performances are reported as being staged in Udvarhely "de nostris Magistris" (probably a Jesuit scholastic) and became a mainstay of the lower divisions or "grammatices" of the Jesuit *collegium* where in many years all classes of the "grammatices" took part.[16] These plays often had a message that went beyond simplistic expositions of virtue and vice, or retellings of familiar Biblical themes. Special attention was devoted to themes from Hungarian history, particularly those that supported the above-mentioned argument that Hungary had a special mission as a Catholic nation, as a bulwark against infidels or as a model polity functioning as *Regnum Marianum*, or rule of the Virgin Mary. Another reference from the history of the Jesuit community, partially illegible, indicates that in 1702 a drama was staged in honor of the daughter of the Governor of Transylvania.[17] In 1713, shortly after the unsuccessful Rákóczi rebellion, during which the town itself was occupied by kuruc troops, an "exhibitio comica" was staged the day following the graduation of the first baccalaureate class of the *collegium*. This play also dealt with the conversion of St. Stephen, the first Christian king of Hungary, and with the conversion of his uncle

---

[12] The Cluj Jesuit press occasionally published summaries of plays produced by other Catholic orders, such as the Piarists. One such summary, of a production in Bistriţa, is OSzK, Carton 4, Pro. 32, *DVX ConspICVVs fIDe IdantYrsVs a qVo phILoMVsVs heLICona a DIVtVus fVIt* [=1735] *honori, ac venerationi Perillustris a generosi domini Stephani Sehy ...* (Claudiopoli, [1735]).

[13] ARSI, *Aust. 155, An. Prov. Aust. 1697*, folio 71.

[14] Zoltán Ferencz, *Kolozsvári színtészet és színház története* (Kolozsvár, 1897), p. 48.

[15] OSzK, 2039 FMI/1608 *Historia anno 1711*, p. 104.

[16] ARSI, *Austria 155, An. Prov. Aust. 1697*, folio 78r; *Austria 187, An. Prov. Aust. 1730*, folios 68v–9r.

[17] OSzK, 2039 FMI/1608, *Historia SJ Claudiopoli*, p. 30.

the Duke or Gyula. These historical events have defining importance in Hungary's relationship to the Holy See, for it was the pope who sent Stephen a Christian king's regalia, which helped construct the tradition in which kings of Hungary (including the Habsburgs) were denominated "Apostolic," a title that Maria Theresia took for herself in 1759.[18] The piety and rectitude of Hungary's first Christian rulers was of added significance in Transylvania, where a large percentage, if not an absolute majority, of the population claimed descent not from Catholic Hungarians, but from Roman legionaries and Dacian settlers, while at the same time the Principalities' new rulers derived their moral authority from the historic relationship between the Crown of St. Stephen and Rome.[19] The differing claims of Hungarians and Romanians on Transylvania places the production of a play on Stephen and Gyula by the mostly ethnic Hungarian Jesuits in multiple contexts. Like other Jesuit dramas, this play promoted morality and what Szkefű Gyula calls the "baroque ideal," but in addition the retelling of the conversion of the House of Árpád reinforces the moral and spiritual legitimacy of the Hungarian crown's authority (even when it is held by a foreign dynasty) over Transylvania.[20] The same theme of Hungarian history intertwined with patriotism and piety is evident in a three-act drama entitled "Emericus Bebekus et Joannes Zápolya, Roxiae Gubernatores a Ludovico I Hungariae Rege constituti," written by Koloszvári (sic) Paulus and produced in 1723.[21] The chief characters of this drama are somewhat more difficult to identify than those of the foregoing play. János Zápolya, King of Hungary (1526–40), ruled during the final years of Hungary's collapse as the Turks advanced following the battle of Mohács. Known in his own lifetime as the "pious" ("jámbor") king, János is a plausible candidate as one of the play's protagonists.[22] Another heroic figure from Hungarian history to appear on a Jesuit school stage in Cluj was Matthias Corvinus, whose marriage to the daughter of the Bohemian King George of Podiebrad was celebrated in a production that may have been bilingual, Latin and Hungarian, in 1702.[23] The anonymous playwright crafted a drama showing the influence of Hungarian and Slovenian folklore, thereby showing that while one of the goals of these historical dramas was to foster a sense of Hungarian national identity as reflected in the histories and devotional literature produced by Jesuits, the Society's playwrights were capable of reaching into the reservoir of popular culture to find motives that would have wide appeal. References to patriotic Hungarian themes were a permanent feature of the Cluj Jesuit playbill, something Jesuit chroniclers acknowledged when they referred to the "solitum è patria historia tentamen" undertaken by the "syntaxis" class that in 1754 was supplemented by an additional production.[24]

---

[18]   3 June 1759. Hungarian constitutional law required the empress to be styled "king" of Hungary. *Magyarország történeti kronológiája*, vol. 2, p. 577.

[19]   Kürti, *Borderland*, p. 42ff.

[20]   Gyula Szekfű, *Magyar története IV. kötet* (Budapest, 1935), pp. 384–5.

[21]   József Takács, *A jezsuita iskoladráma* (Budapest, 1937), p. 56.

[22]   John is referred to as a "jámbor" ruler by a contemporary diarist, who praised the king's piety, *Mindszenti Gábor Diariuma Öreg János Király Haláláról* (Budapest, 1977).

[23]   Kríza Idilkó, "Egy jezsuita Mátyás-dráma folklor vonakozásai" in Demeter and Kilián (eds), *Színhaz*, pp. 74–87.

[24]   ARSI, *Aust. 211, An. Prov. Aust. 1754*, folio 76v.

Martyred heroes were often a popular theme for plays produced in the Society's schools. The title of a play produced in 1741, "Alexius Japon [Alexius the Japanese]" refers one of the Japanese martyrs of the seventeenth century, whose story was well known to all Jesuits and their students in the eighteenth century.[25] Alexius Nakamura was the scion of a royal family in Firando, and after converting to Catholicism was either beheaded or burned alive in Nagasaki on 27 November 1619.[26] Although he was not a Jesuit himself (instead he was a Dominican novice) and was not beatified until the nineteenth century, Alexius was a logical candidate for a Jesuit drama since he also possessed, in addition to piety and youth, another characteristic held in high esteem by the Society: noble blood. The story of the Japanese martyrs, as retold in Jesuit devotional literature and visual art, not only contained dramatic incidents but also provided examples of fortitude and devotion to the Church in a remote and hostile environment, a lesson that would not be lost on the tiny minority of Catholics in central Transylvania. The Jesuits made the most of the exotic setting of the play: a surviving program lists "musici" among the performers and the audience was not allowed to forget that the location of the action took place "in urbe Tunkinense."[27] The theme of martyrdom in far-off lands itself occupied a special place in the Baroque psyche, and was also the subject of public declamations made by Jesuit students.[28] While martyrs had been part of the history of the Church from its earliest years, Baroque sensibility increased the focus on their physical sufferings and their ultimate triumph over the world and over enemies of the Faith.[29] Situated in a community where only a small percentage of the population was Catholic, the performers in "Alexis" would have identified with the noble and youthful martyrs whose victory was assured. An exotic setting and a virtuous youth of distinguished (in this case royal) blood likewise figure in "Cumte è Latrebirs In Thronum Sublimatio," produced in Cluj in 1762. Mixing Chinese and Japanese terminology, the cast of characters includes a "Bonzius" and takes place in the forest, presumably somewhere in China, where Cumte's family derived its royal (but not imperial) lineage.[30]

Among the plays identified as Jesuit dramas held in the collection of the Romanian Academy Library in Cluj are several that point to other classic themes in the Baroque Jesuit playwright's repertoire. These include "Apollo ab Aula Regis Midae Exul," and "Lucius Brutus in Aula Tarquini Superbi."[31] While the texts of these plays have not survived, it may be surmised that the character of Junius Lucius

---

[25] Takács, *Iskoladráma*, p. 78. An "imago" of three Japanese martyrs had been erected in the Jesuit church in the óváros in 1713. OSzK, 2039 FMI/1608 *Historia anno 1713*, p. 125.

[26] *The Book of Saints*, 6th edn, compiled by the Benedictine monks of St. Augustine's Abbey, Ramsgate (London, 1994), p. 26 http://www.katolsk.no/biografi/anakmur.htm.

[27] OSzK, Theatre Karton 4, Pro 83.

[28] In 1725, a declamation was offered on the subject of beheaded martyrs Justus and Jacob in Japan. OSzK, 2039 FMI/1608, 1608, *Historia anno 1725*, p. 290.

[29] A similar theme seems implied in *Innocentia vulnerata sive Pietas* (1717). Varga, "Színjátszás," p. 238.

[30] OSzK, Theatre Karton 4, Pro. 100. Bonzius is the Latinate rendering of the Japanese "Bozo," meaning Buddhist priest.

[31] OSzK, 2039 FMI/1608, *Historia anno 1721*, p. 249.

Brutus, a legendary sixth-century BCE Roman hero identified with opposition to tyranny and civic virtue, was offered to the public as a moral model. Brutus had the added advantage of having feigned madness in order to escape the grasp of the tyrannical Tarquinus, and as the leader of the avengers of the rape of Lucrece would have had an opportunity to display righteous anger. Sex, pagan virtue, fortitude and the protagonist's skill at outwitting an evil opponent together provided a potentially riveting plotline. Other times the central character would be drawn from Imperial Rome. "Constantinus Magus post recuperatam ope divina santitatem derutis inamium Deorum fanis vero Deo Augustate erigens," produced by the *Seminarium S. Josephi* in 1724, appears to have combined imperial glory and righteousness in a manner that would reflect well on Rome's successor, Vienna.[32] "Mitranis," a production offered by the "elementary" class in 1762, may also had have a classical theme, although its text has been lost.[33] Ancient Greece also had a place on the Jesuit playbill. "Kodrus," a tragedy on the "last king of Athens" was produced in Cluj in 1756.[34]

Not all plays produced by the Jesuits of Cluj had plots that would be acceptable to today's audiences. One such drama, produced in 1754, bore the name "Mariophilus," the tale of a youth murdered by the Jews and restored to life through the help of the Virgin.[35] Undoubtedly the theme of this work was the myth of the ritual murder of a young Christian by Jews, to serve as a sacrifice in their Passover celebrations. The origins of this "blood libel" reach back into the Middle Ages, but the Baroque era saw a vigorous return of the view of Jews as murderers, particularly of youths.[36]

Other heroes of Jesuit plays are also often young men in the roles of rescuers or exhibiters of mercy: in "S. Gualbertum amore pendentis è Cruce Christi inimico parcentem," a divine sign is provided to a young Christian seeking to avenge his brother's murder.[37] The legend of Gualbertus relates that the eleventh-century Italian noble was traveling on Good Friday when he came upon the man who had killed his brother. He was about to kill the murderer himself, when he recalled Christ's forgiveness of His own killers. As he embraced the murderer, Gualbertus had a vision of Christ on the Cross nodding in approval. Following the manifestation of this divine *numen*, the Florentine aristocrat entered a Benedictine monastery and later founded the Vallombrosan congregation. Again, youthful virtue, noble birth and decisive action are elements of this drama that may have required some special stage machinery to illustrate the vision of Christ on the Cross.

Scholars of Jesuit plays have included other types of performances, often produced in connection with public events that were not offered on stage. In 1715,

---

[32] OSzK, 2039 FMI/1608, *Historia anno 1724*, p. 272.

[33] ARSI, *Aust. 217, An. Prov. Aust. 1762*, folio 51v.

[34] OszK, Karton 4, Pro. 52. *Kodrus keserves játék a mely Kolosvarott à JESUS Társágának Académiai oskoláiban Hitünk, Házunk 's Királyunknak reményére ... M.DCC. LVI esztendöben.*

[35] Géza Staud, *Magyar iskolai színjátekok forrásai és irodalma* (2 vols, Budapest, 1984–), vol. 1, p. 280.

[36] The *leitmotiv* of the Jew as murderer was complemented in German-speaking regions by the spread of passion plays, after whose performances Jewish ghettoes were sometimes attacked. *Passion Plays and Judaism*, ed. L. Klenicki (New York, 1996).

[37] OSzK, 2039 FMI/1608, *Historia anno 1723*, p. 269.

on the Feast of the Three Kings, three youths dressed as the Magi, performed in the street, where many members of Cluj's Protestant community could watch.[38] Boys costumed as kings and angels also processed through the streets on Epiphany in 1709, paying homage to the baby Jesus. Similar performances were staged in 1711 and 1713, and in the latter case a "choro musico" enlivened the proceedings. In each instance the performance included recitations in Hungarian.[39] The same use of the attention-grabbing that the Society employed in its churches was also found in its public performances. Numerous records of Jesuit school dramas make mention of "comediae," a term that need not imply humorous situations and characterizations, but only a happy ending, perhaps with the accompaniment of music and bright costumes.[40] The appearance of dramas during the carnival season may also have played a role in their identification as "comedies."[41] For example, at the time of the scholastic exercises held for the 1709 academic year, three "comicè productae" were a performed in the Jesuit complex in Cluj, two in the Museum Convictorum, and one in the "Auditorium."[42] It is not known whether the students of the *Convictus* joined those of the Academy in this production, but since the overall enrollment of both schools at the time was relatively small, and it seems not improbable that some of the students of the *Convictus* participated in the play.

Jesuit writers happily recorded the popularity of the plays their schools produced. The Society's chroniclers noted when Calvinists and other non-Catholics were in the audience, as well as when a Calvinist was so taken with a play that he requested a copy of the script.[43] Other unnamed plays were performed for the entertainment and edification of audiences in intervals during the dedication of the Jesuit church, or as part of ceremonies at the close of the academic year.[44] Unique among plays noted in Jesuit records is an unnamed work produced by thirty members of the *convictus* and which was written by the students themselves.[45] The majority of the plays whose performances are recorded were performed by students of the *collegium* or the *convictus*, but in 1754 the students of the *Seminarium S. Josephi* also offered an "actionem comicam amoenam."[46] The impact on a community where a significant number of the performers/writers had deep roots can be imagined. Jesuit plays not

---

[38] OSzK, 2039 FMI/1608, *Historia anno 1715*, p. 156.

[39] Jablonkay Gábor, SJ, *Az Iskoladrámák a Jezsuiták Iskoláiban* (Kalocsa: Nyomatott Árpád R.T. Könyvnyomdájában, 1927), p. 3.

[40] "Comice induti" boys speaking German and Hungarian, appeared in church following the reading of the Gospel, and "comice indutae personae" speaking four languages, including Romanian, made up part of a Good Friday flagellant procession in 1711. A summary of the performance in Hungarian was printed and distributed to the population. OSzK, 2039 FMI/1608, *Historia anno 1701*, p. 10; Jablonkay, *Iskoladrámák*, pp. 9–10.

[41] This was the case in Košice, where a comedy was performed "patrio sermone" during Carnival in 1764. Takács, *Jezsuita iskoladráma*, p. 120.

[42] OSzK, 2039 FMI/1608, *Historia anno 1709*, p. 81.

[43] OSzK, 2039 FMI/1608, *Historia anno 1721*, p. 250; *Historia anno 1701*, p. 15.

[44] OzSK, 2039 FMI/1608, *Historia anno 1724*, p. 280; *Historia anno 1722*, p. 260; ARSI, *Austr. 187, An. Prov. Aust. 1730*, folio 78v.

[45] OSzK, 2039 FMI/1608, *Historia anno 1710*, p. 87.

[46] ARSI, *Austria 211, An. Prov. Aust. 1754*, folio 87r.

only provided a cosmopolitan introduction to the values of the dominant dynasty, like all school plays, they also displayed the talents of local youth in structured, formal setting.

While the public declamations offered by students of the Jesuits' schools lacked the costumes and staging of the dramas, these declamations were also important public demonstrations of the same skills and virtues showcased in the plays produced. The themes of these declamations often paralleled those of the dramas, with themes taken directly or indirectly from Hungarian history frequently in the spotlight. Recent history, especially if it glorified the achievements of the Habsburgs, was also the subject of public recitations.[47] In 1725, the "supremae" and "mediae" classes of Grammarians (the first level of *collegium*) declaimed on the Hungarian King Salamon, whose tragic history was part of the folklore concerning medieval Hungary.[48] A drama with a plot taken directly from the Old Testament was "Bathassar Rex Babilonis a Dario Oppressus," presented to an enthusiastic public in 1746.[49] Public recitations might also occur in Hungarian, paralleling the use of the vernacular in drama, and representing an important contribution to the evolution of Hungarian theatre. Students in Cluj offered poetical performances in Hungarian in 1747, 1756 and 1763.[50] Another genre carefully fostered by the Jesuits was the "pásztorjáték," or pastoral piece, which probably was not produced as a staged, costumed drama but instead consisted of a series of recitations on a theme.[51] Finally, another standby of the *Ratio*-derived curriculum was the public disputation, where many of the same skills (mastery of Latin, oral skill, poise and confidence) showcased in a school drama would also be in evidence.[52] In the relatively small Jesuit schools of Cluj, the same students probably participated in several of these

---

[47] László Szörény, "Politikai iskoldráma Savojai Jenőről és konzultació az ideális államformaról," in Demeter and Kilián (eds), *Színház*, p. 246.

[48] ARSI, *Aust. 182, An. Prov. Aust. 1725*, folio 75v. Perhaps not coincidentally, a century and a half earlier a humorous, Hungarian-language story entitled *Salamoun Királynac az David Király fianac Markarkalfal valo trefa beszedek rövid könyve* ... (Colosuaratt: [Heltai Gásperné], 1577) appeared in Cluj. In this dialogue, the proverbally wise Solomon is verbally outmaneuvered by the peasant Markalf in an exchange conducted in Hungarian. "Salamon és Markalf," unsigned article in *Magyar Irodlami Lexikon*. Ványi Ferenc et al., eds (Budapest, [1936?]), p. 700.

[49] OSzK, 2039 FMI/1608, *Historia anno 1746*, p. 610.

[50] Staud, *Színjátékák*, vol. 1, pp. 273, 283, 293. Elsewhere, at other Jesuit schools, dramas might be produced in multiple languages, on at least one occasion including Romanian. *Op. cit.*, p. 249.

[51] Pastoral pieces might deal with the same topics as full-fledged dramas. Such was probably the case in 1759, with the production of "Alexi Felicitas ..." (Mense Augusto Anno M. D. CC. LIX, Claudiopoli: Typis Academicis Societ, Jesu, 1759), 1-MTA Mikrofilmtár Mf. B. 194/I. See Éva Knapp, "A Nagyszebeni Jezsuita színjátszás első szöveges emlékre: Szent Alexius/1709/," in Demeter and Kilián (eds), *Színház*, p. 227.

[52] For example, in 1733, students debated whether philosophy or history was a more useful subject of study. OSzK, 2039 FMI/1608, *Historia anno 1733*, p. 372.

public displays, as well as in choral musical performances, which reinforced the lessons and messages of the school dramas.[53]

In the second half of the eighteenth century, Jesuit school plays were performed less frequently throughout the Habsburg lands. The disruptions of the Seven Years War put an end to performances in the Bohemian Province and what was probably the Jesuit comedy staged at the *collegium* in Breslau (Wrocław) rang down its curtain in 1757.[54] In the years immediately before the Suppression, school plays increasingly became a rarity. Perhaps the last Jesuit dramatic production in the eastern regions of the Habsburg lands occurred in 1771 in Alba Iulia.[55] The general decline of the Jesuit school play can be attributed to changing tastes that rejected the ornate staging and unrealistic declamation characteristic of the Baroque, but the embattled position of the Society on other fronts may also have contributed to the reduction in the number of performances. The traditional alliance between Jesuits and local elites was likewise under increasing strain in the western Habsburg lands, and a similar trend may have been underway in the east as well, although documentation here is far less conclusive than in the west.

The legacy of plays produced in Cluj by Jesuits outlasted the actual presence of the Society in that city. Joannes Illei, born in Komorno in 1725, was serving as the Rector of the *Seminarium S. Josephi* in 1773, when the suppression of the Society compelled him to seek employment as a teacher elsewhere. While his subsequent career is not known in detail, it is reported that sometime before 1775 he wrote "Tornyos Peter," a popular drama that enjoyed numerous productions. In 1789 Illei published a "Bacchanal" play (that is, one performed during carnival season), and two years later offered several "Ludi tragici" to the public.[56] Despite the late dates of these productions, they were probably continuations of the Baroque model that had served the Society for so long, although in at least one case the production seemed to be bidding for the attention of audiences yearning for the cosmopolitan drama of Vienna. Moses Lestyán, long a teacher in Cluj, offered a Hungarian translation of a successful Metastasio play entitled "Attilius Regulus" as late as 1793.[57] The persistence of themes so closely connected to those promoted by the Society in late eighteenth-century Hungarian theatre is not only evidence of the conservatism and isolation that characterized Hungarian literary life well into the next century, but also

---

[53] For example, in 1715, a choral rendition of "Nisi Dominus aedificaverit Domum" was performed in Cluj. OSzK, 2039 FMI/1608, *Historia anno 1715*, p. 1715.

[54] Hans Heckel, *Geschichte der deutschen Literatur in Schlesien. Erster Band: Von den Anfängen bis zum Ausgang des Barock*. (Breslau, 1929), p. 325.

[55] Shore, "Jesuit missions," p. 112. The lack of detailed records for the Cluj community after 1747 makes it more difficult to assess the scope of dramatic productions in the decades immediately before the Suppression.

[56] Sommervogel et al., *Bibliothèque*, vol. 4, p. 553; *Catalogus Per. et Offici. Prov. Aust. 1773*, p. 8.

[57] *Jezsuita iskoladrámák: Ismert szerzők*, eds Alseghy Zsoltné, Czibula Katalin and Varga Imre (Budapest, 1992), p. 289. Born in Csík in 1720, Lestyán received much of his early formation in Cluj, where he taught "Principia" as a scholastic. ARSI, *Aust*. 93, *Catal. I Col. Claud. 1746*), p. 82. "Attilius Regulus" had been performed, possibly in Hungarian, by Jesuit students in Selemeczbánya in 1758. Jablonkay, *Iskolodrámák*, p. 11.

of the potent impact Jesuit drama continued to have on literary conventions even after the Suppression. The volume of Jesuit plays produced was a major factor in this continuing influence (Jablonkay counts 101 dramas produced in Cluj between 1701 and 1747), but the ingenuity and showmanship of the Jesuit producers also deserves credit. The Society's approach to public dramatic performances can be inferred from the scale and tone of other public undertakings that it staged. In 1750, the Tîrgu Mureş mission celebrated a fifty-year jubilee in which the Jesuit church was decorated and served as the setting for public commemorations. The production was significant enough to be recorded in a booklet published in Cluj that same year.[58] Lavish detail, visual "fény" and careful organization were hallmarks of Jesuit productions in even small and remote towns, and were doubtless prominent in the drama produced in Cluj.

The ultimate importance of the Jesuit school dramas produced in Cluj can only be appreciated in the context of all the literary activities and performances offered by the Society, and by assessing the other cultural, and especially, theatrical performances staged in the town. There is evidence of small-scale theatrical productions staged in Cluj before 1693: in 1683, Tofeus Miháhy, the Bishop of Transylvania, made reference to puppet shows being staged in Cluj.[59] The spectators who witnessed these productions encountered on a daily basis the architectural and frequently personal presence of the Society and its message, concentrated within a town where virtually all relationships were face to face. They bought meat and wine that came from Jesuit lands, rose to the tolling of bells in the towers of the Jesuit church, and watched the town's aristocracy publicly demonstrate their connection to the Society. Jesuit-produced plays were an integral part of a total campaign waged by the Society on literary, artistic and theological fronts to draw the community into the ambit of the Catholic Church, and, in the case of Hungary and Transylvania, the larger Habsburg world whose symbolic reference point was Rome and whose potential sphere of influence the entire world. The results of these efforts were also a direct influence on the direction school plays produced by other Catholic religious orders would take.[60] The location of Cluj made the relative significance of these efforts even greater than they would have been in metropolises such as Vienna or Prague, and the ongoing efforts of the Society to convert the local population or bring it into union with Rome would have created a significantly different context from that of Austrian or Bohemian productions. Within the narrower horizons of this small Transylvanian city, the Society was able to redefine the cultural life of the region, and through the production of plays, the Jesuits left a permanent mark on the relations between the Catholic Church and other faiths.

---

[58] *Anno Jubilaeo Missionis Societatis JESU Maros-Varheliensis. Post exactum Deo propitio dimidium Saeculum. Templi fabricam felicibus auspiciis dedicantis* ... (Claudiopoli, [1750]).

[59] György Székely, "A vásári színjátszás kezdetei hazánkban," in Demeter and Kilián (eds), *Színház*, p. 19.

[60] *A magyarországi katholikus tanitézmények színjátszásának forrásai és irodalma 1800–ig*. Kilián István, Pintér Márta Zsuzsanna and Imre Varga (eds), Imre Varga (chief ed.), *Fontes Ludorum Scenicorum in Scholis Institutisque Catholicis Hungariae* (Budapest, 1992), pp. 238–9.

In a larger context, the plays produced in Cluj during the decades following the return of the Jesuits to the region are best understood as part of the multi-sided effort on the part of the Society to introduce a new aesthetic to a community and to an entire region to which they now had formal entree. While this fact has been recognized by some European scholars, studies of Jesuit drama as a world-wide phenomenon have paid little attention to the connection with the Habsburgs.[61] This aesthetic had its roots far from Transylvania, in the reaches of the Upper Danube, in the piazzas of Rome and in the elaborate ritual of academic debates held in the Jesuit-dominated universities of the western Habsburg realms. The reference points of this aesthetic without exception lay to the west, and its vocabulary was drawn from the narrative of the Church Triumphant and of its champions, the House of Austria. The tone, one might even say the "attitude" expressed by the Habsburg Baroque seemed confident, even if the actual position of the dynasty was frequently less than secure. While elements of this expression of the Baroque achieved an accommodation with some of the local decorative traditions within the Habsburg lands, there was much about it that was transnational, even transcontinental. This visible transformation was an outward sign of external efforts to effect a profound reorientation of the entire Principality. Since Transylvania in the seventeenth century had been a semi-independent political entity, its formal relationship to the great powers of the West was influenced in large part by its desire to remain free of foreign control. And as we have noted, its rulers shifted alliances and played off Turk against Habsburg in an effort to prevent domination by either, but there was a serious cultural price attached to such a strategy. In such an environment, the cultural influence of Western Europe, especially as related to any aspect of literature not directly tied to Biblical studies, was attenuated by these political developments. Internal factors also contributed to this isolation and restriction of expression. One of the most significant consequences of a strong Calvinist presence in Transylvania was a retarding of the advance of the most exuberant forms of the Baroque in literature as well as in the visual arts, while the presence of Eastern Rite Christians likewise inhibited the spread of artistic influences from the West. This tension reached far beyond the doctrinal and formal problems discussed in Chapter Two, and colored all aspects of life in the Principality.

When, in the following century, Transylvania was bound to the Catholic dynasty of the Habsburgs, who themselves had turned their ambitions eastward after being thwarted in their attempts to gain control over Central Europe, many of these difficulties began to appear less formidable. The triumph of Austria seemed secure, especially during the years that the Habsburgs extended their control across the Danube into Serbia and into Wallachian Oltenia. Confidence bred reduced acceptance of local cultural variations, albeit within limits that to the twenty-first century seem

---

[61] For example, William McCabe's survey of Jesuit drama offers no discussion of the relationship between the Jesuits and the Habsburgs. William McCabe, SJ, *An Introduction to the Jesuit Theatre* (St. Louis, MO, 1983). The enthusiasm expressed so often for the Austrian dynasty would however seem to have been counterbalanced by the performance given in 1705 in honor of the French envoy to the rebel Ferenc II Rákóczi. Varga, "Színjátszás," in Demeter and Kilián (eds), *Színház*, p. 239.

very restrictive. The newly introduced aesthetic, despite its ability to assimilate elements from places as diverse Mexico or the Philippines, paid as we have seen scant attention to local artistic traditions and ethnic affiliations in Transylvania. Instead the new point of reference in the public expressions of the Baroque was the relationship of the dynasty to Catholicism, and the desire of that dynasty to bind its peoples and territories together into a cohesive and ultimately loyal unit. The role of the Jesuits in promoting this agenda was central. From the first, the Society openly identified with the Habsburgs, praising them from the pulpit, assisting their armies as chaplains, performing diplomatic missions for them and spreading the message and symbolism of *Pietas Austriaca* into a region on the cultural frontier of Western Christendom.[62] In return, the dynasty supported Jesuit literary undertakings and assured the Society of its preeminent position in Transylvania, supporting an arrangement whereby the Society was placed in a much better economic position than any other Catholic religious order.[63] As the Jesuits sought to draw Orthodox Christians into union with Rome, the themes of some of the plays produced in Cluj and elsewhere in the eastern Habsburg realms reflected not the union of equal partners but the triumph of Rome and Vienna, expressed in references to the power and authority of the former city (and presumably reflected in the inheritance of the latter). The references to Rome echoed those found in Jesuit architecture and in the interest demonstrated by the Cluj Jesuits in ancient Dacia. Mythology was not the only element present in these dramas: sometimes Jesuit producers drew on comic and military themes from pre-Christian Roman culture. For example, "Scipio devicta Carthagine sui victor," produced in Oradea in 1761, and "Botfalva Vig Játék," an adaptation of a Plautus comedy, was produced in Cluj sometime during the second half of the eighteenth century.[64] The employment of Pagan comedy might draw disapproving reactions from the Jansenist or Puritan, but in the eighteenth-century world of the Habsburgs, familiarity with these themes could be considered part of the formation of a gentleman. Any potentially deleterious effects of such carefully expurgated productions might be counterbalanced within the bounds presented in the *Ratio*, by a healthy dose of Pagan philosophers, many of whom were Stoics.

The Baroque Latinity of Jesuit school dramas would have been paralleled on an almost daily basis by the public displays of processions, musical performances, missionary undertakings and the supreme spectacle of the Mass itself, each of which were carefully crafted by the Jesuits to produce a powerful affect. As expressed in

---

[62] The connection between the activities of the Jesuits in the Imperial army in the role of chaplains who provided a narrative of historical triumphalism and Jesuit play producers remains unexplored. See Lumperdean, "Nation et confession," p. 65.

[63] Comparative economic statistics for Catholic orders in Transylvania are incomplete; however, in Hungary, the annual income of the Jesuits during the eighteenth century was 350,000 forints, more than twice that of their nearest rival, the Piarists. Kosáry, *Művelődés*, p. 76.

[64] Jablonkay, *Iskoladrámák*, p. 11; BARC-N, MsC 417. The "Botfalva" comedy was an expurgated version. See Demeter Júlia, "Fösvények, parasztok, bohócok (magyar nyelvű iskolai komédiák)," in Demeter and Kilián (eds), *Színház*, p. 322. *Senis deliria*, produced in 1769, appears to have repeated a theme known in both antique and Renaissance drama: the foolish old man in love.

the architecture of the Jesuit church and school buildings, the Habsburg Baroque aesthetic was dramatic and ornamental while simultaneously exhibiting functional qualities – a concise description of the characteristics of Jesuit school dramas. Jesuit school plays, in addition to their sometimes elaborate set designs and lofty moral messages, also conveyed the solid products of Jesuit education to a larger audience: the skills demonstrated by the student performers were built upon a knowledge of grammar and the niceties of Latin syntax and scansion. The mechanics of producing a play were themselves an indication of how Jesuit education could address practical problems, while the ease and elegance with which the performers rendered their lines conveyed the Society's commitment to the development of polished men of the world. Without having the texts of most of these plays that are alluded to in the records of the Society, it is difficult to know what specific role these dramas played in promoting the image of the Society to the general public, either in Cluj or more widely throughout Transylvania. However, we may be sure that virtue and fidelity, both to the Catholic Church and to those secular authorities legitimated by God (for example, the Habsburgs) were recurring themes in these productions. Indirectly, too, the audiences may have sensed that products of Jesuit schooling, now armed with knowledge of the reigning aesthetic, would be better equipped to succeed in the new order.

One of the proudest achievements of a religious order noted for its industry and ambition, if not always creativity, Jesuit school dramas are at the intersection of the technical, linguistic and "public relations" components of the Jesuit undertaking. Yet the content and impact of these productions remain much more elusive than that of Jesuit architecture or homiletics.[65] The sheer number of Jesuit school plays produced in Cluj and elsewhere compels us to consider questions of originality and quality, both in composition and execution, although it is worth recalling that the eighteenth century was an era of mass-produced operas, symphonies and sermons. In Cluj, as in most of the communities where the Society invested heavily in the production of school dramas, there is little conclusive evidence as to the content of the more serious of these plays. Aside from manuscripts of the aforementioned "Botfalva Vig Játék," there is little direct evidence of the dramatic principles employed, the degree of character development, and the possibilities afforded by the musical accompaniment of plays offered by the Jesuit schools of Cluj.[66] Their contribution to the cultural climate of communities such as Cluj merits further study, both from the standpoint of Jesuit schooling and literary activities, and from the perspective of promoting the values and mythology of the dynasty that the Society served. Moreover, as extensions of school curricula, these plays may have been employed to provide

---

[65] The ambiguity of direction that Jesuit school dramas sometimes took is suggested by a play entitled "A' fen héjázó és maga sorsával meg nem elégendő emberek bolondsága" that may have been an adaptation of Molière's "Le bourgeois gentilhomme." Probably first produced in Oradea, the play's text has unfortunately not survived. Gragger Róbert's discussion of this play, "Molière első nyomai amagyar irodalomban" is summarized at http://www.sk–szeged.hu/kiallitas/moliere/magyar.html accessed 19 May 2005.

[66] BARC-N, MsC., p. 418. Also included in the category "Iskolai drámák" in the Cluj library of the Romanian Academy are "Stephanus" and "Fratres Credulus et Incredulus." BARC-N, MsC., pp. 156–9.

concrete evidence of the social hierarchy the Society sought to promote: it is known that Piarist plays, for example, sometimes cast the most aristocratic students in the most prominent roles. Whether the Jesuits of Cluj, who were very sensitive to the social standing of performers and audience did so is not clear. Easier to assess is the ideal world that these performances projected, one where virtue and skill were the possession of key players, where truths could be communicated through the senses, and where sacrifice was ennobled and rewarded. In no other of their enterprises was the Jesuits world-view so unambiguously set forth, or so skillfully presented.

CHAPTER SEVEN

Social Order

Not stopping with building a physical presence in the community, the Society sought to influence directly the lives of rich and poor through example, performance and persuasion. The status of Cluj as one of only two "missionary stations" in Transylvania placed the Jesuit community in a spotlight in which it might be expected to accomplish much.[1] The connections the Society fostered with the elites of the community aided it in its contacts with the wealthiest, while the absence of any sort of public support for the indigent provided an open terrain for acts of charity.[2] In addition to efforts at conversion of those still outside the Church, the fathers attempted to regulate behavior of all individuals, it would seem, throughout the community, sometimes interrupting social patterns that had existed for years. Families who were engaged in loaning money at usurious rates suddenly found their business being "corrected."[3] Duelists, including those of gentle birth, were "impeded" from answering the demands of honor.[4] Victims of depression and other types of mental illness were rescued and returned to health, women who strayed from their husbands were returned to their families, and houses of ill repute were closed.[5] In one year alone, 1717, in addition to the usual litany of troubled marriages, virgins were reported rescued from dire circumstances and polygamists were unmasked.[6] How Jesuits obtained this information on their neighbors is not specified in the Society's documents, but the performance of sacramental penance would have provided the context for the public admission of these faults. In fact, the attention paid to the sacraments was as important an objective of the Society as was the recording of the narratives of reform and repentance themselves, since neglect of the sacraments posed as great a crisis to the community as did any of the specific misdeeds of the penitents. This Jesuit emphasis on the sacraments was, as we have noted, a response to the anti-sacramental stance of Protestant and Unitarian groups

---

[1] Szilas, "Austria," in *Diccionario*, vol. 1, p. 288. Later a "tertia missionis statio haud longe Claudiopolitnai dissita" was established. Nilles, *Symbolae*, vol. 2, p. 972. Gabrielis Kapi, the head of Dacian missions, a responsibility that covered a huge territory, was based in Cluj for one year. *Op cit.*, vol. 2, p. 972.

[2] Typical of wealthy allies of the Jesuits was Ladislaus Mikola, who contributed to the poor during the plague year of 1710. OSzK, 2039 FMI/1608 *Historia S. J. Claudiopoli 1710*, p. 94. Not until the reforms of Joseph II would any systematic relief for the poor be provided by the Habsburg government. John A. Garraty, *Unemployment and History: Economic Thought and Public Policy* (New York, 1978), p. 52.

[3] OSzK, 2039, FMI/1608, *Historia S. J. Claudiopoli 1711*, p. 105.

[4] OSzK, 2039, FMI/1608, *Historia S. J. Claudiopoli 1710*, p. 105.

[5] OSzK, 2039, FMI/1608, *Historia S. J. Claudiopoli 1723*, p. 263; *1715*, p. 161.

[6] OSzK, 2039, FMI/1608, *Historia S. J. Claudiopoli 1717*, p. 195.

throughout the Habsburg lands. Yet there was a special value attached to the actions associated with the sacrament of penance. In the middle of the sixteenth century when the disruption unleashed by the Reformation seemed to be reaching its climax, Pius V had stated explicitly that sacramental penance had value in maintaining "social order."[7] Public acts of penance put the penitent before the community as a warning to others, while also providing a process by which the offender, through considerable exertions, might be restored to the community. The Jesuit emphasis on penance likewise created a connection between the *Spiritual Exercises*, which placed significant emphasis on examination of conscience, and ritual public behaviors that reiterated the relationship between mortification and holiness, a relationship lying at the heart of the Baroque sensibility the Society brought to the community.[8] Through penance, the mental distress felt by the sinner who believed himself to be "in a state of enmity with God" was addressed, and the differences between Catholicism and other faiths practiced in the region thrown into high relief.[9]

Penance, in particular public penance, also reinforced the connection between religious conviction and bodily experience. Like many of his Baroque contemporaries, the Catholic *devot* moreover sought control over his own body, and engagement with the sacraments provided an avenue for reducing suffering.[10] Acts of public penance often echoed the plot lines of Jesuit dramas that might have been witnessed by the same townspeople only a short time before. Others who felt the weight of guilt were encouraged to undertake private acts of penance, which might range from abstaining from wine to the wearing of tattered or uncomfortable garments to bizarre public demonstrations.[11] An obscure passage in the *Historia* of the Jesuit residence from 1713, a year when the plague was particularly deadly, seems to imply that a few women also performed penances, possibly in public on a weekly basis. The outer boundaries of this penitential behavior could verge on what a later era would call pathological, as when it was reported that a man carved the word JESUS into his chest with a knife.[12] Others used chains, nettles or exposure to the elements to mortify the flesh.[13] Such practices point to a tendency in Baroque Catholic piety for public rituals to gain an instrumentality of their own, one which could go beyond or even contradict Church teaching. For example, in southern Italy in the eighteenth century, the blood shed by flagellants was believed to have the power to purify the soul of the one who shed it, a belief that would have been considered sacrilegious

---

[7] W. David Myers, *"Poor, sinning folk": Confession and Conscience in Counter-Reformation Germany"* (Ithaca, NY, 1996), p. 118.

[8] Stephen Haliczer, *Sexuality in the Confessional: A Sacrament Profaned* (New York/Oxford, 1996), p. 177. Laypersons received direction from members of the Cluj community in the *Spiritual Exercises,* trans. ARSI, *Aust. 198, An. Prov. Aust. 1741,* p. 54.

[9] P. Galtier, *Sin and Penance*. B. Wall trans. (St. Louis, MO, 1932), p. 63.

[10] R. Po-Chia Hsia, *The World of Catholic Renewal 1540–1777* (Cambridge, 1998), pp. 194–7.

[11] OSzK, 2039 FMI/1068, *Historia S.J. Claudiopoli 1713*, p. 120.

[12] OSzK 2039 FMI/1068 *Historia S.J. Claudiopoli, 1725*, p. 287.

[13] ARSI, *Aust. 172, An. Prov. Aust. 1715*, p. 56; ARSI, *189, An. Prov. Aust. 1732*, p. 185.

by the standards of Trent.[14] Yet even such extreme measures were viewed with approval by the Society, struggling as it was to combat not only schismatic and heretical beliefs, but also the specter of atheism that seemed to be lurking behind such movements as Pietism.[15] Yet despite the public staging of demonstrations of penance, reliance on the sacraments was sometimes not enough to regulate social behavior. The unstable and at times desperate atmosphere of an eighteenth-century Transylvanian community occasionally shows its shape in the records compiled by the Cluj Jesuit community. An especially vivid instance of this was recorded in 1739, when nocturnal gatherings of "youths of both sexes" were reported in the town and in the countryside: blasphemies and unnamed "certa corruptella" spewed forth that could only be suppressed with grave penalties, and the Society's chroniclers were unable to report any conversions or acts of public penance.[16] Significantly, these disturbances occurred long after the Jesuits had been able to establish institutions to help regulate social conduct. Jesuits in Cluj, like their colleagues elsewhere, went beyond the tools explicitly prescribed by the Council of Trent and found other ways to draw upon the diverse traditions of popular culture as they strove to reach out to the people.[17] Local rituals of childbirth were supplemented if not supplanted by the aid of the Society, which provided relics of St. Ignatius to aid in the process.[18] To further support the combat against the non-sacramental view of religion, be it Unitarian, Lutheran, or Calvinist, the Jesuits also had such weapons as the Society of the Good Death, a fraternal organization whose members prepared for death by reading pious literature, prayer, and through the spiritual guidance of a Jesuit. Franciscus Retz, who would serve as the Father General from 1730 to 1750, took a particular interest in the fraternity, whose activities called attention both to the necessity of leading a life modeled on Christ's, and on the importance of the sacrament of extreme unction.[19] Unlike the public demonstrations that held the attention of the townsfolk, private devotional practices left few records, but the Jesuits of Cluj probably committed significant resources to their promotion. But while a Jesuit visiting the home of a rural aristocrat or the lodging of a army officer could focus attention on the care of an individual soul, there remained all around a

---

[14] Mario Rosa, "The Italian Churches," in Callahan and Higgs (eds), *Church and Society*, p. 75.

[15] A resident of Cluj who had traveled to Germany was reported to have contracted some dangerous contagions, most specifically from Halle. ARSI, *Aust. 178, An. Prov. Aust. 1722*, folio 11v. Imports from Halle, the nerve center of Pietism, were a constant threat to the Jesuit program. Bibles originating in Halle were seized in Buda in 1728. ARSI, *Aust. 185, An. Prov. Aust. 1728*, folio 14v.

[16] PFK, 880.118.E. 10; ARSI, *Aust. An. Prov. Aust. 1739*, folio 16. Perhaps not coincidentally, the plague was so severe in this year that the customary celebrations associated with the feast of St. Ignatius were cancelled. ARSI, *Aust. An. Prov. Aust. 1739*, folio 7.

[17] Po-Chia, *World*, p. 198.

[18] OSzK, 2039 FMI/1608, *Historia S. J. Claudiopoli 1725*, p. 287.

[19] Epistola Vicarii Generalis Franciscus Retz. Romae 3 Junii 1730. ANR-CN, Fond liceul romano-catolic, unnumbered folio.

great sea of unbelievers and the uncommitted, whose uncharted depths were also the object of proselytizing exhortations and dramatic performance.[20]

In addressing the formidable challenge, this Society had four tools, which it used in various combinations as opportunity and resources allowed. First, as we have seen, the rituals and sacraments of the Church were brought to bear on social deviants individually, or to communities at large, in the context of spreading the Gospel. Outrageous behavior might be curbed through exorcisms, and prurient thoughts through less drastic pastoral efforts.[21] Behaviors that might have had their origins in folk customs and which may have been sanctioned – or at least ignored – by other local religious traditions were frequently identified by Jesuits as expressions of "superstitions," or worse. Amulets and "magic pages" were seized, and an elaborate money-making scheme involving the donning of "certain sacred vestments" and recitation of parodies of Christian ritual was suppressed.[22] While some of the users of these occult devices may have been on the fringes of society, others came from more respectable backgrounds. A "vir illustrus," having seen the error of his ways, burned "diabolical" amulets and underwent a tearful repentance under the guidance of the Jesuits.[23] Social order here was promoted through an approach that went beyond the renewed emphasis placed on the sacraments By identifying some behaviors as totally outside the acceptable limits of the community, the Society helped to foster a sense of what was acceptable, both in terms of Church dogma, and relative to the standards of behavior it sought to impose on the community. Consequently misdeeds identified by the Society might seem at times to lie as much in the civil as in the theological realm. Elsewhere in the Austrian Province, Jesuits had helped to unmask a Jew impersonating a physician, or saw to the punishment of a townsman dressed up like St. Nicholas (who was no doubt continuing a long-sanctioned custom), and were on constant patrol to regulate social behavior.[24] While Jesuit records do not indicate which, if any of the unacceptable behaviors suppressed by the Society were viewed as having ties to other religious traditions, it seems probable that some occult practices were understood as "good magic" or even as legitimate expressions of folk religion by their practitioners. The yardstick by which the Society assessed unfamiliar and seemingly deviant behavior was never made explicit in surviving documents, and in fact probably was not explicitly taught as such to individual Jesuits sent to settings such as Cluj, largely because the institutional culture of the Society stressed personal initiative and judgment, within guidelines reinforced throughout the period of a Jesuit's formation. The Jesuit priest, trained in theology and in cases of conscience, was considered competent on his own to determine whether an unfamiliar or questionable practice fell into the category of "diabolical," or "superstitious," or

---

[20] ARSI, *Aust. 172, An. Prov. Aust. 1715*, p. 6.

[21] ARSI, *Aust. 155, An. Prov. Aust.1697*, folio 79v.

[22] ARSI, *Aust. 182, An. Prov. Aust. 1725*, folio 8v; *Aust. 180, An. Prov. Aust. 1723*, folio 4v.

[23] OszK, 2039 FMI/1608 *Historia S. J. Claudiop. 1723*, p. 262.

[24] ARSI, *Aust. 191, An. Prov. Aust.*. 1734, folio 56r; *Diarium Missionis Societatis Jesu Maros-Vasarheliensis,Tomus II ab A, D, MDCCXXVIII Mense Junio.* BB Szentiványi 1958 Nr. 691 xi.68, folio 169v (6 December 1736).

whether it might be tolerated.[25] Yet "superstitions" were very much on the mind of the Jesuit moving among the people. Ignatius Parhamer, one of the most famous Jesuit missionaries of the day, compiled a program for rural missions that included an entire day devoted to "superstitiones."[26] Coupled with the other roles of teacher, leader of sodalities, play producer, preacher, confessor, landlord and employer, the responsibility of judging social practices gave Jesuit priests considerable leverage in regulating the conduct of individual men and women. Jesuits also performed rituals that affirmed Catholic beliefs in public settings, and which did not single out individuals.[27] One of the most common of these rituals was the blessing of wells, a ritual that conveyed a message of security and hope to the entire community, while placing the Jesuit priest in the role of the medium by which this blessing reached the people.[28] Closely related to employment of sacraments and rituals was the use of public events connected with schooling to promote a theological agenda. Jesuit records report that communion was distributed on a mass scale each year, although the totals reported do not tell us how many communicants participated or of course what the understanding of attitudes of these communicants might have been.[29] The importance of Jesuit school theatre in promoting morality and an understanding of Catholic doctrine is discussed in Chapter Six; public debates between students were also utilized as venues for extolling piety, as when, in 1723, philosophy students debated "Whether the Hungarian nation owed its existence to arms, or to piety."[30] In this instance, it seems unlikely that the honors went to the martial virtues.

A second approach to regulation of society was through direct influence over the socially marginalized and disadvantaged. A poor family might be employed as servants by the Jesuits in their *seminarium* or their residence, where they would be exposed to the moral models of the fathers as well as to the strict behavioral

---

[25] Jean Delumeau writes, "In verità, ciò che i missionari, che percorsero le campagne di Francia e d'Europa durante il XVII secolo, chiamarono 'superstizione' non era altero che paganismo." The further east these missionaries ventured, the less familiar some of the manifestations of this paganism were likely to be, and the greater the possibility that these customs would be branded "superstitious" or worse. Jean Delumeau, "Christianizatione e decristianizatione fra il XV e XVIII secolo," in Carla Russo (ed.), *Società, Chiesa e Vita Religiosa nell "ancien régime"* (Napoli: Guida Editora, 1976), p. 58.

[26] ARSI, *Aust.* 229, *Fructus Missionarium, 1686*, folio 170r. For example, in 1765, Franciscan fathers supported and possibly accompanied Jesuits on a rural mission. ARSI, *Aust. 220, An. Prov. Aust. 1765*, folio 41r. Jesuits also trained Franciscans to conduct missions among the Bulgarians. ARSI, *Aust.* 220, *Lit. An. 1765*, folio 66r.

[27] Yet sometimes these public efforts produced theatrical results whose impression on observers is hard to gauge. On one occasion, "heretics" plunged lead into a vessel of "Ignatius water": a "terrific sound" was heard while the vicinity was plunged into darkness, and "lemures insuper et spectra per avia et devia" flew about. ARSI, *Aust. 174, An. Prov. Aust 1717*, p. 53.

[28] Wells in the Cluj area were blessed during the plague year of 1719. ARSI, *Austria 176, An. Prov. Aust. 1719*, p. 90.

[29] For instance, communion was distributed 30,580 times during 1757, a figure that may include communicants encountered during rural missions. ARSI, *Aust. An. Prov. Aust. 1757*, folio 1v.

[30] ARSI, *Aust. 180, An. Prov. Aust. 1723*, folio 41r.

requirements of the Society.[31] Possibly less supervision of morals and religious practice would have been involved when the Society employed local cowherds to watch over the community's livestock.[32] Captives freed from Turkish or Tartar slavery were another group who might receive particular attention from a Society seeking converts.[33] The Jesuit orphanage provided fourteen boys with an education that undoubtedly reinforced the standards of conduct preached from Jesuit pulpits and promoted in the Society's activities in the town.[34] The *Domus Convertiarum* or *Neoconversiarum* was another setting where children, either of noble or common birth, would be exposed to the tenets of Jesuit teaching.[35] The Society found other ways to gain control over the education of youngsters: Father Paul Libenczki, who died in 1733, had been taken at the age of seven from his Unitarian parents and raised by the Jesuits.[36] Jesuit records note the "masculine constancy" of a girl who rejected the Unitarian beliefs of her parents and servants to hold fast to the Catholic faith, but we are not told how she acquired this faith.[37] In somewhat different circumstances, a woman condemned to death was brought back to the Christian faith through the offices of a Jesuit.[38] A less vulnerable group, but one still subject to the influence of Jesuit teaching, were the clergy of other orders and those students destined for vocations as diocesan clergy who studied in the Jesuit *seminarium*. Through decades of training such future clergy, the Jesuits of Cluj were able to put their stamp on the entire Catholic clergy of the region, and thereby extend their indirect influence into every parish.

As we have seen, Jesuit residences might serve as places of refuge for soldiers and fugitives from justice, and prisoners of war. When in 1733 a wounded POW arrived in Cluj on a cart, the Society provided him a place to try to recover, although in this instance he died.[39] And although the Society never established a facility specifically for women, Jesuits had constant interaction with women and girls, who at the time

---

[31] ARSI, *Aust. An. Prov. Aust. 1720*, 239. In 1700, along with five priests, two scholastics and one *coadjutor temporalis*, the Cluj Jesuit community counted twenty members in the category of "familiam." ARSI, *Austria 55, Catal. Claud. III 1700*, folio 86r.

[32] In 1742, fifteen cowherds were employed by the Jesuit community in Cluj; this is exclusive of those *coadjutors temporales* who performed similar chores. MOL, Microfilm roll 32575, F 234, Erdélyi Fiscalis Levéltár, unnumbered folio.

[33] Sometimes captives could be freed in exchange for a modest amount of tobacco. PFK, 118. A.E. 697, *Transylvania Epistolica*, folio 46v.

[34] OSzK, 2039 FMI/1608, *Historia S. J. Claudiopoli 1713*, p. 133.

[35] *Nomina Personarum sexûs muliebris in Domo Neoconversorum existentium anno 1769*, folio 49r.

[36] ARSI, *Aust. 190, An. Prov. Aust. 1733*, p. 229. Conversely, in the difficult times of plague and famine, a Catholic parent might sell his son to a Unitarian family for ten florins. ARSI, *Aust. 1725*, folio 8v.

[37] ARSI, *Aust. 158, An. Prov. Aust. 1701*, folio 23v. A rare reported conversion of a Romanian Orthodox girl to Catholicism in Alba Iulia, again recorded without details, occurred in 1734. BB, Szentiványi 691, XI 68 *Annue Residentiae S. J. Carolinae Annus* [sic]*1734*, folio 26v.

[38] OSzK, 2039, FMI/1608, *Historia S. J. Claudiopoli 1704*, folio 58.

[39] ARSI, *Aust. 190, An. Prov. Aust. 1733*, p. 13.

possessed few legal rights. In particular, women were invited to be part of sodalities set up by the Society, which frequently distributed books to the general population. The Marian Congregations, like the Baroque architecture of the Jesuit complex, were also an import from the Holy Roman Empire and exemplified the brand of Baroque piety found in the Habsburg heartland.[40] Ironically, the Society was expanding its program of sodalities along the eastern frontier of Latin Christendom at exactly the point when the appeal of these organizations where they had first become popular, the Mediterranean, was waning.[41] The relationship of Jesuit-sponsored sodalities to the Society's involvement in social control is less clear, but a list of books owned by one of these sodalities at the time of the Suppression points to the guidance of conduct through teaching, socialization and, significantly, reading.[42] Among the books confiscated by Austrian authorities in 1773 that had been stored in the library of the Jesuit-supported "Congregatio B.V. Mariae" were the *Imitatio Christi* of Thomas à Kempis, Latin lives of Ignatius and Xavier, four copies of *Zodiacus Christianus*, nine copies of *Trimegistus Christianus*, *Septi Collis Daciae*, a Latin grammar, the Ten *Rationes* of Edmund Campion, one of the first direct challenges by a Jesuit to Protestant clergy, calling upon them to debate, and volumes of Polydore Virgil, Cicero, and a work presumably praising the most adamantly Catholic of Habsburg rulers, *Ferdinandi Secundi Virtutes*.[43] Another highly significant evidence of Jesuit support for female literacy is a "Girl's ABC in Hungarian" found among the stocks of the Jesuit print shop in Cluj after the Suppression.[44] Whether this volume (which appears without reference to an author) was intended for private or classroom instruction cannot be determined with certainty, but the production of a primer specifically for girls in the vernacular is in itself evidence of the willingness of the Jesuits to address the needs of the local population. At the same time, Jesuit ambitions for the books produced at their own printing press in Cluj sometimes reached towards populations located far from the community. An introductory text in Latin, intended for for the faithful who had been exposed to the liturgy in Old Church Slavonic or Ruthenian, was produced in 1746, evidence of the broad view

---

[40] Myers, *"Poor, Sinning Folk"*, pp. 168–9.

[41] Haliczer, *Sexuality*, p. 205.

[42] Much work remains to be done on the earlier history of Marian Congregations. The *Prima Primaria*, a governing document of these sodalities, was only approved by Benedict XIV as late as 1751. Joseph de Guibert, SI, *La Spiritualité de la Compagnie de Jésus: Esquisse Historique (Bibliotheca Instituti Historici S. I. vol. IV)* (Romae, 1953), p. 501.

[43] MOL, F477 *Exactoratus*, pp. 185–7. Since the *Imitatio Christi* appears in a list of books housed in the Jesuit print shop under the Magyarized name of the author ("Kempis Tamas"), it may be that this very popular devotional work was available in Hungarian, which would have made it accessible to a much larger readership, including many women. MOL, F477 *Exactoratus*, p. 54. The *Zodiacus Christianus* was by the Jesuit Hieronymus Drexell (Amersterdam, 1634) and offered a theologically acceptable alternative to the horoscopes so popular in the seventeenth century.

[44] Six hundred copies "in crudo" were reported in the possession of the *collegium* in 1773. MOL, F477 *Exactoratus*, p. 52.

Cluj Jesuits took of their mission.[45] Other lay organizations were sponsored by the Society as it solidified its presence throughout Transylvania and all of the eastern Habsburg domains: in about 1699 the "Congregatio Agoniae" of Ungvár paid for a new altar in the Jesuit church.[46]

Beyond the Society's contact with women already confirmed in the Church that was sustained through the promotion of sodalities, conversion of women figured prominently in Jesuit missionary and evangelizing efforts. The relationship of women to the all-male Society was complex, and subject to restrictions occasioned by the limited freedom accorded women and, on the side of the Society, the necessity of avoiding any hint of scandal. No sooner had the Society begun to reestablish its presence in Cluj when it was able to report that the widow of an Austrian army officer had donated eighty lamps to be lit before the Eucharist. Nevertheless, the Society's records show clearly that ministry to women, above and beyond the formal relationship maintained with socially respectable women through the sodalities, was a significant component of the Jesuit mission, a component that was retained even when Jesuit contacts with women provoked criticism from other Catholic clergy.[47] In Cluj, Jesuits were even prepared to enter bordellos to rescue women and to turn a plague sore of the community into something more wholesome.[48] Jesuit engagement in the lives of women was an inevitable consequence of the Society's approach to social order and improvement: it would have been difficult for the fathers to have ignored the needs and problems of marginalized women in their community. Anecdotal evidence points to the presence of many women, possibly single and without a support system, living in the eastern Habsburg lands, who were under pressure to convert to one religion or another.[49] The upheavals of war and conquest had left many women dependent on whatever institutions or organizations could help them, and in a Baroque culture that stressed the importance of making a "good death," the ministrations of the Jesuits were frequently directed specifically at women facing death, sometimes in the context of impending execution.[50] The process of preparing for a good death would normally include confession and perhaps acts of penance, with the groundwork laid through the conscientious reading of one of the many manuals dealing with this subject.[51] Yet the ranks of women encouraged to prepare for a "good death" were by no means limited to the marginalized. The aristocratic

---

[45] This textbook was composed by Uniate Bishop Manuel Olsavsky. *Elementa Puerilis Institutionis in Lingua Latina* (Claudiopoli, 1746). The one surviving copy of this work is in the collection of the Hungarian National Museum, Sign. T-MK L 2490.

[46] ARSI, *Aust. 157, An. Prov. Aust., 1699–1700*, folio 152r.

[47] From the very beginnings of the Society, contacts with women furnished material for a constantly expanding literature criticizing Jesuits. O'Malley, *Jesuits*, pp. 293–4.

[48] ARSI, *Aust. 177, An. Prov. Aust. 1720*, p. 63.

[49] For example, Catharina Bleyn, born a Muslim, became a Lutheran in Sibiu, and converted to Catholicism on her deathbed. ARSI, *Austria 182, An. Prov. Aust. 1725*, folio 15r. During the same year, "missiones vagae per Hungariam" netted ten Turkish converts.

[50] For example, "... mulierem item praestenti amittendae per carnificem vitae periculo." ARSI, *Aust. 187, An. Prov. Aust. 1730*, folio 41v.

[51] For example, *Sodalitatum Marianum in Soc. Jesu gymnasiis erectarum summa utilitas* (Claudiopoli, 1744).

lady or burgher matron were crucial to Jesuit-sponsored congregations, and no doubt made up a major part of the flock who heard Jesuit sermons each Sunday, or who crowded the small school theatre to enjoy a Jesuit comedy.[52]

The conversion of Jews and Roma might also be considered in the context of control or at least influence over marginalized groups. Occasionally Jews would also convert: eight in 1725 (along with ten "Turks" who could have been Muslims of various nationalities), two in 1732, and one in 1733.[53] Sometimes the process of conversion would require a major effort, as in 1736, when the final step of conversion followed the "longo labore" of a Jesuit.[54] The questionable nature of such conversions, however, is evidenced by the large number of Jewish apostates who reconverted; five apostates are reported reconverted the same year as the five Jewish converts of 1730.[55] A Muslim or Tartar captive would also be marginalized in Habsburg Transylvania, and therefore a prime candidate for conversion.[56] In 1717, a Tartar woman held prisoner in the Timoşoara region was converted to Catholicism.[57] Muslim travelers and soldiers also figure in reports of conversions accomplished at unspecified locations throughout the Austrian Province and beyond.[58] The reporting of such conversions from non-Christian faiths was among the most important tasks for the Jesuit chroniclers, for these anecdotes not only demonstrated the accomplishments of the Society, but also provided ammunition for the polemical and pastoral writing of Jesuits struggling against many traditions hostile to Baroque Catholicism. A final example of a conversion story sheds additional light on the Society's approach to the socially outcast and vulnerable. An unnamed Lutheran soldier, captured in 1702, perhaps during the early phase of the Kuruc rebellion, lay bleeding in the street. Taken to a shelter where it was supposed he would die, the soldier was converted by a Jesuit and received into the Church.[59] This narrative, composed by a Jesuit, stresses the inadequacy of the Lutherans who might have cared for the soldier, and the initiative of the Jesuit who cared for his soul, a concise expression of the pattern Jesuits perceived in their community. Beyond these commonplaces is also visible the way in which the Society was constantly on the lookout for the homeless, the vulnerable and those in need, whose numbers were surprisingly high in a town of

---

[52] Jesuit records make specific reference to the women of Cluj who turned to the relics and images of St. Ignatius for relief. ARSI, *Aust. 185, An. Prov. Aust. 1728*, folio 89v.

[53] ARSI, *Aust. 182, An. Prov. Aust. 1725*, folio 15; *Austria 189, An. Prov. Aust. 1732*, folio 125; *Aust. 190, An. Prov. Aust. 1733*, folio 50v.

[54] OSzK, 2039 FMI/1608, *Historia S. J. Claudiopoli, anno 1737*, p. 387.

[55] ARSI, *Aust. 187, An. Prov. Aust. 1730*, folio 10v.

[56] ARSI, *Aust. 155, An. Prov. Aust. 1697*, folio 79r. In this instance the convert was soon married, presumably to a good Catholic. Another possible conversion from Islam is recorded in 1701: "unum it Mahumete partim exactis." Yet it is not clear whether there were other converts to which this reference only alludes to ("partim"). The "unum a Mahumete" claimed for Chrisitnaity in 1701 from among the youths "in seminariis" in Cluj may refer to the same individual. ARSI, *Aust. 158, An. Prov. Aust. 1701*, folio 72r.

[57] ARSI, *Aust. 174, An. Prov. Aust. 1717*, p. 37.

[58] *Diarium* 1719, folio 12r.

[59] "... violens inter rixas iam alto multatus est vulnere, ut platae omnem prope sanguienem profuderet ... ." ARSI, *Aust. 159, An. Prov. Aust. 1702*, folio 26r.

8,000. Nor should this behavior be viewed merely as exploitative or controlling, since Jesuit priestly formation placed great stress on *cura personalis,* the care of the person, bodily and spiritually. There is every reason to suppose that Jesuit treatment of the unfortunates of Cluj was motivated by what the fathers understood as care for others.

The third of these overlapping strategies was the rural mission. Throughout the Habsburg lands, as well as elsewhere in Central Europe, the pre-Suppression Society devoted significant amounts of resources and manpower to its rural missions, where Catholics might be living without a priest nearby, or where peasants lived without any formal religious affiliation or guidance.[60] In Bohemia, M.-E. Ducreaux notes, the twin tactics of these missions were preaching that stressed doctrine and administration of Holy Communion *en masse.*[61] According to the records compiled by the Jesuits of Transylvania, the fruits of this endeavor were considerable. While the Society's missions were part of a unified effort that included the institutions of school and parish church, the rural missions had a distinctly individual character to them reflecting not only the diversity of the Jesuits themselves, but also the fact that the popular cultures with which Jesuit missionaries interacted were far from uniform or monolithic.[62] Obituaries of Jesuit missionaries stress their solitary undertakings, as when we read that Father Stephanus Miksa embarked on a "missione vaga" in remote reaches of Wallachia, or that in 1743, Josephus Nemaj was recovering his health in Cluj after the rigors of missionary work in Bács.[63]

As many as twenty missionary expeditions might be launched during a single year, and while some of these were probably of short duration, the resources and manpower required to carry out these expeditions must have had a significant impact on the day-to-day operations of the Cluj community.[64] Missionary work continued right up until the time of the Suppression, as evidenced by the career of Josephus Horvath, a native of Cluj, who was working in that city in 1773.[65] Other Jesuit missionaries worked much farther afield, in situations where there was not only an absence of supportive Jesuit institutions, but where hostile institutions would have surrounded and circumscribed their efforts. Franciscus Miroslavich, the native of

---

[60] ARSI, *Austria 172, An. Prov. Aust.* 1715, p. 6.

[61] Marie-Élizabeth Ducreaux, "La mission et la rôle des missionaries dans les pays tcheques au xviiie siecle," *Actes du 109 congrès national des societés savantes, Dijon, 1984. Section d'histoire moderne et contemporaine.* Tome I. *Transmettre la foi: xvie–xxe siècles. I. Pastorale et predication en France*, p. 36.

[62] Michael Mullett, *Popular Culture and Popular Protest in Late Medieval and Early Modern Europe.* (London, 1987), pp. 166–7.

[63] ARSI, *Austria 77, Catalogus I Coll. Claud. 1730*, p. 397; Sommervogel et al., *Bibliothèque*, vol. 5, p. 1082. The word "vagum" and its cognates appears repeatedly in accounts of Jesuit missionary work in the hinterlands, as when Paulus Kolosvári was credited with four years of a "missionem vagum [sic] per Transylvania nunc per Hungariam." ARSI, *Austria 77, Catalogus Coll. Claudiop. 1730*, 598. Nemaj, at the time of his convalescence was 44 years old. ARSI, *Austria 96, Catalogus Coll. Claudiop. 1749*, p. 82.

[64] In 1714, twenty expeditions left Cluj "ac vicinos, ac remotos pagos." ARSI, *Aust. 171, An. Prov. Aust. 1714*, folio 45r.

[65] *Catalogus Person. Prov. Aust. 1773*, col. 8.

Belgrade mentioned earlier, performed the service of "Missionarius in legatione ad Portam Ottomanica anno uno et medio," continuing an old tradition of a Jesuit presence in Constantinople.[66] The Transylvanian missions also drew the attention of the Bohemian Province: two Jesuit priests, Matthias Schmidt and Joannes Koffler, were working in Transylvania immediately before the Suppression, apparently independently of the missions directed from Cluj.[67] Mission work was demanding and risky, but there was never a shortage of men ready to carry it out, perhaps because of the personal contacts that ensued, or perhaps because of the greater degree of freedom that might be experienced in the countryside.

In order to see the Jesuit missionary project in Transylvania and Moldavia more clearly, we might compare with the strategies employed by the Society a century earlier in China, for both undertakings were ambitious projects whose long-term objects was the winning for the Church of geographically important regions not under European colonial rule. The four major characteristics of the strategy used in China and in fact throughout the Far East, as identified by Nicolas Standaert, were first, accommodation or adaptation to local culture; second, propagation and evangelization "from the top down"; third, indirect propagation of the faith using European science and technology, and finally, openness to and tolerance of Chinese values.[68] While some obvious parallels between these strategies and those used in Eastern Europe are readily apparent, the differences between the two approaches are more instructive. Far from the direct material support of any European Catholic power, the Jesuits of China turned to the portable evidences of European superiority, such as clocks, telescopes and paintings employing scientific perspective to impress local authorities. By contrast, although some first-rate scientists such as Maximilianus Hell worked in Cluj and undoubtedly studied problems far beyond the understanding of many local residents, this intellectual and technological firepower was never employed to strengthen the Society's position *vis-á-vis* local elites. Again, while the Jesuits of Iaşi actively courted the local prince's favor, the "top down" model could never work as well in sparsely populated regions where central authority remained relatively weak and there did not already exist a sizable cultured elite. Instead, Jesuits working on the frontiers of the Habsburg lands and beyond relied more on the miraculous as it occurred in nature, rather than on technological triumphs, to gain attention and credibility, wonders that could be appreciated by both the relatively well-off urban burgher and the illiterate peasant.

Some of these wonders appear to have impressed the Jesuit fathers greatly: when a cross appeared on the moon over Papa (in western Hungary) on the night of 2 August 1664, an anonymous Jesuit took pains to sketch the various forms it took.[69] Cynics might claim that the Jesuit penchant for discovering symbolic support for Catholic piety in the natural world was a calculated strategy appealing to the credulous, but the enormous body of devotional literature produced by Jesuits

---

[66] Miroslavich found time to write *Lites inter Provincias Daciae*.
[67] *Catalogus Person. Prov. Aust. 1773*, col. 51.
[68] Nicolas Standaert, SJ, "Jesuit corporate culture as shaped by the Chinese," in O'Malley et al. (eds), *Jesuits*, pp. 352–63.
[69] ARSI, *Aust. 229, Opera Missionarium*, folio 268r.

working in Transylvania, including those trained as scientists, would seem to point in another direction. Jesuits who labored in the mountains and remote villages of Transylvania and Moldavia were not chosen – or were not self-selected – to confront a sophisticated urban society distant from their own. Unlike the handful of outstanding individuals who encountered the high civilizations of the Far East, these Jesuits did not serve as ambassadors from another world that sought to engage the elites on their own turf. Instead, in their backgrounds and attitudes, the Jesuits of the eastern Habsburg lands sometimes resembled the Observant Franciscans who were occasionally their companions.[70] Yet these attitudes that placed Habsburg Jesuits in more close relationship with the folk culture around them did not always translate into an openness and tolerance for the values of the peoples they encountered. The relatively modest results of the Uniate undertaking were not the only evidence of the difficulties the Society encountered in its efforts to evangelize in central Transylvania. In 1754, at the peak of the Jesuits' strength, and after decades of building institutions and educating boys, they could only claim an annual 84 converts from Lutheranism, Calvinism, Socinanism and Orthodoxy.[71] Of course, the Chinese mission likewise did not win large numbers of converts, but it had other immediate political objectives, whose success might be ascertained by the degree of influence Jesuits could exercise in the midst of a complex Imperial Court.

In Transylvania, the closest the Society could come to the intimate position that they held for a while in the K'ang Shi Emperor's court was their long-term role as *theologi* of the Uniate bishops or as advisers to Catholic bishops, documentation of which is scanty.[72] In the other areas where the Jesuits of Cluj strove to effect major changes in local society, the long-term impact verged on insignificant. The Society not only lacked the resources to bring about the kind of major transformation in public and private behaviors that it had identified as one of its major goals, but it also did not have missionary intellectuals of the stature of Schall von Bell or Ricci to advance its work. Yet there were several areas where the Jesuit mission did make significant contact with targeted groups. To the modern historian perhaps the most interesting of these was the Roma.

The Roma

Of all the groups living in the district around Cluj, none is more suggestive of the status of Transylvania as a cultural and political borderland than the Roma people.

---

[70] For example, in 1765, Franciscan fathers supported and possibly accompanied Jesuits on a rural mission. ARSI, *Austria 220, An. Prov. Aust. 1765*, folio 41r. However, such an amicable partnership was not always the rule. In Moldavia in the second half of the seventeenth century, rivalry between Jesuit and Franciscan missionaries reached the level of mutual accusation and open hostility. Benda (ed.), *Okmánytár*, pp. 45–6.

[71] ARSI, *Aust., An. Prov. Aust. 1754*, folio 2r.

[72] One of the few contemporaneous records of this connection not produced by members of the Society is Bod Peter's manuscript *Brevis Valachorum Transylvanaiam incolentium historia ...*, a copy of which is preserved in the Romanian Academy library in Bucharest. ARSI, *Austria 155, An. Prov. Aust. 1697*, folio 79r.

SOCIAL ORDER 159

Romanticized by Westerners and persecuted by their neighbors, the Roma have lived in Transylvania for centuries, resisting pressure to assimilate and maintaining their distance from whatever dominant culture sought to control them, both by remaining mobile and by denying outsiders access to their community. Relations between the Jesuits and the Roma are difficult to reconstruct from the surviving records, although some elements of the encounter are easily identified. As with the other groups that the Jesuits interacted with, a basic goal of the Society was conversion, and most of the surviving references to Roma in Jesuit documents relate to proselytizing; the most common acknowledgement of the presence of the Roma merely lists those who converted.[73] Yet within the framework of conversion accounts may be discerned glimpses of the cross-cultural encounter in which the means of negotiating the gulf between Roma and non-Roma must be altered with the arrival of the Jesuits.[74] In 1703, a Romany father brought his child to be baptized by a Jesuit; in the account preserved in the Cluj Jesuit history, the Jesuit performed the sacrament "not for money but for the love of God." The Roma were reportedly "stupefied" by this intelligence, and marveled at the priest's behavior. The emphasis on the exchange of money may also be a Jesuit swipe at Orthodox practices in the region, or it may reflect the nature of relations between Roma and "Gadjo" (non-Roma), in which a price was assigned to most interactions, thereby "buying" the Roma some security. On a deeper level, the encounter between the Jesuit and Roma hints at the gulf of understanding and communication between priest and parent. Conversion for the Roma may have been undertaken sincerely, but may have also been the consequence of pressure applied by ecclesiastical or civil authorities to a people who historically had been prepared to take on religious affiliations in order to survive. Jesuit records hint at these pressures: out of the eighteen Calvinists converted in Cluj in 1708, two are identified as Roma.[75] We cannot know with certainty the motivations of Roma who had become Calvinists, but it is safe to say that Calvinist clergy would not have approved of the way of life of most Roma, and that the Calvinist restrictions on secular music, smoking, drinking and dancing, to name only a few activities commonly pursued by Roma, would have been a severe burden to a Roma convert. It is also unclear to what degree Roma converts or near-converts were instructed in the Faith. When a seventy-year-old Roma was taught the basics of Catholicism by two Jesuit priests, the absence in the account of any mention of an actual conversion suggests that instruction may not have been carried very far.[76]

The actual consequences of a conversion of Roma to Catholicism are equally hard to assess. In 1705, a Romani woman who "had lived for 35 years without baptism in the most obscure darkness and in contempt of salvation," joined the Church.[77] A quarter of a century later, we find a brief reference to a dying Roma (not identified as

---

[73] OSzK, 2039, FMI/1608 *Historia anno 1711*, p. 105. Roma were listed in a 1695 report by Rudoph Bzenszky as a separate religious group, along with Arians, Jews and Anabaptists. PF 118. A. 6. 697, *Transylvania Epistolica*, folio 46v.
[74] OSzK, 2039 FMI/1608 *Historia anno 1703*, p. 50.
[75] OSzK, 2039 FMI/1608 *Historia SJ Claudiopoli 1708*, p. 77.
[76] OSzK, 2039 FMI/1608 *Historia SJ Claudiopoli 1707*, p. 73.
[77] OSzK, 2039 FMI/1608 *Historia anno 1705*, p. 57.

a convert) attended by a Jesuit.[78] Were the Jesuit missionaries more accommodating in their view of Roma culture than Orthodox, Calvinist, or other Catholic clergy, or did the emerging political and social prominence of the Society play a role in the conversion? As a group, the Roma were not viewed as negatively by the Cluj Jesuits in the way the Jews were in other parts of the Habsburg realms; Roma religious beliefs, conveyed orally and in a language not understood by any of their neighbors, to the degree they were understood by Jesuits did not pose the same threat to Christian as the scholarship of the Torah and the anti-Jesus literature of the Talmudic period. Jesuits even loaned money to Roma: "Georg Buffa Zingarus" owed twelve Rhenish florins and fifteen kreuzters, a debt that was still outstanding after the Suppression.[79] While Roma were not infrequently cast as supporting characters of less than sterling morals in dramas related by Jesuit writers, they were not subject to the negative stereotyping suffered by Uniate Romanians, who, through their numbers and ties to a rival religious tradition, did pose a potential threat to the Society's mission.[80] Roma were occasionally found in Jesuit churches, and probably were encountered in many other settings, including the prisons where Jesuits ministered to the condemned.[81]

Records from Jesuit communities elsewhere in Transylvania indicate that Roma conversions were not always undertaken with a great deal of enthusiasm or sincerity. A hint of the fragility of some of these conversions is evident in an entry in the history of Cluj Jesuit community for 1711, where two Roma are reported as converts, of which one was an apostate.[82]

Conclusion

Jesuit mission activities reflect both the bureaucratic and the less structured aspects of the Society's work. The yearly computations of conversions and communions conducted reveal the Jesuits' skill at conducting a large-scale operation in an environment that was, if not actually hostile, at least fraught with many difficulties. Less explicitly outlined in Jesuit records but crucial to the carrying out of the missionary program were the various public performances that all contributed to the propagation of the Society's basic message. Even in years of war and plague, the Jesuits of Cluj labored unceasingly to order the internal and external lives of their

---

[78] OSzK, 2039 FMI/1608 *Historia SJ Claudiopoli 1708, Historia SJ Claudiopoli anno 1731*, p. 347.

[79] MOL, F 477 Erdély Kincstár Levéltár Exactoratus Cameralis. Inventarium Universae Substantiae in Civitate Claudiopoli post suppressionem ibi Collegium Societatis Jesu apprehensae. No. 30, p. 7.

[80] For example, a Muslim apostate was chased into a field by Roma and their dogs, where he died, prey to "crows, dogs, and other wild creatures." OSzK, 2039 FMI/1608 *Historia anno 1715*, p. 168.

[81] A somewhat garbled account from 1743 seems to relate the case of a Rom who was about to have his hand amputated, presumably for theft. ARSI, *Aust. 200, An Prov. Aust. 1743*, folio 16. Another Roma converted from Calvinism the day before he was to mount the scaffold for an unnamed crime. *Aust. 210, An. Prov. Aust. 1753*, folio 32v.

[82] OSzK, 2039 FMI/1608 *Historia anno 1711*, p. 105.

flocks, as well as to bring order to the larger social sphere that included non-Catholics (and Uniates). But the achievement of social order was always only half of the program envisioned by the Jesuits; the inward transformation that was the intended goal of the *Ratio* lay at the center of the entire missionary and educational enterprise and at the heart of the experience of individual Jesuits. We cannot definitively assess the success of the Jesuits according to their own standards; quantitative analysis does not move our understanding of spiritual development of individuals forward, and the Jesuit records, intended as they were to demonstrate the uniform progress of the order, themselves are neither objective nor nuanced enough to shed light on distinguishing characteristics of the Society's missionary achievement in Transylvania.

Faced with these obstacles, historians of Jesuit missionary work elsewhere have either opted for silence on the question of the ultimate success of the Society's religious objectives, or contented themselves with repeating the Jesuits' own descriptions of their work. Here, we offer two observations on the Jesuit missions centered in Cluj, acknowledging that some important aspects of the encounter between Jesuits and local residents can never be known. First, the Society experienced a tension between the obvious roadblocks that confessional politics, physical circumstances and the local power vacuum following 1693 produced, and the Baroque world-view that saw signs of Divine favor and ultimate victory everywhere. Each day, there were ample reasons to feel discouragement, as Jesuits labored to educate, convert, regain and unify the society around them. This much is easily documented from both Jesuit accounts and from our knowledge of large trends (for example, the resistance of the Orthodox clergy and the ambivalence of some of the Uniate priests) underway throughout the region. Harder for the modern reader to see is the world of symbols and portents that revealed the power of the religious message they sought to propagate. While some Jesuits might have been periodically fainthearted or even doubtful about the validity of their mission, most remained committed.

The second element that shaped the Jesuits' missionary project was the unmistakable decline of entire Baroque aesthetic and world-view throughout the eighteenth century. This decline was very gradual and proceeded more slowly than in some of the western Habsburg lands, but by the 1760s, the Baroque understanding of knowledge and beauty would be distanced from not only from that of Viennese intellectuals, but likewise from reformers within the Society and from artists in touch with developments elsewhere in Catholic Europe. This isolation and decline was all the more significant because the Society had not had sufficient time to root the Baroque aesthetic deeply in Transylvanian society. Like a potted plant moved to a distant room, the Baroque wilted quickly when conditions around it ceased to be ideal.

Finally, the makeup of the Society as a celibate male religious order must be reckoned with. The married Orthodox and Uniate clergy were not the only elements of Transylvanian society whose experience of family and community would have differed greatly from that of the Jesuits. Both the urban *Bürgerschaft* of Cluj, with its strong Lutheran or Unitarian ties, or the intermarried aristocracy of the countryside that had long embraced Calvinism, represented notions of relatedness and identity fundamentally at odds with a peripatetic, university-trained band of Catholic clergy who preached loyalty to distant and sometimes abstract entities. The Jesuits of course were very familiar with settings where local values were not particularly harmonious with their own, and the challenges faced in Cluj were modest compared to those encountered in Japan or China, but the effects of this prolonged isolation on the Cluj community cannot be discounted. Like the interior experiences of the laity among whom the Jesuits worked, the cultivation of a corporate identity is not easily dealt with in either quantitative or qualitative analysis. Yet the Cluj community functioned as an organic whole for many years, and produced collective achievements that easily surpass any of the individual efforts of its members. While conducting a mission to the diverse *nationes* of Transylvania, the Society ministered to itself and kept its community healthy enough to remain active and growing, until it was extinguished from afar. Any further investigation into the accomplishments of the Society in Transylvania must take this key fact into account.

CHAPTER EIGHT

Community: Looking Westward?

Gathered on the edge of Habsburg civilization, the Jesuits of Cluj were, as we have seen, simultaneously seeking to extend their mission to the East while remaining influenced by their connections to and encounters with the cultural centers of the West. We have already noted the ties of some of the most conspicuous figures in the community such as Adam Fitter to Vienna and beyond, but the relationship of the Cluj community to the outside world was more complex than a passive connection with the distant Imperial capital. Jesuits, whether they were from Transylvania or from the Habsburg heartland, took the educational and administrative experience they had gained in the West and presumably drew upon it as they shaped the institutions they founded in Cluj. The most common pattern of training and experience had Jesuit teachers moving between sometimes widely separate locations, many of which were in the Habsburg heartland. Adamus Nyirö (1723–84), who studied poetry and rhetoric in Cluj, taught in Zagreb, Buda, Győr and Košice, as well as in Cluj, where he published *Epistolae Herodum et Heroidium* (1747) and *Utopiae Sapientis* (1748).[1] Ioannes Szegedi, a native of Transylvania who was credited in Jesuit records with speaking Romanian "mediocriter," had served as the rector of both the Pazmaneum in Vienna and the *collegium* in Győr before returning to his homeland.[2] Emericus Tolvaj (1694–1781) likewise had served as the rector of the *collegium* in Buda, as well as the *Convictus Nobilium* in Győr, and Franciscus Németi, who taught philosophy in Cluj and died in Trnava in 1748, had also served as the rector of the Pazmaneum.[3] Sigismundus Vorster, who was teaching in Cluj in 1764, had taught poetry and rhetoric in Fiume, Croatia, making him one of the very few Jesuits in the history of the resurrected Cluj mission to have taught in an Italian-speaking region.[4] Another Jesuit who combined experience in the western reaches of the Habsburg

---

[1] Katona, *Historia*, p. 985; Stöger, *Scriptores*, p. 242.

[2] Katona, *Historia*, p. 1005; *A Királyi Pázmány Péter=Tudományegyetem Története. I Kötet. A Hittudomány Kar Története 1635–1935.* Irták Hermann Egyed and Arter Edgár. (Budapest, 1935), p. 77. ARSI, *Austria 80, Catal. I Coll. Claud. 1734*, p. 65.

[3] Katona, *Historia*, pp. 1011–12; Stöger, *Scriptores*, p. 366. Tolvaj's awareness of the larger world of the Baroque Society is reflected in his work *Athanasij Kircheri iter extaticum II in mundum subteraneum. Dialogus III* published in Trnava in 1739. Szinnyei (ed.), *Magyar irók*, 14, pp. 262–3. Németi, who was born on the western border of Hungary with Austria in 1693 was the author of a *Historia Poetica Montium Transylvaniae*. Katona, *Historia*, p. 984; Sommervogel et al., *Bibliothèque*, vol. 5, pp. 1620–21.

[4] ARSI, *Aust. 110, Catal. Coll. I Claud. 1764*, p. 88. Paulus Raiscani, a Hungarian of noble birth, spent over four years in Rome as a "Poenitentarius Hungaricus," hearing the confessions of pilgrims. *Aust. 80, Catal. I Coll. Claud. 1734*, p. 57. Sommervogel et al., *Bibliothèque*, vol. 5, pp. 1386–7.

realms with service as rector of the Cluj *collegium* was Christopher Muesserer, who directed the Pazmaneum and the *collegium* in Soporon.[5] Nicolaus Benkő, born in Transylvania in 1723, studied theology in Graz and mathematics in Vienna in addition to a sojourn in a house of the third probation in Judenburg, high in the Austrian Alps.[6] A generation earlier, Josephus Kelecseni (1693–1744) had studied in Leoben, Austria and completed his philosophical training in Vienna.[7] Franciscus Prekenfeld (1682–1744) was born in Laibach in modern-day Slovenia (although he was probably an ethnic German), and taught in Trnava and Graz before dying in Cluj; his contemporaries, Christophorus Grembs and Paulus Remich, both hailed from the Tirol.[8] Andreas Illia was born in Radgona in Slovenia, and probably spoke Croatian as his mother tongue, as did Franjo Klinic (1697–1763), who taught philosophy, ethics and theology in Cluj and wrote *Dacia Sicula Brevi Compendio Exhibita*, and Stephanus Ilatskó, who was a scholastic in Cluj in 1761.[9] A few other examples of Jesuits working in Cluj will give some picture of the Western influences that in one way or another touched the overwhelming majority of the leaders of the community. Rudolphus Bzenszky, an early Jesuit visitor to Cluj, was a bilingual Bohemian, born in Prague in 1651 with many years' service in the camps of the Imperial army.[10] Michael Lipsits (1704–65), whose career included service in Zagreb and Trnava and wrote a book of devotional verse, an algebra text and a Baroque fusion of science and triumphalist history entitled *Hungaria Coelestis, Astronomiam et Chronologiam in synopsi complectans*, taught theology and philosophy in Cluj.[11] Josephus Göttwald also had served in Zagreb, Trnava, Košice and Győr, and when he died in Cluj in 1727 on the feast day of a Japanese martyr, had spent thirty years in the Society.[12] For some Jesuits trained in the remoteness of Transylvania, the encounter with the West was not a happy one. Franciscus Götze, who taught mathematics and philosophy in Cluj during the earlier part of his career, later died in Vienna from a disease, probably smallpox, contracted while working in a military hospital there.[13] Andreas Sigrai (1681–1734) also died in Vienna, after "rexit domicilium Claudiopoli"; in his career as a Jesuit, he had entered the noviciate in Vienna, taught in Trnava, Erlau,

---

[5] Katona, *Historia*, p. 980. Christophorus Muesser, the son of a Protestant minister, served in a similar capacity.

[6] ARSI, *Aust. 106, Catal. Coll. I Claud. 1761*, p. 91.

[7] ARSI, *Aust. 90, Catal. Coll. I Claud. 1743*, p. 64.

[8] Katona, *Historia*, 993, Sommervogel et al., *Bibliothèque*, vol. 6, p. 1192; Nilles, *Symbolae*, p. 460. ARSI, *Aust. 72, (1723)*, p. 58. Remich underwent his formation in Gorizia, further reflecting the mobility of the priests assigned to Cluj.

[9] Mijo Korade, "The Croats of Gradisčše (Burgenland), Austria and the Society of Jesus from the 16th to the 18th centuries," in Pozaić (ed.), *Jesuits*, pp. 318, 317; ARSI, *Aust. 106, Catal. I Coll. Claud. 1761*, p. 93.

[10] Bzenszky served as a "historicus domûs" and confessor in Cluj. ARSI, *Aust. 59, Catal. I Coll. Claud. 1711*, p. 332.

[11] Katona, *Historia*, p. 974; Sommervogel et al., *Bibliothèque*, vol. 4, p. 1861.

[12] ARSI, *Aust. 184, An. Prov. Aust. 1727*, folio 98r.

[13] Katona, *Historia*, p. 957.

and served as rector in Košice.¹⁴ On balance, however, the experience of members of the Society with the Baroque culture flourishing in Austria was a salutary one with lessons of value in the East. Jesuits such as Adamus Fitter who were sojourning in Vienna, and perhaps in other Western cities as well, would have also been exposed to the political climate swirling around the Imperial court, and only the most obtuse would have failed to grasp the relationship between the political goals of the dynasty and the applied consequences of the Society's undertakings.¹⁵ And it is clear that many Jesuits destined for key roles in the Cluj community had received just that sort of exposure. Father Joseph Kelesceni had the advantage of experiencing both the center of Habsburg power and prestige and the impact of that power on a smaller provincial community: he completed his study of *Humaniores* in Leoben in Styria (a region that had been reclaimed for Catholicism in the previous century), and his philosophical studies in Vienna.¹⁶ Finally, the versatile Paulus Kolosvári, who in his youth had served as the secretary to Jesuit-trained Ferenc II Rákóczi, had received training in Vienna, as had Fitter, entered the Society there in 1711.¹⁷

While the *Monita Patri Theologico* were explicit in forbidding "publicis et saecularibus ... negotiis," the practical realities of an assignment such as Fitter's were quite different.¹⁸ The promotion of the agenda of the Habsburgs was not as straightforward a task as building churches and schools, or even engaging the local elites. Several campaigns had to be waged simultaneously, each reinforcing the larger message in ways that were not excessively repetitive, yet which complemented and reinforced one another. Just such a campaign had been undertaken in the mountains of Styria and the neighborhoods of laborers and court functionaries that crowded around the old city of Vienna, settings that many Cluj Jesuits knew from their travels west. But could the lessons learned close to the Habsburg heartland be transferred to the borderlands of the east? And how did the Jesuits who were exposed to the successes of the Austrian High Baroque understand these lessons? The constantly public or at least formal nature of the writings produced by and for the Cluj Jesuit community inevitably restricts our picture of the intersection of Western and Eastern influences in the Transylvanian missions of the Society, but several observations about the practical application of the Baroque culture can be offered with confidence.

The most obvious of these is the potential lack of familiarity with local conditions and languages among those Jesuits who were not native to the region, and the tendency of those trained in the West to minimize, at least in their public

---

[14] F. Weiser, *Vitae Patrum et Magistorum* (Colozae, 1886), p. 64; Sommervogel et al., *Bibliothèque*, vol. 7, p. 1204.

[15] However, as with any population, we must make allowances for significant individual differences. Paulus Kovács, whose native language was Hungarian, studied philosophy (in Latin) in Vienna for three years, but only a short time later, at the age of 25, could be credited only with speaking German "mediocriter," which could mean that his grasp of day-to-day events in the capital may not have been profound. ARSI, *Aust. 71, Catal. Coll. Claud. 1723*, p. 62.

[16] ARSI, *Aust. 90, Catal. I Coll. Claud. 1743*, p. 64; Sommervogel et al., *Bibliothèque*, vol. 4, p. 978.

[17] ARSI, *Aust. 71, Catal. I Coll. Claud. 1723*, p. 62.

[18] Nilles, *Symbolae*, vol. 1, p. 341; Tóth, *Nacionalismus*, p. 38.

and collective communications, the differences and difficulties of a mission in the East. Many of these men had no doubt been directly influenced by more impressive physical manifestations of the Baroque aesthetic found in the larger cities of the West. In particular, those Jesuits who had spent time in Vienna at the Pazmaneum would have encountered, in addition to their rigorous training and their exposure to Jesuit educational and missionary strategies, the full-blown examples of hierarchy, ritual and symbol that made up the everyday life of the capital, as well as the personal connections between many Viennese Jesuits and the Imperial Court. Such encounters would have provided concrete examples of the connection between the mission of the Society and the ambitions of the Habsburgs whose Austrian branch had experienced a rapid rise in prestige and influence in the first decades of the eighteenth century. The reigns of Leopold I and Joseph I can also be considered high points in both the history of the Society in Central Europe as well as in the evolution of the public expressions of the Baroque, years during which the patterns of Jesuit schooling in the Habsburg lands were still enjoying the widest influence and prestige.[19] Few, if any, observers would have been able in 1720 or even 1740 to foresee the passing of the high noon of Jesuit pedagogical and mission activities. Nor would it have been easy to discern either the gathering storm clouds presaging the downfall of the Society or the challenges to its long-held theological principles, to say nothing of the coming estrangement of its most important family of patrons. Jesuits from the western regions of the Habsburg domains heading east in the last years of the seventeenth and the early decades of the eighteenth century did so confident that their training and world-view complemented civil and ecclesial institutions whose language was one of triumph and success, and whose future seemed assured. The advance of the Counter-Reformation had proceeded for more than a century, and with the decline of the Ottoman Empire and the continual pressure applied to the "acatholici" within the Habsburg domains, more victories seemed possible, if not inevitable. As late as 1746, the Cluj Jesuit press could publish a history of Hungarian cardinals that give prominence to the influences of the Society on those of the Counter-Reformation era, two solid centuries of a close relationship.[20] The connection of the Society to the powerful ecclesiastical and political forces in Hungary seemed secure and unassailable, and if conditions further east were not yet quite so secure, history seemed to suggest that the successful expansion of the Society's mission would continue. This sentiment was coupled with the perception (sometime reinforced by the secular rulers of Moldavia) that the Eastern Church was itself weak or even

---

[19] Ivana Čornejová, "Jezsuitské skolství a Jan Amos Komensky," in *Pocta Univerzity Karlovy J. A. Komenskému.* (Praha, 1991), pp. 74–87.

[20] *Purpurea Pannonica, sive Vitae et Res Gestae S. R. E. Cardinalium* ... D. Sigismundus Henter L. Baro de Sepsi Szent Ivanyi ... propugnaret praeside R. P. Georgio Szegedi ... (Claudiopoli, 1746). At the Jesuit *collegium* in Košice, the mixing and even replacing of theological by Imperial symbolism was carried to even greater heights. The colophon of a collection of Bachelor's degree recipients featured, not the monogram of the Society and the three nails of Christ's passion, but the double-headed eagle of the Habsburgs. *Saeculum praesulum Hungariae de re literaria bene meritorum ... neo-Baccalaureorum* (Cassoivae, 1737), p. 57. The "promotor" of these exercises was Josephus Balogh, who was to become the notorious *theologus* to the Uniate bishop.

decadent, and staffed by unskilled and indifferent priests. Such an institution might eventually be co-opted or overwhelmed by the sheer majesty of the Roman Church. Jesuit reports and records of encounters with Orthodox clergy stop short of outright defamation, but make it clear that the relationship between the two was from the first adversarial and colored by the belief on the Jesuit side that the theology underlying the Eastern Rite was at best benighted and at worst degenerate.

Secondly, while the powerful presence of ethnic Hungarian Jesuits in Cluj is unmistakable, the presence of Jesuits raised or trained in non-Hungarian speaking regions (including some of the most talented members of the community) diluted the immediate impact of a distinctly ethnic Hungarian dominance over all the Jesuit enterprises in the region. Those Jesuits who did identify with Hungarian culture and language were of course expected to accept as an equal a Croatian or German speaker. The extreme difficulty of the Hungarian tongue meant that more Hungarian speakers were likely to have mastered another language than for non-Hungarian speakers to have learned Magyar.[21] Loyalty to the Society and fidelity to its mission, obedience to superiors and attention to the rules that guided the social structure of the Society, each shaped the experience of the Jesuits – and set the tone of the documents in which this experience was recorded – thus preventing ethnic identity from becoming the single most important determinant of the ways in which the Jesuits pursued their goals. This said, the minimal engagement of the Cluj Jesuits with Romanian culture that we have already noted remained a salient characteristic of the Jesuit presence in the region, one which did not change with the passage of years but instead became institutionalized as wave after wave of priests and brothers passed through Cluj after training in the West. The combination of linguistic, cultural and religious differences between the Jesuits of Cluj and Romanians, whether they were Uniate or Orthodox, was too great a gulf for most members of the Society to overcome. And while clear documentation is lacking, this gulf may have been an equally great problem for the Uniates as well.

While the number of Jesuit priests who had had direct experience in communities far from Cluj is striking, the presence of others whose roots were firmly in Transylvania cannot be ignored. Cluj also remained a point of focus for clergy, Jesuit and otherwise, who had been educated there. Emanuel Olšavsky, brother of the Bishop of Munkačevo and a graduate of the Cluj *collegium*, returned to Transylvania in 1746, to try to assist in the project of the Uniate Church.[22] In a few noteworthy instances, Jesuits with ties to Cluj directed their efforts eastward. Jesuit priests who had direct knowledge of regions to the east of Cluj were relatively rare, and

---

[21] The case of Georgius Gyerö, a scholastic in Cluj in 1758, presents an additional twist on the question of language competence and ethnic loyalty. Gyerö, a native of Pécs, a southern Hungarian city, was reported to have mastered, among other languages, "Graecum" to a mediocre level. Would this have been Classical Greek, taught throughout the Jesuit school system, or modern Greek? Since so many Jesuits would have achieved a level of mediocre or better in Classical Greek it seems more likely that Gyerö had knowledge of the modern tongue. But we are left with no notion of how this came to be. ARSI, *Aust. 103, Catal. I Coll. Claud. 1758*, p. 92.

[22] M. Lacko, SJ, "The pastoral activity of Manuel Michael Olšavsky, Bishop of Mukačevo," *OCP 27, 1* (1961), p. 158; Nilles, *Symbolae*, vol. 2, pp. 571–3.

consequently valued. Michael Szalbeck, who was perhaps the only member of the Cluj community to be born in Moldavia, was chosen from among three candidates to be the *theologus* to Uniate Bishop Petru Pavel Aron in 1751, a role he carried out for the next thirteen years.[23] Another connection between the Moldavian principality to the east and the Cluj Jesuits is mentioned in the Society's records for 1743, where we find that a "frequens ea gratia litterarum comercium" was carried on between the rector of the *collegium* and the son of the Prince of Moldavia, Constantine Nicolaus Mavrocordat.[24]

"Charissimi Fratri"

At any point during the eighty years that the Society operated its schools and residences in Cluj, a significant segment of the community was made up, not of priests, but of *coadjutores temporales*. These "helpers" should not be viewed as marginal or poorly trained members of the Jesuit community, for their skills not only maintained the community, but helped build its relations with the outside world. While a clear distinction had always existed between the professed priest, one that grew out of the social structure of the sixteenth century when the *Constitutions* of the Society defined the role of these *coadjutores*, this distinction was not justified in the culture of the Society on the basis of the personal qualities of the temporal helper. Although he remained unequal in education and power within the Society, the temporal helper was not inferior spiritually in this life or in the next before God.[25] The sixteenth- and seventeenth-century Society had frowned on teaching brothers to read and write, but the increasingly complex projects that the Jesuits took on caused a reversal of this attitude.[26] During the eighteenth century, these helpers had a greater visibility within the literate world of the Society and those it cared for than they had enjoyed previously or would experience in the future. A handful of German brothers even received attention for their spiritual and academic attainments.[27] In Cluj, however, as in most of the Jesuit projects that made extensive use of the *coadjutors temporales*, few of these men left complete records of their activities, and their contributions to the community must be pieced together from brief biographical details, obituary

---

[23] Augustin Bunea, *Episcopiĭ Petru Pavel Aron şi Dionisiŭ Novacovacicĭ saŭ Istoria Românilor Transilvanăneni de la 1751 până la 1764*. (Blaş, 1902), p. 16.

[24] ARSI, *Aust. 200, An. Prov. Aust. 1743*, p. 41.

[25] Antonius M. de Aldama, SI, "De coadjutoribus Societatis Iesu in mente et in praxi Sancti Ignatii," *AHSI*, 38 (1969), pp. 389–430.

[26] The sixth *Regulum* of the Fourteenth General Congregation of the Society stated, "Non sunt in Societate Coadjtores temporales literis instituendi," and the advancement of brothers "ad alium statum" was also proscribed. *Modus conficiendi Institutiones de Candidatis et Promovendis ad Gradum, de modo item Docendi in Scholis Soc. Iesu.* BB, Szentiványi 126, R. I.126, 262, 264.

[27] Peter Waldner, *Besonderer Cosiderationes und Erforschungen über die allgemeine Regelen Fratrum Coadiutorum Societatis Iesu*. (Ingolstadt, 1731); Joseph de Guibert, SJ, *The Jesuits: Their Spiritual Doctrine and Practice. A Historical Study*, trans. William J. Young and ed. George E. Ganss, SJ (St. Louis, MO, 1994), p. 426.

notices, and a scattering of records of their labors that they themselves probably wrote.[28] Like the priests of Cluj, the "helpers" not infrequently came from far to the west. *Coadjutores temporales* also might have backgrounds that included formation and work far from Cluj, for the process that led to final vows might take longer than a decade.[29] Mattheus Göth had worked in Trnava before being sent to recover his health in Cluj in 1737. Unfortunately, Göth died the same year, of unknown causes.[30] Joannes Tröger, who appears in the Cluj community in 1740, was born in Ehrenthal in Saxony in 1690 and had entered the Society in Vienna in 1714, before which he had been a tailor.[31] Matthias Langweiler was born in a rural district near Salzburg; Valentine Schertzer, a woodworker, is listed as "Francofurtensis," and Gerogius Martinez was from Amberg in the Palatinate.[32] Antonius Wartmann, who had served as a "socius dispensoris" in the "Domus Professa" in Vienna and a cook in Košice, was born in Switzerland in 1687; in 1723, he was working in Cluj.[33] The surgeon Andres Schmid and the cook Thomas Forst came from Swabia and Carinthia respectively; we are told only that each spoke German well.[34] Like many other of the "helpers," these men may not have understood much of the other languages spoken in and around Cluj, which would have bound them even more closely to the Jesuit community in which they found themselves. Sometimes the *coadjutor* arrived in the Jesuit community with experiences far afield from the routines of life in Cluj. Joannes Herbst was born in Berlin in 1709 (and thus probably as a Protestant), entered the Society in Buda, and served in half a dozen localities before turning up in Cluj in 1764.[35] Georgius Rauch was born in Würzburg in 1725 and entered the Society in Vienna in 1748. Trained as a cook, he served in the Austrian Alps, Zagreb, Gorizia and Vienna, among other places, all before his fortieth birthday.[36] Ferdinandus Moser, "Tyroliensis Ratenbergerensis," appears in the Society's records of 1730 as a thirty-year-old "mercator et pictor" who spoke German well and Hungarian and "Slavonice" (probably Slovenian) "infra mediocriter."[37] How

---

[28] For example, "Bernardus Paumgartner den 3. Juli hab ich dem Keller angedrötten." MOL, Erdélyi Kincstár Levéltár, folios 261v–262r; "Bier vor daβ Hauss," folio 243v. In Crembs in the western region of the Austrian Province, we read that Adamus Prandl, a janitor, in 1711 "pulsat ante et post examen vespertium." Lukács, *Catalogi*, p. 569.

[29] For example, Gerogius Tompai was admitted to the Society in Trenčin at the age of 23, but did not take final vows until almost fourteen years later, in Cluj. ARSI, *Aust. 80, Catal. I Coll. Claud. 1734.*

[30] OSzK, 2039 FMI/1608 *Historia SJ Claudiop. 1737*, p. 431. Why a sickly brother would be sent to a notoriously unhealthy location such as Cluj remains an unanswered question.

[31] ARSI, *Aust. 86, Catal. I Coll. Claud. 1740*, p. 68.

[32] ARSI, *Aust. 77, Catal. I Coll Claud. 1730*, p. 79; *Aust. 74, Catal. I Coll. Claud. 1726*, pp. 74, 72.

[33] ARSI, *Aust. 71, Catal. I Coll. Claud. 1723*, p. 64.

[34] ARSI, *Aust. 93 Catal. I Coll. Claud. 1746*, pp. 83, 86.

[35] ARSI, *Aust. 110, Catal I. Coll. Claud. 1764*, p. 101.

[36] ARSI, *Aust. 110, Catal. I Coll. Claud. 1764*, p. 99.

[37] ARSI, *Aust. 77, Catal. I Coll. Claud. 1730*, p. 77; *Aust. 65, Catal. I. Coll. Claud. 1717*, p. 49. Keller is reported as speaking only German.

the young merchant came to join the Jesuit community is a mystery; the turmoil of war, loss of a spouse, or the desire to travel may have accompanied more spiritual motivations, a hypothesis that can be applied to many other *coadjutores temporales* as well.[38] Yet origins in the west seldom meant exposure to the urban life that was characteristic of the experience of many Jesuit priests trained in the west. Franciscus Ertl, "cellarius," was from Nikolsburg in Moravia, and Matthias Keller was "ex valle S. Petri in Imperio."[39] Christianus Schrantzer had been born in the Tirol but completed his formation in Cluj.[40] A review of *coadjutors temporales* active in Cluj during the eighteenth century reveals few who were from large cities or even from good-sized towns. While the overwhelmingly rural character of the Habsburg lands during this period is surely a major contributor to this pattern, the life of a "helper" may have been especially attractive to a farm boy or village youth whose opportunities for education and advancement were very restricted. And even though a *coadjutor temporalis* never achieved the status of a university-educated man, the prestige and material advantages (including superior medical care) found in a Jesuit community were significant. Some notable "helpers" were from closer to home. Joseph Reiser, who was born in Sibiu in 1694 and died in Cluj in 1768, was a pharmacist renowned for his knowledge.[41] His unpublished manuscripts unfortunately have not survived.

The obituary notices that provide virtually the only details beyond those listed in the Society's *catalogi* say as much about the values of the priests (or in some cases, scholastics) who would have composed them as they do about the brothers themselves. The obituary of Andreas Wagner, who died in 1736, takes note of his "obedience, which was an example to all."[42] This unusual remark, which had it been repeated frequently in other obituaries might be dismissed as a commonplace, gains a little more significance when we read that Guila Cesare Cordara, whose criticisms of Jesuit priests have already been cited, reported that the brothers could be " …puffed up with a certain air of self-importance. They put themselves ahead of other religious, even those who are priests."[43] Given the preeminent position of the Society

---

[38] Georgius Trompai, "in saeculo sartor," entered the Society at the age of 23 in 1694, and Joanes Hoffer of Sopron, "in saeculo cocus," was 25 when he joined in 1732, meaning that both men had some considerable experience in a secular world of work that would have begun in their mid-teens at the latest. ARSI, *Aust. 86, Catal. Col. Claud. 1740*, 66; *Austria 83, Catal. I Coll. Claud. 1737*, p. 62.

[39] ARSI, *Aust. 74, Catal. I Coll. Claud. 1726*, p. 71.

[40] ARSI, *Aust. 59, Catal. I Res. Claud. 1711*, p. 334.

[41] Reiser's entry in the Society's records identifies him as a "transylvanus," a strictly geographical term, and a reminder that such records are not always trustworthy sources of information about the ethnicity of individual Jesuits. ARSI, *Aust. 86, Catal. I Claud. 1740*, p. 68; Stöger, *Scriptores*, p. 298. Franciscus Roys is thus identified as "ungarus" although he "scit solum Germanicè." ARSI, *Aust. 59, Catal. I Claud. 1711*, p. 331. On occasion, however, the Jesuit recording data in the *Catalogus* may have been attempting to note the ethnic background of his confrere. Joannes Brusko, a *coadjutor temporalis* who served as a cook in Cluj, is variously recorded as "slavus" and "hungarus." ARSI, *Aust. 99, Catal. I Claud. 1754*, p. 92.

[42] ARSI, *Aust. 193, An. Prov. Aust. 1736*, folio 122v.

[43] Cordara, *Suppression*, p. 180.

among Catholic (and Uniate) clergy in Cluj and the overwhelming political influence of Jesuits in the community, sincere humility on the part of a brother may have taken on added significance. The literary talents of the helpers left no traces in the records of the Society, while their more practical skills take a backseat in obituary notices to their piety. In some cases these skills appear to have been of a high order. Andreas Spegel, born in Bavaria in 1670, served in relatively unskilled roles in Cluj that included supplier of linen, but he was also the "director horologii" for ten years, a job that would have required considerable knowledge and skill.[44] We would like to know more about the relationship between Jesuit priests and the *coadjutores temporales*; undoubtedly the two groups were in constant contact, although the dynamics accompanying this contact are not easily reconstructed. Father Franciscus Obermeyer, a native of Linz, in 1726 directed some of the brothers through portions of the *Spiritual Exercises* ("dat puncta fratribus"), a process that might have been complicated by the inability of some brothers to read.[45] A somewhat similar relationship may have existed between the brothers and Father Joannes Paki, who served as the "Confessor Domûs" in the same year.[46] When *coadjutores temporales* were assigned to work closely with one particular priest, a position identified usually as a *socius*, the relationship would no doubt have been close in many cases. Such was the case with Paulus Kostyál, who, trained as a printer, served as the "socius Praefecti typographiae" in Cluj.[47] As for the other complex and continual encounters between priests and brothers, the only other clues lie scattered among such records as the "Talenta ad Societatis Ministeria" compiled by an anonymous Jesuit in 1700 that succinctly reviewed the skills of priests, scholastics and brothers .[48]

The Cluj community, like many other Jesuit communities in Europe, had a fluid structure that allowed for the constant influx and exit of priests and brothers as they traveled to new assignments throughout the Austrian Province. The consequences of this structure, which sought to promote uniformity by training priests and brothers to function as interchangeable units, are hinted at in Jesuit records, where the tasks performed by Jesuits in widely various locations are presented in identical terms. The mission of the Society was universal, as was the message it sought to spread, so that the Cluj community always understood itself to be not merely a small replica of larger communities to the west, but a member of the greater company of communities that made up the Society as a whole, whose relationships were duplicated as well. The major advantage of such an approach to community building was that each member had models on which to build his own role within the community. However, in the case of the *coadjutores temporales*, we know next to nothing about how these

---

[44] ARSI, *Aust. 59, Catal. I. Coll. Claud. 1711*, p. 333.

[45] ARSI, *Aust. 74, Catal. I Coll. Claud. 1726*, p. 64. A translation of the *Exercises*, originally composed in Spanish, were among the German-language works owned by the Cluj community in the 1720s: *Exercitum oder geistliche Übungen des heiligen Vatter Ignatius anno 1722*. BARC-N, MsC. 405.

[46] ARSI, *Aust. 74, Catal. I Coll. Claud. 1726*, p. 66.

[47] ARSI, *Aust. 83, Catal. I Coll Claud. 1737*, p. 65.

[48] ARSI, *Aust. 54, Catal. II Coll. Claud. 1700*, folio 108r.

men acquired knowledge about the roles they were expected to fill.[49] On the other hand, the constant rotation of teachers and administrators often encouraged Jesuits who repeatedly found themselves in new situations to fall back on the strategies that they already knew, rather than to develop responses that were grounded in an awareness that their involvement with the community would be long-term. While there were obvious similarities between the assignment Andreas Sigrai undertook as the rector of Cluj community and his next assignment in Košice, the ethnic groups living nearby, the history of each Jesuit community and the importance of the two towns to Habsburg diplomacy were far from identical.[50] Cluj had experienced a much longer hiatus of Habsburg control, the population living in its hinterlands was much more ethnically mixed, and it had less importance militarily. Its situation was also very different from that of Iași, isolated from any predominantly Catholic states and unable to draw upon either bureaucratic or military pressure from a supportive dynasty. Father Antonius Hedri may have undertaken to catechize in Slovak, one of the languages spoken locally in Prešov, but there is little evidence of similar efforts to reach Romanian speakers in Cluj.[51] The outlines of assignments throughout the eastern Habsburg lands were always similar, and this similarity was reinforced by the universal goals of the *Ratio*, but the differences were equally important.

The Jesuit communities of Cluj and Iași illustrate the never-ending process of negotiation that the Society conducted between the specific circumstances of a particular mission of school and the Jesuit vision of universal truth brought to light through an (almost) universally applied curriculum and missionary strategy. Filled with individualists drawn to the opportunities for independent action, the Society felt compelled to identify general principles and apply them where it could.[52] Yet such individualists were also vulnerable to negative interpretations of their actions that might result in setbacks such as their expulsion from Iași "propter neglectam praxim."[53] The most significant of these general principles was the notion of community and a common mission. Working in different directions simultaneously, the members of the Cluj community could see the material fruits of their common labors: the architectural and educational edifices they had erected, the communities of believers they were helping to create, the rising generations of students trained in their schools, and lastly, the agricultural undertakings they had begun. Yet despite the seemingly complex nature of these projects, and the way in which different components of the project supported one another, the edifice was vulnerable, and

---

[49] Aside from catalogues compiled by the Cluj community, records of the *coadjutores temporales* are almost nonexistent. Some Jesuit artisans' names appear in Agghazy Maria, *A barokk szobrászat Magyarországon* (3 vols, Budapest, 1959), vol. 2, p. 145.

[50] Sigrai moved to Košice after three years in Cluj, a typical pattern of assignments. Weiser, *Vitae Patrum*, p. 64.

[51] ARSI, *Aust. 103, Catal. I Coll. Claud. 1758*, p. 85.

[52] Evidence of this individualism can be found beyond the ranks of the Jesuits themselves, as the Society educated the rebel and nonconformist as well as the obedient functionary. Ferenc II Rákóczi, schooled by the Society in Neuhaus, Bohemia is the most conspicuous example from the eastern Habsburg realms of this sort of "product" of Jesuit education, although he is by no means the only one. Murdock, *Calvinism*, p. 302.

[53] Pall, "Controversie," p. 310.

would be toppled quickly and without perceptible resistance or complaint. Does this mean that the community whose existence is described in Jesuit documents in such detail may not have been as firmly established as this evidence suggests? Despite the rapid evaporation of the Jesuit community after 1773, its significance and reality before this date cannot be doubted. Beyond the public ritual and performance which made up an important component of the community's expression of identity lay countless less visible relations woven together in the sacraments of penance and the Eucharist, and reinforced by the general climate that called for examination of conscience which culminated at various points in the year, such as Easter.[54] With the added presence of many Jesuits who had received all or part of their training in the Cluj community, the sense of collective identity would have been further heightened. This identity, we should note, did not always take the form of social relationships, for the Jesuit community was also characterized by ties between men and God. Samuel Timon, who served as rector in both Cluj and Košice, once lamented that in his career he had been "plus humanis, quam divine intentus."[55] In Iaşi, all the difficulties facing the Cluj Jesuits were magnified and multiplied. The internal sense of commitment of any individuals cannot be assessed from this distance, and at any point the Cluj community no doubt included the lukewarm and the careerist. Yet the community created was no artificial construction, but maintained its own momentum and character through times of considerable adversity. A century early, Pázmány, himself a Jesuit, wrote (we may assume without irony) that he was concerned that the great landed families of Hungary were in danger of dying out because so many young nobles were choosing to become Jesuits![56] Baroque devotion may not have burned quite so brightly at all times in the Cluj community of the Society, but the works of the priests and brothers testify to the very real sincerity and commitment that did exist.

---

[54] For Calvinists as well as Catholics, Easter served as a time for "spiritual and social check-ups" that bound participants to the basic theological positions of their faith, and not incidentally in communities such as Cluj, to one another as well. Wieste de Boer, "Calvin and Borromeo: A comparative approach to social discipline," in Comerford and Pabel (eds), *Catholicism*, pp. 84–96.

[55] Weiser, *Vitae*, p. 27.

[56] Summarized in Savái and Pintér (eds), *Documenta Missionaria*, p. 105.

CHAPTER NINE

The 1743 Mission to Moldavia

The Jesuits of the Cluj community never ceased to look to the East, seeking opportunities to further the Society's enterprises in regions that lay beyond the realm of the Habsburgs. The East held the promise both of the extension of the authority of the Roman Church into lands dominated by the Eastern Rite, and, perhaps more importantly, the dream of the conversion of vast heathen despotisms, and the dramatic winning of many souls through the efforts of the Society, an important theme in the first two centuries of the history of the Jesuits. There were significant precedents for a Jesuit foray into the lands that lay on the other side of the Eastern Carpathians. Franciscus Ravasz, who had envisioned all Eastern Rite Churches united under Rome's leadership, had traveled to Bessarabia (modern-day Moldova) as a missionary to lands controlled by the Tartars or Mongols.[1] Paulus Beke, in the middle of the seventeenth century, had seen Moldavia and the lands to its east as a gateway to the heartlands of Tartary, where the Khan himself might be converted.[2] The vulnerability of those Moldavian Armenians who had entered into union with Rome was another reason to launch a mission into the Principality.[3] The ambitions and optimism that animated the Society's work in the "Indies" always remained a part of the climate in which the planting of missions in Moldavia and beyond took place, and it is possible to detect in the reports sent back to Rome or Vienna an excitement not always present in the accounts of the promotion of the Uniate Church in Transylvania, for the Jesuits who had traveled east over the mountains had in fact left Europe and entered into a more exotic world. Iaşi, the most important town in Moldavia, was the seat of a prince who ruled at the pleasure of the sultan, sometimes for only a few months, since the mechanics of being chosen for this post involved huge bribes followed by the squeezing of the local boyars for funds to recoup the bribes, who in turn sought to replace the current prince with another. The connection of this city to Jesuit educational ideals could be traced back at least as far as Pantilimon Ligardis, a Uniate priest from Chios who had studied at Jesuit institutions in Rome before arriving in Moldavia in 1646 to found an academy.[4] Iaşi itself had been part

---

[1] Sommervogel et al., *Bibliothèque*, vol. 6, p. 1498.
[2] Pall, "Controversie," p. 142.
[3] Armenian Catholics under the rule of the Porte faced prejudice and pressure from the authorities. Mijo Korade, "Josip Martinović, an 18th century defender of the Armenians," in Pozaić (ed.), *Jesuits among the Croats*, p. 235. Moldavian Armenian Catholics in particular were susceptible to apostasy. Georgius Cottori ad S. C. P. F., 2.10.1766, in Dumitru-Snagov (ed.), *Românii*, pp. 239–41.
[4] Victor Papacostea, "Originale învăţămîntului superior în Ţara Românească," in *Civilizaţia Românească şi Civilizaţia Balcanică*, Victor Papacostea and Cornelia Papacostea-Danielopolu (eds) (Bucureşti, 1983), p. 266.

of the Austrian Province of the Society in the mid-seventeenth century, but had later been transferred to the Polish Province. Vienna wished to cultivate a relationship with the reigning prince, if only for economic reasons, but was generally thwarted in its efforts by the prince's inability to act independently. Characteristically, Constantinople issued an edict in 1729 forbidding Prince Nicholas Mavrocordat from selling grain to Austria.[5] Relations between Jesuits who appeared at the prince's court and the Orthodox clergy who gathered in Iaşi were, not surprisingly, usually tense. In 1670, Jesuits were accused of intrigues against the prince, and the following years formally rejected the authority of the Vicar Apostolic in Moldavia who wished to pass judgment on charges that some of the fathers had egged on townspeople and precipitated a knife fight.[6] Local Catholic clergy also found fault with the Jesuits; in 1650, Georg Gross, the parish priest in Cotnar, accused them of having obtained possession of a church in Iaşi "arte doloque."[7] Members of the Polish Province of the Society had been in Moldavia through much of the second half of the seventeenth century, but their rivals the Observant Franciscans, who concentrated their efforts among the rural population, wrote to Rome detailing the questionable financial dealings of the Jesuits.[8] The Jesuits responded to this situation by trying to adapt to local customs and by establishing relationships with the boyars through the creation of a Latin school in Iaşi, but these strategies could backfire. Decades later, relations were no better, with Jesuits forbidden in 1723 from preaching in the churches of the city.[9] Finally, the Society was expelled from all of Moldavia in 1731, although the Austrian and Polish provinces continued to hope for better times.[10] The decline of Ottoman power and the strengthening of the House of Habsburg held out the possibility that such a day might be dawning soon.

In the spring of 1743, the Phanariot Prince, Konstantine Mavrocordat, who had reigned eleven times in succession in Iaşi and separately in Bucharest (the capital of Wallachia), invited Carolus Péterffy, the famous Jesuit historian, to his domain, so that he could gather the documentary materials relevant to the history of the Principality and write its history.[11] After this invitation was relayed to the Trnava Jesuit community, two members of the Cluj Jesuit house, Andreas Patai and Georgius Szegedi, joined the proposed expedition so that they might take up the spiritual care of the Moldavian Hungarian population, and with the support of the prince, initiate conversion efforts among the non-Catholic population, the overwhelming majority of whom were Romanian Orthodox.[12] Constantine's father Nicolae had been a

---

[5] Hitchins, *Romanians*, p. 14.

[6] Pall, "Controversie," pp. 248, 253, 273.

[7] Gross to the S. C. P. F., May–June 1650, in Benda (ed.), *Okmánytár*, vol. 2, p. 471.

[8] Jesuits responded by looking down at the Observant Franciscans, who typically lacked the rigorous education of the Society. Juhász (ed.), *Moldvai*, vol. 1, p. 45.

[9] Pall, "Controversie," p. 303.

[10] *Op. cit.*, p. 309. Note the seamless linking of the academic and educational work of the Society.

[11] Born in Bratislava, Péterffy never taught in Cluj, but was a colleague of Paulus Kolosvári during his years in Trnava. Sommervogel et al., *Bibliothèque*, vol. 6, p. 617.

[12] Szegedi had some knowledge of Romanian. ARSI, *Aust. 103, Cat. I Coll. Claud. 1758*, folio 87; Stöger *Scriptores*, pp. 253–4. Patai had previously been a rector of the Cluj *collegium*.

humanistically cultivated man, who was unusually receptive towards Western culture despite the unpromising circumstances in which he had encountered it.[13] In 1716, the Imperial forces that had invaded the Oltenia districts of Wallachia carried him off as a hostage to Sibiu and Alba Iulia. In Alba Iulia, the young prince had formed a close friendship with the Jesuits and maintained connections with them later, when from 1719 until 1730 (an exceptionally long period of time by Romanian standards) he ruled in Moldavia. This complex set of relationships solidified further when his son Constantine turned to the Hungarian Jesuits, asking them to write the history of the country, perhaps wishing to develop the notion of the connection between Romanian culture and Rome.

The three Hungarian Jesuits sent out on 25 May 1743 from Brassó (Braşov) in the direction of Bereck (Breţcu), where they arrived on the afternoon of the second day of their journey. There, Constantine's emissaries were already waiting for them, and the Jesuits continued on with their hosts over the Ojtiz Pass and went to the Tatros region, which was predominantly inhabited by Hungarians. During their brief sojourn there, they began at once to minister to the spiritual needs of the people, who in their isolated setting had seen few Catholic clergy. From there, they journeyed for four days to Iaşi, where one of the prince's counselors, a Count Kalnoky, received them and saw to their needs.

Iaşi was a small Tower of Babel: in the mid-seventeenth century, Marcus Bandinus, the Archbishop of Marcianopolis had counted among its 48,000 residents, Romanians, Hungarians, Armenians, Greeks, Bulgarians, Albanians, Turks, Tartars, Poles, Ruthenians, Saxons, Muscovites and a few Italians.[14] The ruling Phanariots, while they were themselves of mixed ethnic background, took on the culture of the upper classes in Constantinople, even to the point of imitating their dress and eating habits.[15] Thus Iaşi presented a particularly exotic appearance to Jesuits formed according to standards created in Western Europe. Shortly after the Jesuits' arrival in Iaşi, the prince launched into a four-hour-long discourse with them, expressing his surprise that members of the Society would travel long distances and work among heathen peoples, so that they might be won for Christ, but that those who were already of the faith of Christ, such as the Moldavian Catholics, were neglected. Patai offered as an excuse the special difficulties of establishing a permanent mission, especially the lack of materials. The prince responded by pledging extensive support and gave the Jesuits wide-ranging authority to begin their work, making no reference to the half-dozen Franciscans or the two Polish Jesuits already working in his Principality. Perhaps this omission reflected only the desire of the prince to maintain maximum control over his potentially useful guests, but the Cluj Jesuits were mistaken if they believed that long-established rivalries would not affect their visit. Before their stay had lasted many months, Patai and his company completely alienated the well-established Franciscan community to the degree that they were

---

Sommervogel et al., *Bibliothèque*, vol. 6, p. 344; Nilles, *Symbolae*, vol. 2, p. 1025.

[13] The following section is based partially on Barta István, "Az 1743 évi moldvai misszió," *Regnum 5* (1942–43), p. 81.

[14] Benda (ed.), *Okmánytár*, vol. 1, p. 409.

[15] Sugar, *Southeastern*, p. 135.

declared excommunicated. The origins of this conflict could be traced in part to the rivalry between Jesuits and Franciscans in the region in the previous century, but there were also contemporary issues of jurisdiction that reflected the delicate balance maintained between different Catholic orders and between these orders and the Catholic episcopal hierarchy.[16] Patai and his colleagues had been approached by the representatives of a Hungarian Catholic community Sztocsin on the far side of the River Prut, in Ottoman territory, whose members were probably refugees from the failed kuruc rebellion.[17] One of these representatives was a captain serving under the Turkish Pasha Chotim. A mission to the three hundred souls was exactly the kind of undertaking favored by the Jesuits, but the location of the community outside of the Principality and the problem of the loyalties of ethnic Hungarians who had fought against the Austrians and were now Ottoman subjects may have made the project unattractive to the prince. Questions about the authority of the local Franciscans in neighboring Turkish territory further complicated the carrying-out of the Jesuits' plan. In any case, Constantine made no efforts to oppose the ban of excommunication.

The Superior of the Jesuit mission run by the Polish Province, IoannesRęgarski, protested the excommunication, which illustrated that Moldavian rivalries did not extend to differing Provinces of the Society, but to no avail.[18] The difficult situation of Patai and Szegedi grew worse when Constantine was replaced as prince by his brother John, who was reputed to be the uncultured opposite of Constantine. Despite the good will and material support of the prince, the pastoral activities planned by the Fathers faced obstacles. The Franciscan *Praefectus* refused the Jesuits permission to use the church for their services, a setback compounded by the remoteness of the bishop holding jurisdiction over the Polish Jesuit Province, from whom they would have to wait for authorization to begin their work. They were therefore forced to sit in Iași, waiting for permission to begin their work and assisting Péterffy in the collection of materials for his historical project, a project that would never be completed after Péterffy's death in 1746. One of the few tasks that the Jesuits were able to accomplish was to draw up a catalogue of the Hungarian villages in Moldavia, which they numbered at 26.[19] By 8 August 1743, Patai had returned to Cluj, and was writing to the Austrian Provincial that the entire project would have to wait for a more propitious moment: the prince had journeyed to Constantinople, and the Ottoman Empire itself was reeling from a defeat at the hands of the Persians.

Constantine Mavrokordat again became Prince of Transylvania the following year (1744), and later ruled Moldavia on two other occasions, but the plans that he had made with the Hungarian Jesuits never became a reality. Only a few years later, in 1746, he entered into a scheme whereby he was to help the Piarists become

---

[16] For example, in 1733, the Catholic Bishop of Transylvania was responsible for the "deposita" of the Catholic church in Cotnar. Pall, "Controversie," p. 325.
[17] Sztocsin has not been identified.
[18] Pall, "Controversie," p. 328.
[19] Kálmán Benda, "Csöbörcsök, ein ungarisches Dorf am Dnjester-Ufer," in *Forschungen über Siebenbürgen und seine Nachbarn. Festschrift für Attila T. Szabó und Zsigmond Jakó*. Kálmán Benda et al. (eds) (München, 1987), p. 265.

established in Bucharest, a foreshadowing of the role this order would play after 1773 in continuing the work of the Society.[20] Pope Benedict XIV supported this project by sending three Hungarian Piarists to Bucharest under the direction of Innocentius Desericzky.[21] But the discussions soon broke down, and the mission headed home, although one of the Piarists, Conradi Norbert, stayed behind and continued for a time to teach at a school in Bucharest. The prince meanwhile initiated discussions once more with the Jesuits about the establishment of a *collegium* in Bucharest, but this new attempt was likewise unsuccessful. The Italian Franciscans continued the *cura animarum* of the Hungarians of Moldavia, but these priests lacked both the linguistic skills and the opportunities to carry out this mission successfully.[22] By the end of the century, Rome would have more pressing problems closer to home to occupy its attention, and the dream of flourishing Uniate Churches extending far into Eastern Christendom would be set aside. And the Jesuit outpost in Cluj, from which the Moldavian mission had been launched, would not be restored.

---

[20] Late in the eighteenth century, Romanian Catholic parishes would be placed under the jurisdiction of the Archbishop of Esztergom, but the great distances involved meant that the Provincials of the various orders operating in the region continued to play important roles. Király, "Hungarian Church," p. 114.

[21] Barta, "Misszió," p. 75.

[22] In 1776, the Provincial of the Minorite Franciscans wrote to the Vice-Prefect that "I missionari italiani in Moldavia erano inutili ed incapci a lavore per il bene spirituale dei cattolici ... ." Petro Tocanel, *Storia della chiesa Cattolica in Romania. III. Il vicariato apostolico e le missioni dei frati minori conventuali in Moldavia* (Padova, 1960), p. 18.

CHAPTER TEN

Conclusion

The end of the Jesuit era, which had long been anticipated even as the Austrian Province contemplated further expansion, came conclusively in 1773 with the proclamation of *Dominus ac Redemptor Noster*.[1] Its properties confiscated, its priests and brothers pensioned off with small sums, the Society would retreat into the domains of Catherine the Great for four decades until it was allowed to return to Austria.[2] In the cultural centers of the Habsburg Empire, as well as elsewhere in Europe, the end of the Society was viewed favorably by many, but in Transylvania there was little recorded reaction to the Suppression. This was in contrast to the expulsion of the Jesuits in 1608, which had been characterized by fire and sword. This time there was no banishment, no martyrdoms, no violent transfer of properties and no installation of Unitarian educators in what had been the Society's schools. The Jesuit church in Cluj, now in the hands of the Piarists, underwent an audit that reported its total assets at 11,450 Rhenish florins, a relatively modest sum.[3] By November, all former Jesuit properties had been transferred to the Piarists.[4] As was the case in many other parts of the Habsburg Empire, the long-expected papal brief produced its most obvious long-term consequence in the management of educational institutions, which were,

---

[1] The former Jesuits were still referred to as the "PP SJ" several months after the announcement of the papal brief. BB, Szentiványi 595, R XI, 84, *Catalogus Clericorum Transsylvanorum Seminarii Claudiopolitani*. For how the Society's leadership had anticipated the end, even decades before, see Enrico Rosa, SI, *I Gesuiti. Dalle Origini ai nostri giorni*, 3rd edn, ed. Angelo Martini (Roma, 1957), pp. 240ff. Much work remains to be done on former Jesuits in Habsburg territories. The relationship between the Enlightenment and former Jesuits is explored in Antonio Trampus, *I Gesuiti e l'Illuminismo: Politica e Religone in Austria e nell'Europa centrale (1773–1798)* (Firenze, 2000).

[2] *Merkwürdige Nachrichten von den Jesuiten in Weissrussen. In Briefen aus dem Italienischen*. Zweyte Auflage. (Frankfurt und Leipzig, 1786). Jesuit *coadjutores temporales* received 100 florins to purchase clothes, and 12 florins monthly, for firewood, candles and medicine. Maria Theresia m. p., 18 Sept. 1773 in Szilágyi Ferenc, *Közlemények az erdélyi Római Katholikus Egyházi történetből* (Budapest, 1874), pp. 35–6. A general guide, albeit somewhat dated, to the historiography of the Society is found in John Patrick Donnelly, SJ, "Religious orders of men, especially the Society of Jesus," in *Catholicism in Early Modern History: A Guide to Research*, John O'Malley, SJ, (ed.) (St. Louis, MO, 1988), pp. 149–53.

[3] ANR, C-N, Fond Liceul Romano-Catolic, Dosar 1, unnumbered fascicle, folio 17r.

[4] ANR, C-N, Fond Liceul Romano-Catolic, Dosar 1, unnumbered fascicle, folio 1r. This figure should be considered separate from the 10,600 Rhenish florins reported as the annual income of Jesuit properties a few years earlier. ARSI, *Austria 118, Catal. I. Coll. Claud. 1770*, p. 79. See also Biró Vencel, "Kolozsvár és a Piaristák," *Kolozsvári Szemle* 3, 1 (1943), pp. 27–37; here p. 28.

however, not shut down.⁵ But the shift in formal power in Transylvanian schools was not accompanied by an immediate comparable change in the actual teaching faculty of these schools. Jesuits often remained teaching in the schools they had started for some years after formal and legal control of these schools had passed to others, since there simply were not many trained teachers to step into their place. In addition, *coadjutores temporales* often were allowed to remain in the buildings where they had lived and worked. For example, in 1776, Father Georgius Szegedi (a former Jesuit) pleaded the case of Joannes Papp, who "from his childhood had served the rector of the college and who even now lives in Monostor," seeking to assure that the faithful servant would be retained in his position.⁶ The Piarists stepped into the role of successors to the Society's educational enterprise without difficulty, while continuing to employ many former Jesuits as teachers.⁷ The formerly Jesuit schools, mostly located in the larger towns of Transylvania, were rapidly integrated into the newer system put forward by the Habsburgs, which was to be encompassed in the coming decades by Josephinian political and social reforms.⁸ In Transylvania, this transition was less momentous than in many other regions in Central and Eastern Europe, where the suppression of the Society disrupted educational traditions that had matured over several centuries without providing a successor system of schools or sufficient means of funding such schools as were maintained. In the towns of Transylvania, former Jesuit teachers, if they did not stay on the job, sought means to return to their hometowns or to travel to new locations in search of work.⁹

---

⁵ Conservatism in terminology masks the rate at which Jesuit institutions actually ceased to function as such. As late as 1784, reference was made to a "Jesuiták Collegium," possibly in Sibiu. ANR, C-N, Cluj-Napoca, Városi Levéltár Fasc. II, 2035, folios 1r–2v. The "Fundatio Hevenyesiana" in Vienna provided funding for twenty poor students and recent converts for some time after the Suppression. MOL, 4 477, Erdélyi Kinsctár Levéltár, folio 211v, 16.11.1773; Nicolae Bocşan, "Historique de l'Université de Cluj," *Transylvanian Review* 4 (1995), pp. 3–16.

⁶ MOL, F 234 Erdélyi Kinsc., Fiscalis Levéltár Szekrény XXV/B unnumbered folio.

⁷ This transfer had taken place by November 1777. ANC-N, Liceul romano-catolic, Dosar 1, unnumbered fascicle, folio 1r. In 1774, the entire teaching staff of the Cluj *gymnasium* were former Jesuits. In the same year, the university counted eight former Jesuits among its teachers, including Fathers Mártonffi, Liszi, Gönczi, Jurics, Mertz, Gedő and Felszgi. Jakab, *Története*, vol. 3, pp. 336, 337. Curricular continuity was maintained to some degree, since Piarist fathers of "blameless character" were teaching philosophy and theology in Cluj eleven years later when the Bishop of Transylvania, Battyány Ignác, submitted a report on the state of Catholicism in the region. Gróf Battyány Ignác Püspök jelentése, Alba Iulia, 21.6.1788, in Tihamér Aladár Vanyó (ed.), *Püspöki Jelentések. A Magyar szent korona országnak egyházmegyeiről 1600–1800* (Pannonhalma, 1933), p. 103.

⁸ The *Convictus Nobilium* continued to function after the suppression, with Benkő Miklós serving as its regent. MOL, F477, Erdélyi Kinsc., Exactoratus Cameralis: Jesuitica. Protocolum Commisionis Claudio l., folio 176v., 31.8.1773.

⁹ Valentinus Kasskovics, "hactenusm. Universitate Academia Claudiopolitana Sacrosanctae Theologiae Doctor ex ejusdem Facultatis," sought money to travel and a pension a few months after the Suppression. Adamus Kereskény, *praefectus typographiae* in Cluj sought a yearly pension of 70 Rhenish florins. Kereskény's connection with the Cluj Jesuit community was far from over, however: when he died in 1777, he was buried in the crypt of the former

CONCLUSION

Occasionally, a former Jesuit would land a position that would allow him to continue the work he had performed in the Society. Matthias Geiger, born in Cluj in 1720, had taught mathematics and written school plays; he transferred as a teacher to Buda. After the Suppression, Geiger taught in a Catholic school in Győr until Joseph II decreed the closing of many Church-affiliated schools. It is reported that Geiger died "at a great age" in the monastery of Holy Cross, at an unidentified location.[10] Other Jesuits moved into positions quite different from the ones they had occupied prior to 1773. Theophilus Delphini was named abbot of the monastery of the Blessed Virgin in Kolosmănăştur, where Georgius Szegedi would also serve as a canon.[11] Perhaps the most successful career undertaken by a former Jesuit was that of Josephus Mártonfi, who became inspector of normal schools throughout Transylvania and in 1798 was appointed Bishop of Transylvania. Mártonfi survived until 1815, making him one of the handful of former Jesuits working in the Habsburg lands who was still alive when the Society was restored in 1814.[12] But like other former Jesuits, Mártonfi apparently made no effort to reestablish an affiliation with the restored Society. In a few notable cases, the actual job taken on by former Jesuits is hard to determine. Joannes Fridvaldszky, who after the Suppression was identified as "apud universitatem Claudiopolitanam matheseos professor emeritus," is described on the title page of one of his books merely as "presbitero saeculari."[13] Francis Xavier Vizl, who had taught rhetoric and ethics in Cluj, became a parish priest and canon at a now-forgotten location, but found time to compose a funeral oration for Maria Theresia in Hungarian.[14] For many other former Jesuits, obscurity and perhaps poverty were their fate.[15] The departure of these teachers seems to have had little lasting impact on the surviving school structure. In fact, the network of schools developed by the Society in Transylvania, while it was extensive relative to the scattered population, had never approached the scale of the Jesuit school system in the western Habsburg lands or in neighboring Poland and even in 1773 had not yet evolved into an entity having a strong identification with the religious or national groups that it served.[16]

Jesuit church there. MOL, 477 Erdélyi Kincs. Levéltár, Exoratatus Cameralis Jesuitica folios 178r–178v, 179r–179v, 176r. Sommervogel et al., *Bibliothèque*, vol. 4, p. 1008.

[10] Stöger, *Scriptores*, p. 96; Sommervogel et al., *Bibliothèque*, vol. 3, pp. 304–305.

[11] Weiser, *Iskolaügy*, vol. 2, pp. 34–5.

[12] Stöger, *Scriptores*, p. 220.

[13] *Reges Ungariae Mariani ex Antiquissismis diplomatis allisque Mss. Conscripti ...* (Viennae, 1774). Elsewhere we find Fridvaldszky in the months following the Suppression serving in Cluj as a German-language catechist. MOL-F 477 Erdélyi Kinsc. Levéltár, Exactoratus Cameralis Jesuitica, folios 176r, 178r–178v, 179r–179v, 176r.

[14] Stöger, *Scriptores*, p. 384.

[15] Nothing more is known about the post–Suppression career of Stephanus Mihatz, the author of *Christianus Seneca*, than that "soluto Ordine obiit." *Op. cit.*, p. 229. Likewise, Moses Lestyán, who continued a career as a preacher in various locations in Transylvania, is believed to have died in Udvárhely, although details are lacking. Sommervogel et al., *Bibiliothèque*, vol. 4, p. 151.

[16] In 1770, the Society ran 66 schools in Poland, with about 1,400 students; more than two-thirds of all the schools in the kingdom were under Jesuit control, while simultaneously Jesuit tutors exercised considerable influence on the education of the highest nobility. Elzbieta

Calvinist schools and printing presses, for example, continued their work after 1773, in some instances picking up the slack left by the suppression of the Society.

Beyond the structure and administration of the formerly Jesuit schools, there remained the question of what directions the curriculum might take without the weight of several centuries of Jesuit corporate culture to influence it. Under the guidance of the Piarists and with increasing oversight from Vienna, some elements of the Society's secondary school curriculum were preserved, but the *Ratio Educationis*, a reformist document generated in 1777 by the Theresian court for use in Hungary, placed a new emphasis on the cultivation of the citizen, whose services would be more readily available to the dynasty.[17] Law and surgery, practical sciences greatly valued by the Habsburgs, were added to the faculties of the newly reconstituted university, which came into existence in 1776.[18] Other changes originated closer to home. Innovations in the *gymnasia* of Transylvania, put forward by the Uniate Bishop Ioan Bob in 1789 retained much of the Jesuit curriculum, providing for classes in rhetoric, syntax and poetics, although there is no evidence that the dramas and elaborate public rituals that had been a centerpiece of Jesuit education were retained.[19] Lavish tributes to the Habsburgs, a prominent feature of Jesuit educational practice, passed out of fashion as well, even though the dynasty was entering into a period of crisis where an emperor might ask if one of his subjects was "a patriot for me." The moral underpinnings of Jesuit education in the classics were likewise given short shrift in an educational context where Jesuit teachers were no longer to be had. It is probable, however, that the position of Professor of Natural and Civil Law that had existed during the last years of the *collegium* was retained after 1773.[20] The elaborate process of teacher training developed through the province-wide

---

Drogosz, "L'enseignement Jésuite en Pologne Base intellectuelle des réformes adaptées aux besoins et aux conditions polonaises," in F. Guerello and P. Schivone (eds), *La Pedagogia della Compagnia di Gesù. Atti del Convegno Internazionale Messina 14–16 novembre 1991* (Messina: E.S.U.R. Ignatianum, 1992), pp. 129–30.

[17] Of the new *Ratio*, Kaunitz wrote, "former le coeur avant d'employer l'esprit, donner des moeurs au citoyen avant d'en exiger ses services." Quoted in Paul Cornea, "L'eseignment Roumain à la fin de XVIIIe siècle," in *Les Lumières en Hongrie, en Europe Centrale et, en Europe Orientale. Actes du Cinquième Colloque de Mátrafüred 24–28 octobre 1981* (Budapest, 1984), p. 308. See also István Fazakas, "*Ratio Educationis*," *Annuarul Institutului de Istorie Cluj-Napoca* 36 (1997), pp. 243–8; R. J. W. Evans, "Maria Theresia and Hungary" in H.M. Scott (ed.), *Enlightened Absolutism: Reform and Reformers in Later Eighteenth Century Europe* (Ann Arbor, MI, 1990), pp. 196–7; Moritz Csáky, *Von der Aufklärung zum Liberalismus: Studien zum Frühliberlismus in Ungarn* (Wien, 1981), p. 179; Szabo, *Kaunitz*, p. 247.

[18] Pascu et. al., *Clujul*, p. 62.

[19] Ioan M. Bota, *Istoria Bisericii Universale și a bisericii românești de la origini până în zilele noastre* (Cluj-Napoca), p. 178. Bob, a graduate of the Seminarium S. Josephi, had been raised in Szamos-Ujvár, where he had been exposed to Armenian culture. T. Cipariu, *Acte*, p. 21.

[20] In 1767, this post was held by Michael Csomós. *Titulare Dacicum*, 199. A course in canon law, and another on Church history were still being offered by former Jesuits in 1774 at the *collegium*. Jakab, *Története*, vol. 3, p. 336. Degrees in law were never awarded by the Cluj Jesuits, however.

system of the Society could not be sustained in a post-Suppression world. Trnava, the centerpiece of this system, in fact lost its famed university when the institution was moved to Buda. Yet the reputation of what had been the Jesuit *collegium* in Cluj remained high in the coming decades, and in the early nineteenth century, it was considered as good as the school in Buda.[21] The modest library assembled by the Jesuits for the Cluj *collegium* was gradually expanded, becoming the nucleus for the Babeş-Bolayi University, but collections that had been gathered in Jesuit residences in Cluj and elsewhere were dispersed, with some volumes ending up in parishes where they gathered dust.[22]

While the Society as an educational and missionary organization vanished, the Habsburg hold on the region, maintained through military and bureaucratic means, persisted, however, and in fact grew stronger and more exacting in the closing years of the century. The ferocity with which Imperial troops and judges responded to the Horea uprising of 1784 that took place less than a dozen years after the suppression of the Society testified to the dynasty's determination to hold on to what would turn out to be the farthest extension of its power into the south-east.[23] The Uniate Church also survived in Transylvania into the eras of Enlightenment and nationalism and beyond, but it never succeeded in gaining the allegiance of more than a fraction of the Orthodox population of Transylvania.[24] Unitarians, Lutherans and Calvinists, far from being eliminated or assimilated by the aggressive efforts of the Jesuits, emerged after Joseph II's reforms from the shadows once again to build new churches and, in the case of the Lutherans and Calvinists, to enjoy official toleration from Vienna, although the power relationship that had existed in the first part of the seventeenth century, with Calvinists exercising political dominance over Orthodox believers, was broken for good. The Baroque aesthetic introduced early in the eighteenth century lingered as a highly visible if no longer living and evolving element in the urban landscape of Cluj, for the succeeding waves of Neo-Classicism and Romantic Revival architectural styles advanced only very slowly into the region. For over half a century after the suppression of the Society, the physical evidence of its sojourn in Cluj remained conspicuous, sustained in part by the inherent architectural

---

[21] Imre Szentpéter, *A bölcsészettudományi kar története 1633–1935* (Budapest, 1935), p. 231.

[22] A catalogue compiled in 1797 for the "Bibliotheca Regia Claudiopolitana" lists works by Calvin, Newton and Erasmus, as well as Luther's translation of the Bible and an *Apologia Fratrum Uniatarior.* Some of these books may have been in the Jesuit library at the time of the Suppression, but catalogues from the former library have not survived to confirm this possibility. BARC-N, MsC 697v *et passim*. ANC, Fondul Romano-catolic, Dosar 1, folio 17r. The library of the Trnava *collegium*, after its removal to Buda, was converted into a public library for a city that as of yet had none.

[23] The Horea rebellion and its aftermath are reviewed in this standard English-language study: David Prodan, Supplex Libellus Valachorum *or the political struggle of the Romanians in Transylvania in the Eighteenth Century* (Bucharest, 1971).

[24] While actual documentation is scarce, Hitchins maintains that the Orthodox Church remained largely untouched at the village level by the new Uniate hierarchy until 1759. If so, the Society's prospects for establishing a securely rooted Uniate Church in its later years were significantly diminished by its earlier lack of success. Hitchins, *Romanians*, p. 201.

conservatism of the region and by the relatively slow rate of urban growth, but this presence was an afterglow, not a sign of a vital cultural force.

At the same time, the impact of the disappearance of the Jesuit missions in the countryside and in town is harder to assess. The work of active Jesuit missionaries such as Stephanus Josa, who entered the Society in Cluj in 1743 and began his travels throughout Transylvania in 1760, but who disappears from sight after 1773, presumably ceased after the Suppression and was not supplanted by any comparable efforts from other Catholic orders.[25] The post-Josephinian environment of *de facto* religious toleration made mission work seem to Imperial bureaucrats a doubtful expenditure of valuable resources, as well as an activity whose benefit to the dynasty was questionable at best. Kaunitz and his successors saw the principle virtue of the rigorous training given to Jesuit teachers was their capability to convey practical knowledge. An important legacy of Jesuit education was to survive, but without the theological justification that had brought it into existence. But then some observers of the secular careers taken up by former Jesuits elsewhere have wondered how religiously based the real goal of the Society had been to begin with. Whatever the innermost motivations of the Jesuits were, nineteenth-century Habsburg nation building across ethnic and religious lines was incompatible with the original vision of the Society's educators who sought to reclaim Transylvania. The earlier notion promoted by Peter Canisius of a separated, even segregated Catholic culture, supported by its own literary output and self-sufficient intellectually, was out of step with the Habsburg goals of the late eighteenth and early nineteenth centuries, and with the steadily increasing sense among the minorities of the empire that education was linked to national identity and consciousness.[26] The Canisian model moreover was of little value to the restored Society, whose greatly reduced resources and redefined political position could not allow a return to the social ideals of the Counter-Reformation. Stability, conformity and at least the outward forms of toleration that promoted material progress replaced the fervent Counter-Reformation idea of a theologically purified community. Meanwhile, creative expression in Transylvania, both within and beyond the schools, drew its models from Romantic and nationalistic themes popular in Germany and Austria. We can see clear evidence of this in the evaporation of Jesuit-supported notions of drama that for so long had completely dominated the stages of Transylvania. Translations of Shakespeare or dramas based on other foreign models took the place of hagiographic or patriotic theatre in the Baroque mold.[27] Adolescent virgins, exotic martyrs and medieval miracles vanished, and with them the Baroque aesthetic that had informed stage design and costume. Despite the conscious imitation of Germany in literature, no identifiable unifying aesthetic appeared to take the place of the one that had communicated these Counter-Reformation mainstays, and without the powerful alliance of dynasty and Society, the visual language that had spoken to each of the disparate cultural groups that made up the community sank into oblivion without a clear successor. In retrospect,

---

[25] Stöger, *Scriptores*, p. 164.

[26] O'Brien, "Ideas," p. 11.

[27] Ágnes Bartha Katalin, "A Transylvanian Macbeth production (1812) (Practical Training of Acting and Education of Audience)," *Iskola és Színház*, CD-ROM.

the apparent strength and unity of the aesthetic promoted by the Society was never as total as the material accomplishments of the Jesuits in Cluj and in other Transylvanian towns seemed to suggest. Local architectural, dramatic and oral traditions of each of the ethnic groups found in the region were neither assimilated by the Jesuit presences nor denied viability by it.

And while the dynasty remained firmly Catholic in its personal practice, it no longer turned as persistently to the outward symbols of doctrinal fidelity to express its own political mission, perhaps recognizing that its efforts in this direction had met with only very limited success in its eastern territories. The ideas of the Enlightenment penetrated the mountains and forests of Transylvania slowly, but long before these new ideas had taken root, the Habsburgs had abandoned the Baroque aesthetic, not merely as a form of artistic expression, but also as an articulation of religious beliefs and educational practice wedded to dynastic loyalty. The Catholicism of the nineteenth century, while it retained many of its traditional aspects in the practices of the people, was in its public manifestations much cooler, more Classical in its visible forms and completely divorced from the rhetorical traditions that were found everywhere in the pre-Suppression Jesuit school system. Gradually, the loyal bureaucrat supplanted the pious soul as the ideal of the Habsburg regime. The appointment in 1777 of Samuel von Brukenthal, a Transylvanian Saxon raised as a Lutheran and involved in Freemasonry and homeopathy, as governor of the Principality is a concrete example of how far the disconnection of Catholic piety and dynastic loyalty had advanced, even while the devout empress still ruled.[28] Thus while the architectural monuments of Jesuit Baroque triumphalism were still to be seen in Cluj and elsewhere in Transylvania, there was no returning to the climate that gave them birth. Ultimately, the aesthetic, despite its successes elsewhere and the fervor with which the Jesuits sought to foster it, remained an import that never took root.

The same story of visibility and survival sustained to a limited degree by local conditions cannot be told about the intellectual and broader cultural heritage of the Jesuits of Cluj, although establishing criteria for the impact of the Society in these areas is more difficult. In assessing the success of the Jesuits in Cluj, several criteria may be employed. First, we may consider a criterion that the Society itself continually employed, the number of souls brought into the Church, either directly or in union with Rome, and in a broad sense the other souls brought into contact with the Society's message through missionary and related endeavors. In terms of sheer numbers of faithful brought into meaningful connection with the Latin tradition, the Jesuit achievement in promoting union with Rome was modest and is ultimately only a small part of the story of the Uniate undertaking.[29] The Catholic minority in the region was strengthened and enjoyed a permanent increase in visibility during

---

[28] *Quellen zur Geschichte der Siebenbürger Sachsen 1195–1975*, eds Gesammelt und bearbeitet von Ernest Wagner (Wien, 1976), pp. 164–5.

[29] Adrian Fortescue and George D. Smith, *The Uniate Eastern Churches* (Piscataway, NJ, 2001).

the eighty years of Jesuit institutional presence in the city.[30] In the years after the Suppression, important churches in Cluj remained in Catholic hands, but at no point could the region around Cluj be described as predominantly Catholic. The Uniate Church, without the direct support of a powerful organization such as the Jesuits, made little headway in the nineteenth century, and the possibility of defections by Uniates and Catholics to Orthodoxy remained enough of a concern that Joseph II issued a decree in 1782 threatening severe punishment for those who tried to leave these Churches.[31] Yet the struggles of the Transylvanian Uniate Church must be placed in comparison with the experiences of similar projects elsewhere. In Poland, despite the successful establishment of such a Church in the seventeenth century, protests by Orthodox clergy and laypersons were far more violent and resulted in political instability unknown in Transylvania.[32] Thus the mere survival of the Uniate Church and its continuing role as a principle vehicle for the expression of Romanian national identity is evidence of the success of the Jesuits as institution builders, even if this success took an unexpected form.[33]

In a less precise sense we might seek to discover how the combined Catholic and Habsburg cultural orientation that the Society strove to introduce into the region fared after the Society was no longer an organized force. Habsburg political control over Transylvania continued until the end of World War I, with a brief interruption during the short-lived "Republic of Hungary" that appeared after 1848. But as we have seen, the Habsburg presence of the nineteenth and early twentieth centuries had a far different flavor from that of the early seventeenth and eighteenth centuries. While the struggle to promote conformity and loyalty in the face of ethnic diversity continued, the means of promotion ceased to be primarily or even significantly ecclesiastical. In the era of the Napoleonic Wars and after, Vienna viewed its subject peoples increasingly in terms of the tension between the goals of the Imperial court and each group's national aspirations, in which religious heritage played an as of yet minor, if persistent and growing, role. The rationalized bureaucracy that began to emerge in the Theresian era and which was carried to higher levels of efficiency during the reigns of Joseph II and Leopold II imposed its own Imperial symbolism on its subject

---

[30] However, relations between Transylvanian Catholics and the Society were not invariably cordial. A petition sent to Maria Theresia in 1741 by the "Catholic Christians of Transylvania" offers numerous criticisms of the Society's practices. Cited in full in Hurmuzaki, *Documente*, vol. 6, pp. 572–5.

[31] Hitchins, *Romanians*, p. 208.

[32] In Vitebsk in 1623, the Uniate bishop was murdered in the streets, and in Mohilev, Eastern Rite clergy who acknowledged union with Rome were expelled. A.F. Pollard, *The Jesuits in Poland* (New York, 1971), p. 63. Polish Uniate bishops were excluded from the Senate and thereby from any practical influence on the government. Kłoczowski, "The Polish Church," p. 123. Much later, Catherine the Great, who willingly sheltered the Jesuits, suppressed the Uniate Churches within her domains.

[33] The Uniate Church actually profited materially from the suppression of the Society: the *collegium* operated by the Jesuits in Uzhhorod was transferred to the control of the Uniate bishop of Mukachevo in 1776. Fürst Johann Josef Khevenhüller-Metsch, *Aus der Zeit Maria Theresias*, Rudolf Graf Khevenhüller-Metsch and Hans Schlitter (eds), (10 vols, Wien, 1925), vol. 8, p. 151.

CONCLUSION

peoples in the form of the military uniform, the civil servant's vocabulary, rank and range of responsibilities, and the secret police's inquiries, but did not rely primarily on the identification of the dynasty with its Catholic mission or with its historic connection with Rome. The proclamation in 1804 of a manufactured Imperial title unrelated to the claims of the Holy Roman Empire of the German Nation was only the most obvious manifestation of a trend long underway in the eighteenth century in which the symbols of the dynasty and its authority were gradually divorced from their association with the sacral nature of the old and senescent Empire. Continuing its campaign to bring its diverse peoples into *ein Totum*, Vienna did not use the post-1814 Society as a source of authority, intellectual credibility or creative innovation to further its aims, for these aims, formerly clothed in ecclesiastical language, were now nakedly dynastic and could make little use of the old sacral paradigm in which the Society had played such an important role.[34] The resurrected Society, while it clung to the verities of cherished by the *ancien régime* to a greater degree than at any time during the previous century, could no longer supplement its educational role with a diplomatic one. Talented men still joined the Jesuits, but few were innovators in education or the sciences. And any who did dream of such innovation faced implacable opposition from the Society's leadership and from the Holy See. At the same time, only a few prominent educators or political figures in post-1773 Transylvania were former Jesuits, a contrast with the situation found in Austria and Bohemia.[35] At least one former Jesuit, Georgius Szegedi, whom we have already met, served as a parish priest for a dozen years after the Suppression; probably other former Jesuits did as well.[36] Yet Transylvania would never again be the home of Jesuit literati who produced both devotional and scientific works, nor would Jesuits again occupy positions such as *theologus* that exercised such a direct influence on their Eastern Rite neighbors.

The Society that returned to the region in the nineteenth century followed a pattern occurring throughout the Habsburg lands, one that reflected the financially straitened and politically weakened position of the Jesuits. Deprived of its special relationship to the dynasty and its network of schools and missions, the resurrected Society responded cautiously to opportunities to work once more in Transylvania. The post-Suppression Jesuits found a home in Szatmár (Satu Mare), a community that did not possess the prominence or historical importance of Cluj, which was now growing from a medieval town into a significant commercial center. But they did not resume their teaching and missionary work in the Cluj or Alba Iulia regions, where the Society had once enjoyed such high visibility.[37] Nor was the Society able

---

[34] It is now recognized that this rationalization began earlier than had previously been assumed. An example of rationalized tax records dating from the middle period of Maria Theresia is *Methodus Nova super Contributione Magni Principatus Transylvaniae* ... (Viennae, 1767).

[35] One of the few former members of the Cluj Jesuit community who both rose to relatively high station in the post-Suppression Church and continued a literary career was Dominicus Szeredai, who was a canon in Alba Iulia and an archdeacon in Transylvania. In 1790, Szeredai wrote a *Series Episcoporum Transylvaniae*. Stöger, *Scriptores*, p. 355.

[36] Weiser, *Iskolaügy*, vol. 2, p. 34.

[37] P. Lud. Carrez, SJ, *Atlas Geographicus Societatis Jesu* (Paris, 1900), plate 9.

to provide a viable successor to the Baroque sensibility that had been a distinct feature of the Jesuit mission to Cluj but which rapidly came to appear dated; the architectural contribution of the Jesuits to the evolving early industrial landscape of nineteenth-century Transylvania was negligible, while the most significant aesthetic innovations that did emerge in Transylvanian cities retained a strongly secular flavor. Even more important, the "blood and tears" display of religious fervor so characteristic of even the late Baroque likewise vanished from the region, and with it the evidence of the religious preoccupation with the body that had dominated much of the Society's missionary efforts and its methods of recording these efforts.[38] Sodalities, processions, public acts of penance all receded from view with an astonishing rapidity, considering the fervor with which they had been supported. The stream of devotional literature, once a key component of the literary output of the Jesuits and a source of the vocabulary with which they conducted their missions, quickly shrank to a trickle, and remained completely disconnected from the scientific culture of the region. The political leaders of the new era were in no way hostile to the Society's continuing protestations of loyalty to the dynasty or to its pastoral work. These leaders simply no longer saw these activities as crucial to the survival of the dynasty or the furtherance of its goals. The nineteenth-century Habsburg Society, therefore, can be seen neither as a continuation of the pre-suppression order nor as an important player in those developments that flowed from the eighteenth century accomplishments of the Jesuits.

In such a context, the failure of the eighteenth-century Jesuits to establish a deeply rooted Western-looking Catholic culture that took its cues from Vienna and could continue to grow in the Society's absence becomes more significant. The Jesuit contribution to the local scene in Cluj was not systematically obliterated in the way influence of the Society was suppressed after it was expelled from Russia in 1820. The Habsburgs and many of their subjects remained loyal Catholics and Transylvania, unlike the vastness of Russia, might still be seen as a natural geographical extension of the Catholic heartland of an empire whose ruler maintained close ties to Rome.[39] But the Society's program of extending the cultural influence of the West, and thus, of "Europe" as understood by the early eighteenth century as well as the Enlightenment, had only superficial consequences for Cluj and the surrounding region. The interruption of the Society's self-chronicling during the decades of the Suppression also brought an end to the long tradition of editing and preserving documents that had been promoted first by Hevenesi and then continued by other Hungarian Jesuits in the service of the Habsburgs.[40] The heavily rural character of the entire Principality may have played a role in this failure, for while the Society was no stranger to rural missions, it had long possessed a special strength for work in cities and had invested time and talent in architectural undertakings found in urban settings and in educational projects designed to serve city dwellers.

---

[38] R. Po-Chia Hsia, *Social Discipline in the Reformation: Central Europe 1550–1750* (New York/London, 1989), pp. 155–6.

[39] Schlafly, *"Ratio,"* pp. 421–34.

[40] György Hölvényi, *A magyar jezsuita történetírók és a jezsuita rend* (Budapest, 1974), p. 37.

While the persistently Eastern character of the Uniate Church was essential to what acceptance it was able to find among the Romanian population, the image it projected to the West was exotic and far from entirely favorable. There is little evidence that Vienna came to see its Romanian subjects, even if they had joined with the Church of Rome, as more "civilized," more "Western" or more "Christian" as a result of their encounter with the Jesuits. The entire region remained outside the pale of the Europe known to the Imperial court, while the "barbarous" reputation of Transylvania, along with that of its neighbors both within and outside of the Habsburg realms, survived the Society's suppression and may even have been reinforced by the violence of the Horea uprising and by romantic tales of vampires that persisted into the nineteenth century.[41] Too ethnically mixed, too fractious and too far away, Transylvania, despite the writing and preaching of the Jesuits, could not share fully in the heritage of the distinctly Magyar *Regnum Marianum* that inspired devout Hungarian Catholics and drew that country towards the Habsburgs.[42] Originally of doubtful loyalty because of its Hungarian Calvinist population, Transylvania gained a new and questionable reputation in the nineteenth century as a land claimed by Romanian speakers as part of their own homeland while remaining dominated by Hungarian aristocrats who themselves were of less than sterling loyalty. The forces driving this trend towards national consciousness were more powerful than many contemporaries realized, and even with much greater resources and a continuous presence in Transylvania, it is improbable that the nineteenth-century Society could have prevented the rise of Romanian nationalist sentiment, or could have prevented that sentiment from being identified with the Orthodox Church in opposition to Catholicism and the West. Post-Suppression Transylvania was not destined to be another Styria or Bohemia, that is, Habsburg lands formerly lost to heresy but then reclaimed for the Church. Nor could the Principality even be compared with Hungary, whose loyalty throughout the difficult years of the Napoleonic Wars was unwavering. Yet the coming century would show that the region was still far from a complete loss.

We have already noted how the schools established by the Society served as training grounds for the first generation of Romanian intellectuals who helped shape the Romanian Enlightenment. One might assess the contribution of the Society in Cluj by its long-term impact on this Enlightenment, an impact that may be traced through the exposure Romanian students gained to both Catholic piety and Western rationalism. Yet the connection between the nationalism and Enlightenment ideology of early nineteenth-century Romanians and the education and aesthetic proffered by eighteenth-century Jesuits is less distinct than in the western regions of the Habsburg Empire. Training gained in Jesuit schools and the literary and architectural references to Rome left behind by the Society reinforced the growing awareness

---

[41] Wolff references a scene in a French map dating from 1772 that portrays Hungarians leaping about with swords; the map itself combines (inaccurately) Hungary, Transylvania, Wallachia, Bessarabia and Moldavia into one political entity. Wolff, *Inventing*, p. 326. For the violent reprisals initiated by the "enlightened" Joseph II after Horea upring, see Prodan, *Supplex Libellus*, pp. 253ff.

[42] *A magyar irodalom története 1600-tól 1772-ig*, ed. Tibor Klaniczay (Budapest, 1964), p. 560.

among Romanian intellectuals that their culture had Roman roots. But unlike in Austria and Bohemia, the number of Jesuit teachers and scholars in Romanian-speaking regions such as Transylvania who had seriously engaged the ideas evolving in Western Europe since the middle of the seventeenth century was tiny. For every Hell or Fridvaldsky in the Cluj community were dozens of thoroughly schooled men of much more modest ambitions and curiosity, men whose understanding of the mission of the Society was undoubtedly tempered by their own limited experience and ability. And while the presence of even one Jesuit in the Cluj community such as Father Kapi, who had received part of his education in Italy and Vienna, was noteworthy, such men did not linger long enough in Cluj nor were they supported with sufficient resources to enable them to leave a lasting impression the local cultural landscape.[43] The net impact of the considerable skill and intellectual rigor that the Jesuits brought to the region was blunted by the formidable opposition they encountered, and, most importantly, by the necessity of attending to many other matters while they carried out their mission many days' journey from the western heart of the Society's Austrian Province. We must also keep in mind as we review the accomplishments of individual Jesuits, some of whom were very talented, that the culture of the Society firmly discouraged personal ambition of any sort. Men who joined the Society were expected to surrender much of their own identities and desires to the greater goals of the organization, even as they pursued their own areas of interest. Naturally, not all Jesuits lived up to this ideal, but the pervasive power of the ideal of obedience and humility before the goals of the Society should not be underestimated. While the Jesuits who came to Cluj were in no sense interested in promoting a pluralistic culture as we understand it today, we should keep in mind that the century following the high-water mark of the Reformation actually saw the spread of pluralism in many parts of Europe, a trend whose echoes can be detected in Eastern Europe as well.[44] In the end, the image of the Jesuits as exponents of an alien culture posing a threat to indigenous Romanian society probably loomed larger in the imaginations of nineteenth- and twentieth-century Romanian nationalist historians than they probably did to the residents of eighteenth-century Cluj, who saw instead a procession of foreigners, each of whom was identified with a religious order, sojourning briefly in the town and then continuing on to other assignments, usually to the West.[45]

---

[43] Kapi studied in Vienna from 1676 to 1678, and later in Bologna (1684) and Venice (1685). O'Neill and Domínguez (eds), *Diccionario Historico*, vol. 3, p. 2173; Lukács, *Jezsuita tartomány*, p. 98.

[44] Christine Kooi, "*Sub jugo haereticorum:* Minority Catholicism in Early Modern Europe," in Comerford and Pabel (eds), *Catholicism*, p. 159.

[45] For an example of this view of the Jesuit presence, see Daicóviciu, Constainin et al., *Din Istoria Transilvaniei* (București, 1961), vol. 1, p. 247. The occasional presence of a student from far to the west at the Cluj *convictus* does not seem to have branded the institution as an outpost of an alien and occupying culture, but simply as the temporary home of a cosmopolitan aristocracy who might be found in any part of the Habsburg lands. For example, an undated record of probable Bachelor's degree recipients from the middle of the eighteenth century records the name of one Ignatius Dietrich, "Nobilis Austriacus Viennsis." BARC-N, MsC 49, unnumbered folio.

CONCLUSION

Yet this is not the final word on the men who created a community in Cluj for eighty years. The long-range consequences of the Jesuit program to promote union among the Eastern Rite faithful with Rome must be considered separately from the immediate impact of the Baroque aesthetic and the curriculum of the *Ratio*. The former was a largely unintended consequence, while the latter had been carefully thought out before it was undertaken. The Uniate Church, despite the difficulties it faced in its first decades and the shallowness of its support among the masses, ultimately made a significant contribution to the development of Romanian national identity and helped define the direction in which Romanian literary culture would evolve in the coming century. As early as 1779, the Transylvanian Uniate Church was publishing a prayer book in Romanian that used the Roman, not the Cyrillic alphabet, a move that would ultimately have long-reaching consequences in the developing relation between Romania and the West.[46] The rise of a well-trained Uniate clergy, frequently educated in Jesuit schools, was paralleled by a decline in the influence of Protestant schools, thereby altering a pattern of cultural dominance that had lasted for over a century and reinforcing the connection between Transylvanian Romanians and their brethren in Moldavia and Wallachia. The Uniate Church also provided both a theoretical framework and a practical means by which Romanians, both lay and religious, could understand their connection to Imperial Rome while simultaneously envisioning their own national future. In this process the Jesuit historians of Cluj who wrote about "Dacia" undoubtedly played an important role, as did the handful of Eastern Rite believers of various backgrounds who supported the publication of these works.[47] Even non-Romanian residents of the region could recognize this relationship, which was one of the most distinctive features of the historiography produced in Jesuit Cluj.[48] A Uniate graduate of the Cluj *collegium*, Gerontie Cotorea, went even further than some of his teachers, writing a treatise entitled *Despre schismaticia grecilor* (on the Schism of the Greeks) that proposed if Romanians would return to the Church of Rome a spiritual renaissance would follow.[49] This native-born vision of the relationship of Romanians to Rome must be viewed as something separate from the much more tenuous connection of Romanian intellectuals to the Anglo-French inspired Enlightenment that emerged in later decades, for Romanian national identity expressed by Cotorea and other preachers and teachers only grew stronger with each passing decade, and did not need to be fed from the outside, as did ideas imported from the *philosophes*. Cut off from Western Europe, aware of their relative poverty and backwardness, even in comparison with other minorities within the Habsburg domains, and denied a place in the polity of the Principality, the Romanians of Transylvania did not require any prodding to accept the idea that the Roman *patrimonium* was theirs as well. To what degree the

---

[46] Popinceanu, *Religion*, p. 99.

[47] In the list of "Nomina Offerentium" (160), of Andrea Illia's *Ortus et Progressus variarum in Daciâ ...* was "Franscicus Bibics, nobilis Bulgarus Devensis."

[48] Lukácsi, *Historia*, pp. 85–6, *et passim*.

[49] Cotorea (1720–?) was also noted as an orator, but few of his writings have survived. Keith Hitchins, "An East European elite in the eighteenth century," in *The Rich, the Well-Born and the Powerful*, ed. F.C. Jaher (Urbana, IL/Chicago, IL/London, 1973), pp. 144–5.

Jesuits of Cluj, both those few of Romanian ancestry and those who saw themselves as Germans or Hungarians, consciously sought to play the "Roman" card as they promoted the cause of Union, cannot be determined with certainty. But the at best dismissive tone with which Orthodox clergy (and, by implication, Orthodox dogma) are treated in Jesuit records, coupled with the apparent acceptance of Romanian students in Jesuit schools, suggests that, as was the case with the Jews, no matter how offensive a religious tradition might seen to the Society, those who fled from it to the arms of the Roman Church were still welcome as individuals.

To a degree that sometimes surprises Westerners, the Romanian population of Transylvania came to see itself as part of the community of peoples – including Romanians in Wallachia and Moldavia – who legitimately claimed direct descent from the Roman imperium, culturally and "racially" as well as institutionally, and whose national destiny would be shaped by a combination of their unique geographical position and their relationship to ancient Rome. This identification ran and runs far deeper than the constructs of a small intellectual elite who first articulated this idea, and in fact has shaped every facet of life in the region for the past two centuries. For over sixty years after the Suppression, the narratives written by the Jesuits about the Romanians, the vocabulary the Jesuits utilized in these narratives, and the Jesuit understanding of Romanian national history by default became a point of departure for this evolving national consciousness.[50] Unintentionally, the Jesuits of Cluj, while not solely responsible for the evolution of the mature development of this cultural reference point, created the circumstances under which it was able to flourish. However, we must remember that the Jesuit vision of Rome was always a Christian, papal Rome, whereas the starting point of the Romanians' understanding of their Roman heritage drew upon older images, ones often implying pre-Christian cultural or martial achievements rather than ecclesiastical affiliation and papal dominance.

This is of course not what the Jesuits had in mind as they recorded what they knew of local history and society, and drew upon hagiographic legend and Classical literature refined through a Christian moral perspective to explain the relationship of newly reclaimed Transylvania to the history of the Church Triumphant.[51] The role of these semi-amateur historians working with limited resources in a somewhat alien environment is completely unlike that of the Habsburg-supported Austrian Jesuit historians or even the Bohemian Jesuits who assisted at the birth of modern Czech historiography by "rediscovering" documentary evidence of the Bohemian past. In each of these instances, Jesuit writers were themselves members of the

---

[50] Victor Papacostea, "La fondation de l'Académie grècque de Bucharest, les origins del'erreur de datation et sa penetration dans l'historigraphie," in Victor Papacostea, *Civilizaţie Românească şi Civilizaţie Balcanică. Studuii Istorice*, eds Cornelia Papacostea-Danielopolu and Nicolae Serban Tanasoca (Bucureşti, 1983), p. 302.

[51] While Jesuit chronicles and scientific writings produced in Cluj sometimes have a passing resemblance to the encyclopedist approach to recording data, throughout Eastern Europe the Jesuit view of knowledge continued, right up until the Suppression, to resist the form of specialized, independent entries favored by the *philosophes*. This gives many of the publications of the Cluj Jesuits a slightly outdated appearance. See Alisdair MacIntytre, *Three Rival Versions of Moral Enquiry: Encyclopedia, Genealogy and Tradition* (Notre Dame, IN, 1990), pp. 216–17.

communities about which they wrote and they undertook their work aware that a small but important local public would read and react to their work. The Hungarian Jesuits of Cluj, when they wrote and taught about "Dacia," wrote about a culture they understood in a very different way from their own native cultures, and which they typically approached, not through the recent local past, but through the lens of a selective sample of Classical Latin literature that was a foundational element in the Jesuit curriculum.[52] The audience for these Latin works was, in addition to other Jesuits and perhaps some interested outsiders, the small group of local residents who were for the most part the products of Jesuit schools themselves. After the Suppression, a few Jesuits would continue to write and publish works that might have reached a wider readership, but again, the immediate impact of this literature was small in comparison with the influence of former Jesuit authors on the cultural climate of Austria or Bohemia.[53]

Jesuit educational practice also played a key role in the development of Romanian consciousness. The use of written and spoken Latin at a high level of sophistication, as prescribed by the *Ratio* and frequently maintained through the Society's own channels of communication, was another tie to both Romes, the Rome of the papacy and the Rome of ancient Imperial glory. This Rome was not the city of Renaissance humanists who gloried in its role as a transmitter of Pagan Hellenistic culture or even the city of later Romantics who sometimes idealized the law-giving papacy of the High Middle Ages. Nor was it the Rome of Browning and other nineteenth-century Western European travelers who reveled in the ruins of its former splendor as picturesque backdrop to contemporary dramas. Instead, the Rome of the Transylvanian Jesuits (and Jesuits in many other parts of Europe) was mediated in the visual arts through the expressions of Imperial ambition and Roman association found in Vienna, a city that, although it played a role in the education of some Uniates, was always regarded by Romanians as the seat of a foreign and sometimes hostile power.[54] Rome itself, the real Rome of eighteenth-century popes, notoriously provincial and a bit frayed at the edges, would turn out to be a poor ally of Habsburg ambitions and eventually of Jesuit projects as well.[55] But this irony was not apparent to the Jesuits who worked in Cluj down to 1773, busy as they were with

---

[52] Dacia was not only a topic for Jesuit historians; it was also a theme taken up by their students. In the Magister Phil. Acta of the Cluj *collegium* in 1725 was a "Pars Prima pro Veteri Daca" dealing with the deeds of Octavian, Trajan and Antonius. BARC-N, MsC, 49 a–b, folio 209v.

[53] Representative of writings by former Cluj Jeusits is Stephanus Biro, *Odae Augustissimo Romanorum Imperatori Josepho II* ... (Claudiopoli, 1775); Veress, *Bibliographia*, vol. 1, p. 287. Like other Transylvanian Jesuit writers working before 1773, Biro identifies the reigning Habsburg by his title as Holy Roman Emperor, rather than as Prince of Transylvania or King of Hungary.

[54] At a point when modern history was not being taught in Jesuit schools in any systematic or exhaustive way, the Breslau *collegium* included the "Historia Imperii-Romano-Germanici" in its curriculum. BUW, AKC 1968 KN 313, folios 131r–131v.

[55] Benedict XIV supported the Bavarian claimant to the Imperial title, Charles VII, during the War of Austrian Succession, and declared the expulsion of Austrian troops from the Papal States a "liberation." W.R. Ward, "Late Jansenism and the Habsburgs," in James

the multiple tasks they had set for themselves, and blinded, perhaps, to the long-term negative impact on their mission that their lack of sympathy for the Eastern Rite was likely to engender. That the Jesuits themselves were bearers of a tradition that reached back to Rome through very different channels from the ones some of their Uniate students would rediscover is the greatest irony attendant upon the encounter between the Society and their neighbors.

E. Bradley and Dale Van Kley (eds), *Religion and Politics in Enlightenment Europe* (Notre Dame, IN, 2001), p. 158.

Bibliography

Manuscript sources

ANR, C-N: Arhivele Naționale Ale României, Cluj-Napoca Fond Liceul Romano-Catolic

ARSI: Archivum Romanum Societatis Iesu Austria

ASC-N: Academie Științi Cluj-Napoca Colecția

ASV: Archivio Segreto Vaticano, Archivio della Nunziatura di Vienna

BARC-N: Biblioteca Academiei Române Cluj-Napoca

BB: Biblioteca Battyaneum, Alba Iulia, Romania

BUW: Biblioteka Uniwersytecka we Wrocławiu

ELTE: Eötvös Loránd Tudományos Egyetem, Library Manuscript Collection

MOL: Magyar Országos Levéltár, Budapest

MTA: Magyar Tudományos Akadémia, Budapest

NK: Národni Knihovna Prague

OSzK: Országos Széchényi Könyvtár

PFK: Pannonhalma Főapátság Könyvtár, Pannonhalma

Dosiar 1

Austria 47–229
Germania 25
"Aranka György" 74
Városi Levéltár
Fasc. II

196
MsC 49
MsC 156–159
MsC 417–418
MsC 478
MsC 678
MsC 697
MsC 761
Szentiványi 595
Szentiványi 691
AKC 1968 KN 313
Kéz. Kaprin xxvi

F-234
F-447
F-477
Jesuitica E152,
Kéz. Történet. 2 132
Sz. P. 323
Kéz. Történet 2-R 1352
Kéz. 705
Microfilm 23/19
2039 FMI/1608
Carton 4 Színház
118.E.10
118.E.41
118.A.E.687
118.A.6. 697
119.A.2/1–64

Electronic sources

http://www.mek.iif.hu/porta/szint/tarsad/konyvtar/tortenet.gyorgy/html/gyorgy15. htm. Accessed 3 March 2003. Unfortunately, this work does not include citations or bibliography, but is nonetheless valuable because of the inclusion of archival data no longer available. The reader is referred to the chapter entitled "A kolozsvári jezsuita Akadémia könyvtára" (1693-1773)."
http://www.osi.hu./lgi/ethnic/relations/roma.html. Accessed 2 September 1999. Glassman, Elliot H., "Denial and recovery: Legal policies perpetrated against the Roma in the Habsburg Monarchy"
http://www.hungarian-history.hu/lib/tsangos/tsangos.pdf. Accessed 28 March 2007. Pálfay, Bernadette, "Short history of the Tsangos," in S.J. Magyarody (ed.), *The Tsangos of Romania: The Hungarian Minorities in Romanian Moldavia* (Matthias Corvinus Publishing, 1996-9).

Printed and secondary sources

A Győri püspöki papnevelointézet könyvtárának czimjegyzéke (Győr: Suranyi Jakob Könyvnyomdája, 1893).
A katholikus iskolaügy Magyarországban II Literae Authenticae ... Collectae et Editae a sacerdote achidioeceseos Colocensis. Fasiculus secundus (Coloszae: Procudebat Franciscus Holmeyer Typographicus, 1884).
Acte sinodali ale baserecrei romane de Alba Julia [sic] *si Fagarasiu,* ed. J. M. Moldovanu (2 vols, Blasiu, 1872).
Aggházy, Mária, *A barokk szobrászat Magyarországon* (3 vols, Budapest: Akadémiai Kiadó, 1959).
Alexa, Csetri, *Importantia primei lucrari agromice de spcialitate din Transilvania. Studiul inedit al lui Fridvaldksy Dissertatio de agris fimandis et arandis pro M. Principatu Transylvaniae (1771). Studia Universiatis Babes-Bolyai. Series Historica.* Fasc. I (174).
Alfred, Ritter von Arneth, *Geschichte Maria Theresia's* (10 vols, Wien: W. Braumüller, 1863-79).
Andea, Avram, "Everyday life in Romanian society in the century of Enlightenment," in Teodor Pompiliu (ed.), *Enlightenment and Romanian Society* (Cluj-Napoca: Editura Dacia, 1980).
Andea, Susuana and Avram Andea, *Structuri Transylvane în epoca luminor* (Cluj-Napoca: Presa Universitară Clujeană, 1996).
Anno Jubilaeo Missionis Societatis JESU Maros-Varheliensis. Post exactum Deo propitio dimidium Saeculum. Templi fabricam felicibus auspiciis dedicantis ... (Claudiopoli: Typis Academicis Societatis JESU, [1750]).
Apor, Péter, *Metamorphosis Transylvaniae,* ed. Lőrinczy Béka (Bukarest: Kriterion Könyvkiadó, 1978).

Apor, Péter, *Synopsis Mutationum notabiliorum aetete mea in Transylvania et Progressus Vitae Meae*, Kazinczy Gábor (ed.), *Monumenta Hungariae Historica* (ed.), Második Osztály: Irók, 11 (Pest: Eggenberger Ferdinand M. Akad. Könvyárusnál, 1863).

Argenti, *De Societate Jesu*, excerpted in *Jezsuita okmánytár I/1. Erdélyt és Magyarországot érintő iratok*, Bálazs Mihály (ed.) (Szeged: Jószef Attila Tudományegyetem, 1995).

Arhimandrit, Ioan Marin Mălinaş, *Siutuaţia invatamantului bisericesc al Românilor în Contextul Reformelor Scolare din Timpul Domniei împaratesei Maria Tereza (1740–1780) a împaratilor Iosif al II-ea (1780–1790) şi Leopold al II–ea (1780–1792)* (Oradea: Editura Mihai Eminescu, 1994).

Ariès, Philippe, *Centuries of Childhood*, trans. Robert Baldick (New York: Vintage, 1962).

Ascay, Ferencz, *A győri kath. főgymnázium története* (Győrött: Győr egyházmegye könyvsajtója, 1910).

Ashworth, William B., Jr. "Catholicism and early modern science," in David C. Lindberg and Ronald L. Numbers (eds), *God and Nature: Historical Essays on the Encounter between Christianity and Science* (Berkeley: University of California Press, 1986).

Asztalos, Miklós, "Erdély története" in Miklós Asztalos (ed.), *A Történeti Erdély* (Budapest: Kiadja az Erdélyi Férfiak Egysültete, 1936).

Athanasius, P. and G. Welykyj (eds), *Supplicationes Ecclesiae Uniatae Ucrainae et Bielorusjaie Voll II, 1700–1740* (Romae: P.P. Basilani, 1962).

Aubert, R. (ed.), *Dictionanaire D'Histoire et de Geographie Ecclésiastique* (27 vols, Paris: Letousey et Ane, 1912–).

Authenticae ... Collectae et Editae a sacerdote achidioeceseos Colocensis. Fasiculus secundus (Coloszae: Procudebat Franciscus Holmeyer Typographicus 1884), pp. 306–307.

Barta, János, "A felvilágosult abszolutiszmus fogatatása Erdélyben," in István Rácz (ed.), *Tanulmányok Erdély történétről*, Szakmai Konferencia Debrecen, 9–10 Október 1987 (Debrecen: Csokonai Kiadó, 1988).

Bahktin, Mikhail, *Rabelais and his world*, trans. H.I. Swolsky (Cambridge, MA: MIT Press, 1968).

Bailey, Gauvin Alexander, *Art on the Jesuit Missions of Asia and Latin America 1542–1773* (Toronto: University of Toronto Press, 1999).

Baker, Robin, "On the origins of the Moldavian Csangos," *Slavonic and East European Review 75* (1997).

Bahlcke, Joachim. "*Status Catholicus* und Kirchenpolitik in Siebenbürgen, Entwicklungsphasen des Römisch-katholischen Klerus, zwichen Reformation und Josephinismus," in Zsolt K. Lengyel and Ulrich A Wien (eds), *Siebenbürgishces Archiv 34: Siebenbürgen in der Habsburgermonarchie: Von Leopoldinum bis zum Augleich (1690–1866)* (Köln/Weimar/Wien: Böhlau Verlag, 1999).

Bahlcke, Joachim, "Catholic identity and ecclesiastical politics in early modern Transylvania," in Maria Crăciun, Ovidiu Ghitta and Graeme Murdock (eds), *Confessional Identity in East-Central Europe* (Aldershot: Ashgate, 2002).

Balázs, Eva H., *Hungary and the Habsburgs 1765-1800: An Experiment in Enlightened Absolutism* (Budapest: Central European University Press, 1997).
Balázs, Orban, *Torda Város és környéke* (Budapest: Pesti Könyvnymoda-Részvény Társág, 1889).
Bálint, Sándor and Barna Gábor, *Búcsújáró magyarok: A magyarországi búcsújárás története és néprajza* (Budapest: Szent István Társulat az Apostoli Szentszék Könyvkiadója, 1994).
Balogh, Jolán, *Kolozsvár müemlékei* (Budapest, 1935).
Balogh, Jolán, *Kolozsvár régi lakói* (Kolozsvár: Minerva, 1942).
Bangert, William V., SJ, *A History of the Society of Jesus*, 2nd edn (St. Louis, MO: The Institute of Jesuit Sources, 1986).
Barbier, Frédéric, "Problématique d'une recherché collective," in I. Monok and P. Ötvös (eds), *Lesestoffe und kulturelles Niveau des niedrigen Klerus: Jesuiten und die nationalen Kulturverhältnisse* (Szeged: Scriptum Rt., 2001).
Bărbat, Vasile S.I., *Instituirea Functiei Teologuilui în Biserica Română Unită Extras din teza de doctorat* (Roma: Institutul Pontifical de Studii Orientale, 1963).
Bârlea, Octavian, *Ioannes Bob Episcopus Fagarasisnsis (1783-1830)* (Frankfurt/Main: Im Kommissonsverlag Josef Knecht, c. 1950).
Bârlea, Octavian, *Ostkirchliche Tradition und westlicher Katholicizmus: Die rumänische unierte Kirche zwischen 1713-1727, Acta Historica Tomus VI* (Monachii: Societats Academicia Daco-Romana, 1966).
Bârlea, Octavian, "Biserica Română Unită şi ecumenismul Corifeilor Renasterii culturale," *Perspective* v, 3-4 (19-20) (Ianuarie-Iunie, 1983): 1-242.
Barta, István, "Az 1743 évi moldvai misszió," *Regnum 5* (1942-43): 70-90.
Barta, János, "A felvilágosult abszolutiszmus fogatatása Erdélyben," in István Rácz (ed.), *Tanulmányok Erdély történétről Szakmai Konferencia Debrecen 1987 Október 9-10* (Debrecen: Csokonai Kiadó, 1988).
Bartal, Antonius, *Glossarium Mediae et Infimae Latinitatis Regni Hungariae* (Lipsiae: In Aedibus B. G. Teubneri, 1901).
Bartha Katalin, Ágnes, "A Transylvanian Macbeth production (1812) (Practical Training of Acting and Education of Audience)," *Iskola és Színház*, CD-ROM.
Bauer, Stephen, "Shrines, curiosities and the rhetoric of relics," in Lynne Cooke and Peter Woolen (eds), *Visual Display: Culture beyond Appearances* (Seattle, WA: Bay Press, 1995).
Beju, Ioan N. and Keith Hitchins, *Biserica Ortodoxa Romana in secolul XVIII: conscriptii, statistic* (Urbana, IL/Sibiu: [s.n.], 1991).
Bence, Szabolcsi, "Musicology," in *Science in Hungary* (Budapest: Corvina Press, 1965).
Benkö, Joseph, *Imago Inclytae in Transylvania Nationis Siculicae Historico-Politica* (Cibii and Claudiopoli: Typis Martini Hochmeister, 1791).
Beöthy, Zsolt (ed.), *A Magyar Irodalom Története* (4 vols, Budapest: Az Athenaeum Irodalmi és Nyomdai R. Társulat Kiadasa, 1896).
Bérenger, Jean, "The Austrian church," in William J. Callahan and David Higgs (eds), *Church and Society in Catholic Europe of the Eighteenth Century* (Cambridge: Cambridge University Press, 1979).

Bernard, Paul P., "Poverty and poor relief in the eighteenth century," in Charles W. Ingrao (ed.), *State and Society in Early Modern Austria* (West Lafayette, IN: Purdue University Press, 1994).

Bethlen, István, *A Companion to Hungarian Studies* (Budapest: The Society of the Hungarian Quarterly, 1943).

Birely, Robert, *The Refashioning of Catholicism, 1450–1700* (Basingstoke: Macmillan, 1999).

Biro, Stephanus, *Odae Augustissimo Romanorum Imperatori Josepho II ...* (Claudiopoli: Franc. Kollman Typ., 1775).

Biró, Vencel, "Kolozsvár és a piaristák," *Kolozsvári Szemle* 3, 1 (1943): 27–37.

Biró, Vencel, "A kolozsvári jezsuita egyetem szervezete és épitkezései a XVIII században," *Erdélyi Tudományos Füzetek* 192 (1945).

Bitskey, István, *Hitviták tüzében* (Budapest: Gondolat, 1978).

Blaga, Lucian, *Gîndirea Românească în Transilvania în Secolul al xviii-lea* (Bucharest: Ed. Stiintifica, 1966).

Blume, Jerome, *The End of the Old Order in Rural Europe* (Princeton, NJ: Princeton University Press, 1978).

Boak, Arthur E.R., *A History of Rome to 565 A. D.* (New York: Macmillan, 1929).

Bocşan, Nicolae, "Historique de l'Université de Cluj," *Transylvanian Review* 4 (1995): 3–16.

Bod, Péter, *Magyar Athenas* (Budapest: Magveto, 1982).

Bodea, Cornelia and Virgil Cândea, *Transylvania in the History of the Romanians*. (Boulder, CO/New York: East European Monographs; distributed by Columbia University Press, 1982).

Boia, Lucia, "Romania," in Georg G. Igges and Harold T. Parker (eds), *International Handbook of Historical Studies: Contemporary Research and Theory* (Westport, CT: Greenwood Press, 1978).

The Book of Saints, compiled by the Benedictine monks of St Augustine's Abbey, Ramsgate, 6th edn (London: Cassell, 1994).

Born, Gyöngyös, *Prima JESV Societas Claudiopolitania* (Claudiopoli, 1715).

Bota, Ioan M., *Istoria Bisericii Universale şi a bisericii româneşti de la origini până în zilele noastre* (Cluj-Napoca: Casa de Editura Viaţa Creştină, 2003).

Brady, Thomas A., "'You hate us priests': Anti-clericalism, communism and the control of women in Strasbourg in the age of Reformation," in Peter Dykema and Heiko Oberman (eds), *Anticlericalism in Late Medieval and Early Modern Europe* (Leiden/New York/Köln: E.J. Brill, 1993).

Briggs, Robin, "Embattled faiths: Religion and philosophy in the seventeenth century," in Euan Cameron (ed.), *Early Modern Europe: An Oxford History*, ed. Euan Cameron (Oxford: Oxford University Press, 1999).

Brucker, Joseph, *La Compagnie de Jésus: Esquisse de son Institute et son Histoire (1521–1773)* (Paris: Gabriel Beauchesne, 1919).

Buckley, Michael, SJ, "What have we learned," in John W. O'Malley, SJ et al. (eds), *The Jesuits: Cultures, Sciences and the Arts, 1540–1773* (Toronto: University of Toronto Press, 1999).

Bucsánsky, Georgius, *Epitome Historiae Religionis et Ecclesiae Christianae* (Posonii: Typis Simonis Weber, 1801).

Bunea, Augustin, *Episcopu – Ioan Inocentiu Klein (1728–1751)* (Blaş: Episopul Tipographia Seminarului Archidiecesan gr.-cat., 1900).
Bunea, Augustin, *Episcopiĭ Petru Pavel Aron şi Dionisiŭ Novacovacicĭ saŭ Istoria Românilor Transilvanăneni de la 1751 până la 1764* (Blaş: Tipografia Seminariului Archidiecesan, 1902).
Burn, A.E., *Niceta of Remsiana: His Life and Works* (Cambridge: Cambridge University Press, 1905).
Campbell, Ted, *The Religion of the Heart: A Study of European Life in the Seventeenth and Eighteenth Centuries* (Columbia: University of South Carolina Press, 1991).
Câmpeanu, Remus, *Elitele Românesti din Transilvania veacului al xviii-lea* (Cluj-Napoca: Presa Universitară Clujeana, 2000).
Capros, Carol and Flaviu Popan, "Biserica Unita între anii 1700–1718," in *Biserica Unita: Doua Sute Cinci Zeci de Ani de Istorie* (Madrid, 1952).
Carrez, P. Lud., SJ, *Atlas Geographicus Societatis Jesu* (Pariis: Apud Georgium Colombier, 1900).
Cartojan, N., *Istoria Literaturii Române Vechi* with an afterword and bibliography by Dan Simonescu and a preface by Dan Zamfirescu (Bucureşti: Editura Minerva, 1980).
Castellan, Georges, *A History of the Romanians*, trans. Nicholas Bradley (Boulder, CO/New York: East European Monographs: Distributed by Columbia University Press, 1989).
Catalogus Bibliothecae Hungaricae, Tom. I Supplementum I A–Z (Posoni: Typis Belnaianus, 1803).
Catalogus Provinciarum, Collegiorum, Residentiarum, et Missionum universae Societatis Jesu ... (Tyrnavae: Typis Academicis Societatis Jesu, 1750).
Cernovodeanu, Paul, "L'histoire universelle dans l'historiographie Roumaine," *Revue Romaine d'Histoire* 10 (1972): 53–77.
Cesta Maximiliána Hella do Värdo pri Laponsku a jeho pozorovani prechodu Venuše v Roku 1769, prologue by Jan Tibenský and trans. František Hattala (Bratislava: Tatran, 1977).
Chapple, Christopher (ed.), *The Jesuit Tradition in Education and Missions: A 450-Year Perspective* (Scranton, PA: University of Scranton Press; London/Toronto: Associated University Press, 1993).
Châtellier, Louis, *The Religion of the Poor: Rural Missions in Europe and the Foundation of Modern Catholicism*, trans. Brian Pearse (Cambridge: Cambridge University Press, 1997).
Cicaj, Viliam and Othmar Pickl (eds), *Städtisches Alltagsleben in Mitteleuropa vom Mittelalter bis zum Ende des 19. Jahrhunderts* (Bratislava: Academic Electronic Press, 1998).
Cipariu, T., *Acte si fragmente Latine Romanesci pentru istori'a beserecei romane mai alesu unite*(Blasiu: Cu Tipariulu Semin. diecesanu, 1855).
Ciski, P. Marcellus, "Status Armenorum in Transilvania ... ," in I. Dumitriu-Snagov (ed.), *Românii în arhivele Romei (Secolul XVIII) Romeni in archiviis Romanis (Saeculum XVIII)* (Bucureşti: Cartea românească, 1973).

Comerford, Kathleen M. and Hilmar M. Pabel (eds), *Early Modern Catholicism: Essays in Honour of John W. O'Malley, S. J.* (Toronto: University of Toronto Press, 2001).

Cordara, Guilio Cesare, *On the Suppression of the Society of Jesus: A Contemporary Account,* translated and notes by John P. Murphy, SJ (Chicago, IL: Loyola Press, 1999).

Coreth, Anna, *Pietas Austriaca,* trans. William D. Bowman and Anna Maria Leitgeb (West Lafayette, IN: Purdue University Press, 2004).

Cornea, Paul, "L'enseignment Roumain à la fin de XVIIIe siècle," in *Les Lumières en Hongrie, en Europe Centrale et, en Europe Orientale. Actes du Cinquième Colloque de Mátrafüred 24–28 octobre 1981* (Budapest: Akadémiai Kiadó; Paris: Éditions du CNRS, 1984).

Čornejová, Ivana, "Jezsuitské skolství a Jan Amos Komensky," in *Pocta Univerzity Karlovy J. A. Komenskému* (Praha: Karolinum: 1991).

Čornejová, Ivana (ed.), *Dějiny Univerzity Karlovy II: 1622–1802* (Praha: Univerzita Karlova, 1996).

Costa, Ioanna, "Supplex Libellus Valachorum 'E quatuor [sic] receptis non est,'" Unpublished paper presented at the East-West Seminar, Berlin, July 1997.

Craciun, Maria and Ovidui Ghitta (eds), *Ethnicity and Religion in Central and Eastern Europe* (Cluj: Cluj University Press, 1995).

Craciun, Maria and Ovidui Ghitta (eds), *Church and Society* in *Central and Eastern Europe* (Cluj-Napoca: European Studies Foundation Publishing House, 1998).

Crétineau-Joly, J., *Clement XIV et les Jésuites ou histoire de la destruction de la Compagnie de Jésus* (6 vols, Paris: P. Mellier Frères, 1848).

Cross, F.L. (ed.), *The Oxford Dictionary of the Christian Church* (Oxford: Oxford University Press, 1997).

Csáky, Moritz, *Von der Aufklärung zum Liberalismus: Studien zum Frühliberlismus in Ungarn* (Wien: Verlag der Österreichschen Akademie der Wissenschaften, 1981).

Csapodi Csaba "Newtonianizmus a nagyszombati jezsuita egyetemen," *Regnum. Egyháztörténeti Évkönyv,* 6 (1944–6): 50–68.

Csetri, Alexa, *Importantia primei lucrari agromice de specialitate din Transilvania. Studiul inedit al lui Fridvaldksy* Dissertatio de agris fimandis et arandis pro M. Principatu Transylvaniae *(1771),* Studia Universiatis Babes-Bolyai. Series Historica.

Csikszentmihályi, Mihaly and Isabella Selega Csikszentmihályi (eds), *Optimal Experience: Psychological Studies of Flow in Consciousness* (Cambridge: Cambridge University Press, 1988).

Csóka, Gaspár, Kornél Szóvak and Imre Takács, *Pannonhalma: History and Sights of the Benedictine Abbey,* trans. Catherine Roman and Judith Pokoly (Pannonhalma: Abbey 1996).

Csomós, Michael, *Titulare Dacicum ...* (Cibinii: In Typographia Publica, Sumptibus Samuelis Sardi, 1767).

Cuciuc, Constantin, *Atlasul Religiilor şi al Monumentilor Istorice Religioase din Romania* (Bucureşti, 1997).

Daicoviciu, Constantin and Miron Constaninescu (eds), *Brève histoire de la Transylvanie* (Bucarest, 1965).
Daicoviciu, Constantin, et al., *Din Istoria Transilvaniei* (Bucureşti: Editura Acadmiei Republicii Popular Romîna, 1961).
Daniel-Rops, H., *The Church in the Eighteenth Century*, trans. John Warrington (New York: E.P. Dutton, 1964).
Darorczi, Georgius, *Ortus et Progressus Collegii Academici Societatis Jesus Claudiopolitani ab Anno M. D. LXXVI* (Claudiopoli: Typis Acad. Societatis Jesu, 1737).
de Aldama, Antonius M.S.I., "De coadjutoribus Societatis Iesu in mente et in praxi Sancti Ignatii," *AHSI*, 38 (1969): 389–430.
de Boer, Wieste, "Calvin and Borromeo: A comparative approach to social discipline," in Kathleen M. Comerford and Hilmar M. Pabel (eds), *Early Modern Catholicism: Essays in Honour of John W. O'Malley, S. J.* (Toronto: University of Toronto Press, 2001).
de Certeau, Michel. "History, ethics, science and fiction," in Norma Haan, Robert Bellah, Paul Rainbow and William M. Sullivan (eds), *Social Science as a Moral Inquiry* (New York: Columbia University Press, 1983).
de Guibert, Joseph, SJ, *La Spiritualité de la Compagnie de Jésus: Esquisse historique (Bibliotheca Instituti Historici S. I. vol. IV)* (Romae: Institutum Historicum S. I., 1953).
de Guibert, Joseph, SJ, *The Jesuits: Their Spiritual Doctrine and Practice. A Historical Study*, trans. William J. Young and ed. George E. Ganss, SJ (St. Louis, MO: The Instititute of Jesuit Sources, 1994).
Deák, Ernő, "Ethnisch-nationale Probleme in den königlichen Freistädten," in Viliam Cicaj and Othmar Pickl (eds), *Städtisches Alltagsleben in Mitteleuropa vom Mittelalter zum Ende des 19. Jahrhunderts* (Bratislava: Academic Electronic Press, 1998).
Delumeau, Jean, "Christianizatione e decristianizatione fra il XV e XVIII secolo," in Carla Russo (ed.), *Società, Chiesa e Vita Religiosa nell' "ancien régime"* (Napoli: Guida Editora, 1976).
Demeter, Júlia, "Fösvények, parasztok, bohócok (magyar nyelvű iskolai komédiák)," in Júlia Demeter and István Kilián (eds), *A magyar színház születése* (Miskolc: Miskolci egyetemi kiadó, 2000).
Dercsény, Balázs, Hegyi Gábor, Marosi Ernő and Török József, *Katolikus templomok Magyarországon* (Budapest: Hegyi & Társa Kiadó, 1991).
D'Eszlary, Charles, *Histoire des institutions publique [sic] hongoises* (3 vols, Paris: Librairie Marcel Rivière et Cie., 1959–65).
de Vries, Wilhelm, "L'Unione dei rumeni (1697–1701)," *Transylvanian Review* 6, 1 (1997): 3–26.
Dickson, P.G.M., *Finance and government under Maria Theresia* (2 vols, Oxford: The Clarendon Press, 1987).
Dionesi, Aurelio, *Il Gesù di Roma: breve storia e illustrazione della prima chiesa eretta dalla Compagnia di Gesù* (Roma: Residenza di Gesù, 1982).
Diplomata, Bullae, Priviligia Libertates, Immunitates, Constitutiones ... (Viennae: Typis Joannis Thomae nobilis de Trattnern, MDCCXCI).

Diplomatarium Italicum. Documenti racolti negli Archivi Italiani (4 vols, Roma: Libraria di scienze e lettere, 1939).

Dizionario di Erudizione Storico-Ecclesiastica (109 vols, Venezia: Dalla Tipografia Emiliana, 1850–79).

Dobrescu, N., *Istoria bisericii Române din Oltenia în timpul ocupatiune austriace (1716–1739) Cu 200 acte și fragmente inedite culese din Arhivelel din Viena* (București: Inst. De arte Grafice, 1906).

Documenta Missionaria Hungariam et Regionem sub Ditione Turcia Existentem Spectantia I. Ex Tabulario Romano Sacrae Congregationis de Propaganda Fide, eds Joannes Sávai and Gabrielis Pintér (Szegedini, 1993).

Documenta Missionaria I/I. Ex Tabulario Romano Sacrae Congregationis de Propaganda Fide, eds János Sávai and Pintér Gábor (Szeged, 1993).

Documente Privatóre la Istoria Romanilor, Vol. 7, 1756–1818 (Bucuresti, 1897).

Domanovsky, Sándor (ed.), *Magyar művelődéstörténete* (Budapest: Magyar Történelmitársulat, c. 1940).

Dominorum Dominorum Neo-Baccalorum ... Promotore R. P. Andrea Patai è Soc. Jesu ... (Claudiopoli: Typis Academicis Societ. Jesu, 1731).

Donnelly, John Patrick. SJ, "Religious orders of men, especially the Society of Jesus," in John O'Malley, SJ (ed.), *Catholicism in Early Modern History: A Guide to Research* (St. Louis, MO: Center for Reformation Research, 1988).

Donnelly, John Patrick, SJ, "Antonio Possevino, SJ as Papal Mediator between Emperor Rudolph II and King Stephen Báthory," *ARSI* 59 (2000): 3–56.

Donohoe, John, W., SJ., *Jesuit Education: An Essay on the Foundations of its Idea* (New York: Fordham University Press, 1963).

Dordea, Ioan, "Les archives transylvaines," *Transylvanian Review* 4.3 (1995).

Doyle, William, *The Old European Order* (Oxford: Oxford University Press, 1978).

Dragomir, Silvius. *Istoria dezrobirii religioase a Românilor din Ardeal în secolul al XVIII-lea* (2 vols, Sibiu: Editura și Tiparul Tipgrafiei arhdiecezanie, 1920–30).

Dragomir, Sylvius, *The Ethnical Minorities in Transylvania* (Geneva: Sonor Printing Co., 1927).

Drexell, Hieronymus, SJ, *Zodiacus Christianus* (Amsterdam, 1634).

Driediger, Michael, *Obedient Heretics: Mennonite Identities in Lutheran Hamburg and Altona during the Confessional Age* (Aldershot: Ashgate, 2002).

Drogosz, Elzbieta, "L'enseignment Jésuite en Pologne Base intellectuelle des réformes adaptées aux besoins et aux conditions polonaises," in F. Guerello and P. Schivone (eds), *La Pedagogia della Compagnia di Gesù. Atti del Convegno Internazionale Messina 14–16 novembre 1991* (Messina: E.S.U.R. Ignatianum, 1992).

Ducreaux, Marie-Élizabeth, "La mission et la rôle des missionaires dans les pays tchèques au xviiiie siecle," *Actes du 109 congrès national des societés savantes, Dijon, 1984. Section d'histoire moderne et contemporaine*, Tome I: *Transmettre la foi: xvie–xxe siècles, I. Pastorale et predication en France*.

Duhr, B., *Geschichte der Jesuiten in den Ländern deutscher Zunge* (4 vols, Freiburg in Breisgau: Herder, 1907–28).

Duindam, Jeroen, "The court of the Austrian Habsburgs," in John Adamson (ed.), *The Princely Courts of Europe 1500-1750: Ritual, Politics and Culture under the Ancien Régime* (London: Weidenfeld and Nicolson, 1999).

Dumitran, Ana, Gúdor Botond and Nicolae Dănila, *Relaţii interconfessionale româno-maghiare în Transilvania (mijlocul secolului XVI-primele decenii ale secolui XVIII)/ Román-magyar felekezetközi kapcsolatok Erdélyben a XVI. század közepe- a XVIII század első évtizedei között* (Alba Iulia/Gyulafehévár: Muzeul Naţional al Unirii Biblioteca Mvsei Apulensis, 2000).

Dumitru-Snagov, Ion (ed.), *Românii în Arhivele Romei* (secolul xviii). I. (Cluj-Napoca: Clusium, 1999).

Dümmerth, D., "Les Combats et la Tragédie du Père Melchior Inchofer," *Annales Universitatis Scientarum Budapestiensis de Rolando Eötvös nominate: Sectio Historica* 27: 81-112.

Đurđica Cvitanović, "Jesuit Baroque architecture in Croatian lands," in V. Pozaić (ed.), *Jesuits among the Croats* (Zagreb: Institute of Philosophy and Theology, 2000).

Dykema, Peter and Heiko Oberman (eds), *Anticlericalism in Late Medieval and Early Modern Europe* (Leiden/New York/Köln: E.J. Brill, 1993).

Egyed, Hermann and Arter Edgár, *A Királyi Pázmány Péter=Tudományegyetem Története. I Kötet. A Hittudomány Kar Története 1635-1935* (Budapest: Királyi Magyar egyetemi Nyomda, 1935).

Elementa Puerilis Institutionis in Lingua Latina (Claudiopoli: Typis Academ. Soc. JESU per Andream. Feij, 1746).

Eliade, Mircea, *The Sacred and the Profane: The Nature of Religion*, trans. Willard R. Trask (New York: Harcourt, Brace, 1959).

Eliade, Mircea, *A History of Religious Ideas*, eds Alf Hiltenbeitel and Diane Apostolos (3 vols, Chicago, IL/London: University of Chicago Press, 1985).

Ember, Victor, "The Eighteenth Century," in *A Companion to Hungarian Studies* (Budapest: The Society of the Hungarian Quarterly, 1943).

Endes, Miklós, *Erdély három nemzet és négy vallása autonmiájának történet* (Budapest: Sylvester Irodalmi és Nyomdai Intezet, 1953).

Engel, Christian, *Disquititio Critica, Quo in Loco Nunc Adhuc Cognitio Nostra de Hungarorum Origine et Cum Aliis Gentibus Affinitate Postia Sit?* (Viennae: Sumtibus Stahelianis, 1791).

Entz, Geza, "Cluj-Napoca," in Jane Turner (ed.), *The Dictionary of Art* (34 vols, New York: Grove, 1996).

Epitome chronologica rerum hungaricarum et transsilvanicarum a divo Stephano ad an M.D.CC.XVII ... (Anno M.D.CC.XXXVII. mense ... die ... (Claudiopoli, Typis Academicics Soc. JESU, per Simonem Thadaeum Weicheberg).

Epitome Instituti Societatis Jesu (Pragae: Universitatis Carolo-Ferdinanadaea M.DC. XC).

Eulochion adeca Mltvník (Bucurest, 1729).

Evans, R.J.W., *The Making of the Habsburg Monarchy 1550-1750: An Interpretation* (Oxford: Clarendon Press, 1979).

Evans, R.J.W., "Maria Theresia and Hungary," in H.M. Scott (ed.), *Enlightened Absolutism: Reform and Reformers in Later Eighteenth Century Europe* (Ann Arbor: University of Michigan Press 1990).

Evans, R.J.W., "Die Grenzen der Konfessionisierung: Die Folgen der Gegenreformation für die Habsburgländer (1648–1781)," in Joachim Bahlcke and Arno Stromeyer (eds), *Konfessionaliserung in Ostmitteleuropa: Wirkung des religösen Wandels im 16. und 17. Jahrhundert in Staat, Gesellschaft und Kultur* (Stuttgart: Franz Seiner, 1999).

Every, George, *The Byzantine Patriarchate 451–1204* (London: London Society for Promoting Christian Knowledge, 1947).

Facultates, Exemptiones, et Privilegia Concessa Collegis Germanico et Ungarico Alexander Papa VIII (Romae: Ex Typographia Reverendae Camerae Apostolicae, 1720).

Fagiolo, M., É. Knapp, I. Kilián and T. Bardi, *The Sopron Collection of Jesuit Stage Designs*, trans. D. Stanton et al. (Budapest: Enciklopédia Publishing House, 1999).

Farrell, Allan P. (trans.), *The Ratio Studiorum of 1599* (Washington, DC: Conference of Major Superiors of Jesuits, 1982).

Farkas, Gábor (ed.), *Magyarországi jezsuita könyvtárak 1717-ig: Nagyszombat 1632–1690* (Szeged: Scriptum Kft, 1997).

Fazakas, István, "Ratio Educationis," *Annuarul Institutului de Istorie Cluj-Napoca* 36 (1997).

Ferencz, Zoltán, *Kolozsvári színtészet és színház története* (Kolozsvár: Ajtai Albert Magyar Polgár Könvynyomodája, 1897).

Ferrone, Vincenzo, *The Intellectual Roots: Newtonian Science, Religion and Politics in the Early Eighteenth Century*, trans. Sue Brotherton (Atlantic Highlands, NJ: Humanities Press International, 1995).

Fessler, I.A., *Die Geschichte der Ungern und ihren Landsassen* (10 vols, Leipzig: Bey Johann Friedrich Gleditsch, 1814–25).

Fessler, I.A., *Relatio historica de Daco-Romanis in Transylvania et Hungaria cum Ecclesia Romana unitis vel uniendis* (București: Monitorul official și imprimerilile statului impermeria Națională, 1942).

Félegházy, Joseph, "Hongrie: Temps moderns," in Marcel Viller and André Rayer (eds), *Dictionnaire de spiritualité ascetique et mystique, doctrine et histoire* (21 vols, Paris: Beauchesne, 1951–1995).

Fidler, Petr, "Několik poznámek k fenoménu jezuitské architektury," in Jan Skutil (ed.), *Morava a Brno na sklonku Třicetiletí Valky* (Brno: Magistrát Města Brna, 1995).

Fischer, Karl A.F., "Jesuiten-Mathematiker in der deutschen Assistenz," *Archivum Historicum Societais Iesu* 47 (1978): 159–224.

Fleming, David, L., SJ., *The* Spiritual Excercises *of St. Ignatius: A Literal Translation and Contemporary Reading* (St. Louis, MO: The Institute of Jesuit Sources, 1978).

Florescu, Radu R., *Essays on Romanian History* (Iași/Oxford/Portland, OR: The Center for Romanian Studies, 1999).

Fortescue, Adrian and George D. Smith, *The Uniate Eastern Churches* (Piscataway, NJ: First Gorgias Press, 2001).
Foucault, Michel, *Religion and Culture*, ed. Jeremy R. Carrette (Manchester: Manchester University Press, 1999).
Frazee, Charles A., *Catholics and Sultans: The Church and the Ottoman Empire 1453–1923* (Cambridge: Cambridge University Press, 1983).
Freyberger, Andreas, *Historica Relatio Unionis Ecclesiae Walachiae Cum Romana Ecclesia* (Cluj-Napoca: Clusium, 1996).
Fülöp-Miller, René, *The Power and Secret of the Jesuits*, trans. F.S. Flint and D.F. Tait (New York: Viking, 1930).
Gábor, Jablonkay, SJ, *Az Iskoladrámák a Jezsuiták Iskoláiban* (Kalocsa: Nyomatott Árpád R.T. Könyvnyomdájában, 1927).
Gabriel, Stan, *Ioannes Patachi, Episcopus Fogarasiensis (1721–1729)* unpublished MS Thesis, in collection of Pontifical Oriental Institute, Rome, 1929.
Gadovits, Miklós, *Az Erdély örmények történetéből* (Kolozsvár, 2000).
Galtier, P., *Sin and Penance*, trans. B. Wall (St. Louis, MO: Herder, 1932).
Garraty, John A., *Unemployment and History: Economic Thought and Public Policy* (New York: Harper and Row, 1978).
Garter, Alfred, *Die Volkszählungen Maria Theresias und Josef II. 1750–1790* (Innsbruck: Verlag der Wagner'schen Universitäts-Buchhandlung, 1909).
Gáspár, Csóka, Kornél Szóvak and Imre Takács, *Pannonhalma: Pictorial Guide to the History and Sights of the Benedictine Abbey*, trans. Catherine Roman and Judith Pokoly (Pannonhalma: Abbey, 1996).
Gates-Coon, Rebecca, *The Landed Estates of the Esterházy Princes: Hungary during the Reforms of Maria Theresia and Joseph II* (Baltimore, MD: Johns Hopkins University Press, 1994).
Ganss, George E., SJ (trans. and introduction), *The Constitutions of the Society of Jesus* (St. Louis, MO: The Institute of Jesuit Sources, 1970).
Georgescu, Vlad, *The Romanians: A History*, ed. Matei Calinescu and trans. Alexandra Bley-Vroman (Columbus: Ohio University Press, 1984).
Géza, Rajka, *Kolozsvári szabó céh története* (Kolozsvár: Stief Jenő és Társa Könyvsatója, 1913).
Gherman, Mihai (ed.), *Lexicon Compendiarium Latino-Valachicum* (3 vols, Roma: Università di Sapienza, 1994–96).
Ghibu, Osnifor, *Catolicismul Unguresc în Transilvania și Politica Religioasă a Statului Român* (Cluj: Instiutut de arta grafice "Ardealul," 1924).
Giuescu, Constintin C., *Transylvania in the History of the Romanian People* (Bucharest: Meridiane Publishing House, 1968).
Gordon, R.J., "Patronage and parish: The nobility and the recatholization of Lower Austria," in Karin Maag (ed.), *The Reformation in Eastern and Central Europe* (Aldershot: Scolar Press, 1997).
Gragger, Robert, "Die ungarische Universität," *Ungarische Jahrbücher* 5 (1925).
Grancea, Mihaela, "Western travelers on Romanians' religiosity: 1683–1787," in Maria Craciun and Ovidui Ghitta (eds), *Central and Eastern Europe* (Cluj-Napoca: European Studies Foundation Publishing House, 1998).

Griffin, Nigel, *Jesuit School Drama: A Checklist of Critical Literature, Supplement No. 1* (London: Grant and Cutler, 1986).
Grueber, Antonius, SJ, *Secunda deiparae Virginis laudum minuta post laudes Laurentanas* (Claudopoli: Typis Academ. S. J. per Thad. Weichenberg, 1736).
Gudea, Nicolae, *Biserica Româna Unita (Greco-Catholica – 300 de ann i– februarie 1697–februarie 1997)* (Cluj-Napoca: Editura Viaţa Creştina, 1994).
Guerello, F. and P. Schivone (eds), *La Pedagogia della Compagnia di Gesù. Atti del Convegno Internazionale Messina 14–16 novembre 1991* (Messina: E.S.U.R. Ignatianum, 1992).
Guoth, Kálmán, "Kolozsvár város és a magyar színügy kapcsolati a xix. a xix. század elején," *Kolozsvári szemle* 1.1 (1942).
Gyémánt, Ladislau, "The Jews from Romania – A historical destiny," *Nouvelles études d'histoire* 9 (1995): 81–5.
Gyémánt, Ladislau, "Religious domination and national Renaissance. The Transylvanian Romanians in the xviiith–xixth centuries," in Maria Craciun and Ovidui Ghitta (eds), *Ethnicity and Religion in Central and Eastern Europe* (Cluj-Napoca, 1995): 276–83.
Gyenis, András, *A Jezsuita rend hazánkban: Rendtörténeti Vázlat* (Budapest: Stephaneum Nyomda, 1940).
Hadas, Peter I, "The role of Greeks, Armenians and Jews in the economic life of Transylvania in the eighteenth century," *Tanulmányok Danyi Dezsö 75 születésnapjára* (Budapest: KHS Könyvtár Dokumentációs Szolglat, 1996).
Haliczer, Stephen, *Sexuality in the Confessional: A Sacrament Profaned* (New York/ Oxford: Oxford University Press, 1996).
Hamann, Günther, "Zur Wissenschaftspflege des aufgeklärten Absolutisms," in Erich Zöllner (ed.), *Österreichischer im Zeitalter des aufgeklärten Absolutismus* (Wien: Österreichischen Bundesverlag, 1983).
Handler, Andreas, *Principes tredecim Transylvaniae, Carmine Elegiaco* (Claudiopoli: Typ. Acad., 1733).
Haner, Georg, *Historia Ecclesiarum Transylvanicarum inde a Primis Popularum Originibus ...* (Francofurti et Lipsae: Apud Ioh. Christoph Fölginger, 1694).
Haraszti, Endre, *The Ethnic History of Transylvania*, (Astor Park, FL: The Danubian Press, 1971).
Harris, Stephen J., "Confession-building, long-distance networks, and the organization of Jesuit science," *Early Science and Medicine* 1, 3 (1996): 287–318.
Heckel, Hans, *Geschichte der deutschen Literatur in Schlesien. Erster Band: Von den Anfängen bis zum Ausgang des Barock* (Breslau: Ostdeutscher Verlaganstalt, 1929).
Heer, Friedrich., *The Intellectual History of Europe*, trans. Jonathan Steinberg (Cleveland, OH/New York: The World Publishing Company, 1966).
Heiss, Gernot, "Princes, Jesuits and the Origins of the Counter-Reformation," in R.J.W. Evans and T.V. Thomas (eds), *Crown, Church and Estates: Central European Politics in the Sixteenth and Seventeenth Centuries* (Basingstoke: Macmillan, 1991).
Hell, Maximillianus, *Elementa mathematica Naturalis Philosophiae Ancillantia* (Claudiopoli, 1755).

Hengst, Karl, *Jesuiten an Universitäten und Jesuitenuniversitäten* (Paderborn/ München/Wien/Zürich: Ferdinand Schönigh, 1981).
Herm, Gerhard, *Aufstieg, Glanz und Niedergang des Hauses Habsburg* (Düsseldorf/ Wien/New York: ECON Verlag, 1994).
Hets Aurelián J., *A Jezsuiták iskolái Magyarországon a 18. század közepen* (Pannonhalma: Pray Rendt, 1938).
Hevenesi, Gabriel, *Parvus Atlas Hungariae* (Vienna, 1696).
Historia Critica Regnum Hungariae stirpis Austriacae ... a Stephano Katona (Budae: Typis et Sumptibus Regiae Universitatis Pestanae, 1809).
Hitchins, Keith, *The Romanian national movement in Transylvania* (Cambridge, MA: Harvard University Press, 1969).
Hitchins, Keith, "An East European elite in the eighteenth century," in F.C. Jaher (ed.), *The Rich, the Well-Born and the Powerful* (Urbana/Chicago/London: University of Illinois Press, 1973).
Hitchins, Keith, "Religion and Rumanian National Consciousness in Eighteenth Century Transylvania," *The Slavonic and East European Review* 57 (1979): 214–39.
Hitchins, Keith, *The Romanians, 1744–1866* (Oxford: Clarendon Press, 1996).
Hofmann, Paul, *The Viennese* (New York: Anchor/ Doubleday, 1988).
Hollis, Christopher, *The Jesuits: A History* (New York: Macmillan, 1968).
Hölvényi, György, *A Magyar Jezsuita történetírók és a Jezsuita rend* (Budapest: A budapesti egyetemi könyvtár kiadványai, 1974).
Hóman, Bálint and Szekfű Gyula, *Magyar történet* (Budapest: Királyi Magyar Egyetemi Nyomda, 1935).
Horváth, Joannes Baptista, "Csapodi, Newtonianizmus a nagyszombati jezsuita egyetem," *Regnum* 6 (1944/46): 58–68.
Hubners, Johann, *Neu=vermehrtes und verbessertes Reales Staats=Zeitungs und Conversations Lexicon* (Regenspurg und Wien: Im Verlegung Emerich Felix Baders, Buchhandlers, 1759).
Idilkó, Kríza, "Egy jezsuita Mátyás-dráma folklor vonakozásai," in Júlia Demeter and István Kilián (eds), *A magyar Színház Szülétese* (Miskolc: Miskolci egyetemi kiadó, 2000).
Ignatius of Loyala, *The Constitutions of the Society of Jesus*, trans. George E. Gans (St. Louis, MO: The Institute of Jesuit Sources, 1970).
Illia, Andrea, SJ, *Ortus et Progressus variarum in Dacia Gentium et Religionum cum Principalum ejusdem usque ad a. 1722* (Claudiopoli: Typis Acadmicis Societatis Jesu 1730, reprinted in 1767).
Imago Primi Saeculi Societatis Iesu (Antwerp, 1640).
Împaratesei Maria Tereza (1740–1780) a împaratilor Iosif al II-ea (1780–1790) și Leopold al II-ea (1780–1792) (Oradea, 1994).
Institutum Societatis Iesu Volumen Tertium (Florentiae: Ex Typographia A SS. Conceptione, 1893).
Inventarul Archivelor Statului (București: Monitorul Oficial și Imprimerile Statului Imprimeria Centrală, 1939).

Ionesco, Grigoire, *Historie de l'Architecture en Roumanie: De la préhistoire à nos jours* (Bucurest: Éditions de l'Académie de la République Socialiste de Roumanie, 1972).
Iorga, Nicolae, *Istoria Bisericii Românești* (2 vols, București: Editura Ministeriului De Culte, 1928–30).
Iorga, Nicolae, *Istoria literaturii romậne in secolul al XVIII-lea (1688–1821) Vol. II* (Bucuresti: Editura Didactică și Pedagogică, 1969).
Iorga, Nicolae, *Istoria poporului românesc*, ed. Georgeta Penela (București: Editura Științifica și Enciclopedica, 1985).
Iorga, Nicolae, *Istoria Romanilor din Ardeal și Ungaria. Volumul I. Până la mișcarea lui Horea (1784)* (Bucuresti: Editura Casei Scoalelor, 1915).
Ivi, Aurel, "Seventeenth century Romanian Orthodox confessions of Faith," in Auril Jiji (ed.), *Orthodox, Catholics, and Protestants: Studies in Romanian Ecclesiastical Relations* (Cluj-Napoca: Cluj University Press, 1999).
Jablonkay, Gábor, SJ., *Az iskoladrámák a jezsuiták iskoláiban* (Kalocsa: Nyomatott Árpád R.T. Könyvnyomdájában, 1927).
Jadin, R., "Fagaras," in R. Aubert (ed.), *Dictionanaire D'Histoire et de Geographie Ecclésiastique* (27 vols, Paris: Letouzey et Ane, 1912–).
Jakab, Elek, *Prima quinque Saecula Regni Mariani Apostolici ethicae adumbrata* (Budapest: Nyomtatott a Magyar Királyi Egyetemi Könyvnyomdában, 1870–85).
Jakab, Elek, *Kolozsvár története* (3 vols, Budapest: Nyomtattot a Magyar Királyi Egyetemi Könyvnyomdában, 1870–88).
Jakab, Elek, *Kolozsvár Története elötti világositó rajzai* (Budapest: Nyomattak Kellner és Mohrlüder Müintézetében, 1888).
Jakó, Klára, *Erdélyi könyvesház. I. Az első kolozsvári egyetemi könyvtár története és állományának rekonstrukciója 1579–1604* (Szeged: Scriptum Kft., 1991).
Jedin, Hubert, Kenneth Scott Latourette and Jochen Martin, *Atlas d'histoire de l'Église* (Bruxelles: Brepols, 1990).
Johnson, Trevor, "Blood, tears and Xavier-Water: Jesuit missionaries and popular religion in the eighteenth century Upper Palatinate," in Bob Scribner and Trevor Johnson (eds), *Popular Religion in Germany and Central Europe, 1400–1800* (Basingstoke: Macmillan, 1996).
Johnstone, William M., *The Austrian Mind: An Intellectual and Social History 1848–1938* (Berkeley: University of California Press, 1972).
Jones, Martin D.W, *The Counter-Reformation: Religion and Society in Early Modern Europe* (Cambridge: Cambridge University Press, 1995).
Josephus Accrescens sat. Publica Parentatio sat. a Quodam Societate Patre ... mens. Jul. die VIII a. 1711 (Claudiopol.: Impr. Sam. P. Telegdi) *Régi magyar könyvtár* II k. 2418 sz.
Josupeit-Neitzel, Elke. *Die Reformen Josephs II. in Siebenbürgen* (München: Dr. Rudolf Trofenik, 1986).
Kálmán, Benda, "Csöbörcsök, ein ungarisches Dorf am Dnjester-Ufer," in Benda Kálmán et al. (eds), *Forschungen über Siebenbürgen und seine Nachbarn. Festschrift für Attila T. Szabó und Zsigmond Jakó* (München: Dr. Rudolf Trofenik, 1987), pp. 253–66.

Kálmán, Benda, *Magyarország történeti kronológiája* (Budapest: Akadémiai Kiadó, 1983).
Kálmán, Benda, (ed.), *Moldvai Csángó-Magyar Okmánytár 1467–1701* (Budapest: Magyarságkutató Intézet, 1989).
Kálmán, Guoth, "Kolozsvár város és a magyar színügy kapcsolati a xix. a xix. század elején," *Kolozsvári szemle* 1.1 (1942).
Kann, Robert, *A History of the Habsburg Empire 1526–1918* (Berkeley: University of California Press, 1974).
Kapossy, Johann, "Die Stellung des ungarlandischen Barock in der europäischer Kunstentwicklung," *Ungarische Jahrbücher* 1 (1931), pp. 38–55.
Katalin, Péter, "Vie de la societé transylvanaine dans la première moitié de XVIIIe siècle," *AHASH* 27 (1981).
Katalin, Péter, "The later Ottoman period and royal Hungary," in Peter F. Sugar (ed.), *A History of Hungary* (Bloomington and Indianapolis: Indiana University Press, 1990).
Katona, Stephanus, *Historia Critica Regum Hungariae Stirpis Austriacae* (23 vols, Budae: Typis et Sumptibus Regiae Universitatis Pestae, 1794–1817).
Kaufmann, Thomas DaCosta, *Court, Cloister and City: The Art and Culture of Central Europe* (Chicago, IL: University of Chicago Press, 1995).
Kaufmann, Thomas DaCosta, "Jesuit art: Central Europe and the Americas," in John O'Malley et al. (ed.), *The Jesuits: cultures, sciences, and the arts, 1540–1773* (Toronto: University of Toronto Press, 1999), pp. 274–304.
Kenton, Edna (ed.), *The Jesuit Relations and Allied Documents: Travels and Explorations of the Jesuit Missionaries in North America (1610–1791)*, with an introduction by Reuben Gold Twaithes (New York: The Vanguard Press, 1954).
Khevenhüller-Metsch, Fürst Johann Josef, *Aus der Zeit Maria Theresias*, Rudolf Khevenhüller-Metsch and Hanns Schlitter (eds), (10 vols, Wien: Holzhausen, 1925), 8, 151.
Kilián, István, "Church, school, drama and stage in the 17th–18th centuries," *Publicationes Universitatis Miskolciensis. Sectio Philosophica Tomus IV* (Miskolc, 1998).
Kilián, István, Pintér Márta Zsuzsanna and Varga Imre (eds), *A magyarországi katholikus tanitézmények színjátszásának forrásai és irodalma 1800-ig, Fontes Ludorum Scenicorum in Scholis Institutisque Catholicis Hungariae* (Budapest: Argumentum Kiadó, 1992).
Király, Béla K., *Hungary in the Eighteenth Century: The Decline of Enlightened Despotism* (New York: Columbia University Press, 1969).
Király, Béla K., "The Hungarian Church," in William J. Callahan and David Higgs (eds), *Church and Society in Catholic Europe of the Eighteenth Century* (Cambridge: Cambridge University Press, 1979).
Király, Béla K., "The Transylvanian concept of liberty and its impact on the Kingdom of Hungary in the seventeenth and eighteenth centuries," in John F. Cadzow, Andrew Ludanyi and Louis J. Elteto (eds), *Transylvania: The Roots of Ethnic Conflict* (Kent, OH: The Kent State University Press, 1983), pp. 61–87.
Kirschbaum, Stanislav J., *A History of Slovakia: the Struggle for Survival* (New York: St. Martin's Press, 1995).

Kisban, Emil, "Hell Miska: A magyar csillagász," *Publicationes ad Historiam S. J. In Hungaria Illustrandum* 27 (1942): 5–20.
Klaniczay, Gábor (ed.), *Monumenta Hungariae historica*, vol. 2 (Pest: Eggenberger Ferdinand M. Akad. Könyvárusnál, 1863).
Klaniczay, Tibor (ed.), *A Magyar irodalom története 1600-tól 1772-ig* (Budapest: Akadémiai Kiadó, 1964).
Klenicki, L. (ed.), *Passion Plays and Judaism*, New York: Anti-Defamation League, 1996).
Kligman, Gail, *The Wedding of the Dead: Ritual, Poetics and Popular Culture in Transylvania* (Berkeley: University of California Press, 1988).
Klima, H., "Die Union der Siebenbürger Rumänen und der Wiener Staatsrat im theresianischen Zeitalter," *Südost Forschungen* 6 (1941): 249–56.
Kloczowski, Jerzy, "The Polish Church," in William J. Callahan and David Higgs (eds), *Church and Society in Catholic Europe of the Eighteenth Century* (Cambridge: Cambridge University Press, 1979).
Knapp, Éva, "A nagyszebeni jezsuita színjátszás első szöveges emléke: *Szent Alexius* (1709)," in Demeter Júlia and Kilián István (eds), *A magyar színház születése* (Miskolc: Miskolci egyetemi kiadó, 2000).
Knapp, Éva and Tüskés Gábor, "Barokk társulati kiadványok grafikai ábrázolásai," *Magyar Könyvszemle* 115 (1999): 1–34.
Knatchbull-Hugessen, C.M., *The Political Evolution of the Hungarian Nation* (2 vols, London: The National Review Office, 1908).
Koch, L., *Jesuitenlexikon* (Paderborn: Bonifacius Druckerei, 1934).
Kocsis, Károly and Eszter Kocsis-Hodosi, *Hungarian Minorities in the Carpathian Basin: A Study in Ethnic Geography* (Toronto/Buffalo, NY: Matthias Corvinus, 1995).
Kooi, Christine, "*Sub jugo haereticorum:* Minority Catholicism in Early Modern Europe," in Kathleen M. Comerford, and Hilmar M. Pabel (eds), *Early Modern Catholicism: Essays in Honour of John W. O'Malley, S. J.* (Toronto: University of Toronto Press, 2001).
Köpeczi, Béla (ed.), *Erdély Rövid Története* (Budapest: Akadémiai Kiado, 1989).
Korade, Mijo, "The Croats of Gradisčše (Burgenland), Austria and the Society of Jesus from the 16th to the 18th centuries," in Valentin Pozaić (ed.), *Jesuits Among the Croats: Proceedings of the International Symposium: Jesuits in the Religious, Scientific, and Cultural Life among the Croats, October 8–11, 1990* (Zagreb: Institute of Philosophy and Theology, 2000).
Korade, Mijo, "Josip Martinović, an 18th century defender of the Armenians," in Valentin Pozaić (ed.), *Jesuits Among the Croats: Proceedings of the International Symposium: Jesuits in the Religious, Scientific, and Cultural Life among the Croats, October 8–11, 1990* (Zagreb: Institute of Philosophy and Theology, 2000).
Kosáry, Domokos (Dominic), "Gabriel Bethlen: Transylvania in the xvii Century," *The Slavonic and East European Review* 17 (1938–39): 162–72.
Kosáry, Domokos, *Bevezetés a magyar történelem forrásaiba és irodalmába (1711–1823)* (Budapest: Művelt nép könyvkiadó, 1951–).

Kosáry, Domokos, *Művelődés a XVIII századi Magyarországon* (Budapest: Akadémiai Kiadó, 1980).
Kosáry, Domokos, "L'education en Europe Centrale et Orientale a l'âge des Lumières," in *Les Lumières en Hongrie, en Europe Centrale et en Europe Orientale* (Budapest: Akadémia Kiadó, 1984), pp. 213–42.
Kosáry, Domokos, *Culture and Society in Eighteenth-Century Hungary*, trans. Zsuzsa Béres (Budapest: Corvina, 1987).
Kotkowska, Elżbieta and Monika Raczyńska-Sęzikowska, *Die Kirche zum allerheiligen Namen Jesu*, trans. Bernadetta Szyszka (Wrocław: Studio Sense, 1997).
Kürti, László, *The Remote Borderland: Transylvania in the Hungarian Imagination*. (Albany: State University of New York Press, 2001), pp. 13ff.
Lacko, M., SJ, "Unio Uzhorodensis Ruthenorum Carpatorum cum Ecclesia Catholica," *OCA* 143 (1955): 1–279.
Lacko, M., SJ, "Documenta spectantia regimen episcopi Munkačevensis Michaelis Olšavsky, Manuelis," *Orientalia Christiana Periodica* 25 (1959): 54–89.
Lacko, M., SJ, "The pastoral activity of Manuel Michael Olšavsky, Bishop of Mukačevo," *OCP* 27, 1 (1961): 150–61.
Ladić, Zoran, "Students from Croatia at Universities in Graz, Austria and Trnava," in Valentin Pozaić (ed.), *Jesuits among the Croats: Proceedings of the International Symposium: Jesuits in the Religious, Scientific, and Cultural Life among the Croats, October 8–1, 1990* (Zagrabiensis: Institutum Philosophico-Theologicum Societatis Jesu; Vindobonensis: Institutum Historicum Croaticum, 2000).
Lampe, John R. and Marvin R. Jackson, *Balkan Economic History 1550–1950: From Imperial Borderlands to Developing Nations* (Bloomington: Indiana University Press, 1982).
László, Heinrich, *Az első koloszvári csillagda* (Bukarest: Kriterion, 1978).
Lechinţan, Vasile, *Instituţii şi edifice istorice din Transilvania* (Cluj-Napoca: Editura Carpatica, 2000).
Lewis, J., "Ignatian spirituality," *The New Catholic Encyclopedia*, (15 vols, New York: McGraw Hill, 1967) vol. 7, pp. 349–51.
Lowe, Heinz-Dietrich, Gunther Tontschand and Stefan Troebst (eds), *Siebenbürgisches Archiv, 35. Minderheiten, Regionalbewusstsein und Zentralismus in Ostmitteleuropa* (Köln/Weimar/Wien: Böhlau Verlag, 2000).
Lowenthal, David, *The Heritage Crusade and the Spoils of History* (London: Viking, 1997).
Lucas, Thomas M., SJ, *Landmarking: City, Church and Urban Strategy* (Chicago, IL: Jesuit Way/Loyola Press, 1997).
Lukácsi, Kristof, *Historia Armenorum Transsilvaniae a primodris gentis usque nostram memoriam e fontibus authenticis et documentis antea indeitis ...* (Viennae: 1859).
Lukács, Lázsló, *A független magyar Jezsuita rendtartomány kérdése és az osztrák abszolutizmus (1649–1773)* (Szeged: Istituto Storico della Compagnia di Gesù; Szegedi: I. sz. Magyar Irodalomtörténeti Tanszék együttműködés keretében, 1989).Lukács, Ladislaus, *Catalogi Personarum et Officiorum Provinciae Austria S. I. VI (1700–1717)* (Romae: Institutum Historicum S. I., 1993).

Lukács, Ladislaus, *Catalogi Personarum et Officiorum Provinicae Austria S. I. VII (1717–1733)* (Romae: Institutum Historicum S. I., 1993).

Lukinich, Imre, *A History of Hungary in Biographical Sketches* (Budapest: Dr. George Vajna & Co.; London: Simkin Marshal Ltd, 1937).

Lumperdean, Ioan, "Nation et confession au XVIIIe siècle. Options et preoccupations pour l'union ecclésiastique de Roumains de Transylvanie," in Nicolae Bocsan, Ioan Lumperdean and Ioan-Aurel Pop (eds), *Ethnie et Confession en Transylvanie (du XIII au XVIII Siècles)* (Cluj-Napoca: Central de Studii Transilvanie Fundaţia Culturală Română, 1996).

Lupaş, I., *Sfârşitul suzeraniţii otomane şi începutul regimului habsburgic în Transilvania. Analele Academiei Române Memorile Secţiunii Istorice Serie III Tomul XXV Mem. 19* (1943).

Macartney, C.A., *Hungary: A Short History* (Chicago, IL: Aldine Publishing Co. 1962).

Macartney, C.A., *The Habsburg and Hohenzollern Dynasties in the Nineteenth and Eighteenth Centuries* (New York: Harper, 1970).

MacDonnell, Joseph, SJ, *Jesuit geometers: a study of fifty-six prominent Jesuit geometers during the first two centuries of Jesuit history* (St Louis, MO: Institute of Jesuit Sources, 1989),

Mach, Josef, SJ, "Ecclesiastical unification: A theoretical framework together with case studies from the history of the Latin-Byzantine relations,"*Orientalia Christiana Analecta*, 198 (1974): 1–388.

MacIntytre, Alisdair, *Three Rival Versions of Moral Enquiry: Encyclopedia, Genealogy and Tradition* (Notre Dame, IN: University of Notre Dame Press, 1990).

Magnus manes TransylvaiaPrincipatu, honoriReverendorumNobiliumacEruditorum Dominorum DD. AA. LL. Et Philosophiae Neo-Doctorum (Claudiopoli, 1722).

Magocsi, Robert Paul, *Historical Atlas of East Central Europe* (Seattle/London: University of Washington Press, 1993).

Magyar művelődés történet. Barokk és felvilágosodás ([Budapest?]: Magyar Történelmi Társulat, 1940[?]).

Magyari, András, "Kolozsvár az 1703–1711 évi habsburgellenes szabaságharc első szakaszában," *Studia Universitatis Babeş–Bolyai* Series VI. Fasciculus I (1959): 45–56.

Magyarody, S.J. (ed.), *The Tsangos of Romaina: The Hungaian Minorities in Romanian Moldavia* (Matthias Corvinus Publishing, 1996-9) http://www.hungarian-history.hu/lib/tsangos/tsangos.pdf.

Magyarország bibliográfiája 1712–1860 (Vol. 8, Budapest: Az Országos Széchény Könyvtár, 1991).

Mansi, A.M., "Le icone di Maria: Un camino teologico," in C. Giraudo (ed.), *Liturgia e spiritualità nell'Oriente cristiano* (Milano: San Paolo, 1997): 237–47.

Marczali, Henrik (ed.), *Enchiridion Fontium Historiae Hungarorum* (Budapestini: Sumptibus et Typis Societatis Athenaei, 1901).

Marczali, Henrik, *Hungary in the XVIII Century* (Cambridge: Cambridge University Press, 1910).

Marczali, Henrik, *Magyarország története a szatmári béketöl a bécsi congressusig* (Budapest: Laudo Kiadó, n. d.).
Mărtinaş, Dumitriu, *The Origins of the Changos*, eds Vasile M. Ungureanu, Ion Coja and Laura Treptow (Iaşi/Oxford/Portland, OR: The Center for Romanian Studies, 1999).
Mârza, Eva, *Tipografia de la Alba Iulia 1577–1702* (Sibiu: Editura Imago, 1998).
Matkai, László Pál, Szász Zoltán and Köpéczi Béla, *Erdély története*, vol. 2: 1606-tól 1830–ig. ed. (Budapest: Akadémiai Kiadó, 1982).
McCabe, William H., SJ, *An Introduction to the Jesuit Theatre*, ed. Louis A Oldani, SJ (St. Louis, MO: The Institute of Jesuit Sources, 1983).
McCartney, C.A. "The Habsburg Dominions," in *The New Cambridge Modern History.* Volume 7: *The Old Regime 1713–1765* (Cambridge: Cambridge University Press, 1963).
McEvedy, Colin, *The Penguin Atlas of Modern History (to 1815)* (London: Penguin, 1972).
McGucken, William, SJ, *The Jesuits and Education* (New York: The Bruce Publishing Company, 1932).
McNaspy, Clement J., "Art in Jesuit life," in *Studies in the Spirituality of Jesuits* 5, 3 (April, 1973).
Melling, David J., "Council of Florence (1438–49)," in Ken Parry et al. (eds), *The Blackwell Dictionary of Eastern Christianity* (Oxford: Blackwell, 1999).
Melton, James Van Horn, *Absolutism and the Eighteenth Century Origins of Public Schooling in Prussia and Austria* (New York: Cambridge University Press, 1988).
Merkwürdige Nachrichten von den Jesuiten in Weissrussen. In Briefen. Aus dem Italienischen. Zweyte Auflage. (Frankfurt und Leipzig, 1786).
Metamorphoses seu Natales Poëtici submontianarum Superioris Hungaria Urbium et Vinearum honoribus ... A Reverendo Patre Bartholomeo Zarubal è S. J. ... (Cassoviae: Typis Academ. Per J. H. Frauenheim, 1728).
Metempsychosis sive Animalium in alia Corpora Transmigratio ... (Claudiopoli: Typis Acad. Soc. JESU, 1729).
Meteş, Étienne, "La vie menée par les Roumains du XVIe au XVIIIe siècle," in *La Transylvanie* (Cluj: L'Institut d'histoire nationale de Cluj, 1938): 260–68.
Meteş, Stefan, *Domni şi Boieri din Ţările Românii in Oraşul Cluj şi Românii din Cluj* (Cluj: Tipografia Astra, 1935).
Methodus Nova super Contributione Magni Principatus Transylvaniae ... (Viennae: Typis Ioannis Thomae de Trattern, 1767).
Methodus quam in Collegio Reformatorum Helveticae Confessionis Debrecensi, Omnes Scholas Inferiores Docentes ... (Debreceni: Per Stephanum Margitai Typogr., 1770).
Michalski, Sergiusz, *The Reformation and the Visual Arts* (London and New York: Routledge, 1993).
Mindszenti Gábor Diarium öreg János Király haláláról, with an afterword by Markkái Laszló (Budapest: Magyar Helikon, 1977).
Minerologia magnae Principatus Transylvaniae (Claudiopoli, 1767).

BIBLIOGRAPHY

Minor, Petru, *Istoria Beserica Românilor* (La Buda: în kriacka Typograpfie a universitatei din Pesht, 1813).

Mittelstrass, Otto, *Historisch-Landeskundlicher Atlas von Siebenbürgen* (Heidelburg: Arbeitkreis für siebenbürgische Landeskunde, 1992).

Molnar, Antal, "Sándor Dobokai's Autobiographische Aufzeichnungen 1620," *AHSI* 66 (1997): 75-88.

Molnár, Antál, "Rudolf Bzenszky SJ (1651-1715) ein tschechisher Missionar und Geschichtsschreiber in Siebenbürgen," in István Monok and P. Ötvös (eds), *Lesestoffe und kulturelles Niveau des niedrigen Klerus: Jesuiten und die nationalen Kulturverhältnisse* (Szeged: Scriptum Rt., 2001), 67-77.

Molnár, Erik, "Historical Science," in *Science in Hungary* (Budapest: Corvina Press, 1965).

Monok, István, *A Rákóczi-család könyvtárai 1588-1660* (Szeged: Scriptum Kft., 1996), XXV.

Monok, István, "Libri ecclesiae pastorumque – Zeugniss der Protocolle der Kirchenvisitatoren," in Monok and Ötvös (eds), *Lesestoffe*, 43-54.

Monok, István and P. Ötvös (eds), *Lesestoffe und kulturelles Niveau des niedrigen Klerus: Jesuiten und die nationalen Kulturverhältnisse* (Szeged: Scriptum Rt., 2001).

Monumenta Hungaricae Historica Vol. 11. Altorjai B. Apor Péter Munkái (Pest: Eggenberger Ferdinánd M. Akad. Könyvárusnál, 1863).

Mout, Nicolette, "Introduction," in Charles W. Ingrao (ed.), *State and Society in Early Modern Austria* (West Lafayette, IN: Purdue University Press, 1994).

Müller, Konrad, *Siebenbürgische Wirtschaftspolitik unter Maria Theresia* (München: Buchreihe der Südostdeutchen historischen Kommision, 1961).

Mullett, Michael, *Popular Culture and Popular Protest in Late Medieval and Early Modern Europe* (London: Croom Helm, 1987).

Mullett, Michael, *The Catholic Reformation* (London and New York: Routledge, 1999).

Münch, Paul, *Lebensformen in der frühen Neuzeit* (Frankfurt am Main/Berlin: Propayläen, 1992).

Murdock, Graeme, *Calvinism on the Frontier 1600-1660: International Calvinism and the Reformed Church in Hungary and Transylvania* (Oxford: Clarendon Press, 2000).

Myers, W. David. *"Poor, sinning folk": Confession and conscience in Counter-Reformation Germany* (Ithaca, NY: Cornell University Press, 1996).

Newton, Isaacus, *Arithemetica Universalis* (Amstelod., 1761).

Nicoara, Toader, *Transilvania. La începtulurile timpurilor moderne (1680-1800). Societate rurală și mentalitati colective* (Cluj: Presa Universiată Clujeană, 1997).

Nicolas Premier Jésuite et roi de Paraguai (Buenos Aires: Aux depéns de la compagnie, 1761).

Nilles, Nicolaus, *Symbolae ad Illustrandam historiam ecclesiae orientalis in terris coronae S. Stephani* (2 vols, Oenioponte: Typis et Sumptibus Felciani Rauch, 1885).

Nouzille, Jean, *La Transylvanie: Terre de contacts et de conflicts* (Strasbourg: Revue d'Europe Centrale, 1993).
Nouzille, Jean. "Les Jésuites en Transylvanie aux XVIIe et XVIIIe siècles," *Dix-Septième Siècle* 199 (1998).
O'Brien, Charles, "Ideas of religious toleration at the time of Joseph II," *Transactions of the American Philosophical Society,* New Series 59.7 (1969): 1–80.
O'Malley, John W., SJ, *The First Jesuits* (Harvard: Cambridge, 1993).
O'Malley, John W., "The Historiography of the Society of Jesus," in John W. O'Malley, SJ, Alexander Bailey Gauvin, Stephen J. Harris and T. Frank Kennedy, SJ, (eds), *The Jesuits: Cultures, Sciences and the Arts, 1540–1773* (Toronto: University of Toronto Press, 1999), p. 26.
O'Malley, John W., SJ, Alexander Bailey Gauvin, Stephen J. Harris and T. Frank Kennedy, SJ (eds), *The Jesuits: cultures, sciences, and the arts, 1540–1773* (Toronto: University of Toronto Press, 1999).
O'Neill, Charles E. and Joaquín Domínguez (eds), *Diccionario histórico de la Compañia de Jesús: biográfico-temático* (Roma: Institutum Historicum; Madrid: Universidad Pontificia Comillas, 2001).
Ogden, Alan, *Revelations of Byzantium: The Monasteries and Painted Churches of Northen Moldavia,* with an introduction by Kurt W. Treptow (Iași/Orford/Palm Beach, CA/Portland, OR: The Center for Romanian Studies, 2002).
Ogilvie, R.M., *Latin and Greek: A History of the Influence of the Classics on English Life from 1600 to 1918* (Hamden, CT: Archon, 1969).
Oliva Pacis a Dva Hungariae Patrona haereditariarvum domûs Austriae provinciarvm votes retenta (Claudiopoli, 1746).
Ormanian, Malachia, *The Church of Armenia* 2nd edn, trans. G. Marchar Gregory and ed. Terenig Poladia (London: A.R. Mowbray, 1955).
Pâclișanu, Zenobie, *Istoria Bisericii Române Unite,* ed. O. Bârlea (Editura Galaxia Gutenberg München: Rumänische Unierte Mission der Bundesrepublik Deutschland, 1996).
Păcurariu, Mircea, *Pages de l'histoire de l'église roumaine. Considerations au sujet de uniatisme en Transylvanie,* trans. M. Alexandrescu (Bucarest: Editions de l'Institut Biblique de Mission de l'Eglise Orthodoxe Roumaine, 1991).
Păcurariu, Mircea, *Istoria Bisericii Românesti din Transilvania, Banat, Crisina și Maramureș până în 1918* (Cluj-Napoca: Arhiepiscopia Vadului, Feleacului și Clujului, 1992).
Padberg, John W., SJ, *Colleges in Controversy* (Cambridge, MA: Harvard University Press, 1969).
Padberg, John W., SJ, "The General Congregations of the Society of Jesus: A brief survey of their history," *Studies in the Spirituality of Jesuits* 6, 1 & 2 (January and March, 1974): 1–127.
Pál, Judit, "Armenier in Donau-Karpaten-Raum, im besonderen in Siebenbürgen," in Heinz-Dietrich Lowe, Gunther Tontschand and Stefan Troebst (eds), *Siebenbürgisches Archiv, 35. Minderheiten, Regionalbewusstsein und Zentralismus in Ostmitteleuropa* (Köln/Weimar/Wien, 2000).
Papacostea, Victor, *Civilizația Românéscă și Civilizația Balcanică,* ed. Cornelia Papacostea-Danielopolu (București: Eminescu, 1983).

Papacostea, Victor, "La fondation de l'Académie grècque de Bucharest, les origins del'erreur de datation et sa penetration dans l'historigraphie," in Victor Papcostea, Cornelia Papacostea-Danielopolu and Nicolae Serban Tanasoca (eds), *Civilizaţie Românească şi Civilizaţie Balcanică. Studii Istorice* (Bucureşti: Editura Eminescu, 1983).

Papacostea-Danielopolu, Cornelia and Lidia Demény, *Carti şi Tipar în Societata Romanească şi sud-est Europeană (secole XVII–XIX)* (Bucureşti: Editura Eminescu, 1985).

Parvev, Ivan, *Habsburgs and Ottomans between Vienna and Belgrade* (Boulder, CO/ New York: Eastern European Monographs distributed by Columbia University Press, 1995).

Pascu, Ştefan, *L'Université de Babeş-Bolyai de Cluj*. (Cluj: Dacia Verlag, 1971).

Pascu, Ştefan, *Die Babeş-Bolyai Universität aus Cluj* (Cluj: Dacia Verlag, 1972).

Pascu, Ştefan, (ed.), *Istoria Clujul* (Cluj: Concilul Popular al municiului Cluj, 1974).

Pascu, Ştefan, *A History of Transylvania*, trans. D. Robert Ladd with a foreword by Paul E. Michaelson (Detroit, MI: Wayne State University Press, 1982).

Pascu, Ştefan, Josif Pataki and Vasile Popa, *Cujul* (Cluj: Intreprinderea Poligrafica Cluj, 1957).

Pastor, Ludwig, *History of the Popes,* ed. Frederick Ignatius Antrobus (29 vols, London: Kegan Paul 1938).

Patacsi, Gabriel, SJ, "Die unionsfeindlichen Bewegungen der orthodox Rumänen in Siebenbürgen in den Jahren 1726–1729," *Orientalia Christiana Periodica* 26, 2 (1960): 349–400.

Patai, Andreas, *Historia Thaumaturgae Virginis Claudiopolitanae* ... (Claudiopoli, 1737).

Patrides, C.A., "Hierarchy and order," in Philip P. Wiener (ed.), *Dictionary of the History of Ideas* (New York: Charles Scribner's Sons, 1973).

Paulsen, Friedrich, *Die Geschichte des gelehrten Unterrichts* (2 vols, Leipzig: W. Schultze & Riemenschneider, 1919–1921).

Periş, Lucien, *Le missioni Gesuite in Transilvania e Moldavia nel seicento* (Cluj-Napoca, Editura Fundatiei pentru studii Europene, 1998).

Petri, Anton Peter, *Die Jesuiten in der Belgrader Mission, Neue Benater Bücherei XVIII* (Mühldorf/Inn: A.P. Petri, 1985).

Petri, Anton Peter, *Die Jesuiten in der Perwardeiner Mission (1716–1773) Neue Benater Bücherei XIX* (Mühldorf/Inn: A.P. Petri, 1985).

Pirigyi, István, *A magyarországi görögkatolikus története* (Nyiregháza: Görögkatolikus hittudományi föiskola, 1990).

Pirri, Pietro, SJ, "*Giovanni Tristano e i primordi della Architettura Jesuitica*" (Roma: Institutum Historicum S. J., 1955) (Biblioteca Instituti Historici S.J. VI).

Pius, Gams P. (ed.), *Series episcoporum Ecclesiae Catholicae* (Ratisbonae: Typis et sumtibus Georgii Josephi Manz, 1873).

Po-Chia Hsia, R., *Social Discipline in the Reformation: Central Europe 1550–1750* (New York/ London: Routledge, 1989).

Po-Chia Hsia, R., *The World of Catholic Renewal 1540–1770* (Cambridge: Cambridge University Press, 1998).

Polgár, László, *Bibliographia de Historia Societatis Jesu in Regnis olim Corona Hungarica Unitis 1560–1773* (Romae: Institutum Historicum S. J., 1957).
Pollard, A.F., *The Jesuits in Poland* (New York: Haskell House, 1971).
Pompiliu, Teodor, "The Romanians from Transylvania between the Tradition of the Eastern Church, the Counter Reformation and the Catholic Reformation," in Maria Crăciun and Ovidiu Ghitta (eds), *Ethnicity and Religion in Central and Eastern Europe* (Cluj: Cluj University Press, 1995).
Pompiliu, Teodor, "The confessional identity of the Transylvanian Greek Catholic Church," in Maria Crăciun, Ovdiu Ghitta and Graeme Murdock (eds), *Confessional Identity in East-Central Europe* (Aldershot: Ashgate, 2002).
Pop, Ioan-Aurel, "Medievalism and Enlightenment in Romanian Historiography," in Teodor Pompiliu (ed.), *Enlightenment and Romanian Society* (Cluj-Napoca: Editura Dacia, 1980).
Pop, Ioan-Aurel, "Ethnie et confession. Genèse médiévale de la nation roumaine moderne," in Nicole Bocsan, Ioan Lumperdean and Ioan-Aurel Pop (eds), *Ethnie et Confession en Transylvanie (du XIII au XVIII Siècles)* (Cluj-Napoca: Central de Studii Transilvanie Fundaţia Culturală Română, 1996).
Pop, Ioan-Aurel, *Romanians and Romania: A Brief History* (Boulder, CO/New York: East European Monographs, Distributed by Columbia University Press, 1999).
Popinceanu, Ion, *Religion, Glaube, und Aberglaube in der rumänischen Sprache* (Nürenberg: H. Carl, 1964).
Porter, Roy and Mikuláš Teich (eds), *The Enlightenment in National Context* (Cambridge: Cambridge University Press, 1982).
Pozaić, Valentin, *Jesuits Among the Croats: Proceedings of the International Symposium – Jesuits in the Religious, Scientific, and Cultural Life among the Croats, October 8–11, 1990*, ed. Valentin Pozaić (Zagreb: Institute of Philosophy and Theology, 2000).
Pray, Georgius, *Historia Regum Hungariae* (3 vols, Budae: Typis et Sumtibus Regiae Universitatis Pestanae Typographiae, 1801).
Précline, E. and E. Jarry (eds), *Storia della Chiesa XIX/I : Le lotte politiche e dottrinale nei secoli XVII e XVII (1648–1789)*, Edizione italiana a cura di Luigi Mezzadri (Milano: Edizione Paoline, 1991).
Prima JESV Societatis Claudiopolitana (Claudiopoli, 1715).
Proceedings of the international conference "Iskola és Színház" (School and Theatre) Miskolc, Hungary September 7–9, 2002), CD rom.
Prodan, D., *Supplex Libellus Valachorum; or The political struggle of the Romanians in Transylvania during the 18th century* (Bucharest: Pub. House of the Academy of the Socialist Republic of Romania, 1971).
Prodan, D., *Din istoria Transilvaniei: Studii şi evocări* (Bucuresti: Editura enciclopedica, 1991).
Prunduş, Silvestru Augustin and Clemente Plainanu, *Catolicism şi Ortodoxie Românească* (Cluj-Napoca: Casa de Editură Viaţa Creştină, 1994).
Purpurea Pannonica, sive Vitae et Res Gestae S. R. E. Cardinalium ... D. Sigismundus Henter L. Baro de Sepsi Szent Ivanyi ... propugnaret praeside R. P. Georgio Szegedi ... (Claudiopoli: Typis Acad. Soc. JESU 1746).

Puskely, Mária, *Kétezer év szeretesége: Szeretség és müvelődéstörténenti enciklopédia* (2 vols, Budapest: Dinasztia, 1998).

Quellen zur Geschichte der Siebenbürger Sachsen 1195-1975, Gesammelt und bearbeitet von Ernest Wagner (Wien: Böhlau Verlag 1976).

Rabe, Carsten, *Alma Mater Leopoldiana: Kolleg und Universität der Jesuiten in Breslau* (Köln: Böhlau, 1999).

Rácz, István (ed.), *Tanulmányok Erdély történétről*, Szakmai Konferencia Debrecen, 1987.

Rădutiu, Aurel, "Les institutions rurales dans les pays roumains au xviiie siècle," *Revue Roumaine d'histoire* 20, 3 (1981): 503–15.

Rădutiu, Aurel and Ladislau Gyémánt, *Reportoriul Izvoarelor Statistice privind Transilvania 1690-1847* ([Cluj?]: Editura "Univers Enciclopedic," 1995[?]).

Ratiu, Ion, "Contribuția Biserice Române Unite cu Roma la dezvoltarea vieții romaniești de la 1697 incoace," in *Un Destin Istoric: Biserica Română Unită* (Targu-Mureş: Revista Vatra, 1999).

Redlich, Oswald, *Weltmacht des Barock: Österreich in der Zeit Leopolds I.* 4th edn (Wien: Rudolf M. Rohrer Verlag, 1961).

Reges Ungariae Mariani ex Antiquissismis diplomatis allisque Mss. Conscripti ... (Viennae: Typis Thomae nob. De Trattern, 1774).

Reingrabner, Gustav and Gerald Schlag (eds), *Reformation und Gegenreformation in Pannonischen Raum. Schlaininger Gespräche 1993/1994* (Eisenstadt: Burgenländisches Landesmuseum, 1999).

Richter, Václav, "Poznámky k barokní uměni," in *O Barokní kultuře: Sborník statí*, ed. Milan Kopecký (Brno: Universita J.E. Purkyně, 1968).

Riedl, Frederick, *A History of Hungarian Literature*, trans. C. Arthur Givener and Ilona de Gjögy Givener (London: Heinemann, 1906).

Ritzer, R. and P. Serfin, *Hierarchia Catholica Medii et Recentoris Aevi Vol. VI 1730-1799* (Patavii: Typis et Sumptibus Domus Editorialis "Il Messagero di San Antonio" apud Basilicum S. Antonii, Patavii, 1958).

Robertson, Ronald G., "Romanian Catholic Church" in *The HarperCollins Encyclopedia of Catholicism* (New York: HarperCollins, 1989).

Rohwerder, Max (ed.), *Historia Residentiae Walcensis Societatis Jesu ab anno 1618 avo* (Köln/Graz: Böhlau Verlag, 1967).

Roider, Karl E., Jr., *Austria's Eastern Question 1700-1790* (Princeton, NJ: Princeton University Press, 1982).

Rosa, Enrico, SI, *I Gesuiti. Dalle Origini ai nostri giorni*, ed. Angelo Martini, 3rd edn (Roma: La Civiltà Cattolica, 1957).

Rosa, Marion, "The Italian Churches," in William J. Callahan and David Higgs (eds), *Church and Society in Catholic Europe of the Eighteenth Century* (Cambridge: Cambridge University Press, 1979).

Rózsa, Gy., "Thesenblätter mit ungarischen Beziehungen," *Acta Historica Artium Hungaricarum* 33 (1987–88): 257–89.

Rtizler, R and P. Sefrin, *Hierarchia Catholica Media et Recentioris Aevi*, vol. 5 (Monasterii, sumptibus et typis librariae Regensbergianae, 1898–1978).

Ruha, Michael J., *Reinterpretation of History as a Method of Furthering Communism in Romania* (Washington, DC: Georgetown University Press, 1961).

Sacher, Abram Leon, *A History of the Jews*, 5th edn (New York: Alfred Knopf, 1964).
Sacra Congregazione per la Chiesa Orientale, *Oriente Cattolico: Cenni storichi e statistiche* (Città del Vaticano: Sacra Congregazione per la Chiesa Orientale, 1962).
Saisselin, Remy, *The Enlightenment against the Baroque: Economics and Aesthetics in the Eighteenth Century* (Berkeley: University of California Press, 1992).
Salbeck, Michael, *Prima 5. saecula regni Mariani* (Claudiopoli: Typ. Acad. Soc. IESU, 1746).
Sallay, Mariane, "Koloszvár," in Zádor Anna and Genthon István (eds), *Művészeti lexikon* (4 vols, Budapest: Akadémia Kiadó, 1965).
Sandius, Chistopher, *Nucleus historiae ecclesiasticae exhibitus in historia Arianorum* (Coloniae: Apus Joannem Nicolia, 1676).
Sándor, Bálint and Barna Gábor, *Búcsújáró magyarok: A magyarországi búcsújárás története és néprajza* (Budapest: Szent István Társulat az Apostoli Szentszék Könyvkiadója, 1994).
Sas, Péter, *A koloszvári Szent Mihály templom* (Kolozsvár: Gloria, 1998).
Sas, Péter, *A koloszvári ferences templom* (Kolozsvár: Gloria, 1999).
Sas, Péter, *A koloszvári piarista templom* (Kolozsvár: Gloria, 1999).
Schlafly, Daniel L., Jr., "True to the *Ratio Studiorum*? Jesuit colleges in St. Petersburg," *History of Education Quarterly* 37, 4 (1997): 421–34.
Schöpflin, George, "Transylvania: Hungarians under Romanian rule," in Stephen Borsody (ed.), *The Hungarians: A Divided Nation* (New Haven, CT: Yale Center for International and Area Studies, 1988).
Schwicker, J.H., *Geschichte der oe. Militärgrenze* (Wien: K. Prochazka, 1883).
Secunda deiparae Virginis laudum minuta post laudes Laurentanas ... per R. P. Antonium Grueber è S. J. (Claudopoli: Typis Academ. S. J. per Thad. Weichenberg, 1736).
Selecta Heroum Daciae Spectacula. Honori Reverendum, Nobilorum ac Eruditorum Dominorum Dominorum Neo-Baccalorum ... Promotore R. P. Andrea Patai è Soc. Jesu ... (Claudiopoli: Typis Academicis Societ. Jesu, 1731).
Seton-Watson, R.W., *A History of the Romanians* (Cambridge: Cambridge University Press, 1963).
Seton-Watson, R.W., *Racial Problems in Hungary* (New York: Howard Fertig, 1972).
Shore, Paul, "Cluj: A Jesuit Educational Outpost in Transylvania," *Catholic Education* 5, 1 (2001): 55–71.
Shore, Paul, "Jesuit missions and schools in eighteenth century Transylvania and Eastern Hungary," in I.I. Monok and P. Ötvös (eds), *Lesestoffe und kulturelles Niveau des niedrigen Klerus: Jesuiten und die nationalen Kulturverhältnisse I. I.* (Szeged: Scriptum Rt., 2001).
Shore, Paul, "Universalism, Rationalism and among the Jesuits of Bohemia (1770–1800)," in D. Dawson and V.Cossy (eds), *Progrès et violence au xviii siècle* (Paris: Slatkine: 2001).

Shore, Paul, "The activities of the Society of Jesus in an eighteenth century Transylvanian city: The Jesuits of Cluj," *Proceedings of the Fourth International Congress on Romanian Studies* (Iaşi: Center for Romanian Studies, 2002).

Shore, Paul, *The Eagle and the Cross: Jesuits in Late Baroque Prague* (St. Louis, MO: The Institute of Jesuit Sources, 2002).

Shore, Paul, "The several lives of St. John Nepomuk," in J. Chorpenning (ed.), *"He Spared Himself in Nothing": Essays on the Life and Thought of John N. Neumann, C. Ss. R., Fourth Bishop of Philadelphia, on the Occasion of the 25th Anniversary of his Canonization* (Philadelphia, PA: St. Joseph's University Press, 2005).

Simeghi, Joannes, *Genuina de Lacrimosa Virgine Claudiopolitana* (Claudiopoli, 1714).

Simon Melina and Ágnes Szabó, *Bethlen Kata könyvtárnak rekonstruckiója* (Szeged: Scriptum Kft, 1997).

Skutil, Jan (ed.), *Morava a Brno na sklonku Třicetiletí Valky* (Brno: Magistrát Města Brna, 1995).

Sodalitatum Marianum in Soc. Jesu gymnasiis erectarum summa utilitas (Claudiopoli: 1744).

Someşan, Maria, *Începtulurile Bisericii Române Unite cu Roma* (Bucuresti: ALL Istoric, 1999).

Sommervogel, Carlos, Augustin de Backer, Auguste Carayon and Pierre Bliard, *Bibliothèque de la Compagnie de Jésus: nouvelle edition* (10 vols, Bruxelles: Oscar Schepens, 1890–1932).

The Sopron Collection of Jesuit Stage Designs, with a preface by Marcello Fagiolo, studies by Éva Knapp and István Kilián, iconography by Terézia Bardi (Budapest: Enciklopédia Publishing House, 1999).

Standaert, Nicolas, SJ, "Jesuit corporate culture as shaped by the Chinese," in John W. O'Malley, SJ et al. (eds), *The Jesuits: Cultures, Sciences and the Arts, 1540–1773* (Toronto: University of Toronto Press, 1999).

Staud, Géza, *Magyar iskolai szinjátekok forrásai és irodalma* (2 vols, Budapest: Magya Tudományos Könyvtáránák Kiadása, 1984–).

Ştefănescu, Ştefan, "Cuvînt înaninte," in S Ştefănescu (ed.), *Reflectarea Istoriei Universale în Istoriografia Românescă* (Bucuresti: Editura Academiei Republicii Socialiste România, 1986).

Ştefănescu, Ştefan, *Romaneasccă şi sud-est Europeană (secole XVII–XIX)* (Bucuresti: Editura Academiei Republicii Socialiste România, 1986).

Stöger, Johann Nepomuk, *Scriptores Proviniciae Austriacae Societatis Jesu* (Viennae: Typis Cong. Mechit.; Ratisbonnae: Georg Joan. Manz, 1856).

Ştriban, Marcel, "L'église des Roumains Uniates sous l'évêque Petru Pavel Aron," *Transylvanian Review* 6, 1 (1997): 36–50.

Stoye, John, *Marsigli's Europe: The Life and Times of Luigi Ferdinando Marsigli, Soldier and Virtuoso* (New Haven, CT: Yale University Press, 1994).

Sudetic, Charles, "Historical Setting," in *Romania: A Country Study* (Washington, DC: US Government Printing Office, 1989).

Sugar, Peter, *Southeastern Europe under Ottoman Rule, 1354–1804* (Seattle/London: University of Washington Press, 1977).

Sugar, Peter, "Ethnicity in Eastern Europe," in Peter Sugar (ed.), *Ethnic Diversity and Conflict in Eastern Europe* (Santa Barbara, CA/Oxford: ABC-CLIO, 1980).

Sugar, Peter, "The historical role of religious institutions in Eastern Europe and their place in the Communist Party state," in P. Ramet (ed.), *Religion and Nationalism in Soviet and East European Politics* (Durham, NC: Duke University Press, 1989).

Sulzer, Franz Joseph, *Geschichte der transalpinischen Daciens* ... (Wien: R. Graeffer, 1781–82).

Svatoš, Martin, "Antonín Koniáš SJ von seinen Ordensbrüdern dargestellt," *Humanistica Lovaniensia* 43 (1994): 411–24.

Szábo, Ferenc, *A teologus Pázmány* (Budapest, 1998).

Szabo, Franz, AJ, *Kaunitz and Enlightened Absolutism, 1753–1780* (Cambridge/ New York: Cambridge University Press, 1994).

Szabó, Károly, *Régi Magyar könyvtár* (3 vols, Budapest: Magyar Tudományos Akadémia, 1879–98).

Szabó, Péter, *Az Erdélyi fejedelemség* (Budapest: Kulturtrade Kiadó, 1997).

Szegedi, Johann Baptist, *Tripartitum Iuris Hungarici Tirocinium* (Tyrnaviae, Typis Academicis Societatis JESU, 1754).

Székely, György, "A vásári színjátszás kezdetei hazánkban," in Júlia Demeter and István Kilián (eds), *A magyar Színház Szülétese* (Miskolc: Miskolci egyetemi kiadó, 2000).

Székely Oklevéltár, Csíkvármgye költégén, ed. Lajos Szádeczky (8 vols, Kolozsvár: Ny. Gombos Ferencz Lyceum–Nyomdájban, 1898) vol. 7, 1696–1750, pp. 269–71.

Szekfű, Gyula, *Magyar Története IV. kötet* (Budapest: Királyi Magyar Egyetemi Nyomda, 1935).

Szent Biblia az az Istennek o es uj Testamentomban Foglaltataott (Varadon: MDCXI). (Exhibit 169, Ráda Collection, Bible Museum, Budapest).

Szent-Ivanyi, Béla, *A pietizmus* (Budapest: Királyi Magyar egyetemi nyomda, 1936).

Szentkatolnai, Bakk Endre, *A Bak és Jancsó család* (Budapest: Nyomatott a Hunyadi Máttyas Intézetben, 1883).

Szentkatolnai, Bakk Endre, *Altojai gróf Apor István* (Cluj: Erdélyi Katolikus Kiadása, 1935).

Szentpéter, Imre, *A bölcsészettudományi kar története 1633–1935* (Budapest: A királyi magyar egyetemi nyomda, 1935).

Szigetváry, Ferenc, "Die Apotekengründungen der Jesuiten," in Gustav Reingrabner and Gerald Schlag (eds), *Reformation und Gegenreformation in Pannonischen Raum. Schlaininger Gespräche 1993/1994* (Eisenstadt, 199).

Szilágyi, Ferenc, *Közlemények az erdélyi Római Katholikus Egyházi történetből* (Budapest, 1874).

Szilas, L., "Baranyai Pál László," in Charles E. O'Neill and Joaquín Domínguez (eds), *Diccionario histórico de la Compañía de Jesús: biográfico-temático* (Roma: Institutum Historicum; Madrid: Universidad Pontificia Comillas, 2001).

Szilas, Ladislaus, SI, "Die Österreichische Jesuitenprovinz im Jahre 1773. Eine historische-statistische Untersuchung," *AHSI* 47 (1978).

Szinneyei, József (ed.), *Magyar írók élete és munkái* (14 vols, Budapest: Hornyánszky, 1891–1914).
Szlilagyi, Ferencz, *Közlemények az erdélyi romái katholikus egyházi történetből* (Budapest: Hoffmann és Molnár, 1874).
Szörény, László, "Politikai iskoldráma Savojai Jenőről és konzultació az ideális államformaról," in Júlia Demeter and István Kilián (eds), *A magyar Színház Születese* (Miskolc: Miskolci egyetemi kiadó, 2000).
Takács, József, *A Jezsuita iskoladráma* (Budapest: Korda Részvénytárság Nyomdája, 1937).
Tanner, Mathias, *Societas Jesu usque ad Sanguinis et Vitae Profusionem* ... (Pragae: Typis Universiatis Carlo-Fernandeae, 1675).
Tapié, Victor L., *The Rise and Fall of the Habsburg Monarch*, trans. Stephen Hardman (New York/Washington/London: Praeger, 1971).
Tazbir, Janusz, "Les Frères polonais en Transilvanie," *Revue Romane d'Histoire* 8, 3 (1969): 697–704.
Tetlow, Joseph, *Ignatius Loyola: Spiritual Exercises* (New York: Crossroad, 1992).
Toca, Mircea, *Cluj Baroc* (Cluj-Napoca: Dacia, 1983).
Tocanal, Petru, "Attestamento delle missioni in Bulgaria, Valachia, Transylvania e Moldaviam," in *Sacrae Congregationis de Propaganda fide Memoria Rerum. Vol. II 1700–1815* (Roma/Freiburg/Wien: Herder, 1973).
Tocanel, Petro, *Storia della chiesa Cattolica in Romania. III. Il vicariato apostolico e le missioni dei frati minori conventuali in Moldavia* (Padova: Edizioni Messaggero, 1960).
Tótfalusi, Kis Miklos, *Szent Dávid Királynak és Profetanak Szazötven Soltari* ... (Amstelodaman: M. Totfaulsi Kis Miklos által, 1686).
Tótfalusi, Kis Miklos, *Új Testmentom* (Amestelodámban, Kis Miklos által, 1687).
Tóth, I.G. (ed.), *Relationes Missioniarum de Hungaria et Transilvania (1627–1707)* (Roma/Budapest: MTA Történettudomány Intéztében, 1994).
Tóth, Zoltán, *Az Erdélyi Román Nacionalizmus első százada 1697–1792* (Budapest: Athaneum, 1946).
Toynbee, Arnold, *An Historian's Approach to Religion*, 2nd edn (Oxford: Oxford University Press, 1979).
Trampus, Antonio, *I Gesuiti e l'Illuminismo: Politica e Religone in Austria e nell'Europa centrale (1773–1798)* (Firenze: L.S. Olschki, 2000).
Treptow, Kurt W. (ed.), *A History of Romania* (Boulder, CO/New York: East European Monographs, distributed by Columbia University Press; Iaşi: Center for Romanian Studies, 1996).
Trevor-Roper, H.R., *The Crisis of the Seventeenth Century: Religion, Reformation and Social Change* (New York/Evanston, IL: Harper and Row, 1968).
Trevor-Roper, H.R., *The European Witch-Craze of the 16th and 17th Centuries* (Harmondsworth: Penguin, 1969, 1967).
Trósanyi, Zsolt, *Habsburg politika és Habsburg kormányzat Erdélyben 1690–1740* (Budapest: Akadémia Kiadó, 1982).
Ungarisches Magazin (Pressburg: bey Anton Löwe, 1781).
Universae Matheseos Brevis Institutio Theoretico-Practica ex Operibus P.P. Societatis Jesu. (Tynaviae: Typ. Acad. S. J., 1752).

Valentin, Jean-Marie, *Le theâtre des Jésuites dans les pays de langue allemand. Répertoire chronologique des pièces représentées et des documents conserves* (2 vols, Stuttgart: Anton Hiersmann Verlag, 1984).
Valjavec, Fritz, *Geschichte der deutschen Kulturbeziehungen zu Südosteuropa. III Aufklärung und Absolutismus* (München: R. Oldenbourg, 1958).
Valley-Radot, J., "Le recueil des Plans d'Édifices de la Compagnie de Jésus conservé à la Biblithèque National de Paris" (Roma: Instiutum Historicum S. J., 1960) (Biblioteca Instituti Historici S.J., XV).
Ványi, Ferenc et al. (eds), *Magyar irodalmi lexikon* (Budapest: A "Studium" Kiadása, [1936?]).
Vanyó, Tihamér Aladár (ed.), *Püspöki Jelentések. A Magyar szent korona országnak egyházmegyeiről 1600–1800* (Pannonhalma, 1933).
Vardy, Stephen Bela, *Historical dictionary of Hungary (European historical dictionaries, no. 18)* (Lanham, MD/London: Scarecrow Press, 1997).
Varga, Imre, "A Kolozsvári Jezsuita Színjátszás," in Demeter Júlia and Kilián István (eds), *A magyar Színház születése* (Miskolc: Miskolci egyetemi kiadó, 2000).
Várkonyi, Á.R., "Historical personalities, crisis and progress in 17th century Hungary," in *Études Historiques 1970 publiées a l'occasion du XIIIe Congrès International des Sciences Historiques par la Commission Nationale des Historiens Hongrois* (Budapest: Akadémiai Kiadó, 1970): 265–299.
Várkonyi, Á.R., "Repopulation and the system of cultivation in Hungary after the expulsion of the Turks," *Acta Historica Academiae Scientarum Hungaricae* 16 (1970): 151–70.
Várkonyi, Á.R., "Handelswesen und Politik in Ungarn des 17–18 Jahrhunderts Theorien, Monopole Schmugglerbewegungen 1600–1711," *Acta Historica Academiae Scientarum Hungaricae* 17 (1971): 207–24.
Vasile Lechințan, *Instituții și edifice istorice din Transilvania* (Cluj-Napoca: Editura Carpatica, 2000).
Venard, Marc, "Popular religion in the eighteenth century," in William J. Callahan and David Higgs (eds), *Church and Society in Catholic Europe of the Eighteenth Century* (Cambridge: Cambridge University Press, 1979).
Veress, Andrai, *Bibliografia Romano-Ungară Românii în literatura ungară și literatura română. Vl. I 1473–1780* (București: Editura Cartea Românescâ, 1931).
Verus Patriae Pater etc. Oratio Funebris ab uno Societate Presbytero Celebrata (Claudiopol.: Impr. Sam. P. Telegdi, 1710).
Viețața Agrară , Economică Românilor din Ardeal și Ungaria: Documente Contemporane. Vol. I 1508–1820, ed. Ștefan Meteș (București: Tipografia România Nouă Th. Volnea Calea Griviței, 41, 1921).
Viller, Marcel, Charles Baumgartner and André Rayez (eds), *Dictionnaire de spiritualité ascétique et mystique, doctrine et histoire* (17 vols, Paris: G. Beauchesne et ses fils, 1937).
Vols, Ernestus, *Architecturae militaris tyrocinium* (Claudiopoli, 1738).
Vorbuchner, Adolf, *Az erdélyi püspökség* (Brassó: Az Erdélyi Tudósító kiadása, 1925).

von Engel, Johann Christian, *Geschichte des Ungrischen Reichs* (Wien: In der Camesinaschen Buchhandlung, 1814).

Wagner, Ernest, "The Saxons of Transylvania," *The Transylvanian Saxons: Historical Highlights* (Cleveland, OH: The Alliance of Transylvanian Saxons, 1982).

Waldner, Peter, *Besonderer Considerationes und Erforschungen über die allgemeine Regelen Fratrum Coadiutorum Societatis Iesu* (Ingolstadt, 1731).

Walker, Alan, "Romanian Christianity," in Ken Parry et al. (eds), *The Blackwell Dictionary of Eastern Christianity* (Oxford: Blackwell, 1999).

Wangermann, Ernest, *The Austrian Achievement* (London: Thames and Hudson, 1973).

Wangermann, Ernest, "Reform Catholicism and political radicalism in the Austrian Enlightenment," in Roy Porter and Mikuláš Teich (eds), *The Enlightenment in National Context* (Cambridge: Cambridge University Press, 1982).

Wappenbuch des Adels von Ungarn samt den Nebenländern der Stephans–Krone (Nürnburg: Verlag von Bauer und Raspe, 1885–1887).

Ward, W.R., *Christianity under the ancien régime 1648–1789* (Cambridge: Cambridge University Press, 1999).

Ward, W.R., "Late Jansenism and the Habsburgs," in James E. Bradley and Dale Van Kley (eds), *Religion and Politics in Enlightenment Europe* (Notre Dame, IN: University of Notre Dame Press, 2001).

Weiser, F., SJ, *Tabulae exhibentes Sedes Antiquae Societatis Jesu: Missionum Stationes et Collegia, 1556–1773 Provinciae Bohemiae et Silesiae* (Viennae: Sumptibus Monastarum Societatis Jesu, 1899).

Weiser, F., SJ, *A katholikus iskolaügy magyarországon* (Colozae: Francisus Holmeier, 1985).

Weiser, F., *Vitae Patrum et Magistorum* (Colozae: Franciscus Holmeyer, 1886).

Wellmann, Imre, "Erdély népsége és agrárfejlödése 1660–1830," in István Rácz (ed.), *Tanulmányok Erdély történétről. Szakmai konferencia Debrecen 1987 Október 9–10* (Debrecen: Csokonai Kiadó, 1988).

Welykyj, Athanasius G. (ed.), *Litterae Episcoparum Historiam Ucrainae Illustrantes (1600–1900)* Vol. V 1711–1740 (Romae: P.P. Basiliani, 1981).

Welykyj, Athanasius G. (ed.), *Supplicationes Ecclesiae Uniatae Ucrainae et Bielorusjaie Voll II, 1700–1740* (Romae: P.P. Basilani, 1962).

Whaley, Joachim, "Austria, 'Germany,' and the dissolution of the Holy Roman Empire," in *The Habsburg Legacy: National Identity in Historical Perspective*, eds Richie Robertson and Edwads Timms (Edinburgh: Edinburgh University Press, 1994).

de Vries, Wilhelm, "L'Unione dei rumeni (1697–1701)," *Transylvanian Review* 6, 1 (1997): 3–26.

Witkower, Rudolf and Irna B. Jaffe (eds), *Baroque Art: The Jesuit contribution* (New York: Fordham University Press, 1972).

Wolff, Lawrence, *Inventing Eastern Europe: The Map of Civilization on the Mind of the Enlightenment* (Stanford, CA: Stanford University Press, 1994).

Wolff, Lawrence, "Parents and children in the sermons of Père Bourdaloue: A Jesuit perspective on the early modern family," in *The Jesuit Tradition in Education and Missions: A 450-year Perspective*, ed. Christopher Chapple (Scranton, PA: University of Scranton Press; London/Toronto: Associated University Press, 1993).

Woodrow, Alain, *The Jesuits: A Story of Power* (New York: Geoffrey Chapman, 1995).

Zádor, Anna and István Genthon, *Művészeti lexikon* (4 vols, Budapest: Akadémia Kiadó, 1965).

Zelliger, Aloysius, *Pantheon Tyrnaviense* (Tyrnaviae: Typis Soc. S. Adalberti, 1931).

Znayenko, Myroslava T., *The gods of the ancient Slavs: Tatischev and the beginnings of Slavic mythology* (Columbus, OH: Slavica, 1980).

Zsoltné, Alseghy, Czibula Katalin and Varga Imre *(eds), Jezsuita iskoladrámák: Ismert szerzök* (Budapest: Argumentum: Akadémai Kiadó, 1992).

Zsomoborde, Szász, *The Minorities in Romanian Transylvania* (London: The Richards Press, Ltd, 1927).

Index

Adamovich, Paulus 90
Alba Iulia 56, 60, 141, 177
    Catholics in 71
    Romanian-Latin school 57
    Synod 55
Anabaptists 43, 159
Anghel, Atanasie, Bishop 56, 57, 58, 59
    funeral 65
animism 5
Antalffi, Joannes 112
Apáczai Csere, János 112
Apafi II, Mihály 46, 47
Apor, István, Count 90
Apor, Péter 90, 123, 135
Apor, Stephanus, Count 122–3
Arians *see* Unitarians
Armenians
    Jesuits, good relations 76–8
    Transylvania 4–5, 75
Aron, Petru Pavel, Bishop 85, 168
Aulic Council of Transylvania 73

Bács 125, 156
Balásovics, Georgius 84
Balogh, Ladislaus 50, 86
Bandinus, Marcus, Archbishop 177
Báranyi, Paulus Ladislaus 55, 89
Barbier, Frédéric 44
Bathory, Stephen, King 100–1
Bayr, Matthais 120
Beke, Paulus 175
Belgrade 1, 15, 157
Benedict XV, Pope 179
Benkő, Nicolaus 164
Bible, in Hungarian 63
Blaj 63, 80
    school 57
Bob, Ioan, Bishop 184
Bobâlna 56
Boér, Jozsef 82
Bogor 125
Borgia, St Francis, *Praepostius Generalis* 135
Borromeo, St Charles 135

Bourdaoue, Louis 97
Brady, Thomas A. 70
Breslau (Wroclaw) 141
Brukenthal, Samuel von 187
Bucharest, Piarists 178–9
Buckley, Michael 105
Buda 94
    collegium 163
    liberation 1
Buitul, Georgius 84
Búza 125
Bzenszky, Rudolphus 94, 164

Calvinism, Transylvania 45–6, 57, 74
    conversion 82
    Orthodox Church, fears of 57–8
Calvinist-Reformed 4
Campion, Edmund, *Rationes* 153
Canisius, Peter 186
catechism 34, 84
Cantimir, Dimitrie, *Incrementa* 67
Carolina Resolutio (1731) 39
Chalcedon, Council (451) 76
Charles VI, Emperor 46–7, 92–3, 101
Chotim, Pasha 178
Cluj (Kolozsvár) 4, 5, 7, 11
    Bánffy palace 131
    Baroque architecture 113–14, 124, 129, 130, 185
    Calvinist
        academy 99, 112
        community 125
    coadjutores temporales
        individuals 169–71
        Jesuits, relationship 171
        obituary notices 170–1
        origins 169–70
        post-Jesuit suppression 182
        role 168
    community characteristics 172
    Convictus Nobilium 68, 96, 126
    food shortages 115
    Franciscan boarding school 99
    guilds 112

historiographical issues 13
and Hungarian identity 12
Jesuit
   aesthetics 124, 129–30
      drama as 143
   bookshop 106
   churches 105
   historians 93–4
   landowners 127
   orphanage 152
   reading 153
Jesuit Church 114–15
   architecture 115–16
   crypt 122
   Mary column 123
   setting 123
   statues 117
   Viennese influences 117
   'Weeping Madonna' image 118–21
Jesuit *collegium* 59–60, 69, 73, 77, 84, 86, 91, 92, 94
   curriculum 96, 97, 184
   distinguised alumni 103–4
   drama productions 135
   facilities 126
   Hebrew instruction 106
   library
      expansion 185
      extent 96
   music education 96–7
   scholarship 103
Jesuit drama 24, 35, 101, 133–46
   about St Stephen 135–6
   cosmopolitanism 134
   decline 141, 186
   and educational goals 134
   Hungarian history 136
   influence 141–2
   Latin, Baroque 144–5
   martyrs 137
   as new aesthetic 143
   non-theatre performances 138–9
   play summaries 134–5
   public
      declamations 139–40
      disputations 140–1
   themes 135–8
      Roman 144
   values, projection of 145–6
   volume 133–4, 142
Jesuit schools 24, 85, 125–6
   curriculum 91–2, 94, 95
   educational dominance 99–100
   fees 91
   history teaching 92
   influence 107
   learning environment 102
   library 94
   non-Jesuit teachers 95
   popularity 100
   text books 94
   theatre in 133–46
   thesis topics 95
Jesuits
   blessing of wells 151
   common mission 172
   conversions 155
   heritage 187–8
   instability 172–3
   reports to Rome 20–1
   sacramental penance 147–9
   social control 147, 149, 150–2
   sources on 20–3
   women, ministry to 154–5
Jews, conversion 155
Marian Congregations 153
Moldavia, connections 168
Orthodox cathedral 36
Piarists 181, 182
plague 115, 119
Polish Brethren 112
pre-1693 Jesuit presence 89–90, 111–12
printing press 153, 166
Protestantism 106
publishing 12
St Michael's Church 112–13, 114
Seminarium S. Josephi 98–9, 126, 141
seminarum pauperum 97–8, 126, 139
   students' revolt 98
sodalities 153, 154
Collegium Germanicum (Rome) 8, 43, 72
Collegium Hungaricum (Rome) 43, 72
Congregatio de Propaganda Fide 31, 52
Convictus Nobilium
   Cluj 68, 96, 126
   Győr 163
Cordara, Guila Cesare, criticisms of Jesuits 170
Corvinus, Matthias 136
Cotorea, Gerontie, *Despre schismaticia grecilor* 193
Counter-Reformation 30, 166

INDEX

Crăcium, Gheorghe 6
Csisco 125

Dacia 40, 50, 67, 83, 122, 144, 193, 195
Danube Basin 38, 39, 87
de Felvinczi de Harasztos, Sigismundus 122
Delphini, Theophilus 183
Desericzky, Innocentius 179
Dobner, Stephanus 100
Dobra, Ladislaus 84, 100
Dobra, Vasile 84
Ducreaux, Marie-Elizabeth 40, 156
Dunod, Antonidus 30

Eger 94
Elidae, Mircea 10
Enlightenment ideas, Transylvania 187
Enyedi, Benedek Samuel 106
Ertl, Franciscus 170
Esztergom 1
Evangelical-Lutheran 4

Făgăraș 80, 82
Fasching, Franciscus, *Nova Dacia* 83
Ferdinand I, Emperor 41
Ferdinand II, Emperor 41
Ferdinand III, Emperor 41
Ferenc II Rákóczi 165
    uprising against Habsburgs 39, 80, 115, 135
Ferenczi Medobéri, András 99
Fitter, Adam 73–4, 163, 165
    reforms 74–5
Florence, Council (1439) 31, 33
Forst, Thomas 169
Franciscans, Moldavia 178; *see also* Observant Franciscans
Freyberger, Andreas 68
Fridvaldszky, Joannes 103–4, 183
    Reges Ungariae Mariani 104

Gegennye 125
Geiger, Matthias 183
George of Podiebrad, King 136
Ghibu, Osnifor 85
Göth, Matteus 169
Göttwald, Josephus 164
Götze, Franciscus 164
Grancea, Mihaela 58
Great Schism (1054) 29, 32
Grembs, Christophorus 164

Gross, Georg 176
Gyerö, 167n21
Gyologi, Joannes 118
    catechism 64
Győr 1, 94
    collegium 163
    Convictus Nobilium 163
Gyula, St Stephen's uncle 136

Habsburgs
    eastern ambitions 143–4
    Jesuits, mutual interests 16–18, 100–1, 144, 165
    Ratio Educationis 184
    Transylvania
        Catholic policy 49–50
        military conquest 59
        policy 40–1
    and Transylvanian Uniate Church 85–6
    unifying vision 7–8
    western preoccupations 48–9
Haller, György, Baron 118
Haller von Hallerstein, Paul, *Epitome chronologica* 93
Hammer, Konrad 115
Hedri, Fr Antonius 172
Heer, Friedrich 129
Heidegger, Martin 129
Hell, Maximilianus 93, 104–5, 157
    Astronomer Royal 104
Herbst, Joannes 169
Horea uprising (1784) 185, 191
Horvath, Andreas 60
Horvath, Josephus 156
Hungarian language 44–5, 167
    Bible in 63
    Jesuits, bias towards 65
    Transylvania, administrative language 65–6
Hungary
    recatholicization 27–8
    as *Regnum Marianum* 42, 135, 191
    theatre, influence of Jesuit drama 133–4
Hunyadi, Matthias 93

Iași 106, 172, 173, 175–6
    ethnic diversity 177
    Latin school 176
Ilatskó, Stephanus 164
Illei, Joannes 141
Illia, Andreas 164

Ortus et Progressus 78
Iorga, Nicolae 57

Jansenism, Jesuits, rivalry 42
Jesuit drama *see under* Cluj (Kolozsvár)
Jesuits
    Armenians, good relations 76–8
    Austrian Province 15–17, 18, 192
    China, missions 157
    in Cluj *see under* Cluj (Kolozsvár)
    Constitutions 7n35, 19, 102, 109, 168
    dress 68, 69
    Habsburgs, mutual interests 16–18,
        100–1, 144, 165
    Hungarian language, bias to 65
    influence, maximum 166
    institutional organization 44
    interchangeability 171–2
    Jansenism, rivalry 42
    Latin, use 82, 107
    Literae Annue reports 20, 67, 71, 78, 82,
        98, 107
    missionary expeditions 156–7, 160–2
    modus operandi 8
    Moldavia, missions 24–5, 33, 34, 157,
        173–9
    motives 9–10
    Orthodox conversions 33–5
    polemical techniques 42–3
    Ratio Studiorum (1599) 19, 22, 23, 43,
        53–4, 116, 172, 193
        distinctiveness 108–9
        linguistic competence 133
        in schools 90, 91–2, 97, 107
    and realism 10–11
    Relations reports 66–7
    Roma people, relationship 159–60
    Romanian, avoidance of 64–5, 66, 167,
        172
    Spiritual Exercises 22, 69, 148, 171
        and Jesuit identity 108
    in Transylvania, *see under* Transylvania
    Uniate Christians
        conversion 52–3, 81, 82–3
        tensions 51–2
        ties 19, 62–3
    Uniate Church, Transylvania, tensions
        167
Jews, Cluj, conversion 155
Josa, Stephanus 186
Joseph I, Emperor 113, 166

Joseph II, Emperor 6, 47, 183, 185, 188
Junius Lucius Brutus, as Jesuit model 137–8

Káldi, Gerogius 63
Kaprinai, Stephanus 93
Kaunitz, Wenzel Anton 186
Kelecseni, Fr Josephus 164, 165
Keller, Matthias 170
Kerestúr 125
Kircher, Athanasius 102–3, 116
Klein (Micu), Inochentie 51, 63, 85, 86
    Supplex libellus 50
Klinic, Franjo, *Dacia Sicula Brevi*
    Compendio Exhibita 164
Koffler, Fr Joannes 157
Kollonitz, Cardinal 51, 52, 59
Kolosmănăştur 89, 128
    Blessed Virgin monastery 183
    Jesuit church 124–5
    school 90
    Synod (1728) 61, 74, 81
Kolosvári (Kolozsvári), Pál (Paulus) 125,
    136, 165
Komárom 101
Koncz, Eva 99
König, Johann 117, 124
Kornis, Sigismund, Count 118
Košice 94
Kostyál, Paulus, *socius* 171

Lajos, György 96
Langweiler, Matthias 169
Latin
    in Jesuit drama 144–5
    Jesuit use 82, 107
    and Roman heritage 195
    Uniate clergy, ignorance of 64
    verses, published in Cluj 92–3
Leopold I, Emperor 46, 49, 90, 126, 166
    Diploma Leopoldinum 47, 85
Leopold II, Emperor 188
Lestyán, Moses 83, 141
Libenczki, Fr Paul 152
Ligardis, Pantilimon 175
Lipsits, Michael, *Hungaria Coelestis* 164
Lwow 106

Maior, Grigore, Romanian–Latin dictionary
    65
Major, Petru 80
Manner, Thadeus 84

INDEX

Maria Theresia 40, 47
  'Apostolic' title 136
  Orthodoxy, toleration 61–2
Martinez, Gerogius 169
Mártonfi, Josephus, Bishop 183
martyrdom, in Jesuit drama 137
Mavrocordat, Constantine 35, 168, 176, 178–9
Mavrocordat, John 178
Mavrocordat, Nicolae 176–7
Mavrocordat, Theophanes 34
Mayer, Joannes 84
Micu, Inochentie *see* Klein, Inochentie
Miksa, Fr Stephanus 156
Mindszenti, Antonius 122
Miroslavich, Franciscus 156–7
Miskolc, Calvinist college 102
Misztótfalusi Kis Miklós 12
Mohács, battle (1526) 1, 136
Moldavia 15, 28
  Cluj, connections 168
  Franciscans 178
  Hungarian villages, number 178
  Jesuits
    expulsion (1731) 176
    missions 24–5, 33, 34, 157
    in 1743: 173–9
    Orthodox rivalry 176
  Phanariots 177
Moser, Ferdinandus 169–70
Muesserer, Christopher 164
Muslims 5, 22, 52, 155

Nakamura, Alexius 137
Napolyi de Félőr, Georgius 122
Nedetzki, Ladislaus 94
Nemaj, Fr Josephus 156
Németi, Franciscus 163
Neuratner, Karl, *theologus* appointment 59
Norbert, Conradi 179
Nyirö, Adamus
  Epistolae Herodum et Heroidium 163
  Utopiae Sapientis 163

Obermeyer, Fr Franciscus 171
Observant Franciscans 158, 176
Okolitsani, Alexius 83
Olšavsky, Emanuel 167
O'Malley, John J. 23
Oradea 34
Orthodox Church

Romanian 37
Rome, key differences 32
Orthodox Church, Transylvania 28, 29, 53
  Calvinism, fear of 57–8
  Maria Theresia, toleration by 61–2
  see also Uniate Church, Transylvania
Ottoman Turks
  decline 59
  retreat from Hungary 1, 27
Ovid, in Jesuit schools 93

Padberg, John W. 92
Paki, Fr Joannes 171
Papp, Joannes 182
Parhamer, Ignatius 151
Pascu, Ştefan 36–7, 50
Patai, Andreas 176, 177, 178
Pataki, Joannes 59–60, 80
Pázmány, Peter 60, 173
Péterffy, Carolus 176, 178
Petrovanu, Serephinus, Bishop 57
Phanariots, Moldavia 177
Piarists
  Bucharest 178–9
  Cluj 181, 182
Pietism 149
Pius V, Pope 148
Poland, Uniate Church 33
Polish Brethren, Cluj 112
Prekenfeld, Franciscus 164
Prešov 94
Prezner, Christopher 122

Rákóczi, Sigmund 92
Rákóczi uprising (1703–11) 39, 80, 115, 135
Rauch, Georgius 169
Ravasz, Franciscus 35, 175
realism, and the Jesuits 10–11
Rednic, Atanasie, Bishop 85
The Reformation, and Transylvanian Uniate Church 72; *see also* Counter-Reformation
Ręgarski, Ionnes 178
Regnum Marianum, Hungary as 42, 135, 191
Reiser, Joseph 170
Remich, Paulus 164
Retz, Franciscus 149
Richter, Václav 129
Roma people 5
  Jesuits, relationship 159–60

Roman Catholics 4, 62
Romania, ethnic identity, and Transylvanian Uniate Church 67–8
Romanian language 56
  Jesuits
    avoidance of 64–5, 66, 167, 172
    knowledge of 84
    publications in 80–1
Romanians, in Transylvania 3
Rome, Orthodox Church, key differences 32
Ruthenia 33, 44

Sabbatarians, Transylvania 58
Salbeck, P. Michalis 83
Sándor, Paulus 101
Satu Mare *see* Szátmar
Schertzer, Valentine 169
Schmid, Andres 169
Schmidt, Fr Matthias 157
Schrantzer, Christianus 170
Serbia 15, 35
Seven Years War (1756–63) 141
Sibiu 49, 56, 177
Sigrai, Andreas 164–5, 172
Sincai, Gheorghe 36
Skalica 94
Slovakia 16
Society of Good Death 149
Socinian movement 112
Socinian-Unitarian 4
Sophronius 61
Soporon, *collegium* 164
Spegel, Anreas 171
Spinola, Giulio 89
Standaert, Nicolas 157
Stephen, St, plays about 135–6
Szalbeck, Michael, *theologus* 168
Szamoroczi, Paulus 90
Szátmar (Satu Mare) 34, 189
  Treaty (1711) 39
Szkefű, Gyula 136
Szegedi, Fr Georgius 61, 176, 178, 182, 183, 189
Szegedi, Ioannes 163
Szeredai, Antonius 95–6
Szinder, Andreas 89–90
Sztocsin 178

Teklie 125
Teofil, Orthodox metropolitan 55
theologus post 46, 57, 75, 80, 84, 189

Karl Neuratner 59
Michael Szalbeck 168
  role 86
Thirty Years' War (1618–1648) 40
Thomas à Kempis, *Imitatio Christi* 153
Thomas, Georgius 84
Timon, Samuel 94, 173
Tirgovişte 34
Tofeus, Mihály, Bishop 142
Tolvaj, Emericus 163
Transylvania 1–2
  Armenian Church 77
  Armenians 4–5, 75
  Bishop, appointment 58
  Calvinism 45–6, 57, 74
  Diet 47, 50, 89, 112
  Enlightenment ideas 187
  ethnic diversity 3–4
  feudalism 3
  Habsburg
    intervention 47
    reconquest 6, 59
  as Habsburg colony 2
  heresies 4
  Jesuits
    churches 125
    ethnic origins 63–4
    expulsion (1608) 181
    failures 5–6
    literary treatment 66–7
    missions 157
    opposition 43–5
    Orthodox clergy, comparison 69–70
    post-suppression
      continuities 181–3
      return 189–90
    Romanian Uniates 83–4
    suppression 7, 14, 86, 100, 173, 181
  land tenure system 54
  landed gentry 45
  literacy 6
  nations 3
  nineteenth-century reputation 191
  Orthodox Church 28, 29, 53
  as recatholicization territory 39, 40
  religious diversity 4–5, 47
  Romanians in 3
  Sabbatarians 58
  strategic location 30
  World War I 13
Trent, Council 19, 126, 149

Trnava 16, 62, 73, 94, 103, 121
  Jesuit library 96
  university 95, 185
Tröger, Joannes 169
Turda, Proclamation (1568) 4
Turks *see* Ottoman Turks

Udvarhely 135
Ungvár, 'Congregatio Agoniae' 154
Uniate Church
  Greek 34
  Poland 33
  Romanian 71
Uniate Church, Transylvania
  clergy
    dress 68
    education 69
    ignorance of Latin 64
    Jesuits, comparison 69–70
    peasant lifestyle 68–9, 74
  continuity 185
  development 38
  educational opportunities 62–3
  establishment 13–14
  and Habsburgs 85–6
  Jesuits
    tensions 167
    ties 19
  opposition 45
  Reformation 72
  Romanian ethnic identity 67–8, 188

Romanian historians 35–8
Romanian prayer book 193
union with Rome 33, 56–61
  motives for 71–2
  opposition to 61, 71, 80
  tenuousness of 72–3
Uniates, Armenian 76–7
  Transylvania 77
  union with Rome 77, 78
Union of the Churches (1697/98) 55, 56, 64
Unitarians (Arians) 4
Uzhhorod (Ungvár) 65, 94
  collegium 63

Varad 61
Vienna, Pazmaneum 163, 166
Vizl, Francis Xavier 183
Vols, Ernestus 127
Vorster, Sigismundus 163

Wagner, Andreas 170
Wallachia 28, 177
  Metropolitan of 58
  Prince of 58
Wartmann, Antonius 169

Zacharyaczewicz, Gregory 76
Zápolya, János 92, 136
Zeller, Martinus 90

CPSIA information can be obtained
at www.ICGtesting.com
Printed in the USA
LVOW13*0344100818
586586LV00006B/66/P